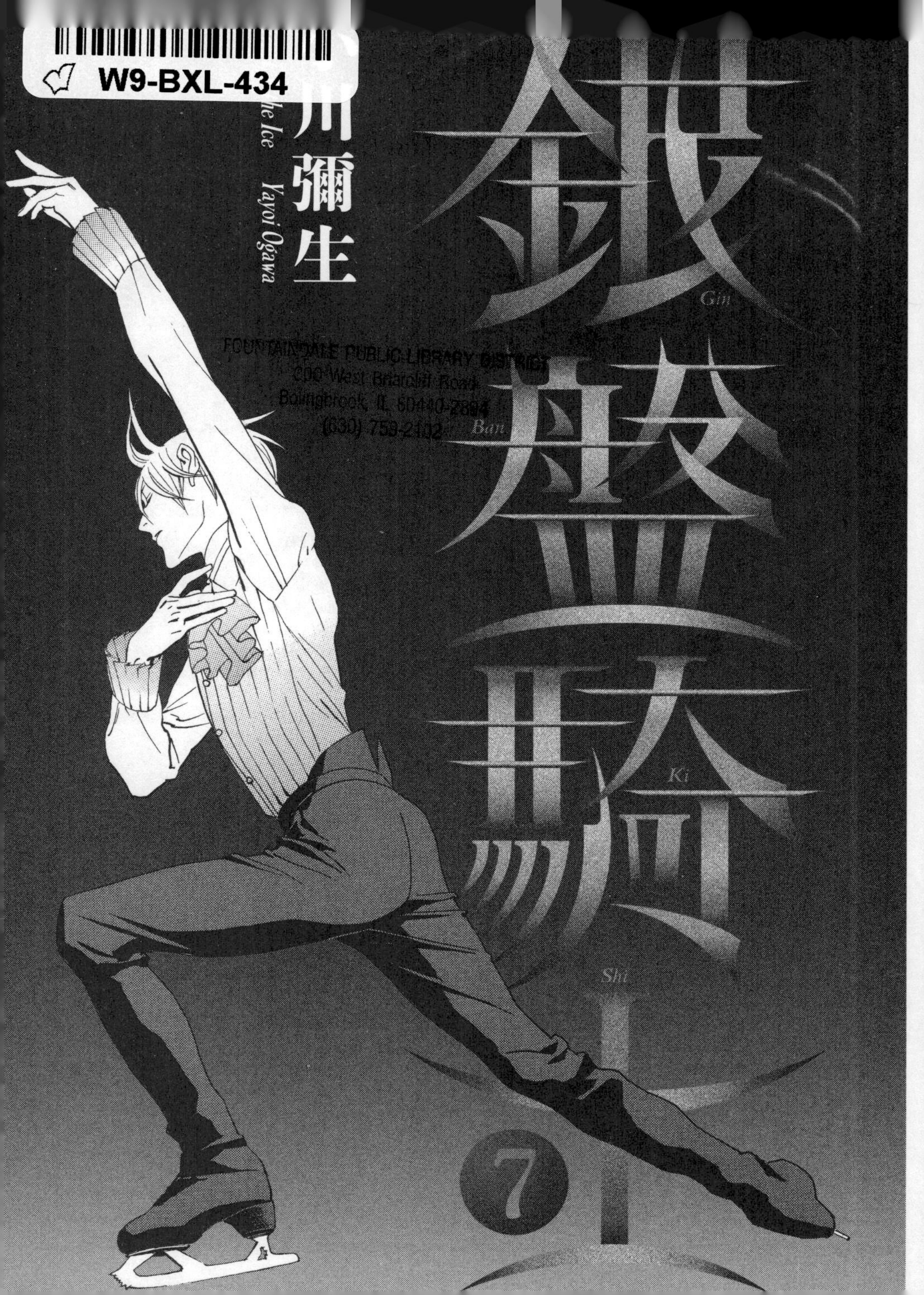
銀
Gin
盤
Ban
騎
Ki
士
Shi
7
川彌生
Yayoi Ogawa
he Ice

Characters

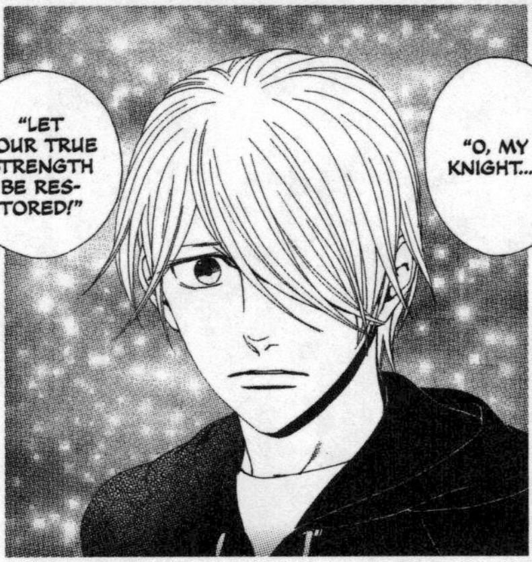

"O, MY KNIGHT..."
"LET YOUR TRUE STRENGTH BE RESTORED!"

Kokoro Kijinami

Japan's top men's figure skater. One of his greatest strengths is the beauty his height lends to his quadruple jumps. He cracks easily under pressure, but he's gotten more consistent since Chitose started reciting their magic spell for him. He and Chitose have been friends since childhood, and he was two years behind her in school.

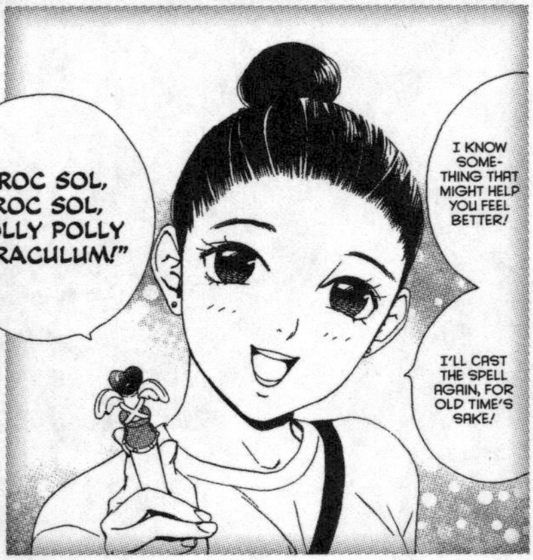

I KNOW SOMETHING THAT MIGHT HELP YOU FEEL BETTER!
"ROC SOL, ROC SOL, POLLY POLLY MIRACULUM!"
I'LL CAST THE SPELL AGAIN, FOR OLD TIME'S SAKE!

Chitose Igari

An editor for the health-and-lifestyle magazine *SASSO* She's so short that she often gets mistaken for an elementary schooler. She also accompanies Kokoro to competitions and pretends to be his personal trainer. It was Moriyama's idea. She seems to be having health problems...

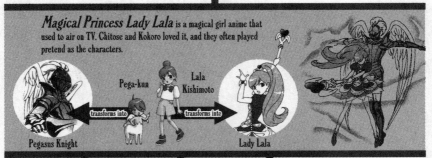

Magical Princess Lady Lala is a magical girl anime that used to air on TV. Chitose and Kokoro loved it, and they often played pretend as the characters.

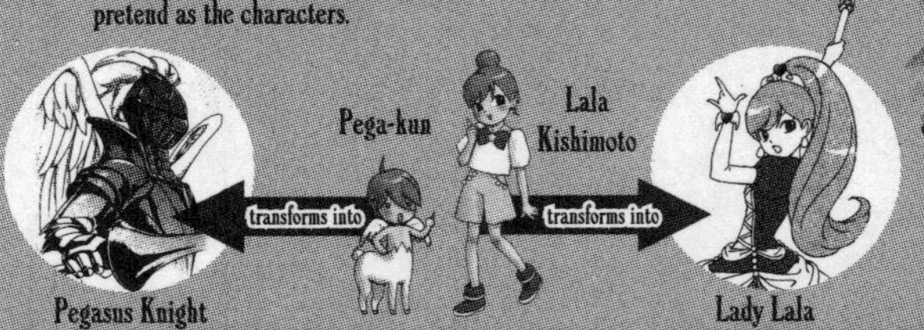

Pega-kun
Lala Kishimoto
transforms into
transforms into
Pegasus Knight
Lady Lala

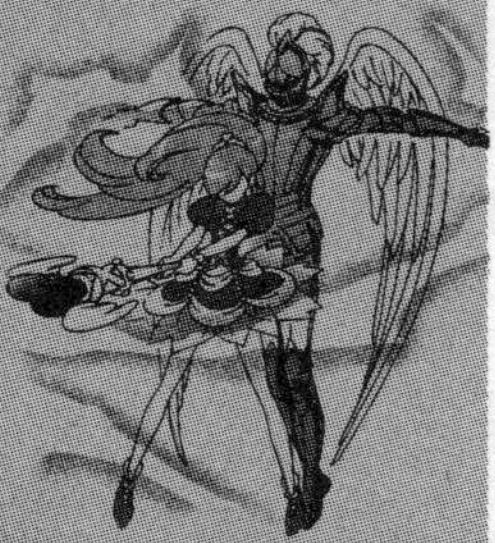

Liza Shibata

A model. Could the reports of her and Kokoro's affair be part of her plot?

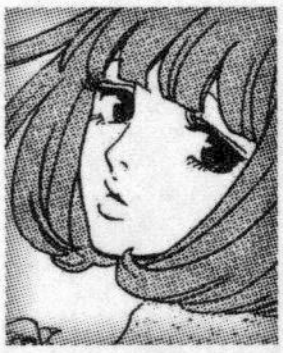

Yayoi Ogata

A manga artist. She went to the same college as Chitose and knows about her relationship with Kokoro.

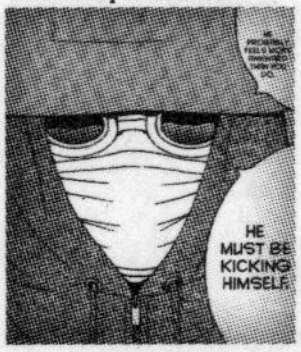

HE MUST BE KICKING HIMSELF.

Reiko Yano

An employee in Kodan Publishing's PR department. She's married, but she's having an affair with Sawada.

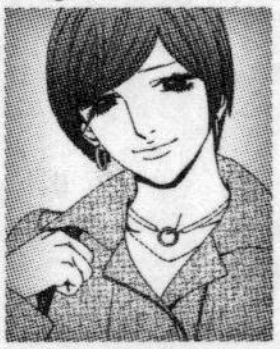

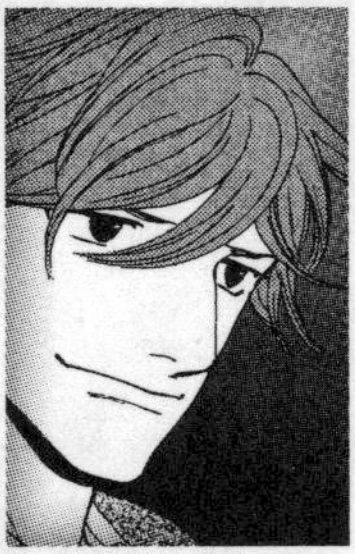

Koichi Sawada

The head of the editorial department for Kodan Publishing's magazine *SASSO.* He's good at his job, but can be somewhat lacking in delicacy...

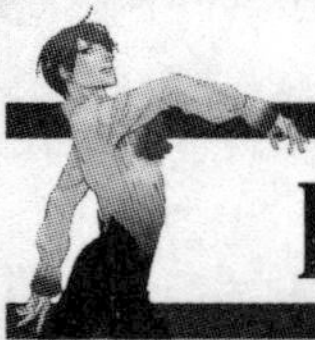

Knight of the Ice

Kokoro's Staff

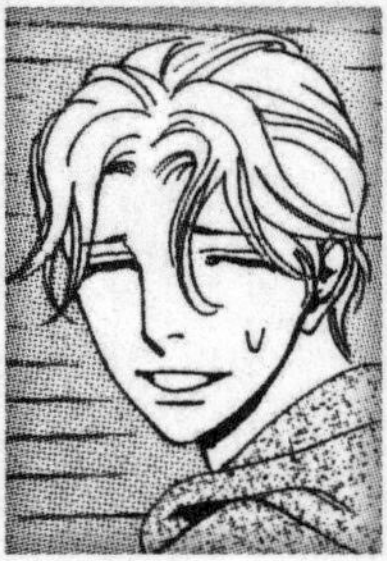

Kenzo Dominic Takiguchi

Kokoro's personal trainer.

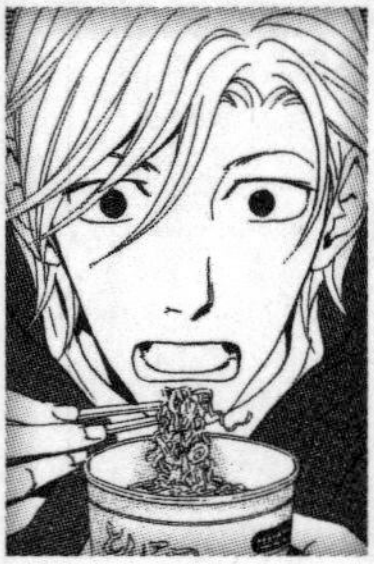

Hikaru Yomota

Kokoro's assistant coach and a former ice dancer.

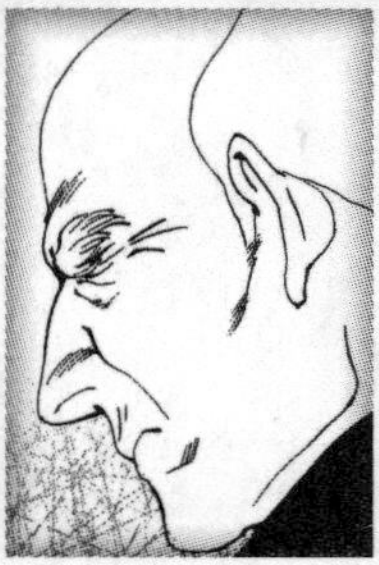

Takejiro Honda

Kokoro's coach and longtime rival of Raito Tamura's grandfather and coach, Masato Tamura.

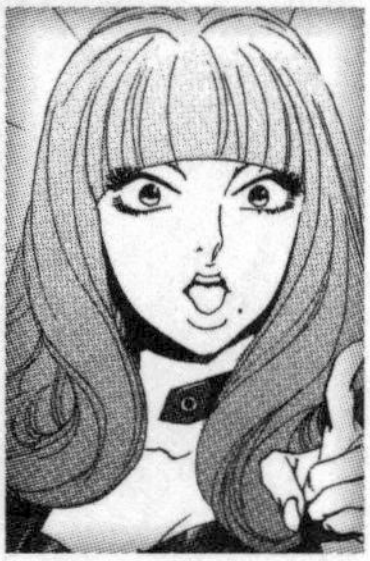

Moriyama

Kokoro's manager. She's not afraid to get a little pushy if that's what it takes to get results.

Kokoro's Rivals

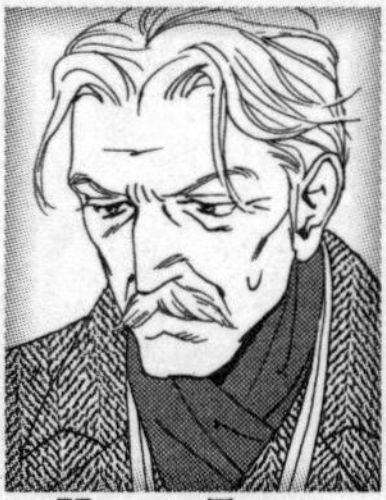

Masato Tamura

Raito Tamura's grandfather and coach.

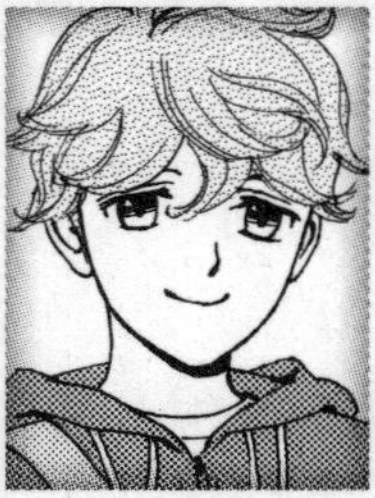

Fuuta Kumano

He can always rely on his speed and his devilish cuteness.

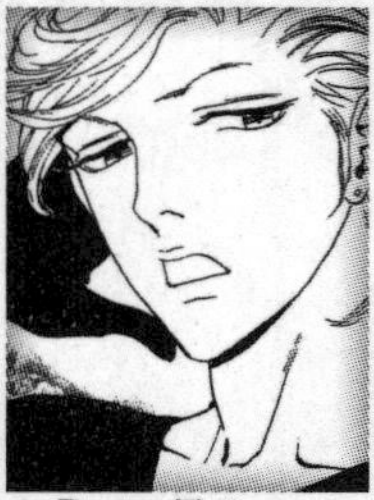

Raito Tamura

He dazzles the crowd with his passion and expressiveness.

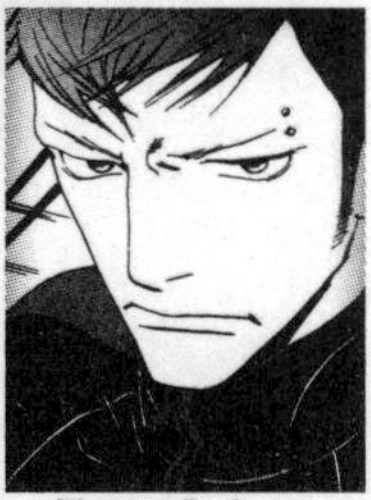

Taiga Aoki

His greatest strength is his ability to land two different quad jumps.

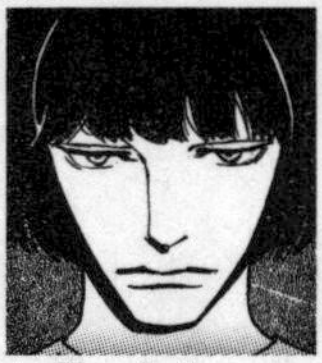

Ilia Sokurov

Russia's young top skater. He's an extreme klutz.

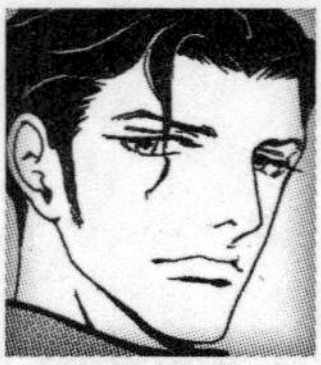

Kyle Miller

An American skater. He and Louis are known together as "KyLou."

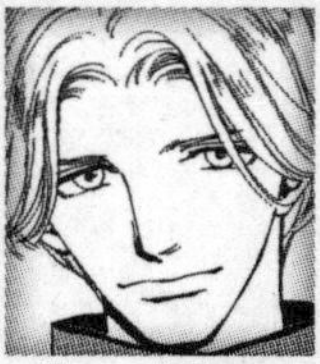

Louis Claire

A Canadian skater. He's a year younger than Kokoro and is the reigning World Champion.

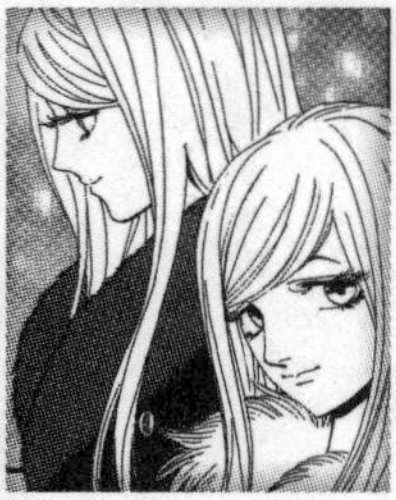

Maria & Anna Kijinami

Kokoro's younger twin sisters.

Contents

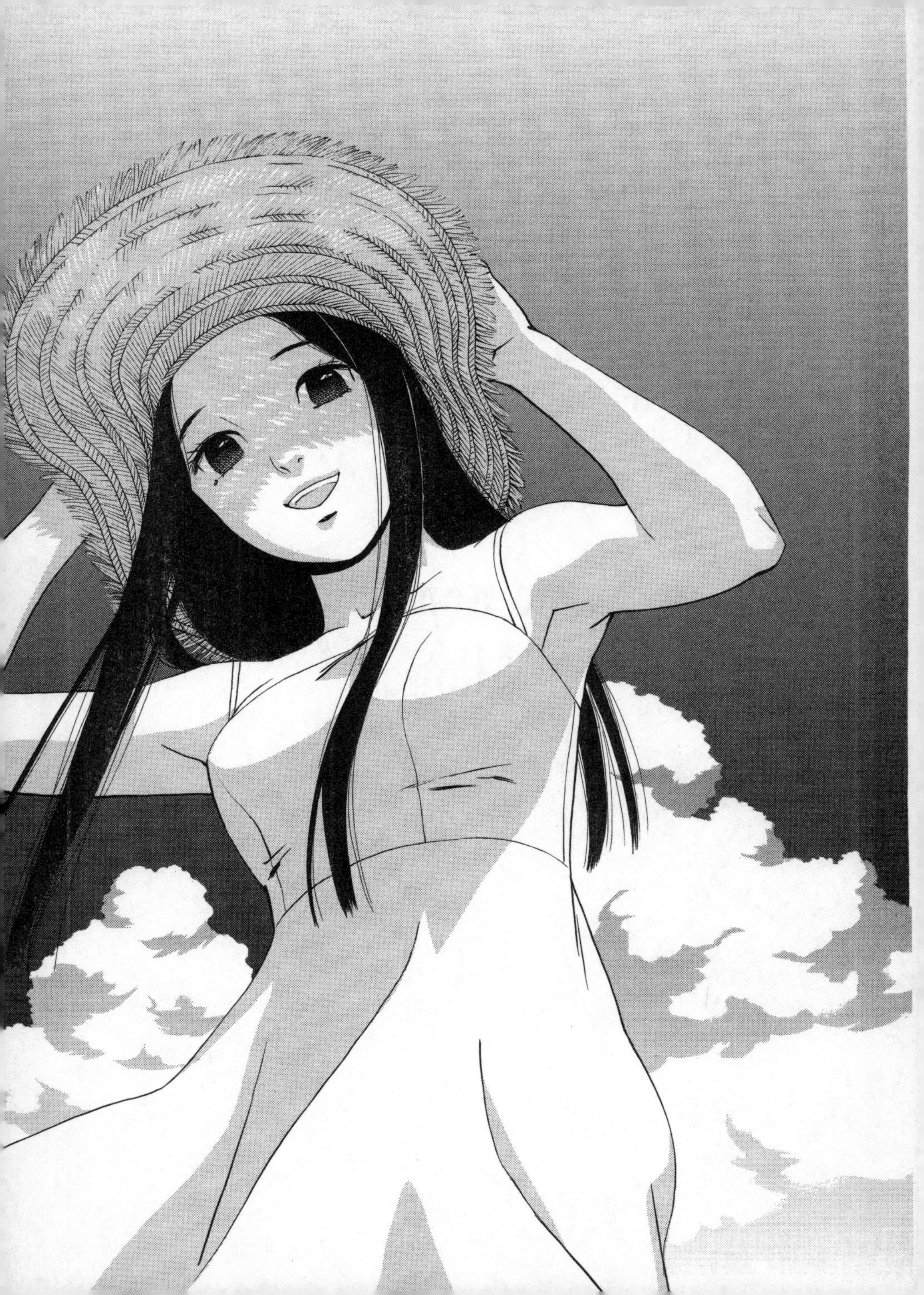

Spell 32
No Romance Allowed

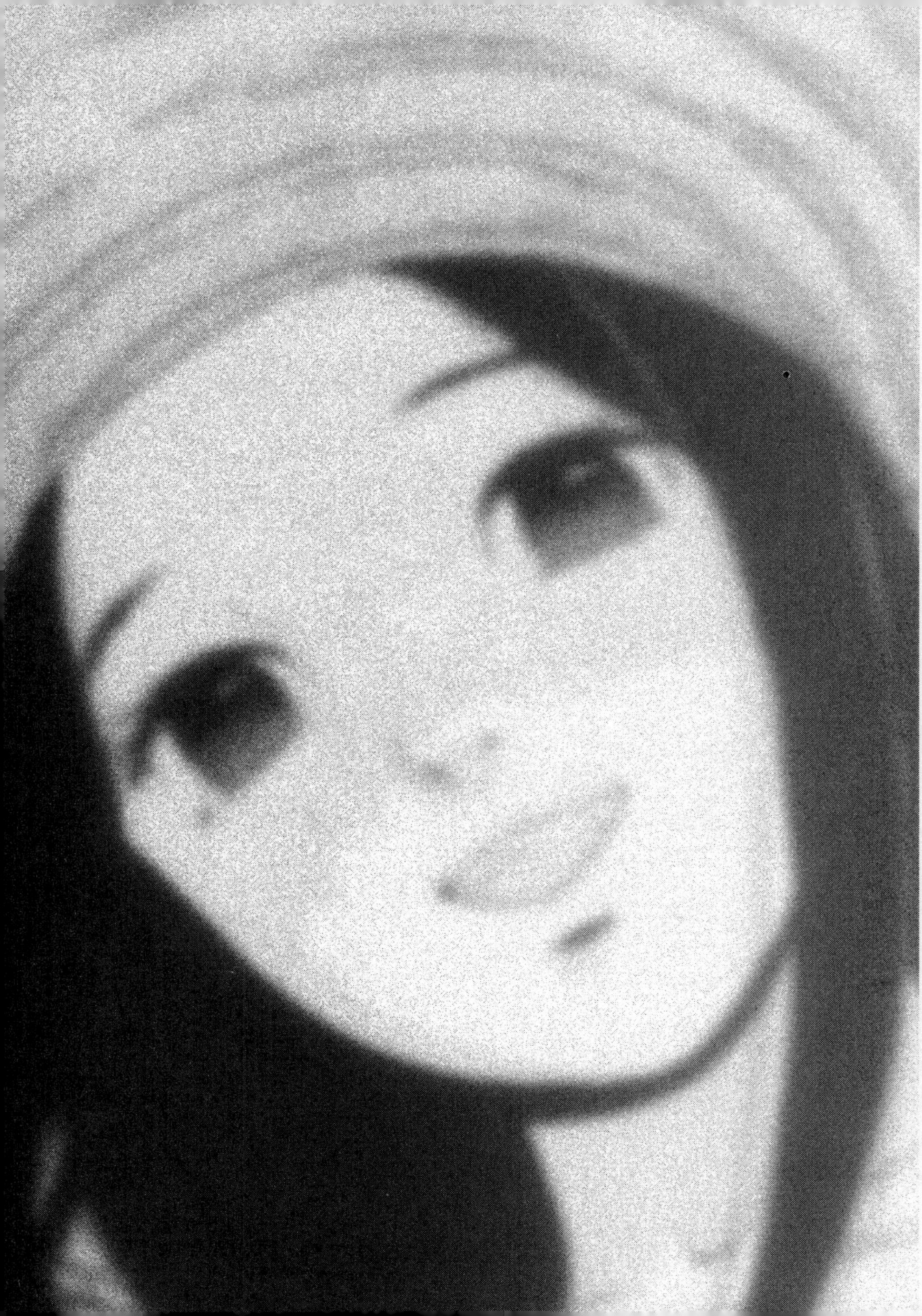

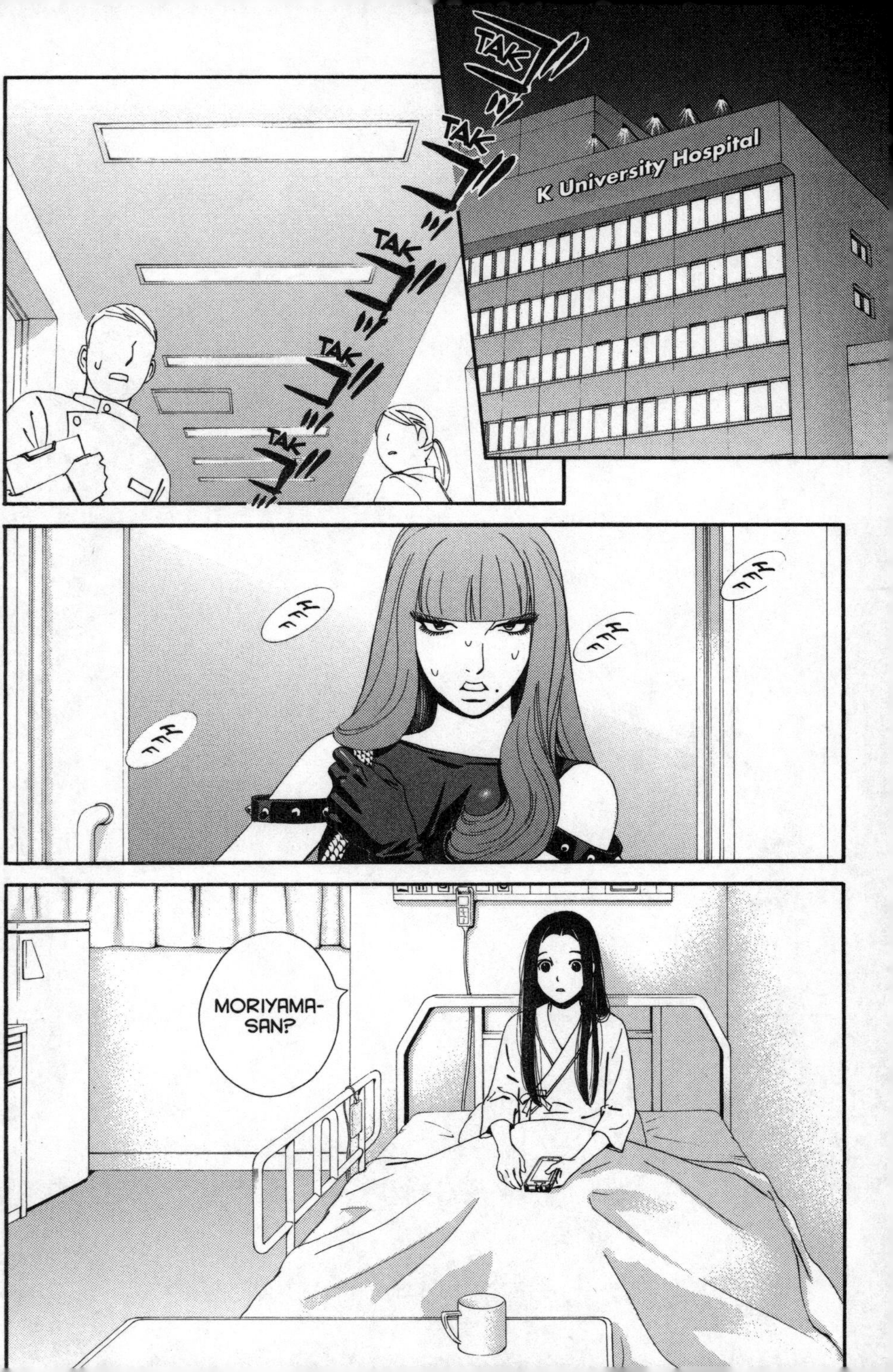
K University Hospital
TAK
TAK
TAK
TAK
TAK
HFF
HFF
HFF
HFF
MORIYAMA-SAN?

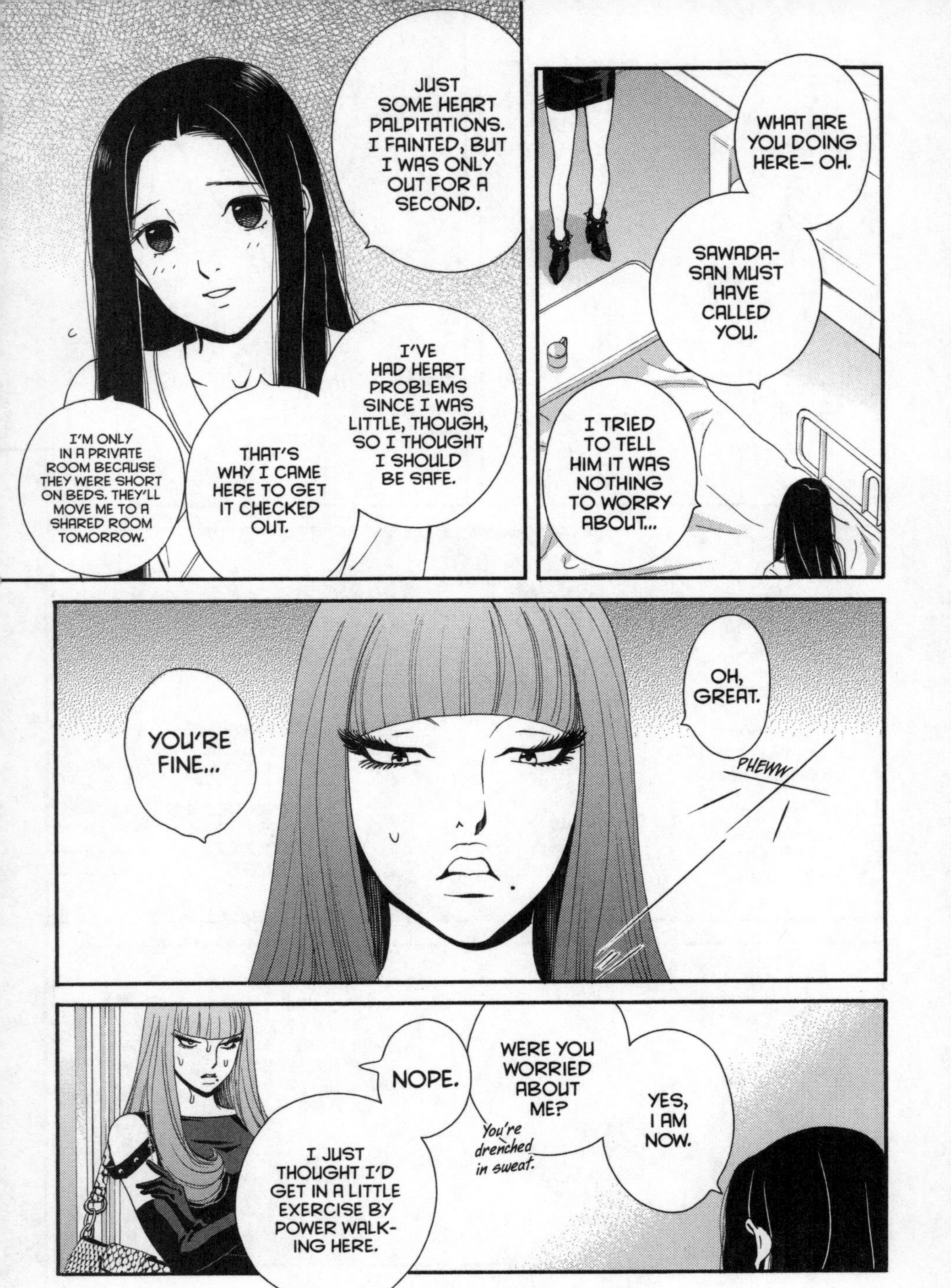
WHAT ARE YOU DOING HERE— OH.
SAWADA-SAN MUST HAVE CALLED YOU.
I TRIED TO TELL HIM IT WAS NOTHING TO WORRY ABOUT...
JUST SOME HEART PALPITATIONS. I FAINTED, BUT I WAS ONLY OUT FOR A SECOND.
I'VE HAD HEART PROBLEMS SINCE I WAS LITTLE, THOUGH, SO I THOUGHT I SHOULD BE SAFE.
THAT'S WHY I CAME HERE TO GET IT CHECKED OUT.
I'M ONLY IN A PRIVATE ROOM BECAUSE THEY WERE SHORT ON BEDS. THEY'LL MOVE ME TO A SHARED ROOM TOMORROW.
OH, GREAT.
PHEWW
YOU'RE FINE...
WERE YOU WORRIED ABOUT ME?
NOPE.
I JUST THOUGHT I'D GET IN A LITTLE EXERCISE BY POWER WALKING HERE.
You're drenched in sweat.
YES, I AM NOW.

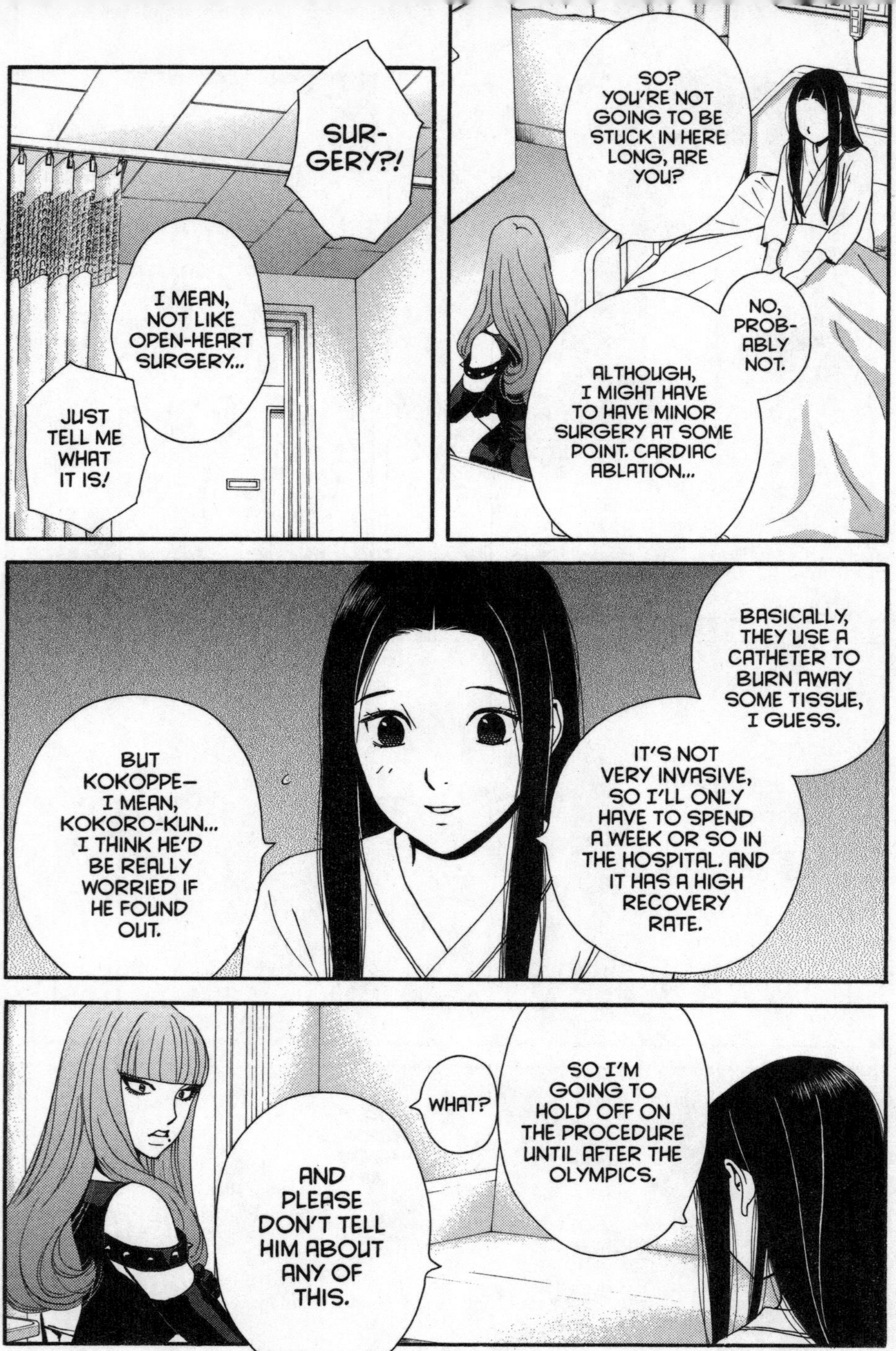
SO? YOU'RE NOT GOING TO BE STUCK IN HERE LONG, ARE YOU?
NO, PROB-ABLY NOT.
ALTHOUGH, I MIGHT HAVE TO HAVE MINOR SURGERY AT SOME POINT. CARDIAC ABLATION...
SUR-GERY?!
I MEAN, NOT LIKE OPEN-HEART SURGERY...
JUST TELL ME WHAT IT IS!
BASICALLY, THEY USE A CATHETER TO BURN AWAY SOME TISSUE, I GUESS.
IT'S NOT VERY INVASIVE, SO I'LL ONLY HAVE TO SPEND A WEEK OR SO IN THE HOSPITAL. AND IT HAS A HIGH RECOVERY RATE.
BUT KOKOPPE— I MEAN, KOKORO-KUN... I THINK HE'D BE REALLY WORRIED IF HE FOUND OUT.
SO I'M GOING TO HOLD OFF ON THE PROCEDURE UNTIL AFTER THE OLYMPICS.
WHAT?
AND PLEASE DON'T TELL HIM ABOUT ANY OF THIS.

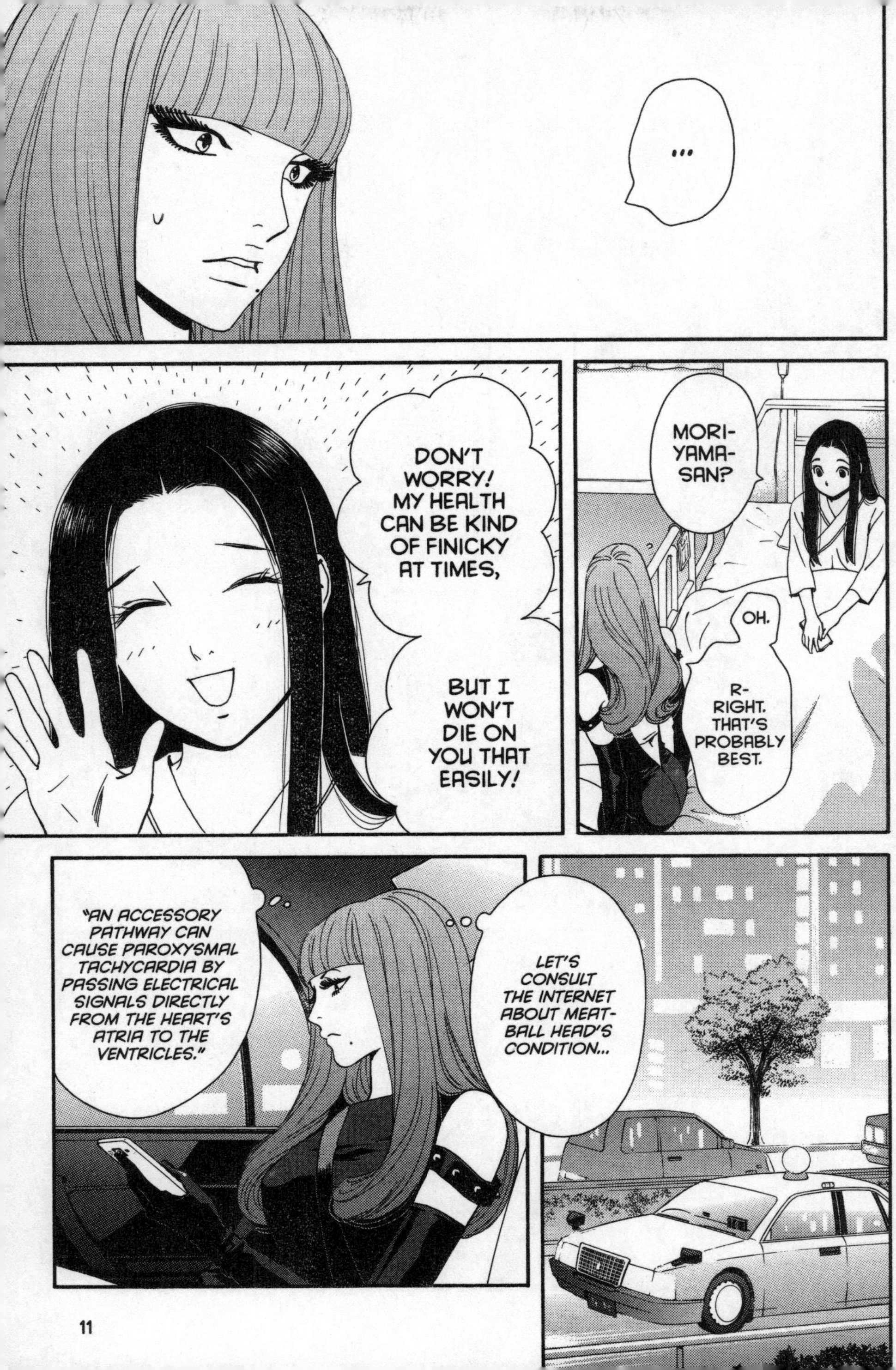
...
MORI-YAMA-SAN?
OH.
R-RIGHT. THAT'S PROBABLY BEST.
DON'T WORRY! MY HEALTH CAN BE KIND OF FINICKY AT TIMES,
BUT I WON'T DIE ON YOU THAT EASILY!
LET'S CONSULT THE INTERNET ABOUT MEAT-BALL HEAD'S CONDITION...
"AN ACCESSORY PATHWAY CAN CAUSE PAROXYSMAL TACHYCARDIA BY PASSING ELECTRICAL SIGNALS DIRECTLY FROM THE HEART'S ATRIA TO THE VENTRICLES."

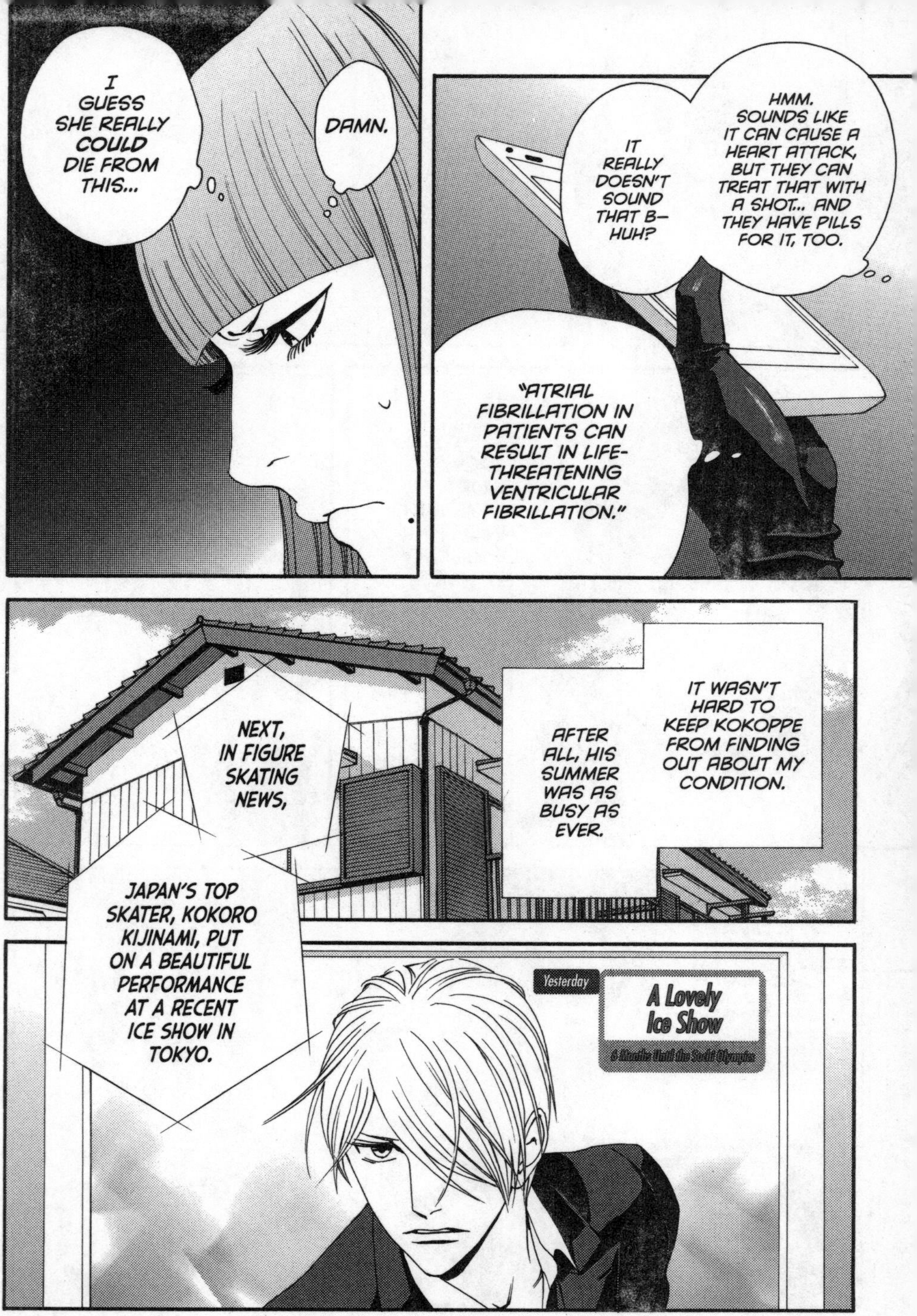
HMM. SOUNDS LIKE IT CAN CAUSE A HEART ATTACK, BUT THEY CAN TREAT THAT WITH A SHOT... AND THEY HAVE PILLS FOR IT, TOO.
IT REALLY DOESN'T SOUND THAT B— HUH?
"ATRIAL FIBRILLATION IN PATIENTS CAN RESULT IN LIFE-THREATENING VENTRICULAR FIBRILLATION."
DAMN.
I GUESS SHE REALLY COULD DIE FROM THIS...
IT WASN'T HARD TO KEEP KOKOPPE FROM FINDING OUT ABOUT MY CONDITION.
AFTER ALL, HIS SUMMER WAS AS BUSY AS EVER.
NEXT, IN FIGURE SKATING NEWS,
JAPAN'S TOP SKATER, KOKORO KIJINAMI, PUT ON A BEAUTIFUL PERFORMANCE AT A RECENT ICE SHOW IN TOKYO.
Yesterday
A Lovely Ice Show

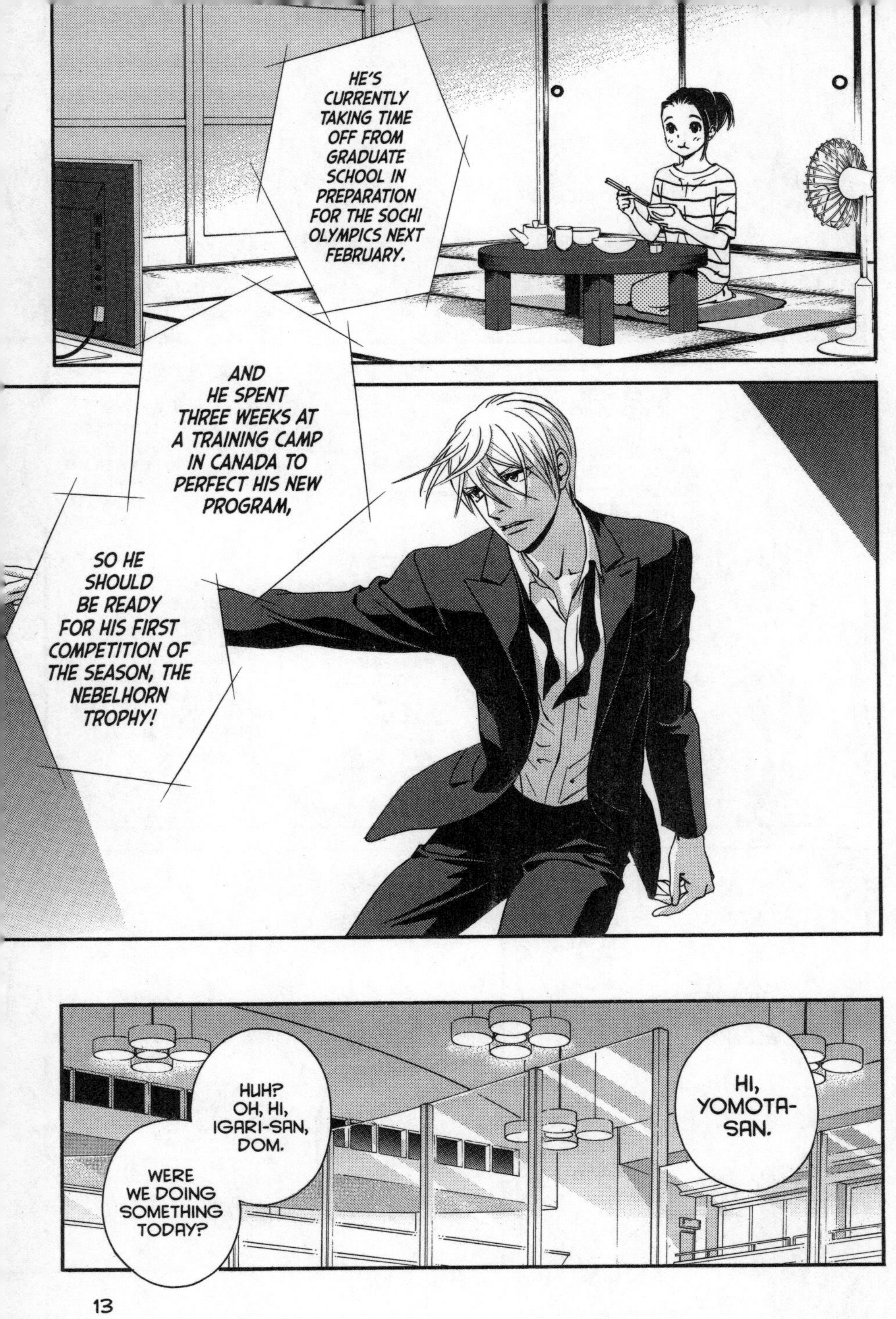
HE'S CURRENTLY TAKING TIME OFF FROM GRADUATE SCHOOL IN PREPARATION FOR THE SOCHI OLYMPICS NEXT FEBRUARY.
AND HE SPENT THREE WEEKS AT A TRAINING CAMP IN CANADA TO PERFECT HIS NEW PROGRAM,
SO HE SHOULD BE READY FOR HIS FIRST COMPETITION OF THE SEASON, THE NEBELHORN TROPHY!
HI, YOMOTA-SAN.
HUH? OH, HI, IGARI-SAN, DOM.
WERE WE DOING SOMETHING TODAY?

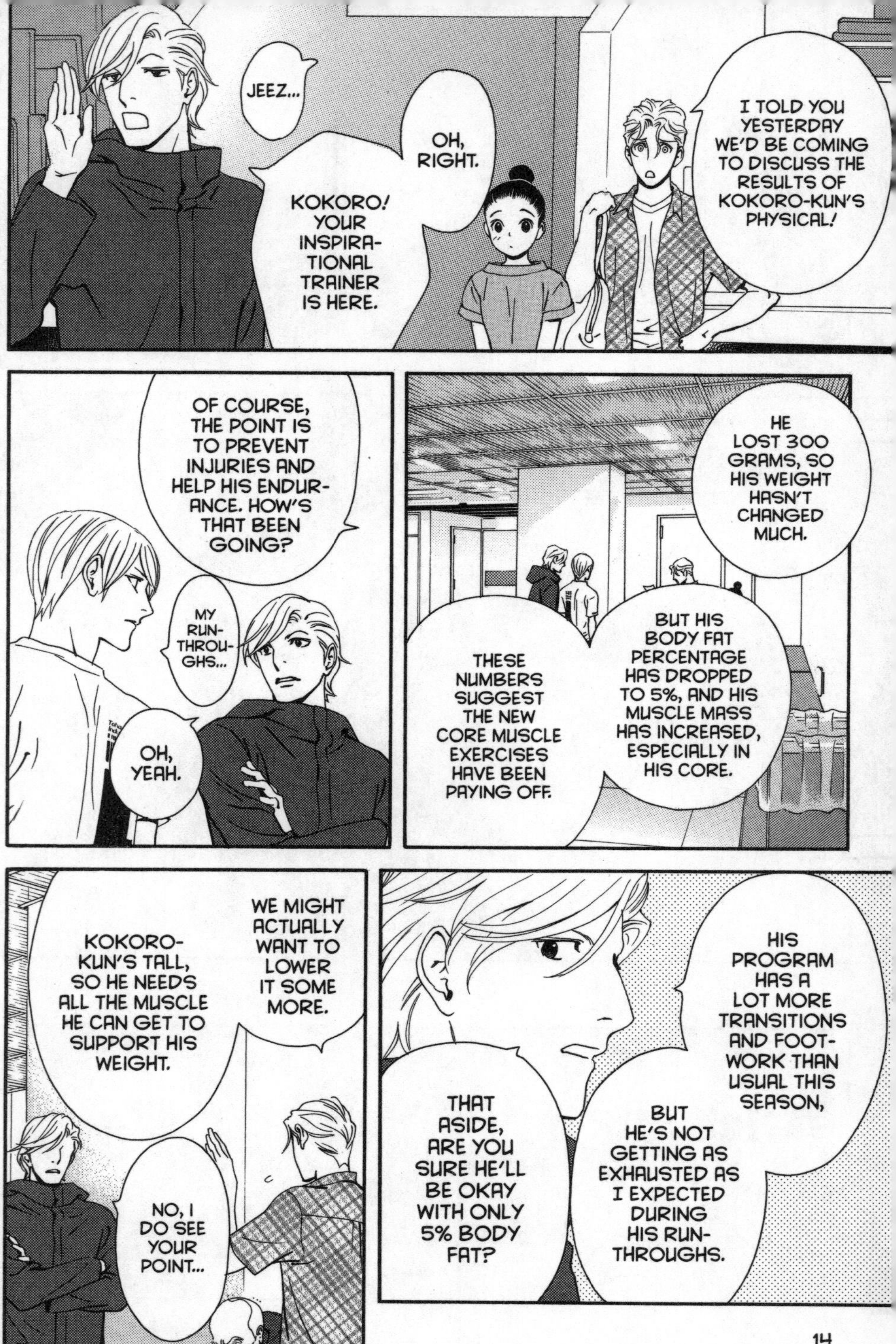
I TOLD YOU YESTERDAY WE'D BE COMING TO DISCUSS THE RESULTS OF KOKORO-KUN'S PHYSICAL!
OH, RIGHT.
JEEZ...
KOKORO! YOUR INSPIRATIONAL TRAINER IS HERE.
HE LOST 300 GRAMS, SO HIS WEIGHT HASN'T CHANGED MUCH.
BUT HIS BODY FAT PERCENTAGE HAS DROPPED TO 5%, AND HIS MUSCLE MASS HAS INCREASED, ESPECIALLY IN HIS CORE.
THESE NUMBERS SUGGEST THE NEW CORE MUSCLE EXERCISES HAVE BEEN PAYING OFF.
OF COURSE, THE POINT IS TO PREVENT INJURIES AND HELP HIS ENDURANCE. HOW'S THAT BEEN GOING?
MY RUN-THROUGHS...
OH, YEAH.
HIS PROGRAM HAS A LOT MORE TRANSITIONS AND FOOTWORK THAN USUAL THIS SEASON,
BUT HE'S NOT GETTING AS EXHAUSTED AS I EXPECTED DURING HIS RUN-THROUGHS.
THAT ASIDE, ARE YOU SURE HE'LL BE OKAY WITH ONLY 5% BODY FAT?
WE MIGHT ACTUALLY WANT TO LOWER IT SOME MORE.
KOKORO-KUN'S TALL, SO HE NEEDS ALL THE MUSCLE HE CAN GET TO SUPPORT HIS WEIGHT.
NO, I DO SEE YOUR POINT...

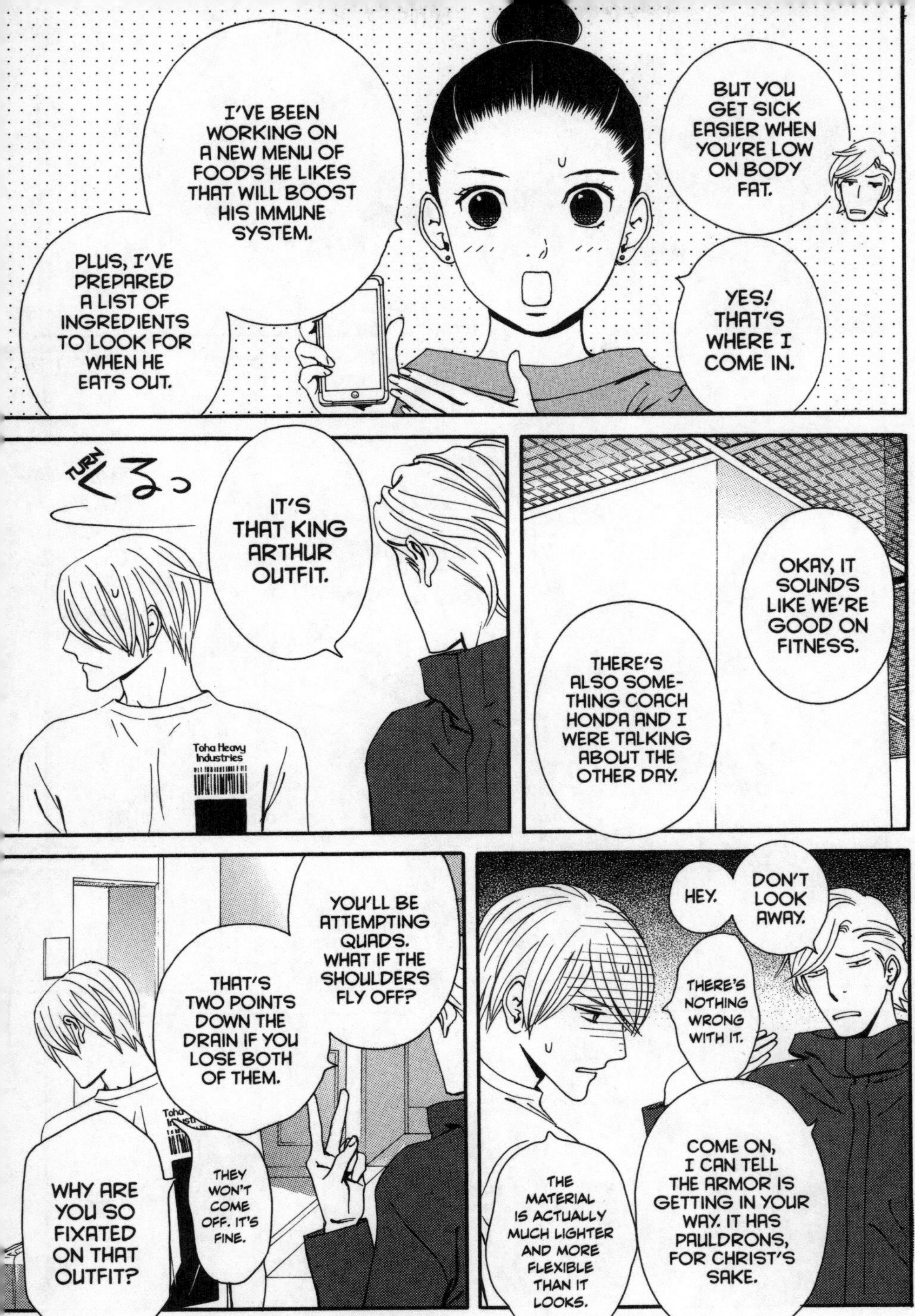
BUT YOU GET SICK EASIER WHEN YOU'RE LOW ON BODY FAT.
YES! THAT'S WHERE I COME IN.
I'VE BEEN WORKING ON A NEW MENU OF FOODS HE LIKES THAT WILL BOOST HIS IMMUNE SYSTEM.
PLUS, I'VE PREPARED A LIST OF INGREDIENTS TO LOOK FOR WHEN HE EATS OUT.
OKAY, IT SOUNDS LIKE WE'RE GOOD ON FITNESS.
THERE'S ALSO SOME-THING COACH HONDA AND I WERE TALKING ABOUT THE OTHER DAY.
IT'S THAT KING ARTHUR OUTFIT.
TURN くるっ
Toha Heavy Industries
DON'T LOOK AWAY.
HEY.
THERE'S NOTHING WRONG WITH IT.
COME ON, I CAN TELL THE ARMOR IS GETTING IN YOUR WAY. IT HAS PAULDRONS, FOR CHRIST'S SAKE.
THE MATERIAL IS ACTUALLY MUCH LIGHTER AND MORE FLEXIBLE THAN IT LOOKS.
YOU'LL BE ATTEMPTING QUADS. WHAT IF THE SHOULDERS FLY OFF?
THAT'S TWO POINTS DOWN THE DRAIN IF YOU LOSE BOTH OF THEM.
THEY WON'T COME OFF. IT'S FINE.
WHY ARE YOU SO FIXATED ON THAT OUTFIT?
No pause

(ACTUALLY, HE'D ONLY LOSE ONE POINT NO MATTER HOW MANY PIECES CAME OFF.)

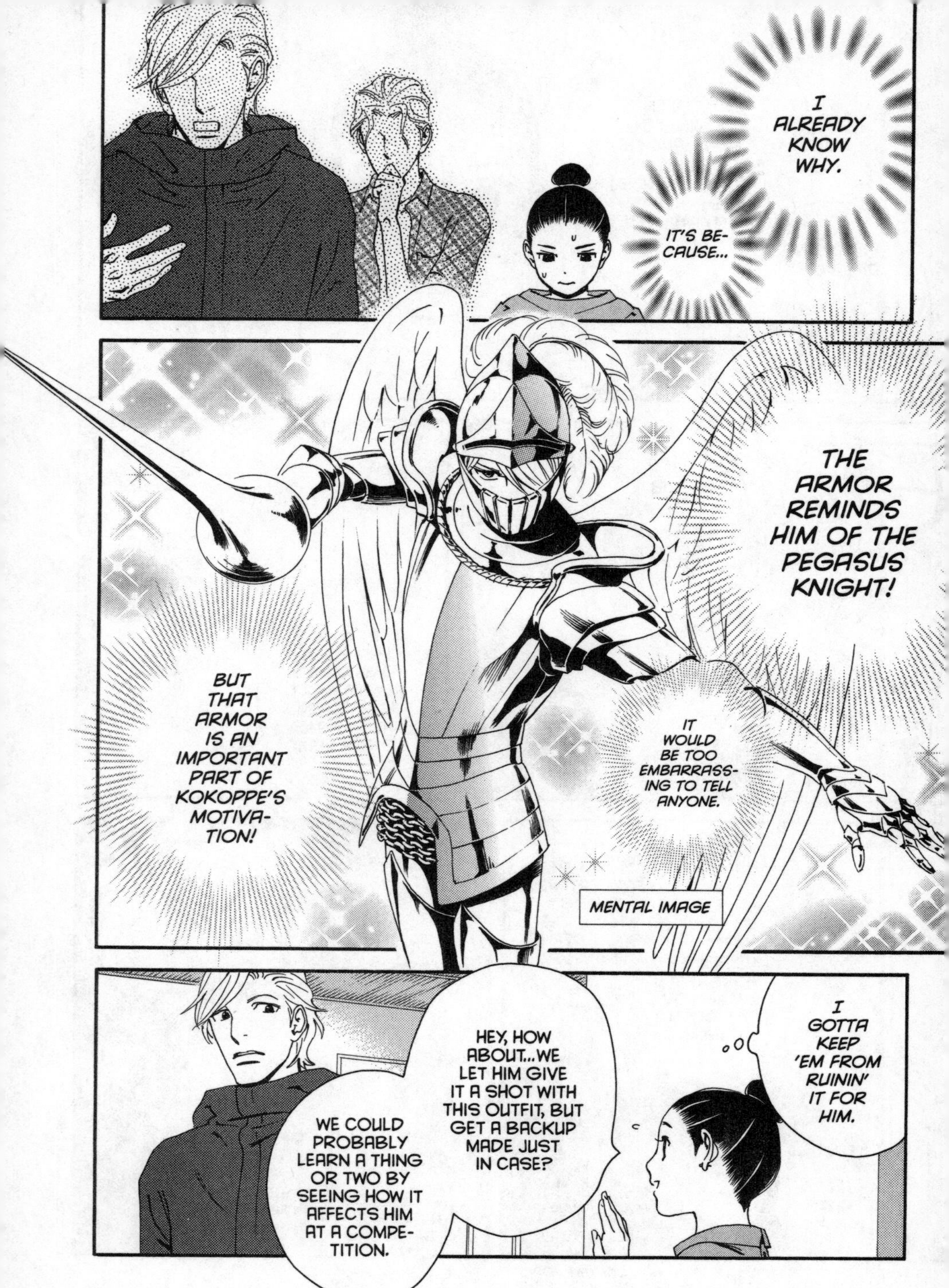
I ALREADY KNOW WHY.
IT'S BE-CAUSE...
THE ARMOR REMINDS HIM OF THE PEGASUS KNIGHT!
IT WOULD BE TOO EMBARRASS-ING TO TELL ANYONE.
BUT THAT ARMOR IS AN IMPORTANT PART OF KOKOPPE'S MOTIVA-TION!
MENTAL IMAGE
I GOTTA KEEP 'EM FROM RUININ' IT FOR HIM.
HEY, HOW ABOUT...WE LET HIM GIVE IT A SHOT WITH THIS OUTFIT, BUT GET A BACKUP MADE JUST IN CASE?
WE COULD PROBABLY LEARN A THING OR TWO BY SEEING HOW IT AFFECTS HIM AT A COMPE-TITION.

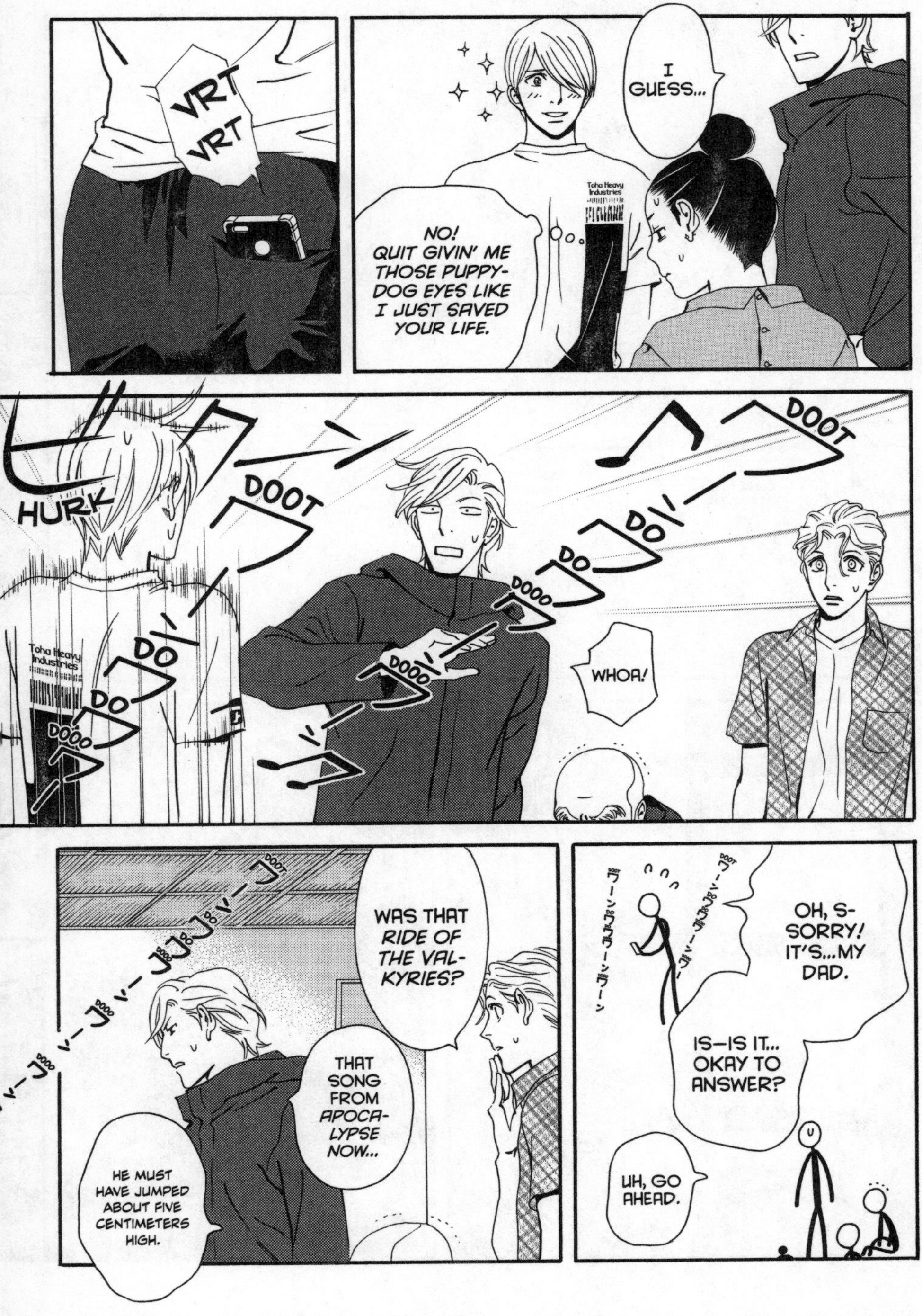

I GUESS...
NO! QUIT GIVIN' ME THOSE PUPPY-DOG EYES LIKE I JUST SAVED YOUR LIFE.
VRT VRT
DOOT
DO
DO
DOOO
WHOA!
DOOO
HURK
DOOT
DO
DO
DOOO
DOOT
OH, S-SORRY! IT'S...MY DAD.
IS—IS IT... OKAY TO ANSWER?
UH, GO AHEAD.
DOOT
WAS THAT RIDE OF THE VAL-KYRIES?
THAT SONG FROM APOCA-LYPSE NOW...
HE MUST HAVE JUMPED ABOUT FIVE CENTIMETERS HIGH.

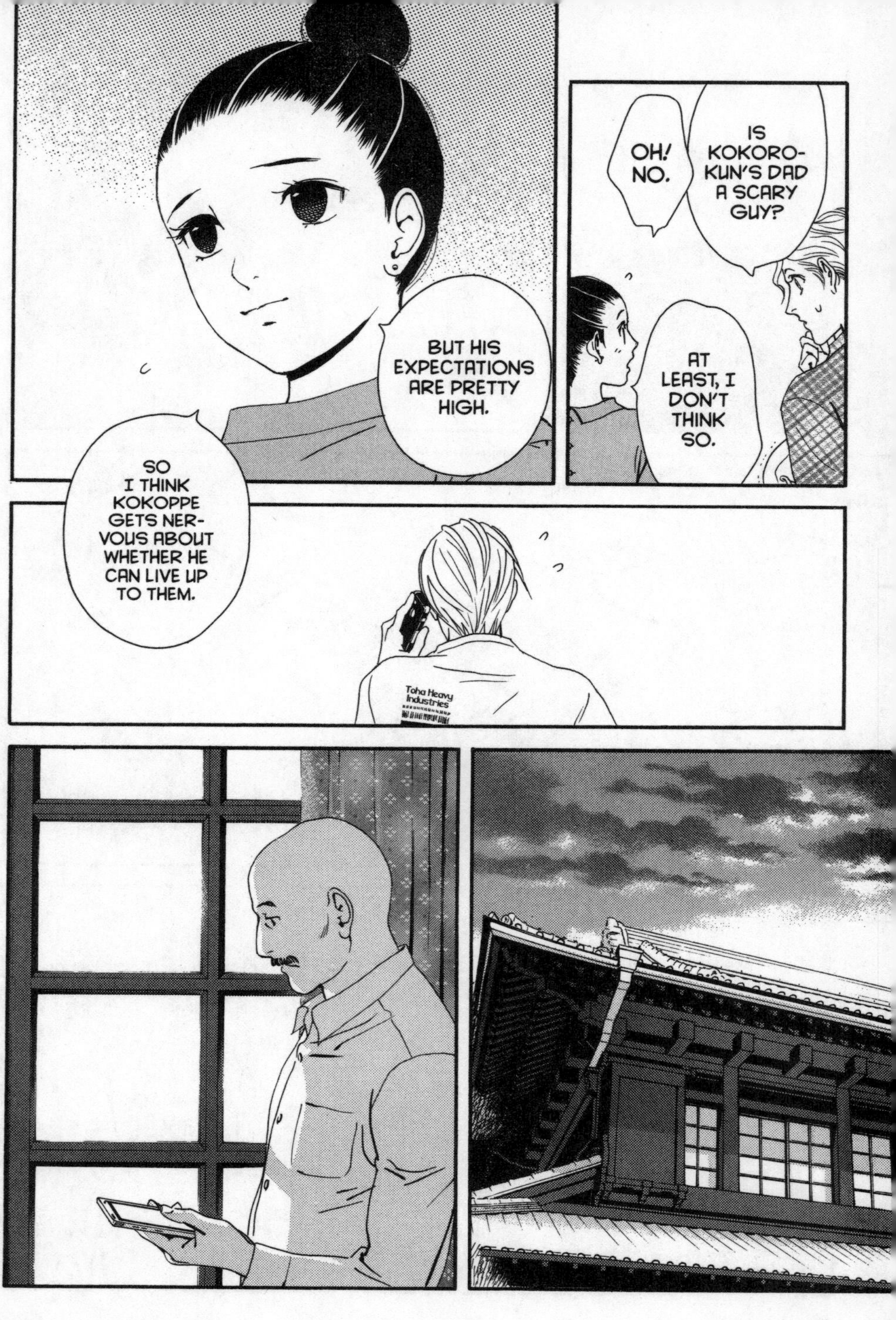
IS KOKORO-KUN'S DAD A SCARY GUY?
OH! NO.
AT LEAST, I DON'T THINK SO.
BUT HIS EXPECTATIONS ARE PRETTY HIGH.
SO I THINK KOKOPPE GETS NERVOUS ABOUT WHETHER HE CAN LIVE UP TO THEM.
Toha Heavy Industries

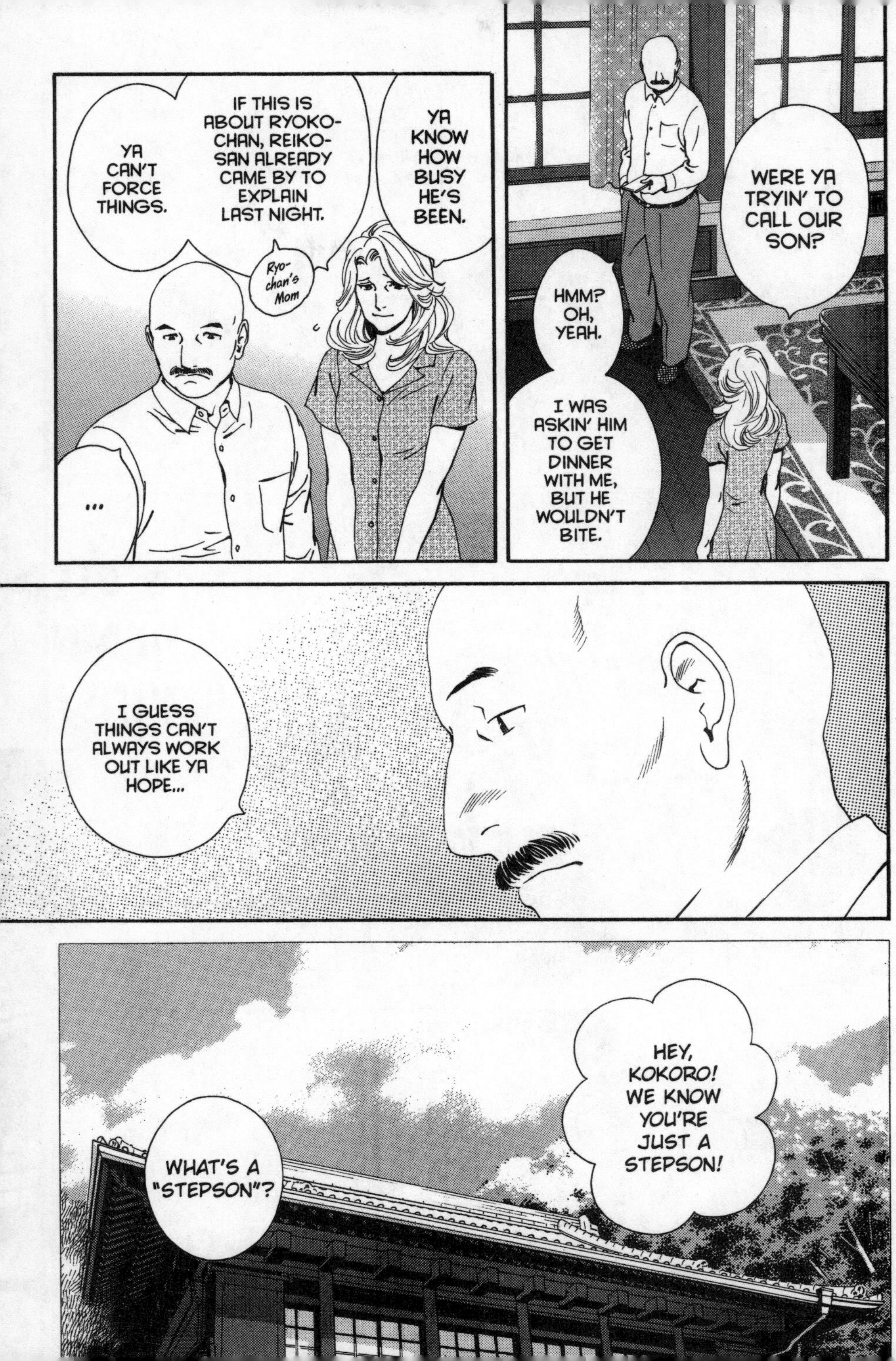
WERE YA TRYIN' TO CALL OUR SON?
HMM? OH, YEAH.
I WAS ASKIN' HIM TO GET DINNER WITH ME, BUT HE WOULDN'T BITE.
YA KNOW HOW BUSY HE'S BEEN.
IF THIS IS ABOUT RYOKO-CHAN, REIKO-SAN ALREADY CAME BY TO EXPLAIN LAST NIGHT.
YA CAN'T FORCE THINGS.
Ryo-chan's Mom
...
I GUESS THINGS CAN'T ALWAYS WORK OUT LIKE YA HOPE...
HEY, KOKORO! WE KNOW YOU'RE JUST A STEPSON!
WHAT'S A "STEPSON"?

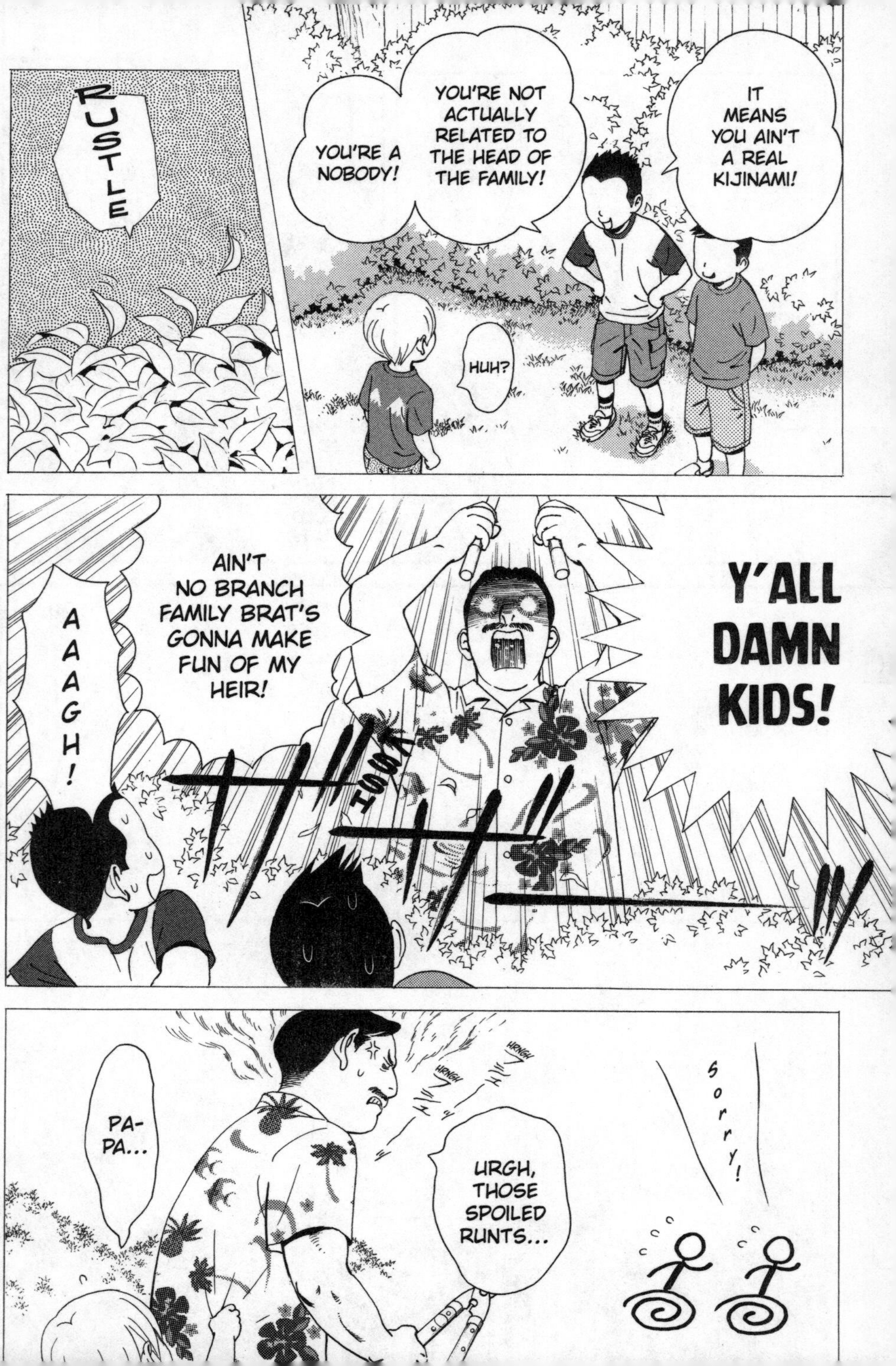
IT MEANS YOU AIN'T A REAL KIJINAMI!
YOU'RE NOT ACTUALLY RELATED TO THE HEAD OF THE FAMILY!
YOU'RE A NOBODY!
HUH?
RUSTLE
Y'ALL DAMN KIDS!
AIN'T NO BRANCH FAMILY BRAT'S GONNA MAKE FUN OF MY HEIR!
AAAAGH!
Sorry!
HRNGH
HRNGH
URGH, THOSE SPOILED RUNTS...
PA-PA...

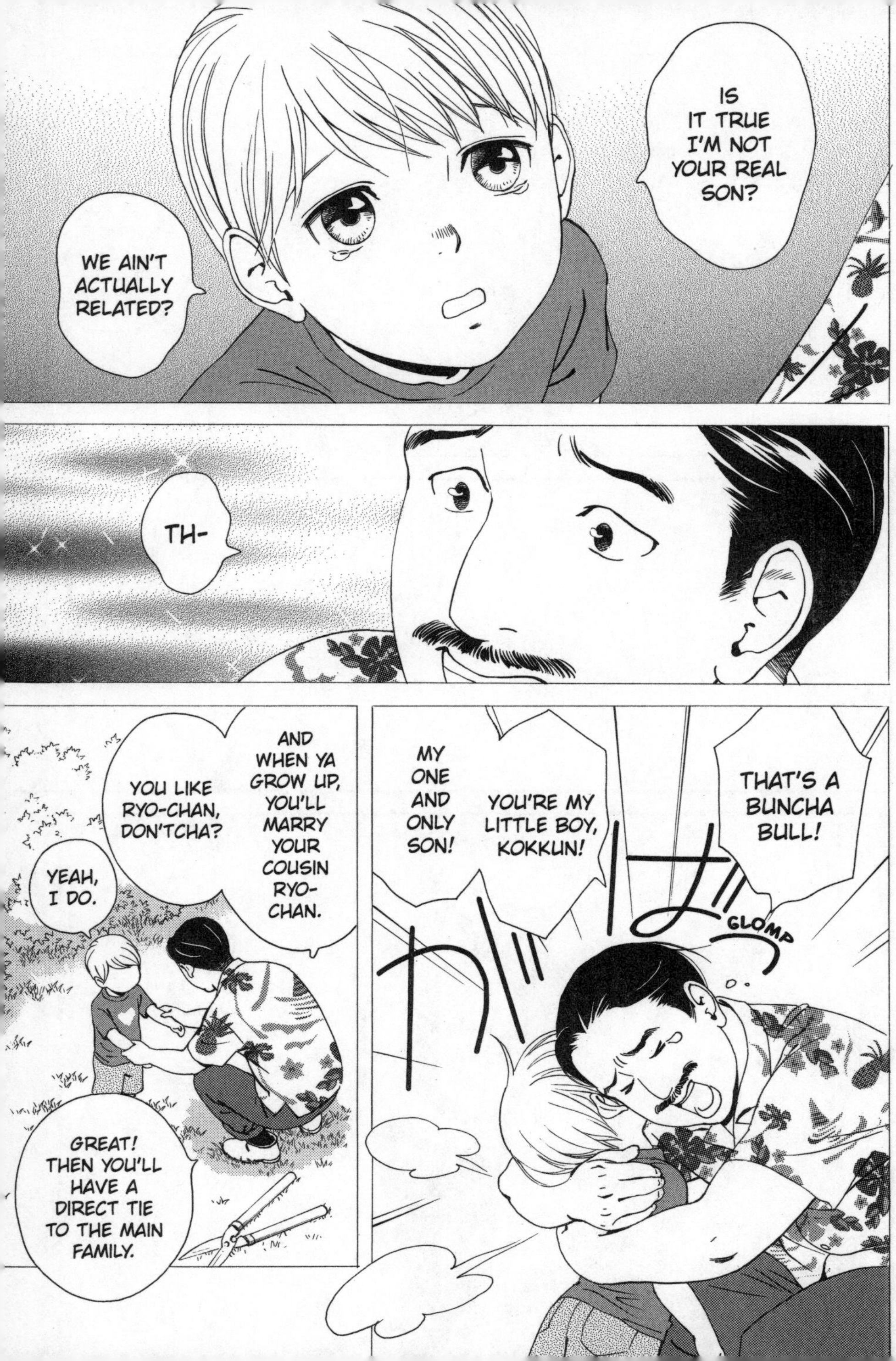
IS IT TRUE I'M NOT YOUR REAL SON?
WE AIN'T ACTUALLY RELATED?
TH-
THAT'S A BUNCHA BULL!
GLOMP
YOU'RE MY LITTLE BOY, KOKKUN!
MY ONE AND ONLY SON!
AND WHEN YA GROW UP, YOU'LL MARRY YOUR COUSIN RYO-CHAN.
YOU LIKE RYO-CHAN, DON'TCHA?
YEAH, I DO.
GREAT! THEN YOU'LL HAVE A DIRECT TIE TO THE MAIN FAMILY.

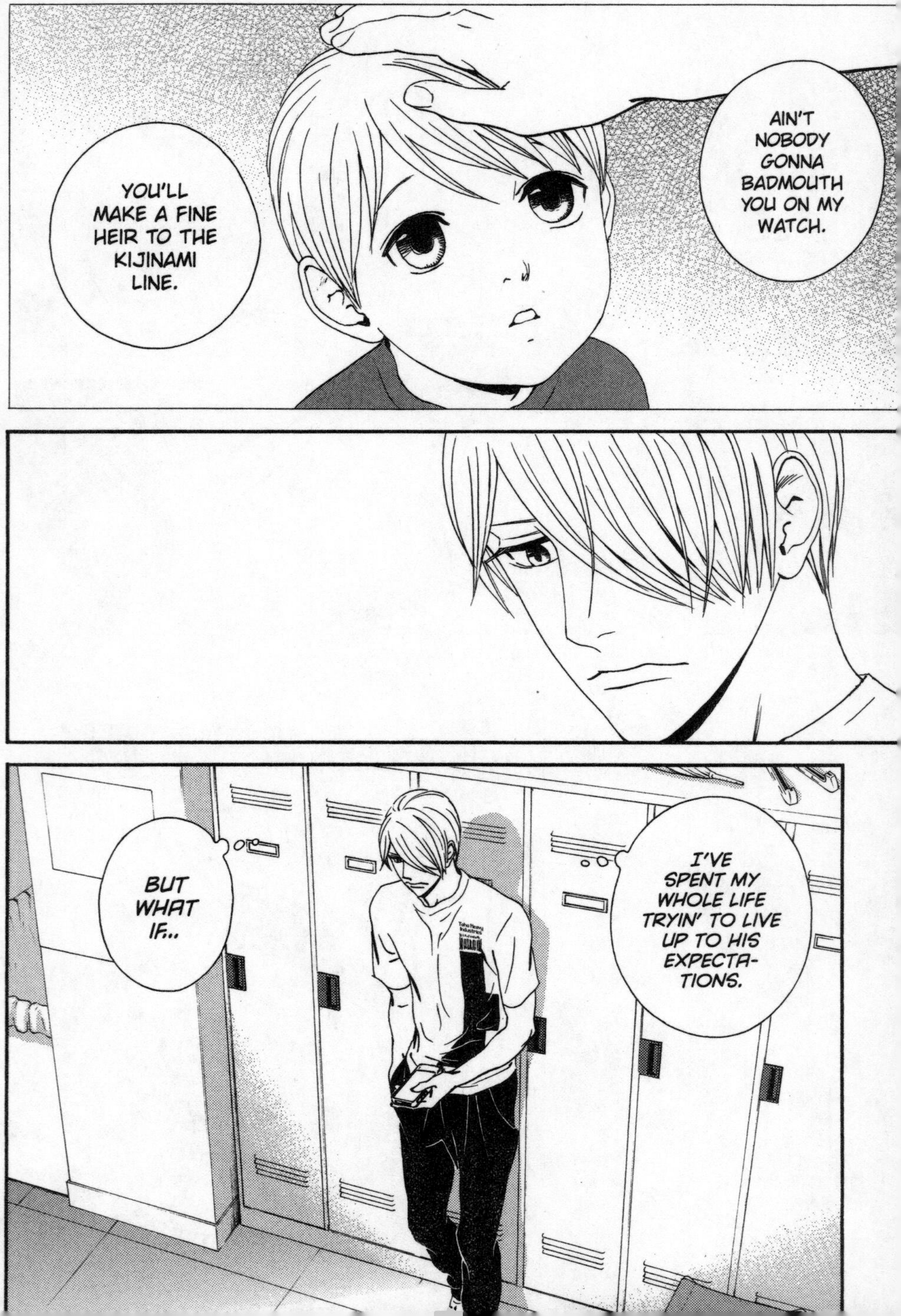
AIN'T NOBODY GONNA BADMOUTH YOU ON MY WATCH.
YOU'LL MAKE A FINE HEIR TO THE KIJINAMI LINE.
I'VE SPENT MY WHOLE LIFE TRYIN' TO LIVE UP TO HIS EXPECTA-TIONS.
BUT WHAT IF...

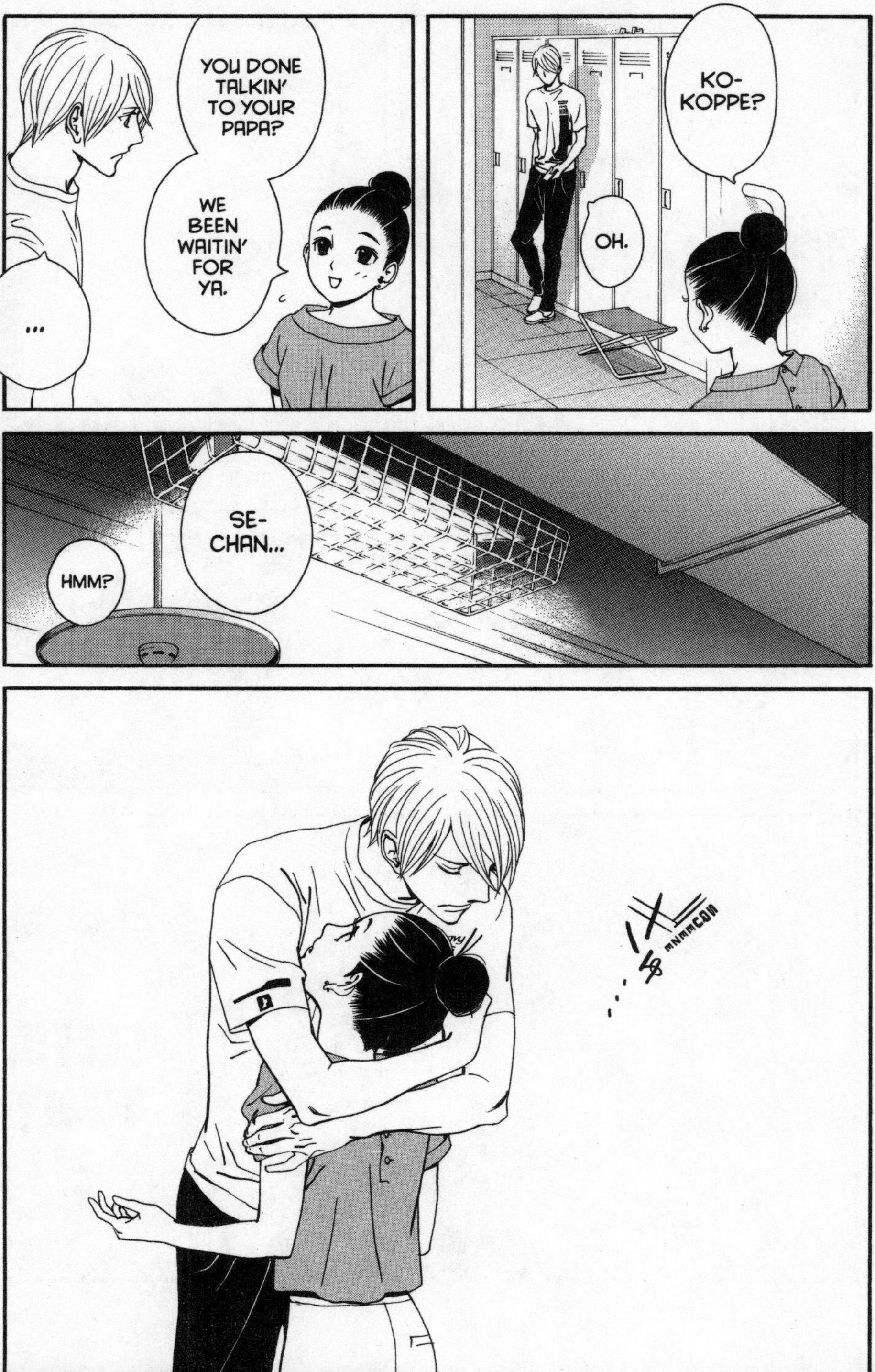
KO-KOPPE?
OH.
YOU DONE TALKIN' TO YOUR PAPA?
WE BEEN WAITIN' FOR YA.
...
SE-CHAN...
HMM?

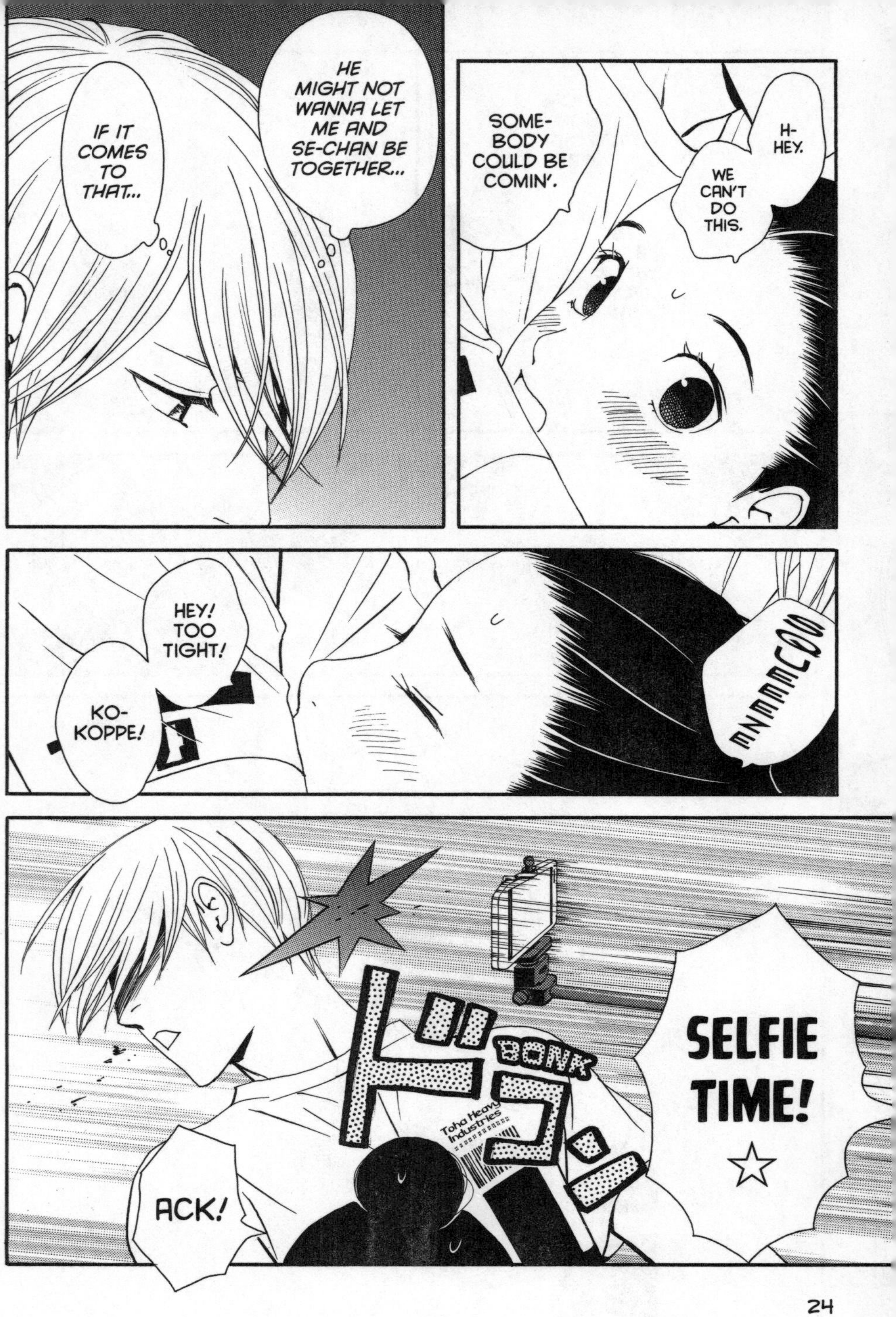
H- HEY.
WE CAN'T DO THIS.
SOME- BODY COULD BE COMIN'.
HE MIGHT NOT WANNA LET ME AND SE-CHAN BE TOGETHER...
IF IT COMES TO THAT...
HEY! TOO TIGHT!
KO- KOPPE!
SELFIE TIME! ☆
BONK
Toha Heavy Industries
ACK!

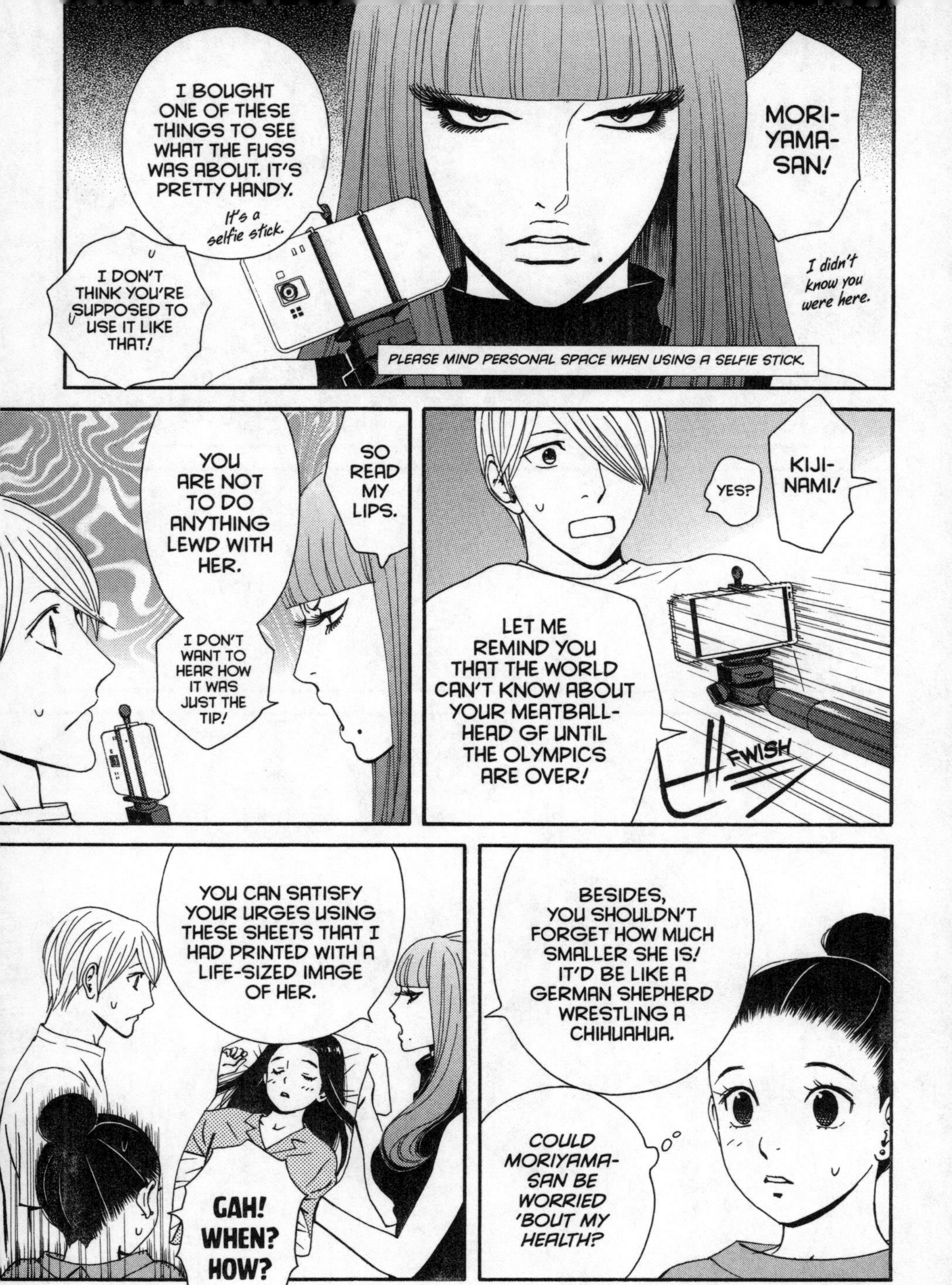
MORI-YAMA-SAN!
I didn't know you were here.
I BOUGHT ONE OF THESE THINGS TO SEE WHAT THE FUSS WAS ABOUT. IT'S PRETTY HANDY.
It's a selfie stick.
I DON'T THINK YOU'RE SUPPOSED TO USE IT LIKE THAT!
PLEASE MIND PERSONAL SPACE WHEN USING A SELFIE STICK.
KIJI-NAMI!
YES?
LET ME REMIND YOU THAT THE WORLD CAN'T KNOW ABOUT YOUR MEATBALL-HEAD GF UNTIL THE OLYMPICS ARE OVER!
FWISH
SO READ MY LIPS.
YOU ARE NOT TO DO ANYTHING LEWD WITH HER.
I DON'T WANT TO HEAR HOW IT WAS JUST THE TIP!
BESIDES, YOU SHOULDN'T FORGET HOW MUCH SMALLER SHE IS! IT'D BE LIKE A GERMAN SHEPHERD WRESTLING A CHIHUAHUA.
COULD MORIYAMA-SAN BE WORRIED 'BOUT MY HEALTH?
YOU CAN SATISFY YOUR URGES USING THESE SHEETS THAT I HAD PRINTED WITH A LIFE-SIZED IMAGE OF HER.
GAH! WHEN? HOW?

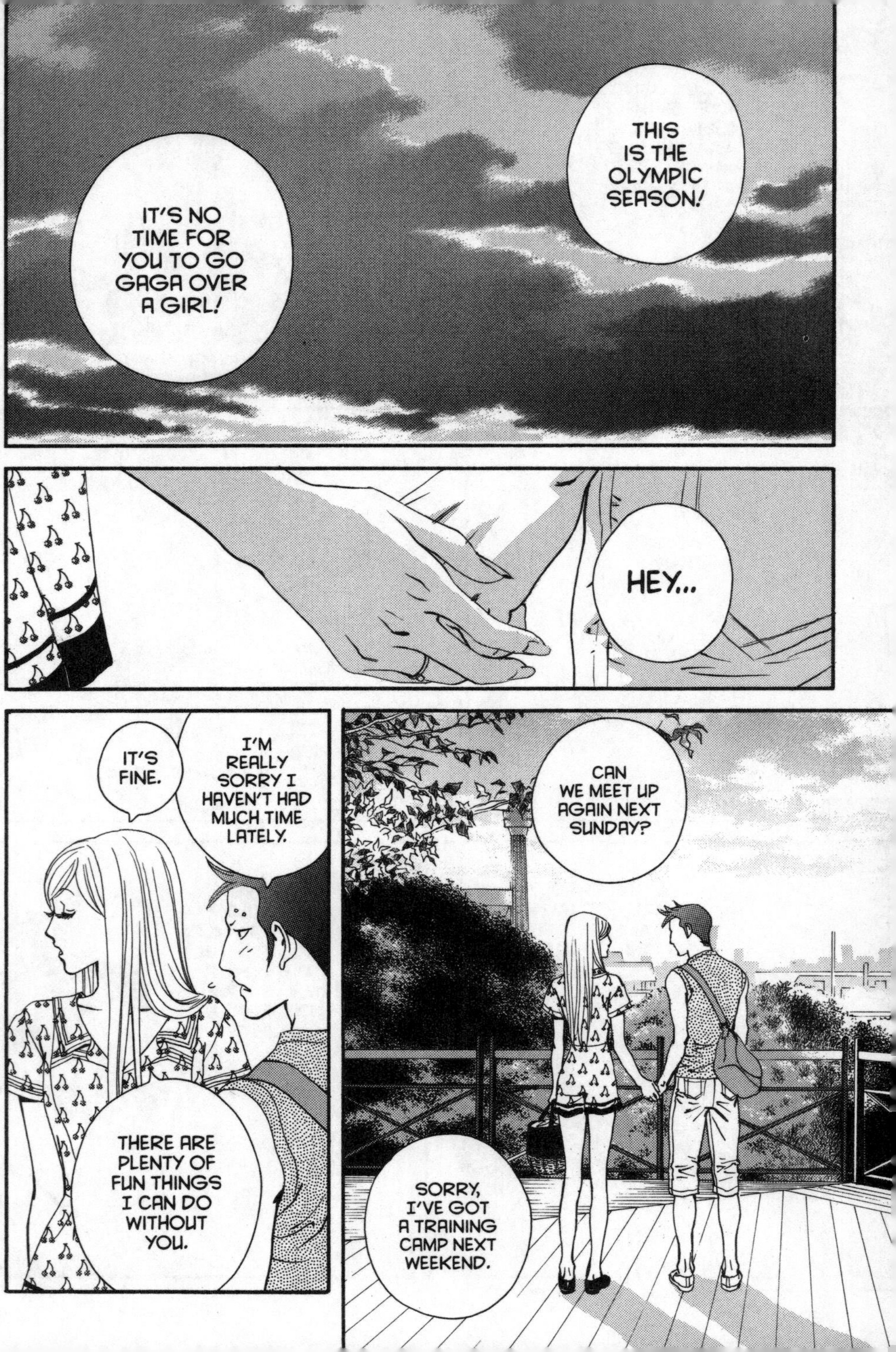
THIS IS THE OLYMPIC SEASON!
IT'S NO TIME FOR YOU TO GO GAGA OVER A GIRL!
HEY...
CAN WE MEET UP AGAIN NEXT SUNDAY?
SORRY, I'VE GOT A TRAINING CAMP NEXT WEEKEND.
I'M REALLY SORRY I HAVEN'T HAD MUCH TIME LATELY.
IT'S FINE.
THERE ARE PLENTY OF FUN THINGS I CAN DO WITHOUT YOU.

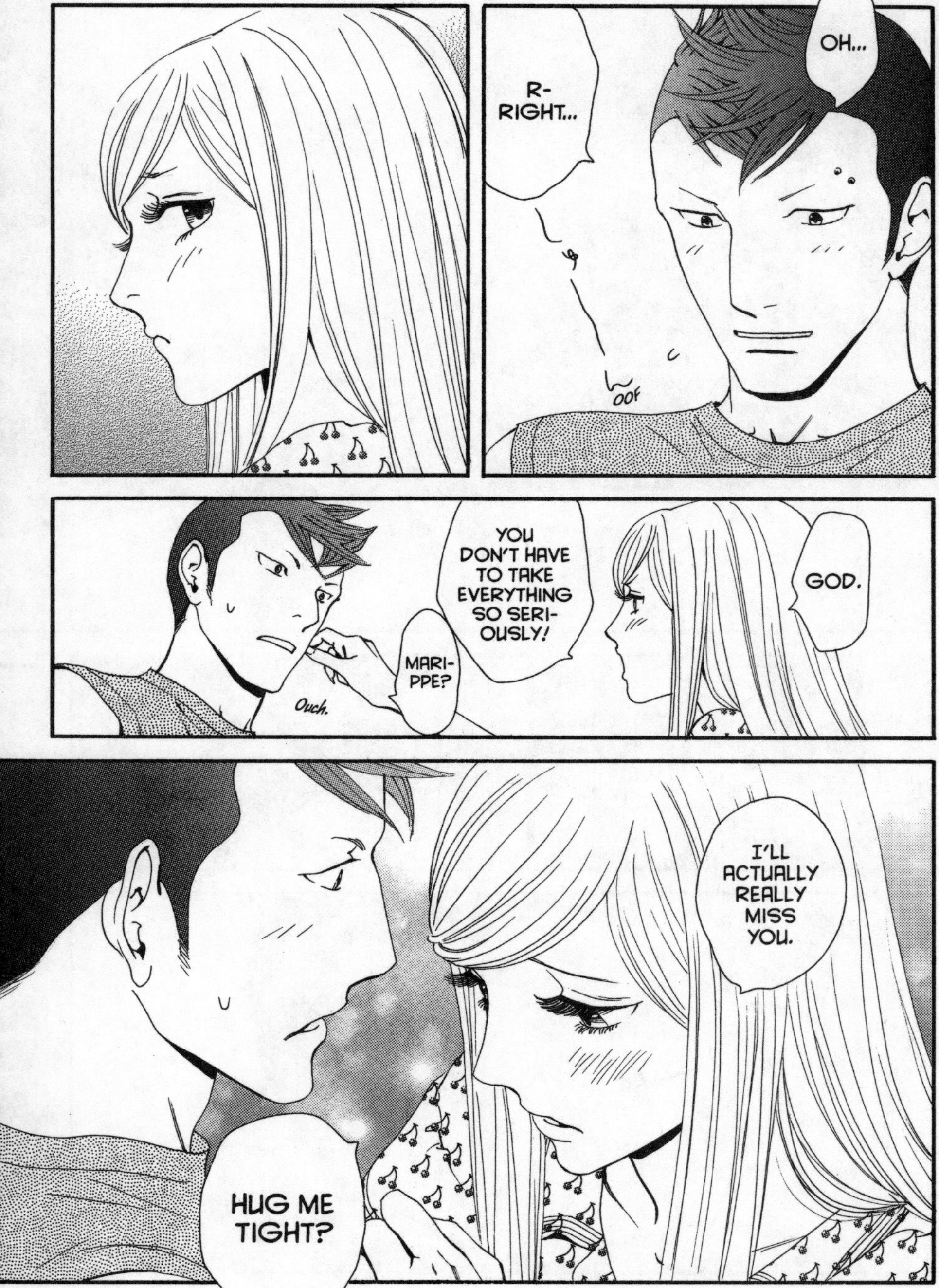
OH...
R-RIGHT...
OOF
GOD.
YOU DON'T HAVE TO TAKE EVERYTHING SO SERI-OUSLY!
MARI-PPE?
Ouch.
I'LL ACTUALLY REALLY MISS YOU.
HUG ME TIGHT?

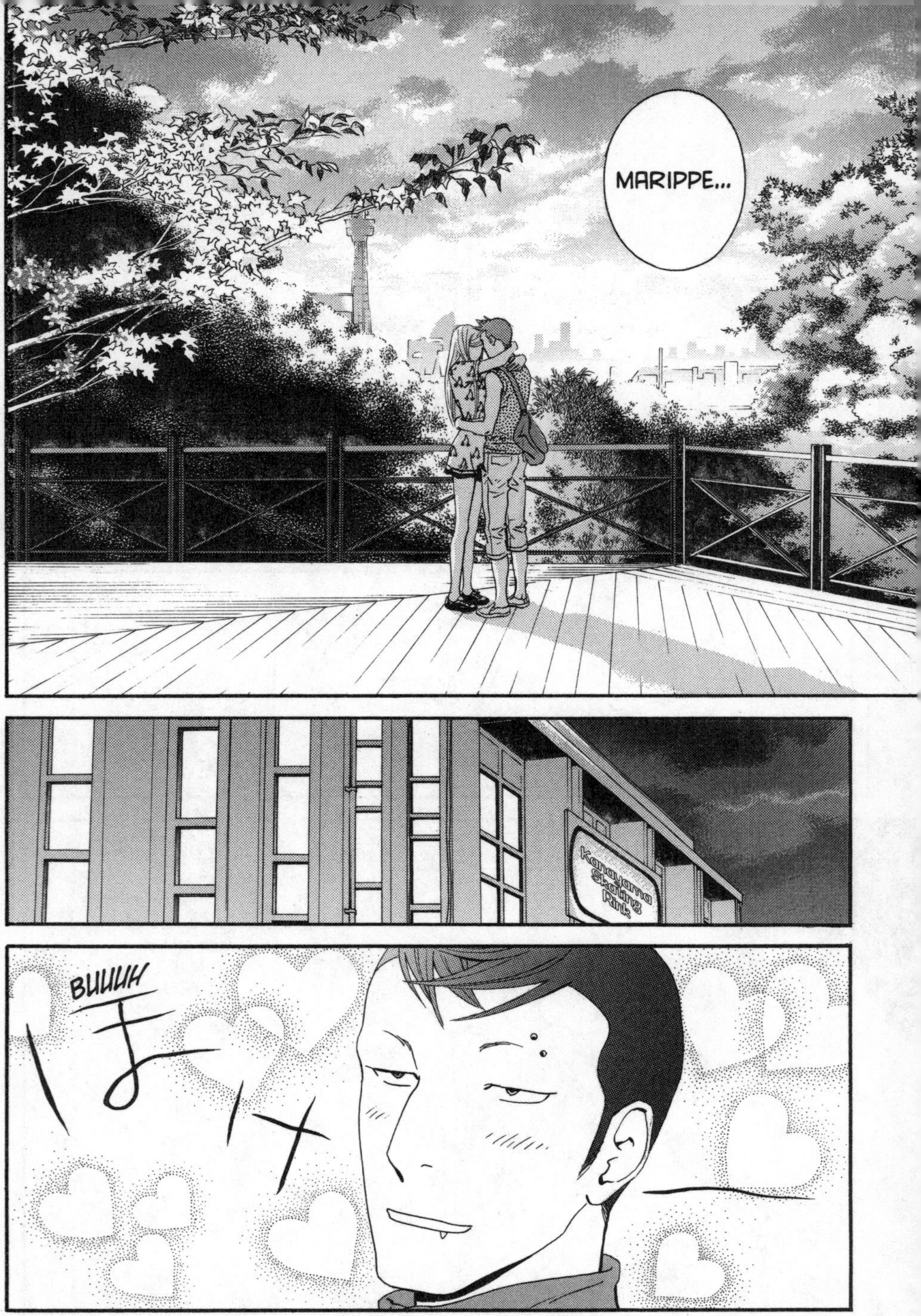
MARIPPE...
Kanayama Skating Rink
BUUUH

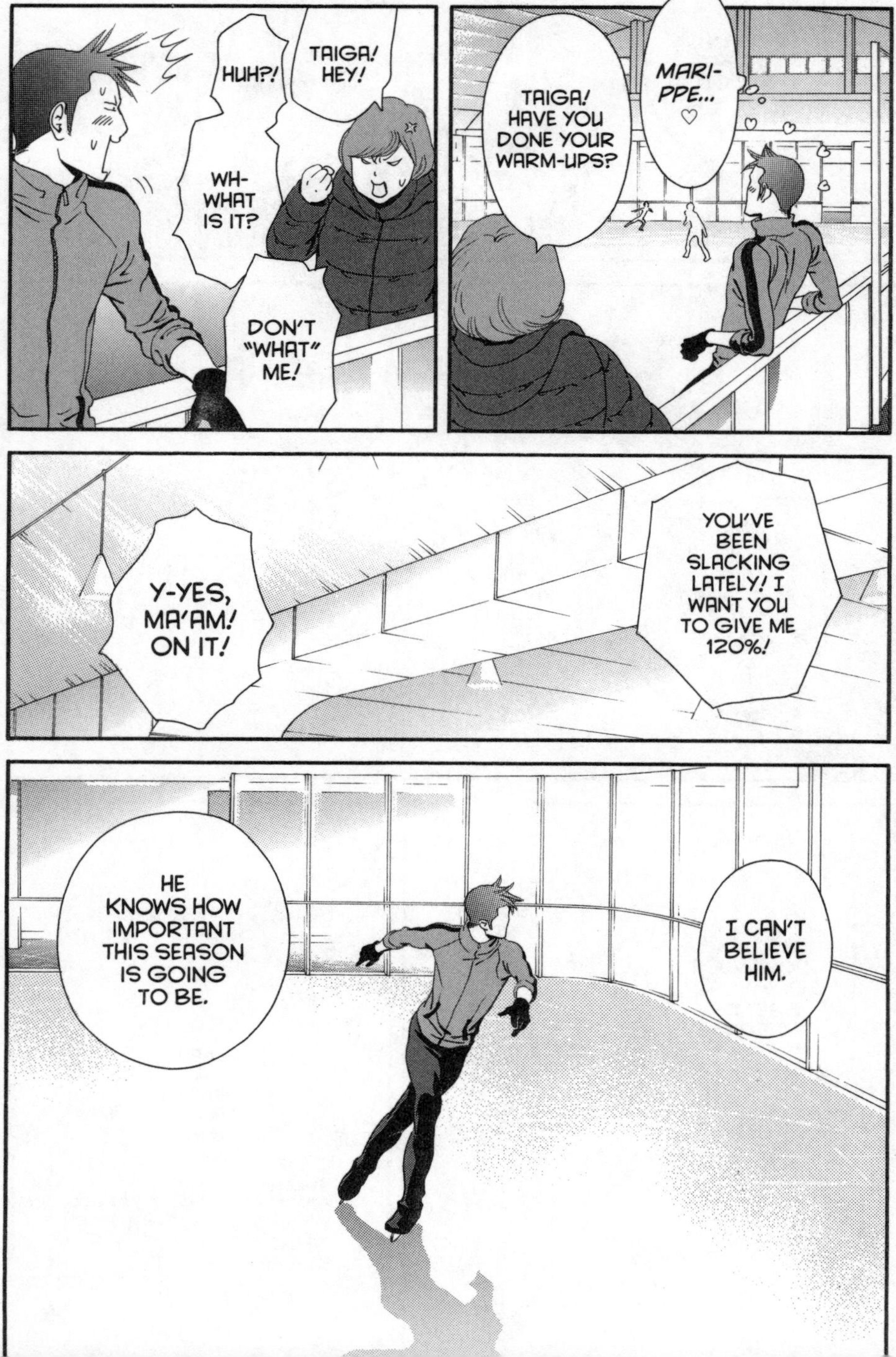
MARI-PPE... ♡
TAIGA! HAVE YOU DONE YOUR WARM-UPS?
TAIGA! HEY!
HUH?!
WH-WHAT IS IT?
DON'T "WHAT" ME!
YOU'VE BEEN SLACKING LATELY! I WANT YOU TO GIVE ME 120%!
Y-YES, MA'AM! ON IT!
I CAN'T BELIEVE HIM.
HE KNOWS HOW IMPORTANT THIS SEASON IS GOING TO BE.

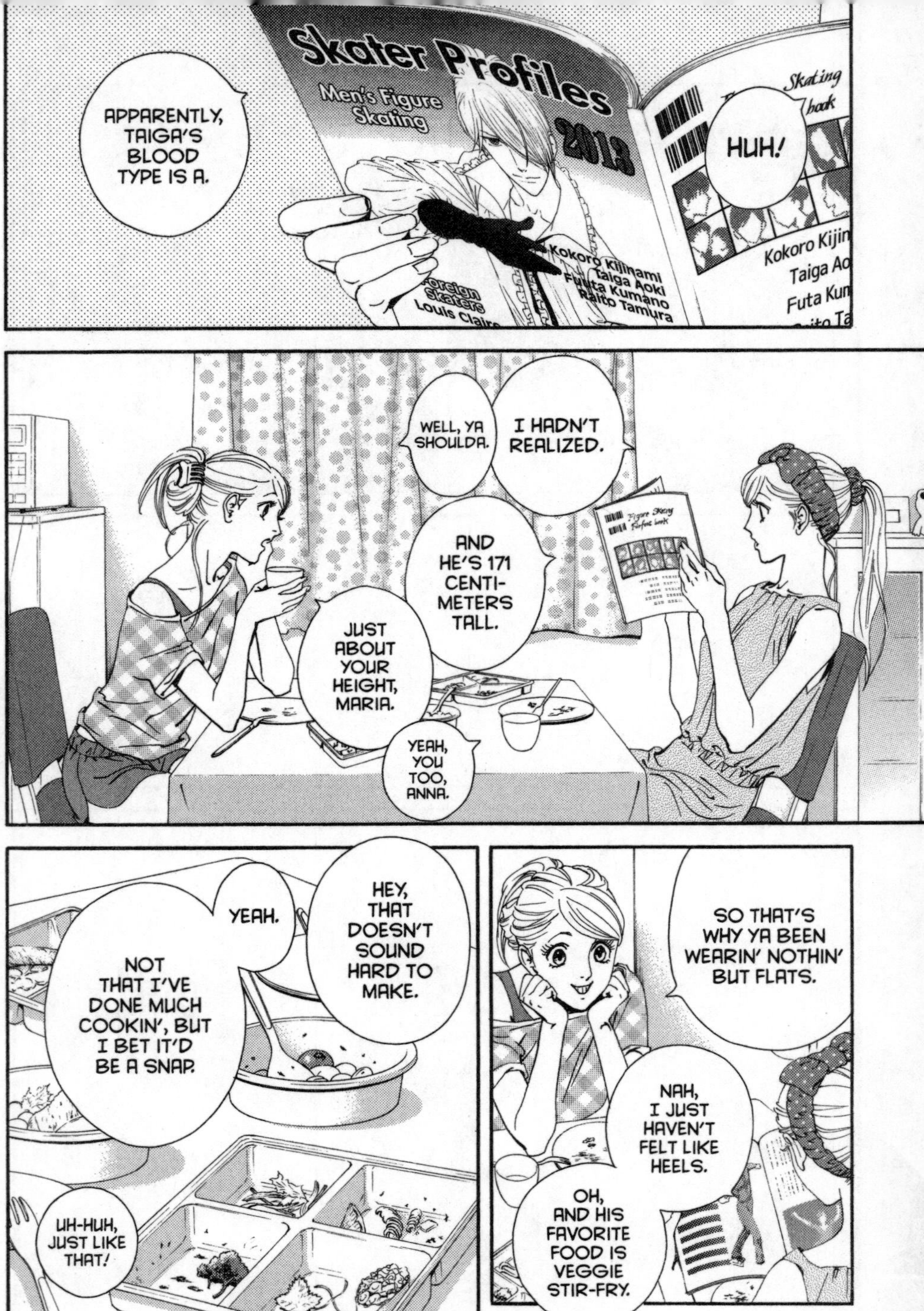
Skater Profiles
Men's Figure Skating
2013
Skating book
HUH!
APPARENTLY, TAIGA'S BLOOD TYPE IS A.
Kokoro Kijinami
Taiga Aoki
Futa Kumano
Raito Tamura
Foreign Skaters
Louis Claire
I HADN'T REALIZED.
WELL, YA SHOULDA.
AND HE'S 171 CENTI-METERS TALL.
JUST ABOUT YOUR HEIGHT, MARIA.
YEAH, YOU TOO, ANNA.
SO THAT'S WHY YA BEEN WEARIN' NOTHIN' BUT FLATS.
NAH, I JUST HAVEN'T FELT LIKE HEELS.
OH, AND HIS FAVORITE FOOD IS VEGGIE STIR-FRY.
HEY, THAT DOESN'T SOUND HARD TO MAKE.
YEAH.
NOT THAT I'VE DONE MUCH COOKIN', BUT I BET IT'D BE A SNAP.
UH-HUH, JUST LIKE THAT!

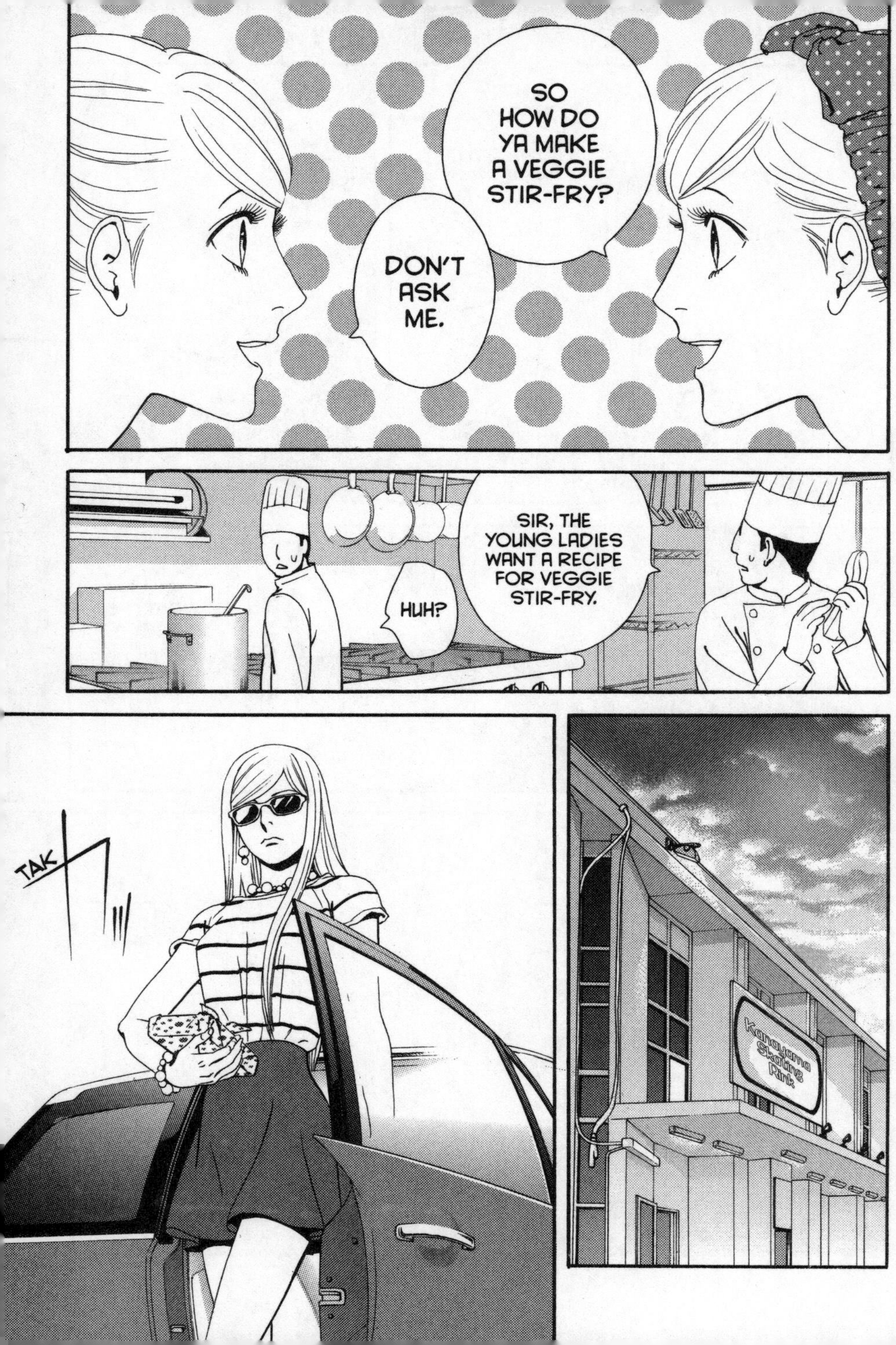
SO HOW DO YA MAKE A VEGGIE STIR-FRY?
DON'T ASK ME.
SIR, THE YOUNG LADIES WANT A RECIPE FOR VEGGIE STIR-FRY.
HUH?
Kanayama Skating Rink
TAK

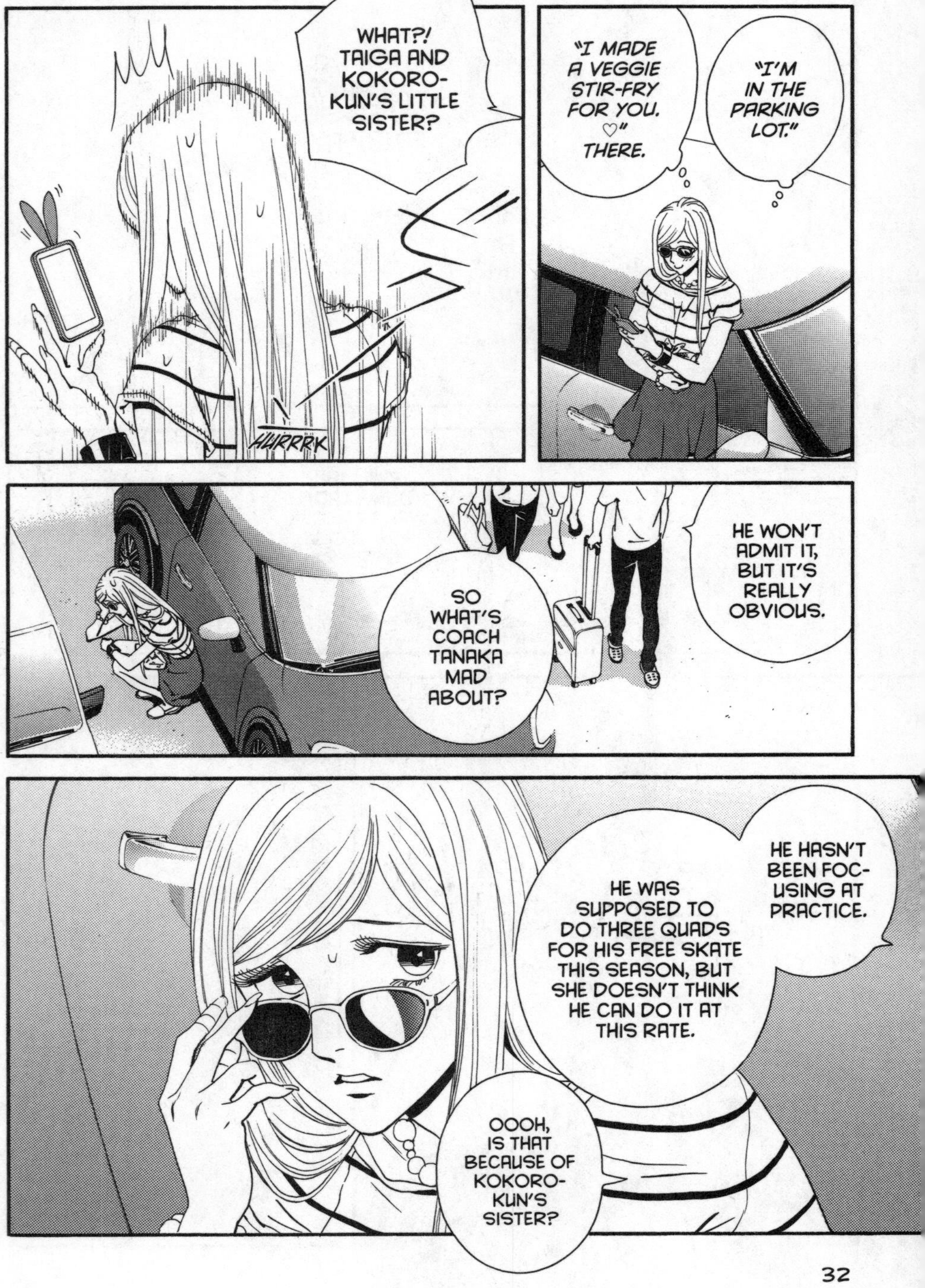
"I'M IN THE PARKING LOT."
"I MADE A VEGGIE STIR-FRY FOR YOU. ♡" THERE.
WHAT?! TAIGA AND KOKORO-KUN'S LITTLE SISTER?
HURRRK
HE WON'T ADMIT IT, BUT IT'S REALLY OBVIOUS.
SO WHAT'S COACH TANAKA MAD ABOUT?
HE HASN'T BEEN FOC-USING AT PRACTICE.
HE WAS SUPPOSED TO DO THREE QUADS FOR HIS FREE SKATE THIS SEASON, BUT SHE DOESN'T THINK HE CAN DO IT AT THIS RATE.
OOOH, IS THAT BECAUSE OF KOKORO-KUN'S SISTER?

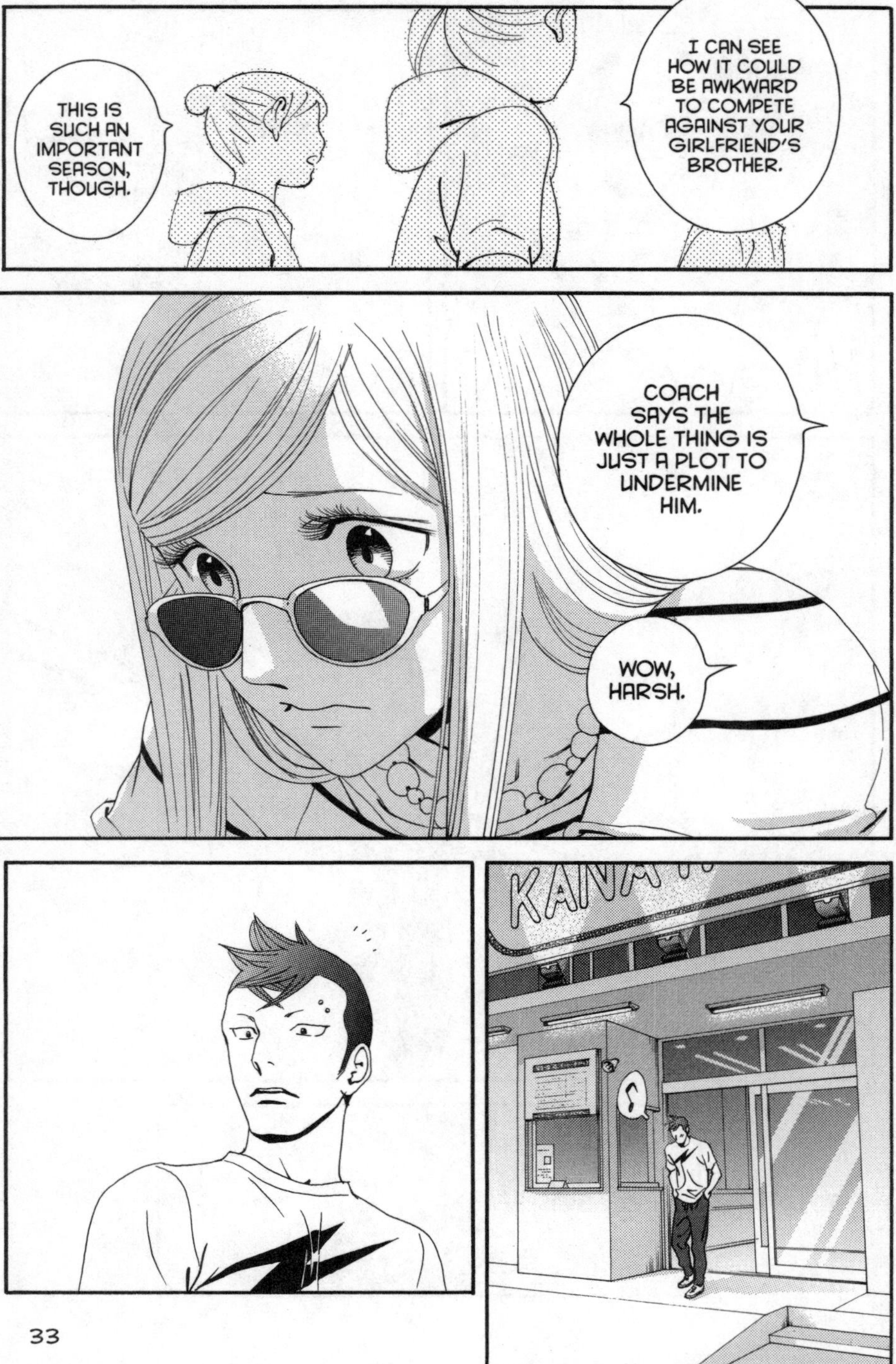
I CAN SEE HOW IT COULD BE AWKWARD TO COMPETE AGAINST YOUR GIRLFRIEND'S BROTHER.
THIS IS SUCH AN IMPORTANT SEASON, THOUGH.
COACH SAYS THE WHOLE THING IS JUST A PLOT TO UNDERMINE HIM.
WOW, HARSH.
KANA

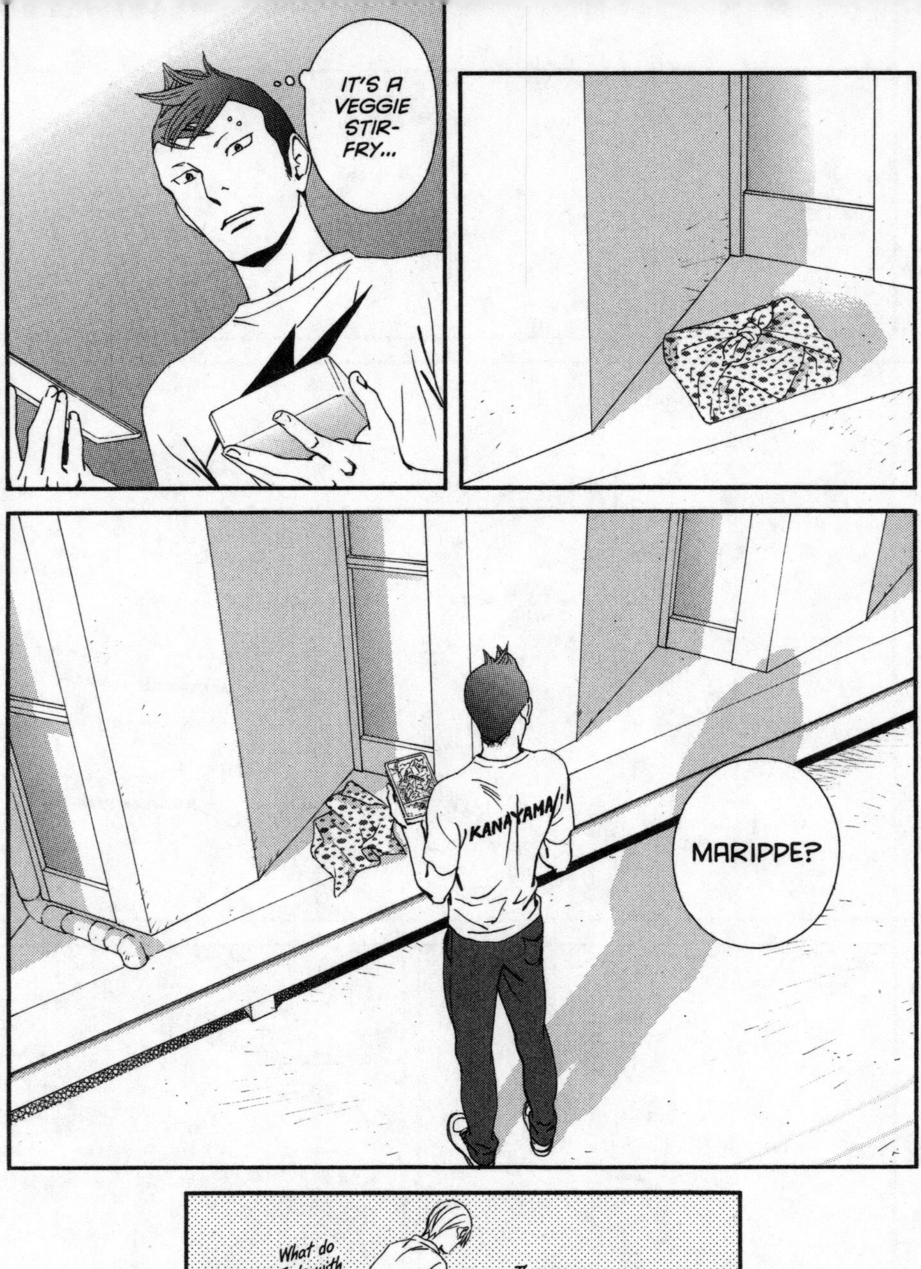
IT'S A VEGGIE STIR-FRY...
MARIPPE?
The custom sheets
What do I do with these?

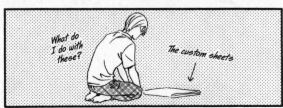

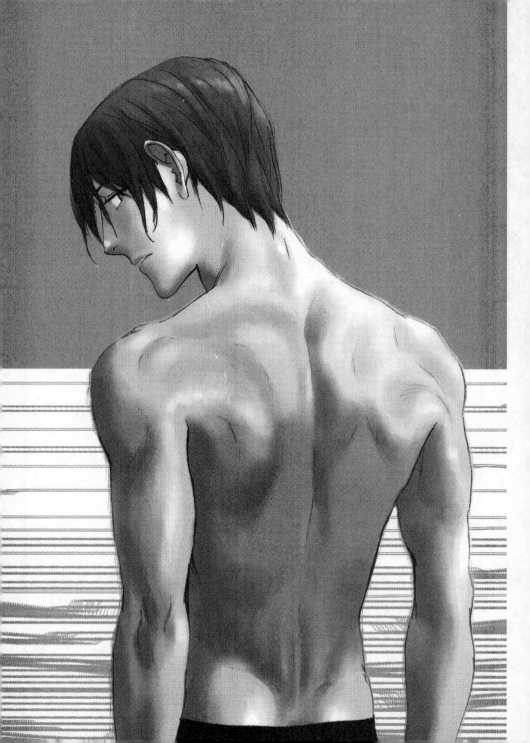

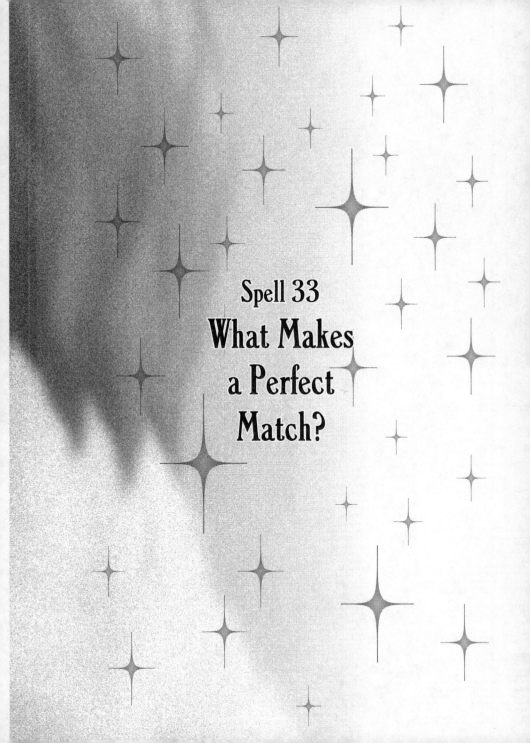

Spell 33
What Makes
a Perfect
Match?

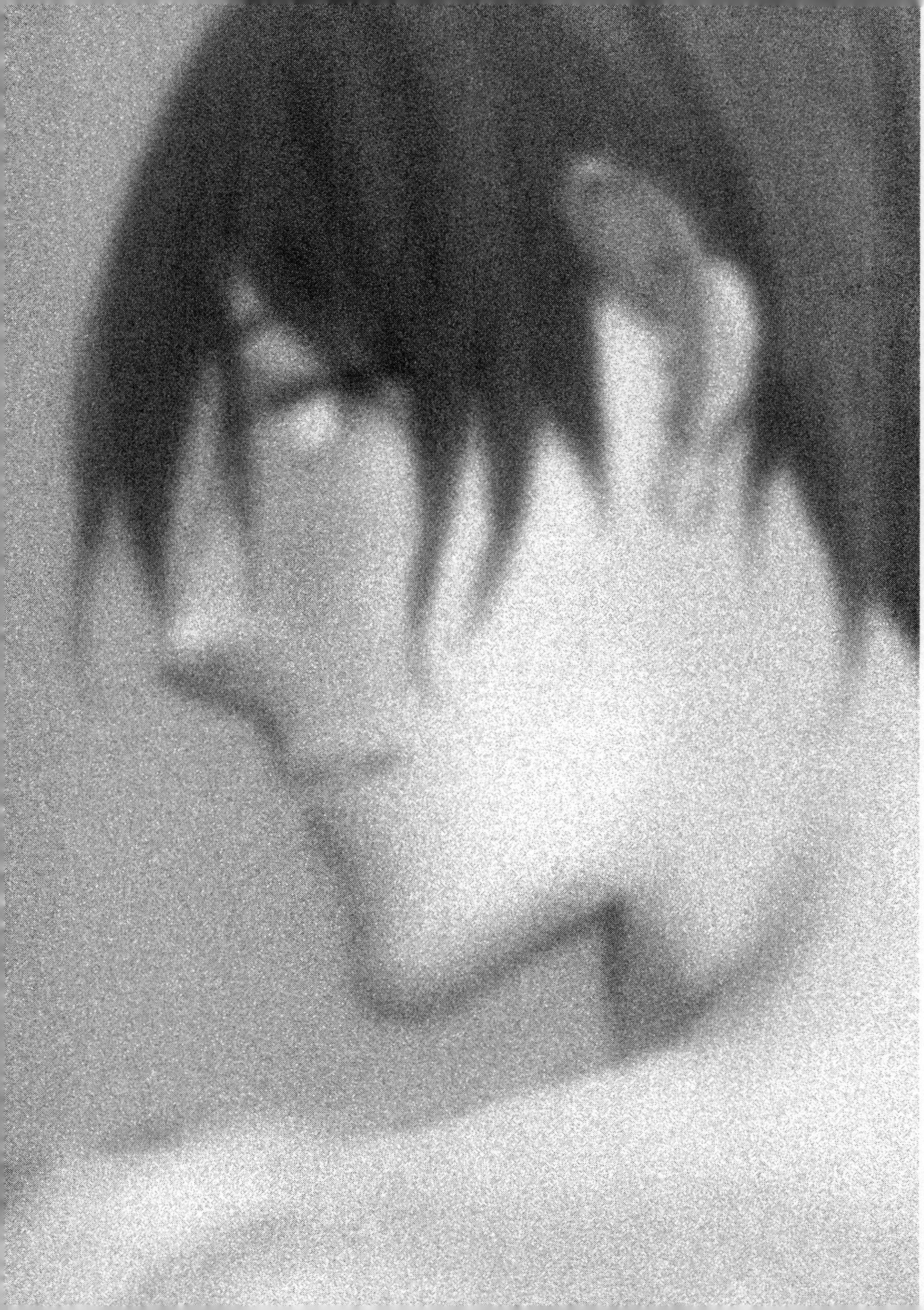

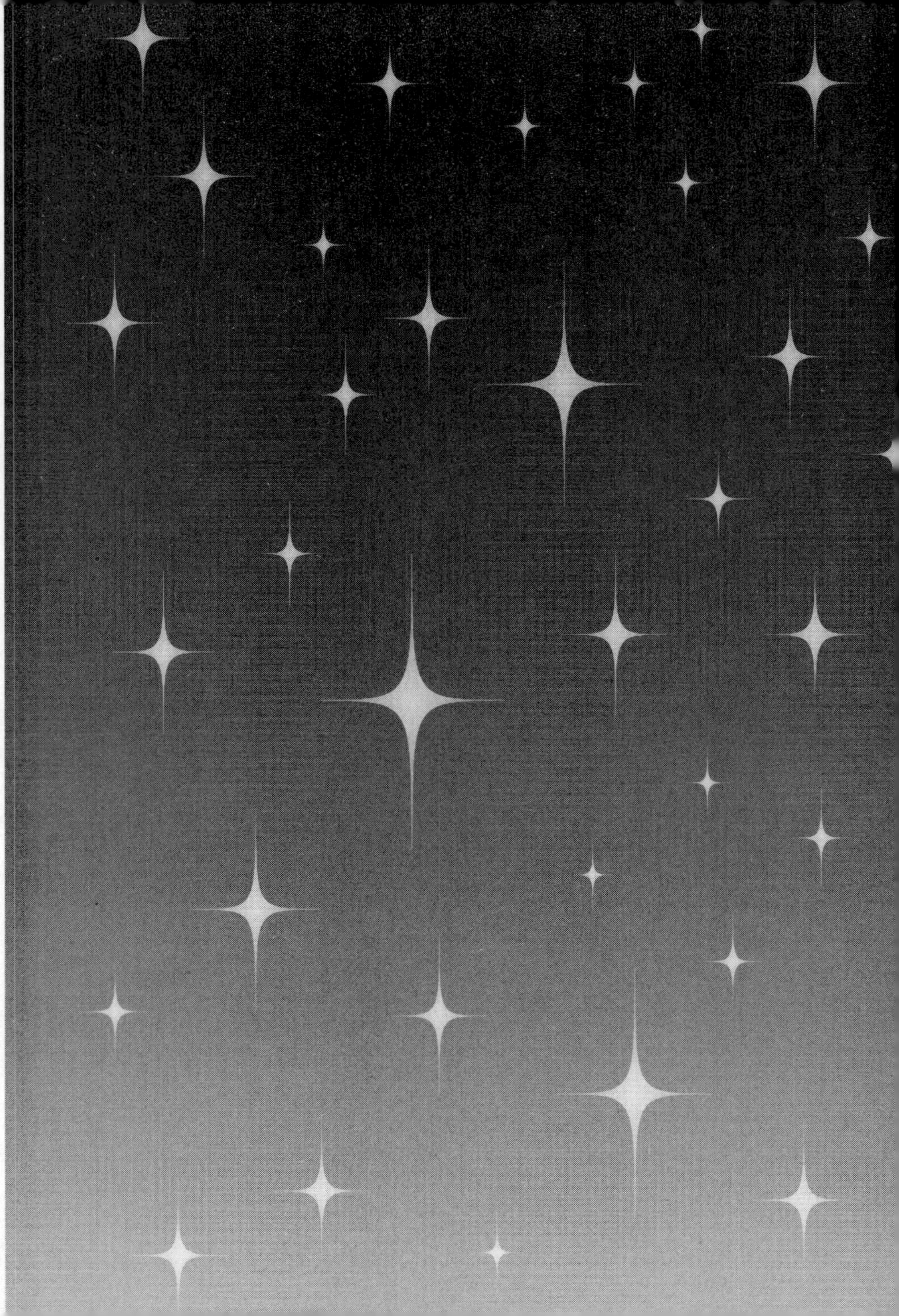

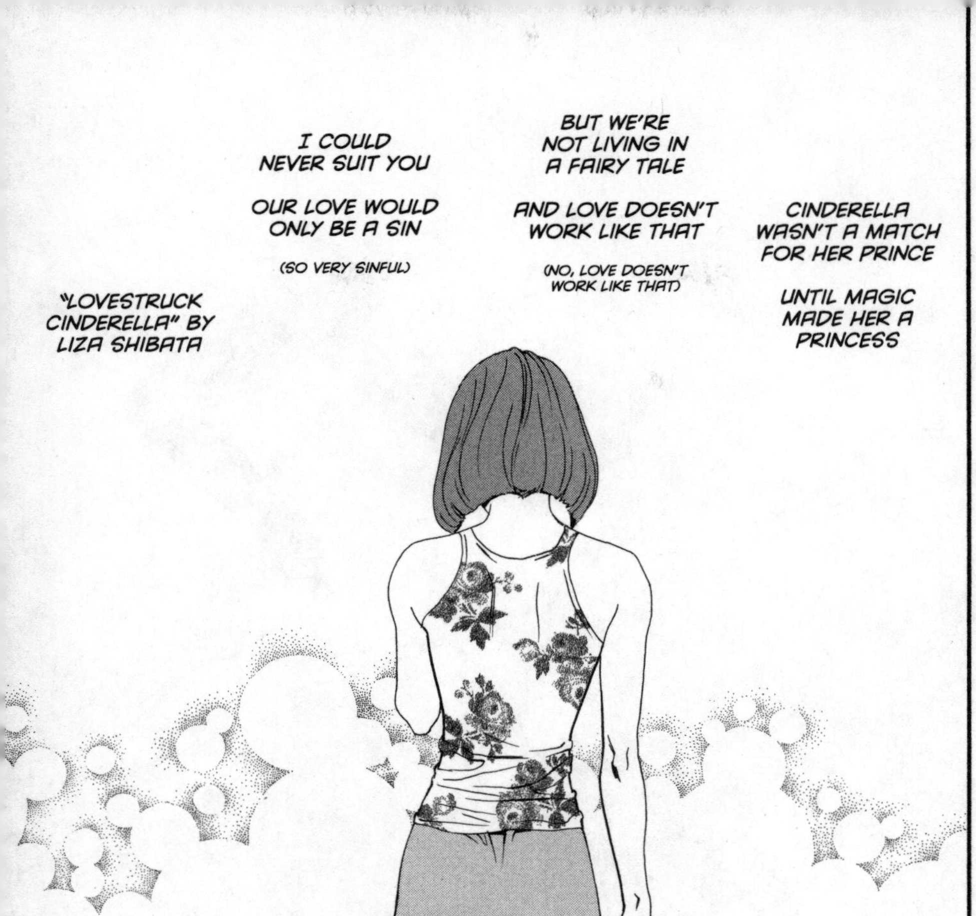
CINDERELLA WASN'T A MATCH FOR HER PRINCE
UNTIL MAGIC MADE HER A PRINCESS
BUT WE'RE NOT LIVING IN A FAIRY TALE
AND LOVE DOESN'T WORK LIKE THAT
(NO, LOVE DOESN'T WORK LIKE THAT)
I COULD NEVER SUIT YOU
OUR LOVE WOULD ONLY BE A SIN
(SO VERY SINFUL)
"LOVESTRUCK CINDERELLA" BY LIZA SHIBATA

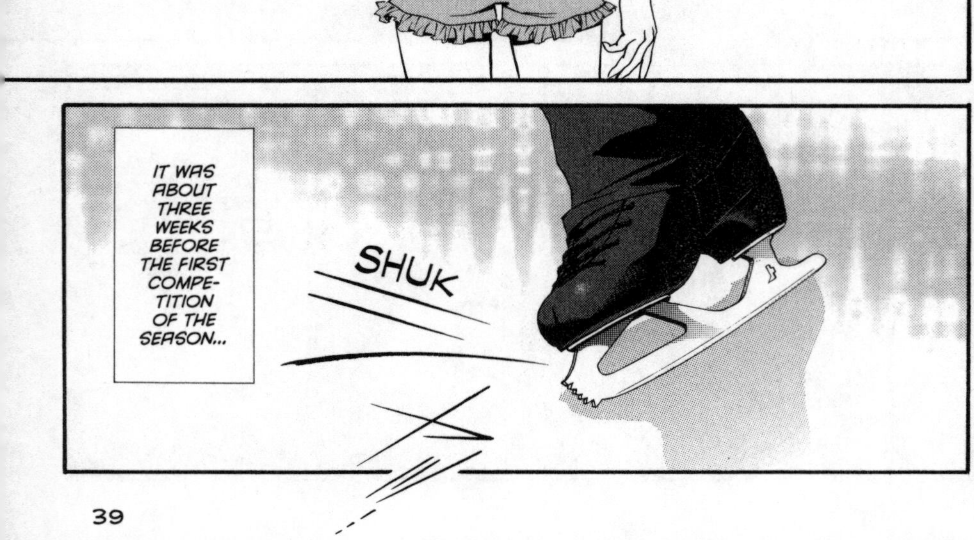
SHUK
IT WAS ABOUT THREE WEEKS BEFORE THE FIRST COMPETITION OF THE SEASON...

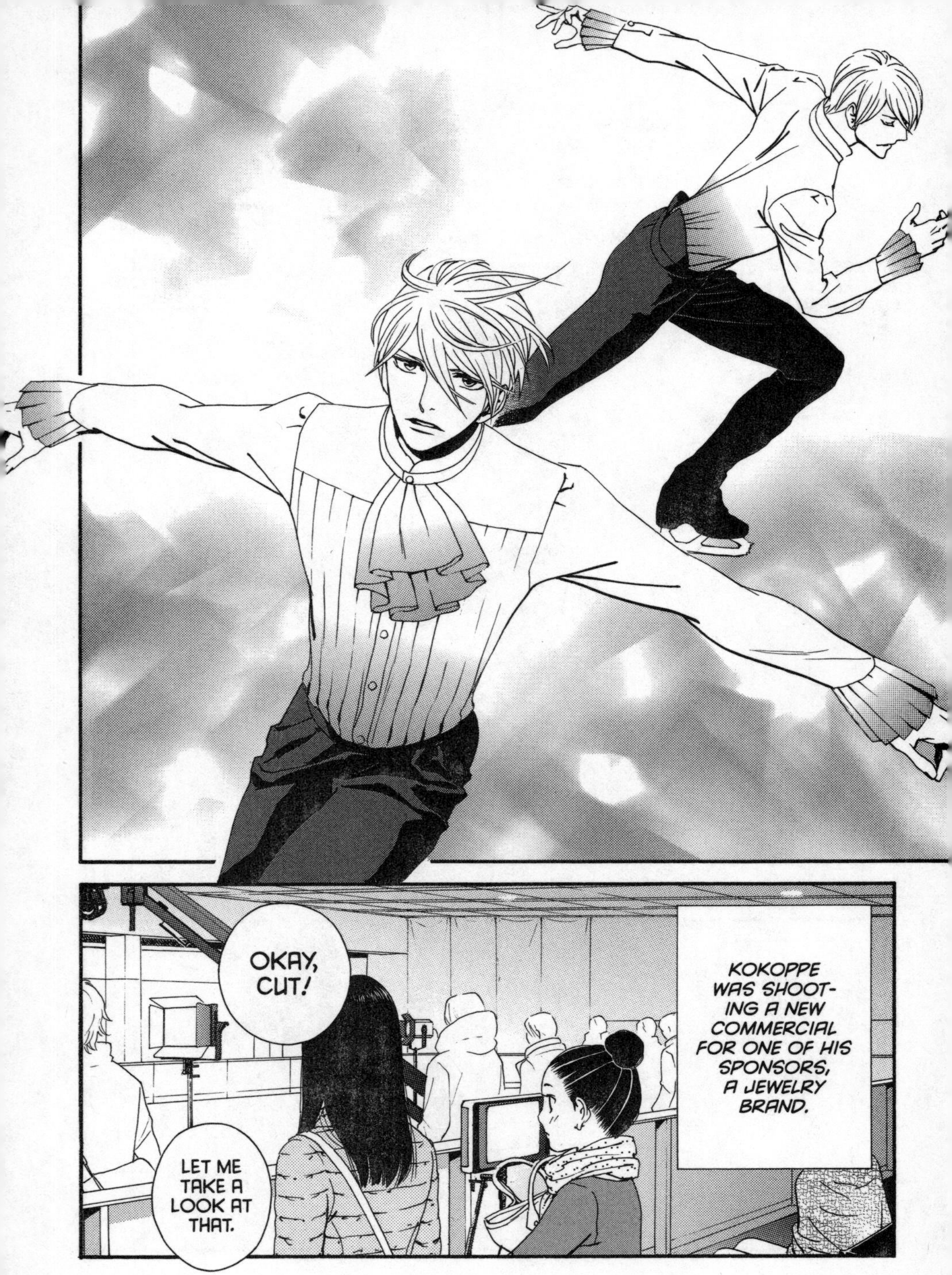
KOKOPPE WAS SHOOTING A NEW COMMERCIAL FOR ONE OF HIS SPONSORS, A JEWELRY BRAND.
OKAY, CUT!
LET ME TAKE A LOOK AT THAT.

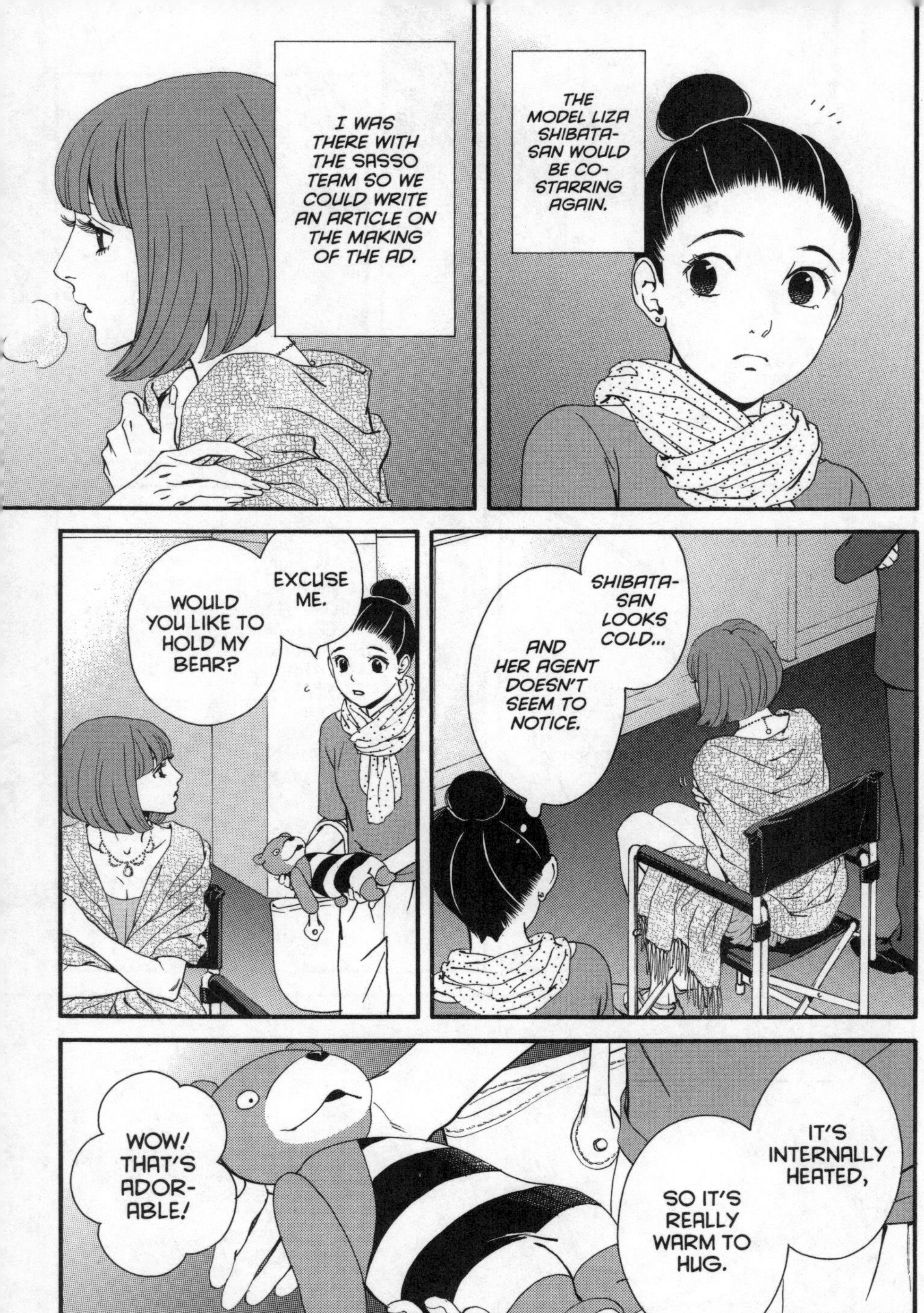
THE MODEL LIZA SHIBATA-SAN WOULD BE CO-STARRING AGAIN.
I WAS THERE WITH THE SASSO TEAM SO WE COULD WRITE AN ARTICLE ON THE MAKING OF THE AD.
SHIBATA-SAN LOOKS COLD...
AND HER AGENT DOESN'T SEEM TO NOTICE.
EXCUSE ME.
WOULD YOU LIKE TO HOLD MY BEAR?
IT'S INTERNALLY HEATED,
SO IT'S REALLY WARM TO HUG.
WOW! THAT'S ADOR-ABLE!

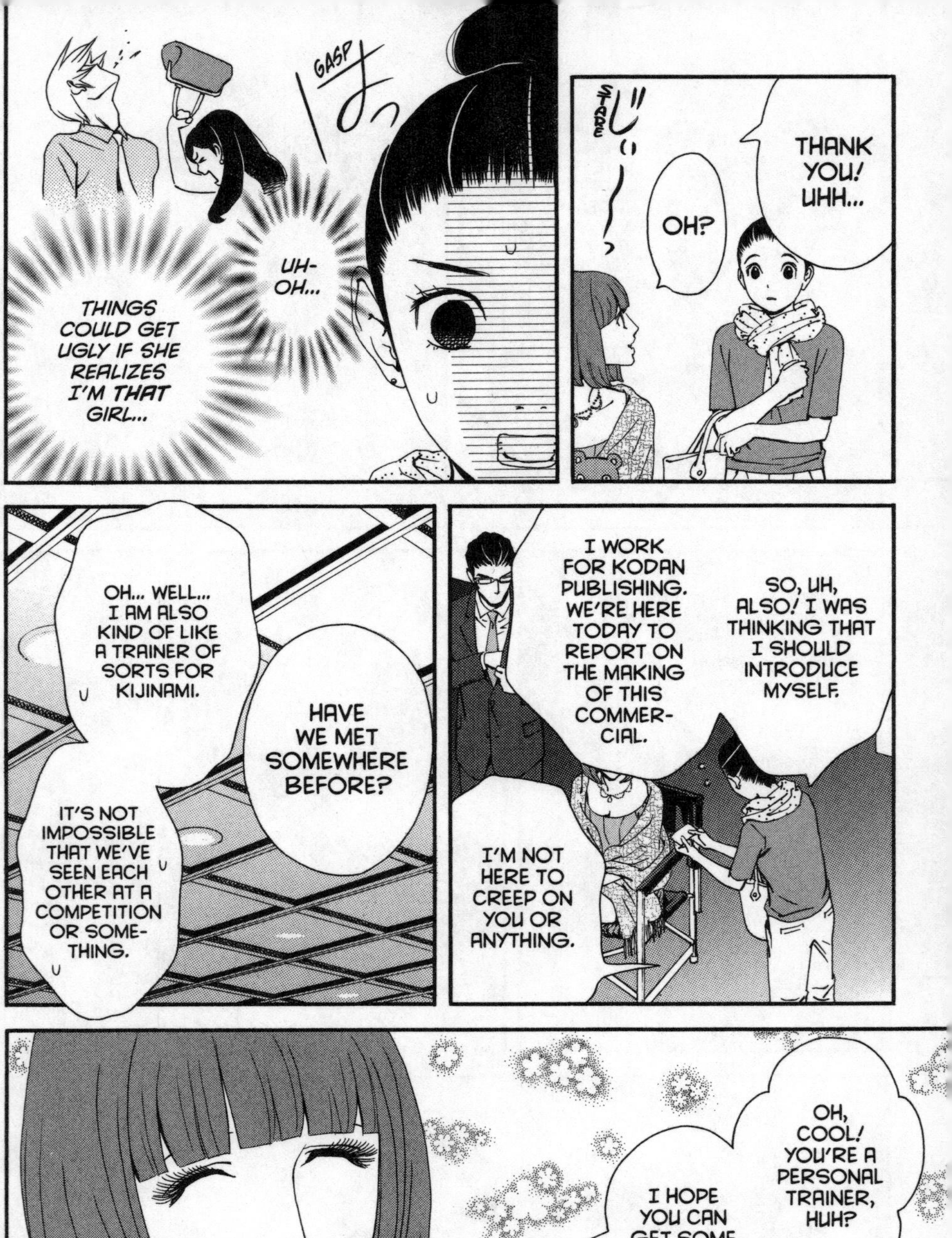
THANK YOU! UHH...
STARE
OH?
GASP
UH-OH...
THINGS COULD GET UGLY IF SHE REALIZES I'M THAT GIRL...
SO, UH, ALSO! I WAS THINKING THAT I SHOULD INTRODUCE MYSELF.
I WORK FOR KODAN PUBLISHING. WE'RE HERE TODAY TO REPORT ON THE MAKING OF THIS COMMERCIAL.
I'M NOT HERE TO CREEP ON YOU OR ANYTHING.
HAVE WE MET SOMEWHERE BEFORE?
OH... WELL... I AM ALSO KIND OF LIKE A TRAINER OF SORTS FOR KIJINAMI.
IT'S NOT IMPOSSIBLE THAT WE'VE SEEN EACH OTHER AT A COMPETITION OR SOMETHING.
OH, COOL! YOU'RE A PERSONAL TRAINER, HUH?
I HOPE YOU CAN GET SOME GOOD MATERIAL TODAY! ♡

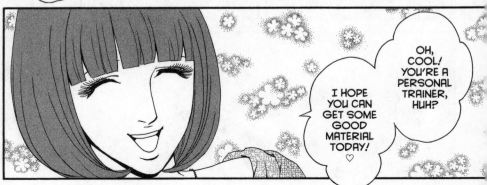

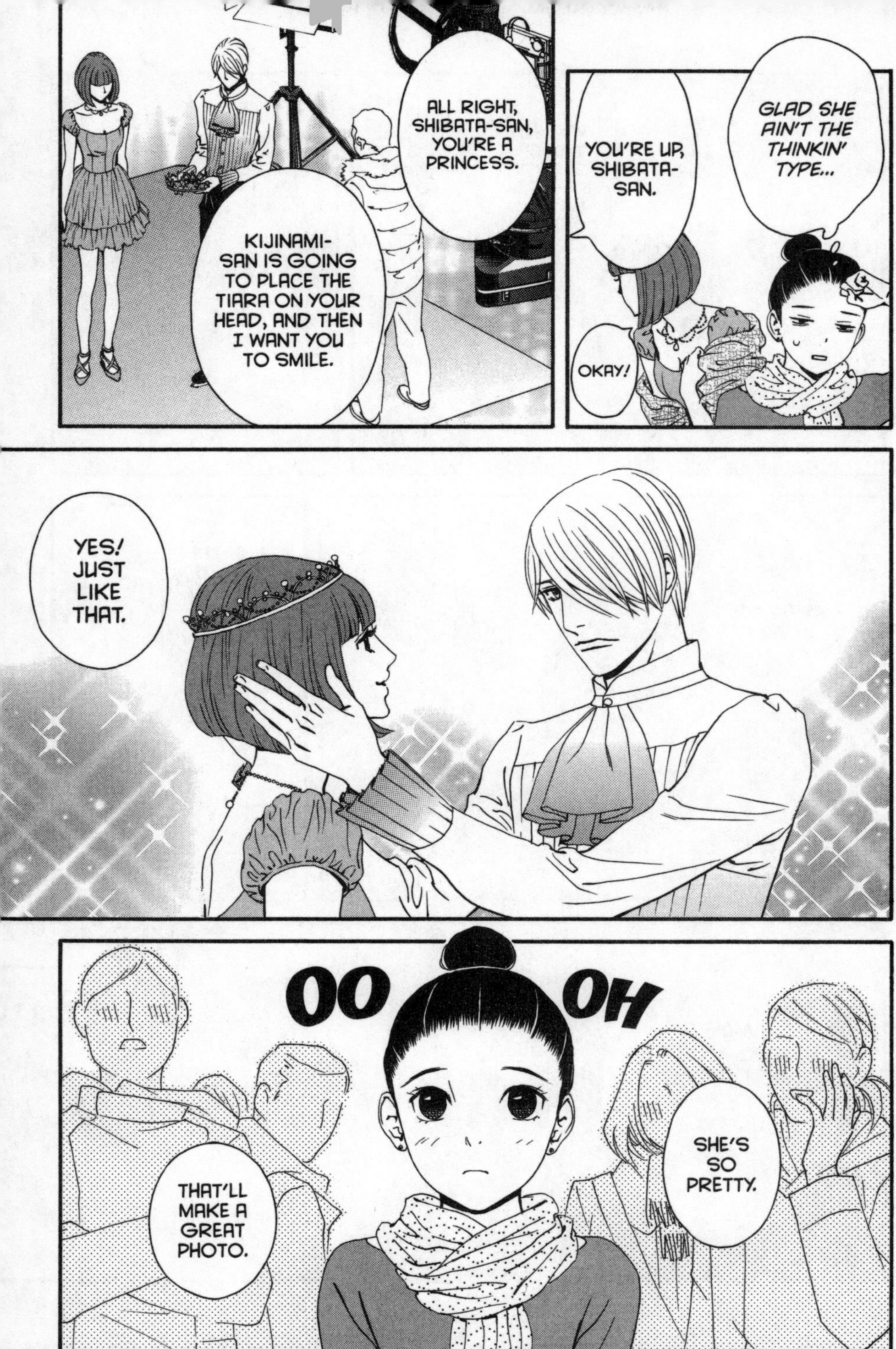
GLAD SHE AIN'T THE THINKIN' TYPE...
YOU'RE UP, SHIBATA-SAN.
OKAY!
ALL RIGHT, SHIBATA-SAN, YOU'RE A PRINCESS.
KIJINAMI-SAN IS GOING TO PLACE THE TIARA ON YOUR HEAD, AND THEN I WANT YOU TO SMILE.
YES! JUST LIKE THAT.
OOOH
SHE'S SO PRETTY.
THAT'LL MAKE A GREAT PHOTO.

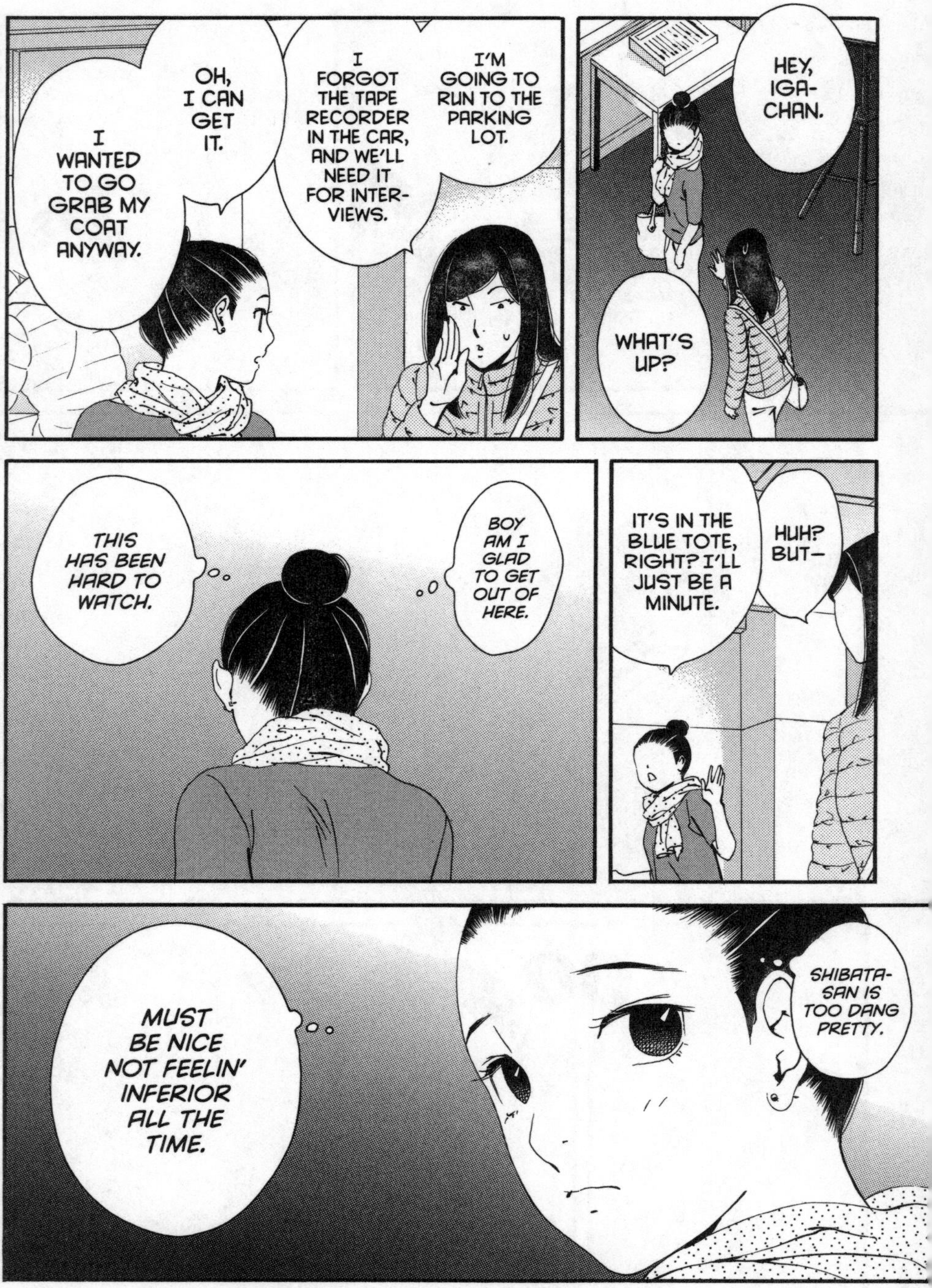
HEY, IGA-CHAN.
WHAT'S UP?
I'M GOING TO RUN TO THE PARKING LOT.
I FORGOT THE TAPE RECORDER IN THE CAR, AND WE'LL NEED IT FOR INTER-VIEWS.
OH, I CAN GET IT.
I WANTED TO GO GRAB MY COAT ANYWAY.
HUH? BUT—
IT'S IN THE BLUE TOTE, RIGHT? I'LL JUST BE A MINUTE.
BOY AM I GLAD TO GET OUT OF HERE.
THIS HAS BEEN HARD TO WATCH.
SHIBATA-SAN IS TOO DANG PRETTY.
MUST BE NICE NOT FEELIN' INFERIOR ALL THE TIME.

SE-CHAN.

HERE IT IS.

WOW, TAKAHASHI-SAN EVEN FORGOT THE PENS AND NOTE-PADS.

HUH?

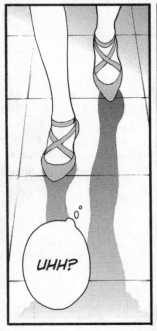
UHH?

KOKOPPE!

WHAT ARE YA DOIN' HERE?

Weird outfit for a parkin' lot!

UH... SHIBATA-SAN'S GOTTA CHANGE CLOTHES AN' GET HER MAKEUP REDONE... SO WE'RE ON BREAK...

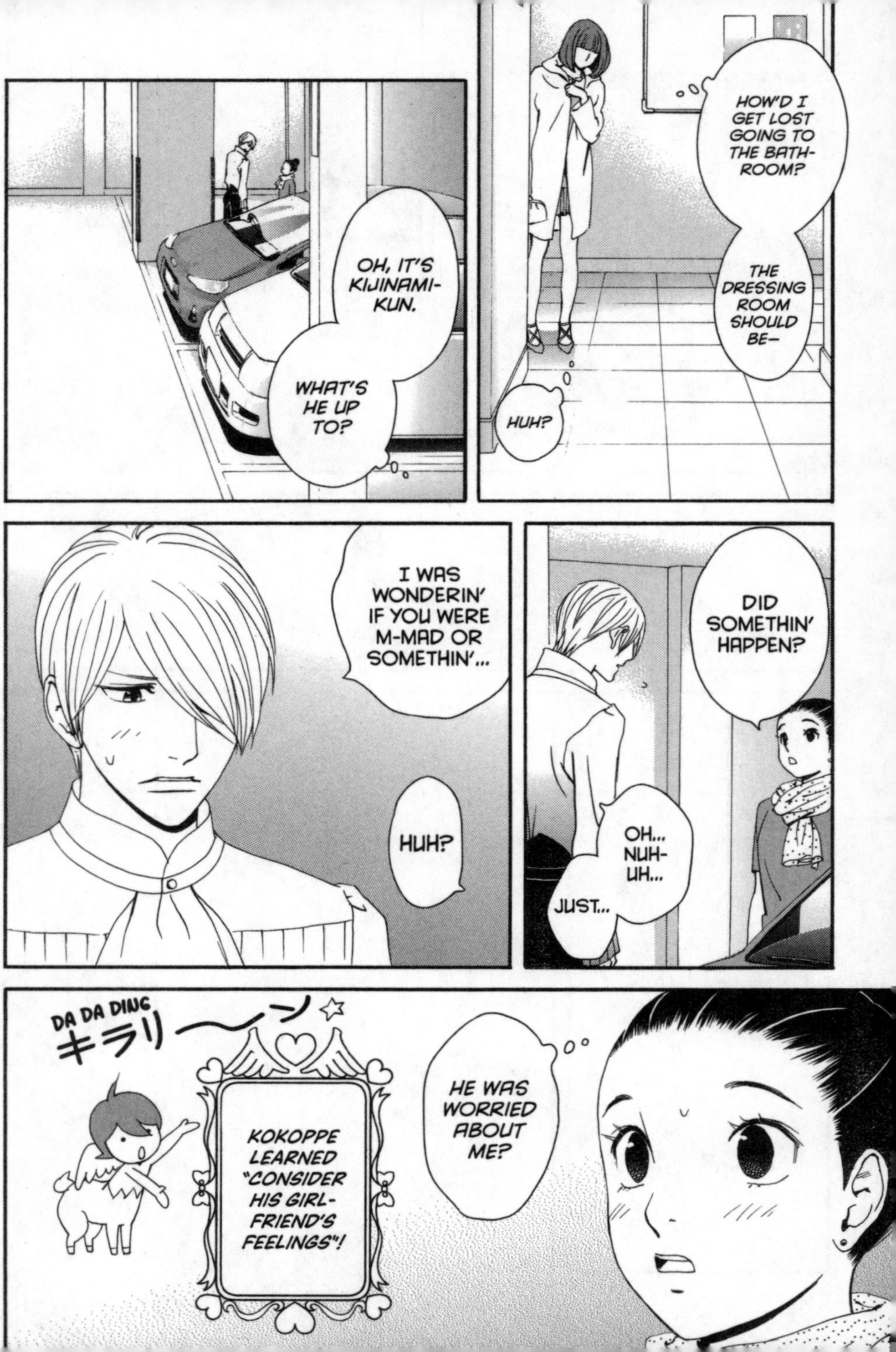
HOW'D I GET LOST GOING TO THE BATH-ROOM?
THE DRESSING ROOM SHOULD BE—
HUH?
OH, IT'S KIJINAMI-KUN.
WHAT'S HE UP TO?
DID SOMETHIN' HAPPEN?
OH... NUH-UH...
JUST...
I WAS WONDERIN' IF YOU WERE M-MAD OR SOMETHIN'...
HUH?
HE WAS WORRIED ABOUT ME?
DA DA DING
キラリ〜ン☆
KOKOPPE LEARNED "CONSIDER HIS GIRL-FRIEND'S FEELINGS"!

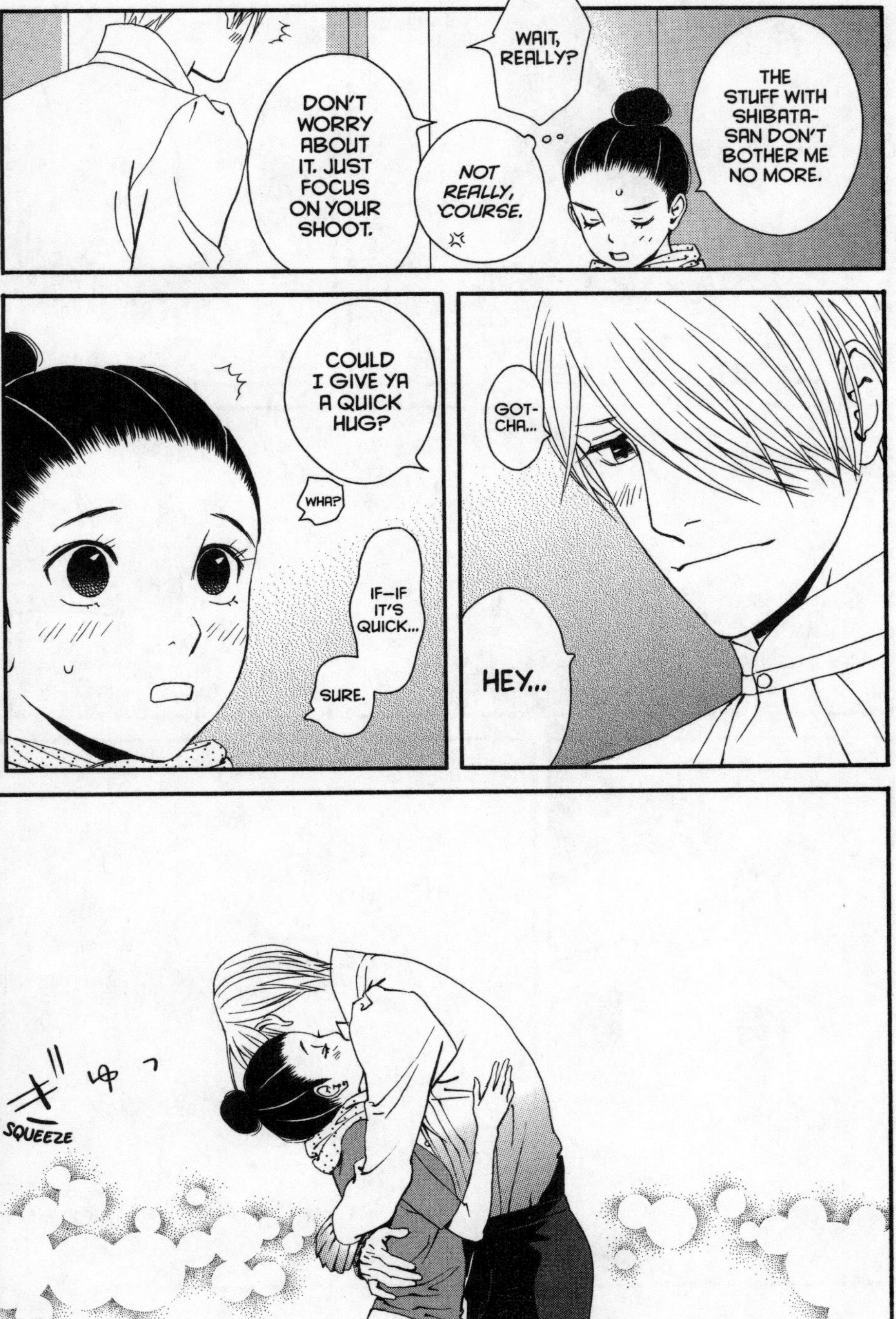
THE STUFF WITH SHIBATA-SAN DON'T BOTHER ME NO MORE.
WAIT, REALLY?
NOT REALLY, 'COURSE.
DON'T WORRY ABOUT IT. JUST FOCUS ON YOUR SHOOT.
GOT-CHA...
HEY...
COULD I GIVE YA A QUICK HUG?
WHA?
IF—IF IT'S QUICK...
SURE.
SQUEEZE

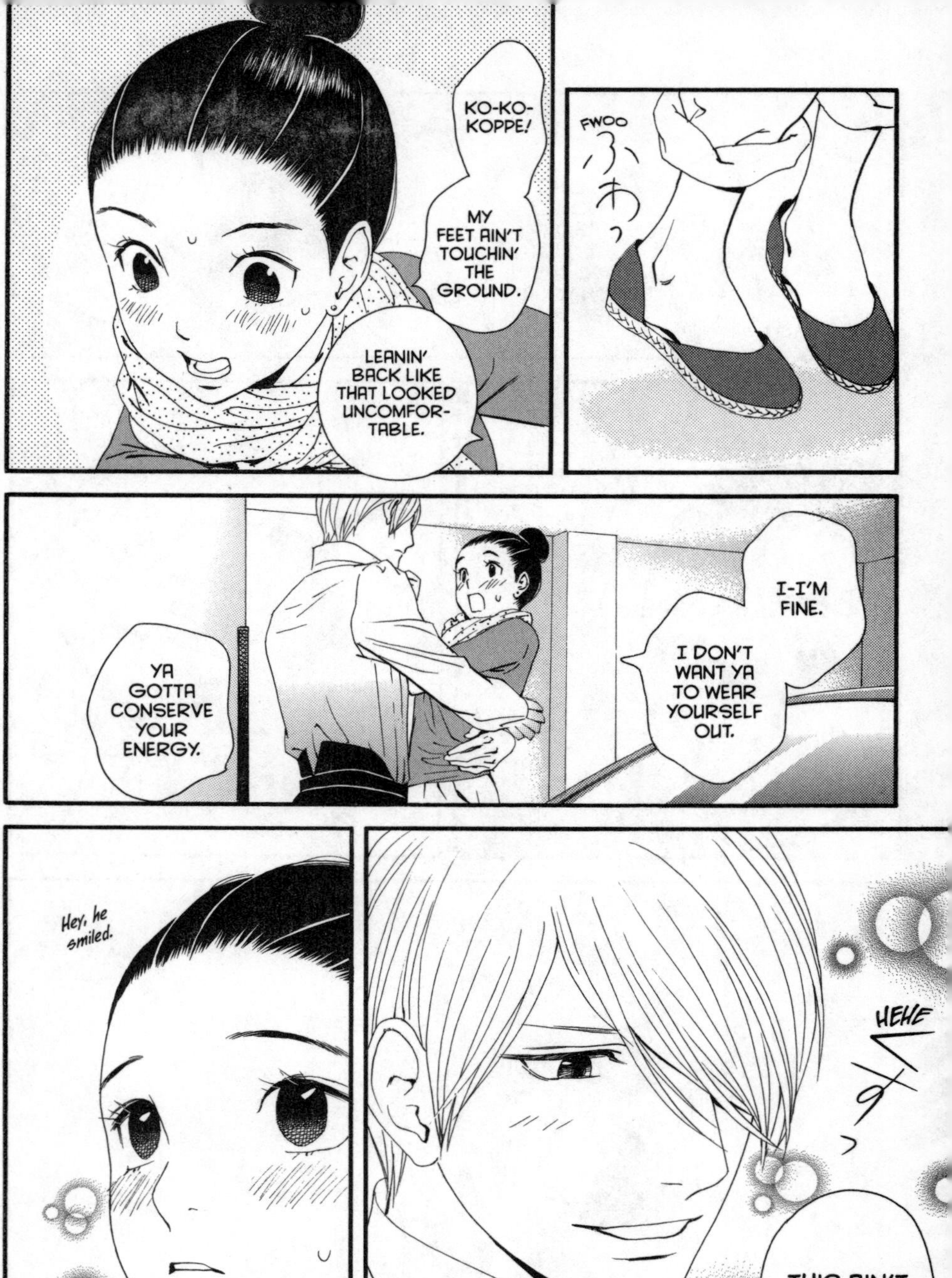
FWOO
KO-KO-KOPPE!
MY FEET AIN'T TOUCHIN' THE GROUND.
LEANIN' BACK LIKE THAT LOOKED UNCOMFOR-TABLE.
I-I'M FINE.
I DON'T WANT YA TO WEAR YOURSELF OUT.
YA GOTTA CONSERVE YOUR ENERGY.
HEHE
THIS AIN'T NOTHIN'.
Hey, he smiled.

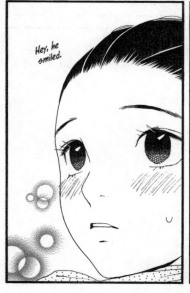

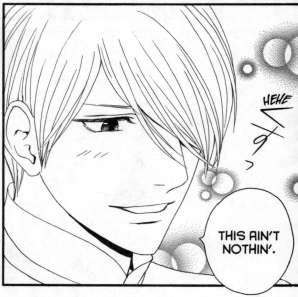

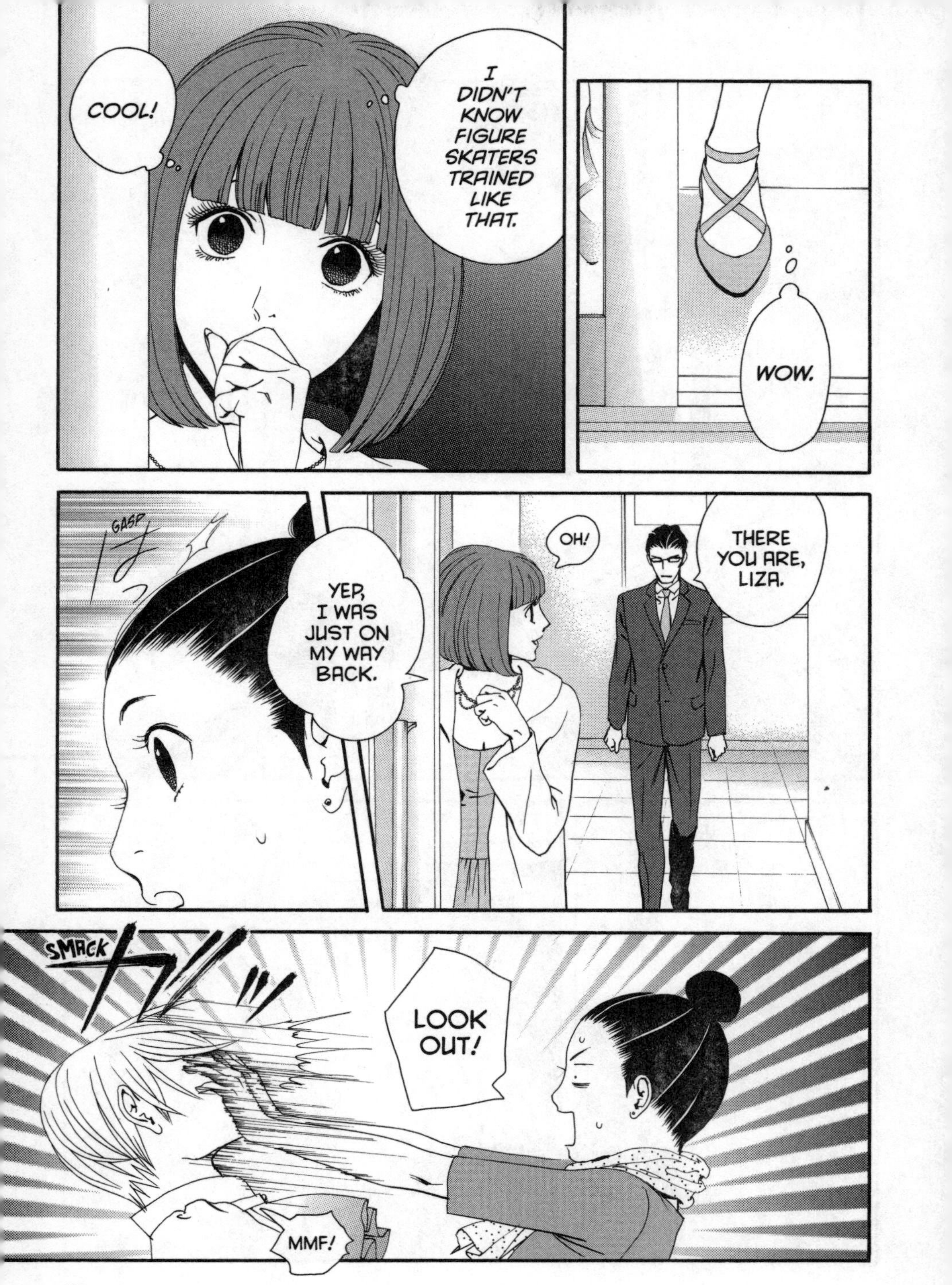
WOW.
I DIDN'T KNOW FIGURE SKATERS TRAINED LIKE THAT.
COOL!
THERE YOU ARE, LIZA.
OH!
YEP, I WAS JUST ON MY WAY BACK.
GASP
LOOK OUT!
SMACK
MMF!

THAT VOICE...

IT WAS LIZA SHIBATA'S!

GOOD WORK, EVERY-ONE!

THANKS, GUYS!

WOULD YOU HOLD ON TO THESE FOR ME, MACHIDA-SAN?

I'LL BE IN THE CAR.

OKAY!

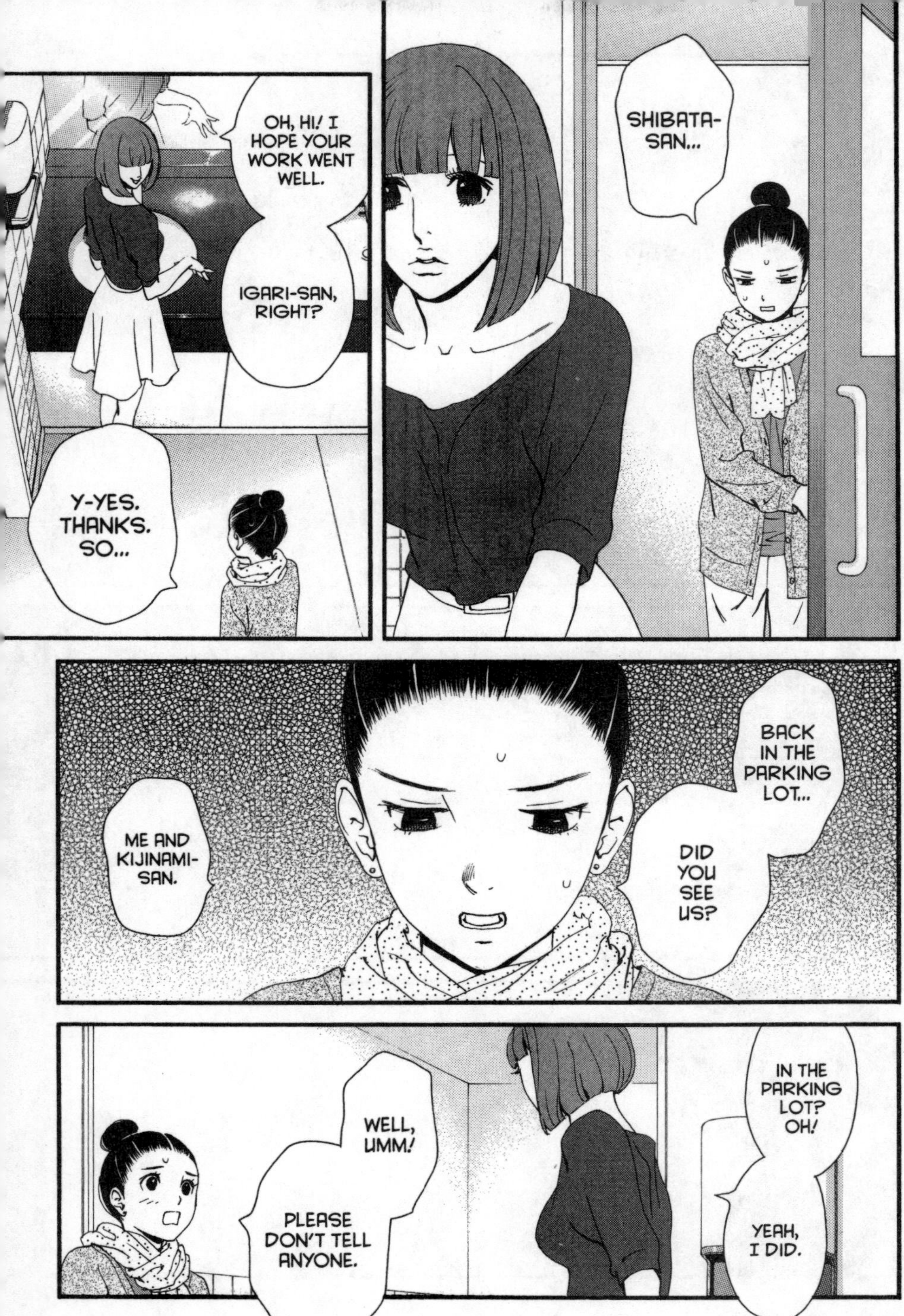
SHIBATA-SAN...
OH, HI! I HOPE YOUR WORK WENT WELL.
IGARI-SAN, RIGHT?
Y-YES. THANKS. SO...
BACK IN THE PARKING LOT...
DID YOU SEE US?
ME AND KIJINAMI-SAN.
IN THE PARKING LOT? OH!
YEAH, I DID.
WELL, UMM!
PLEASE DON'T TELL ANYONE.

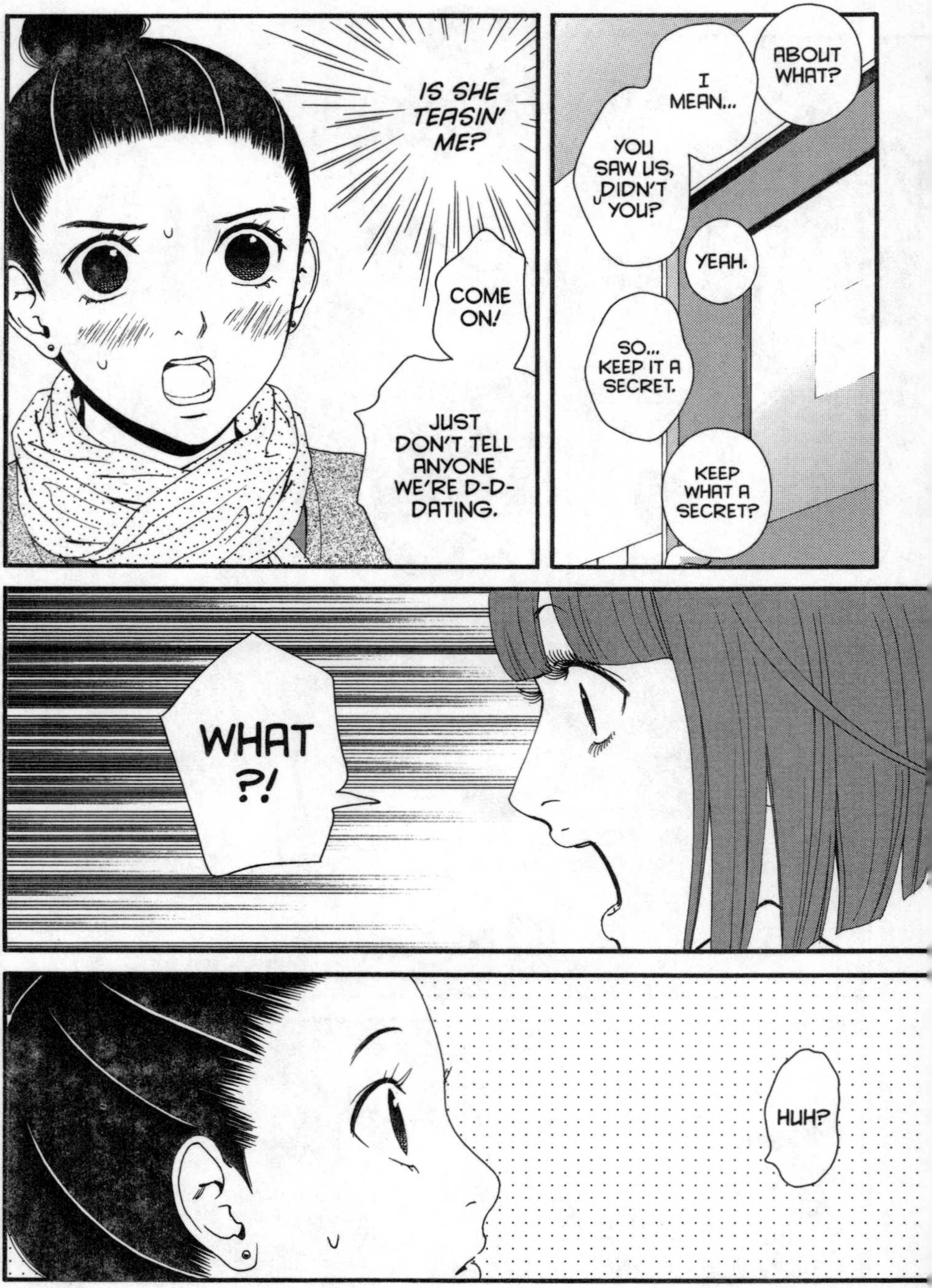
ABOUT WHAT?
I MEAN...
YOU SAW US, DIDN'T YOU?
YEAH.
SO... KEEP IT A SECRET.
KEEP WHAT A SECRET?
IS SHE TEASIN' ME?
COME ON!
JUST DON'T TELL ANYONE WE'RE D-D-DATING.
WHAT ?!
HUH?

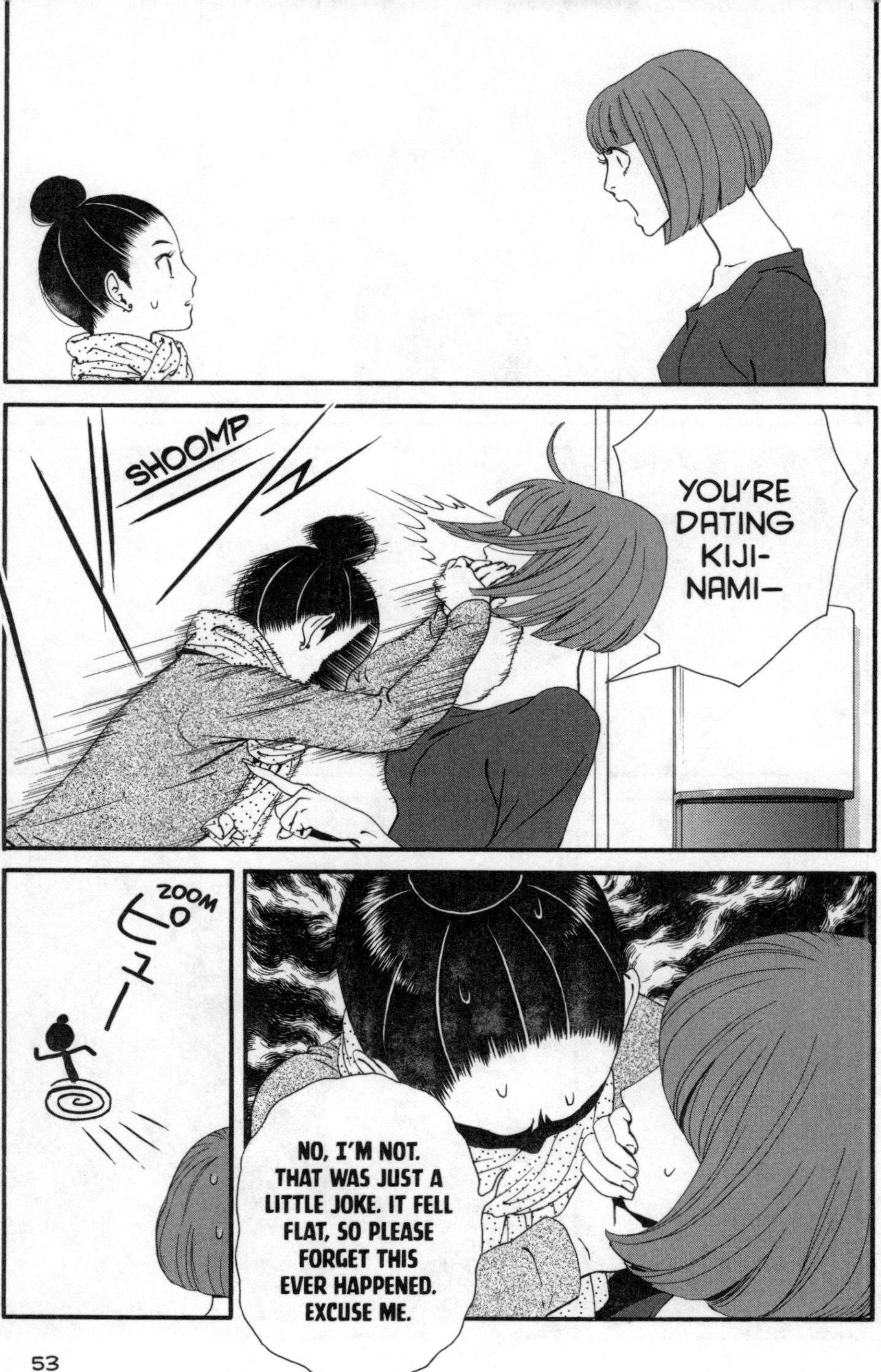
YOU'RE DATING KIJI-NAMI—
SHOOMP
NO, I'M NOT. THAT WAS JUST A LITTLE JOKE. IT FELL FLAT, SO PLEASE FORGET THIS EVER HAPPENED. EXCUSE ME.
ZOOM
ピュー

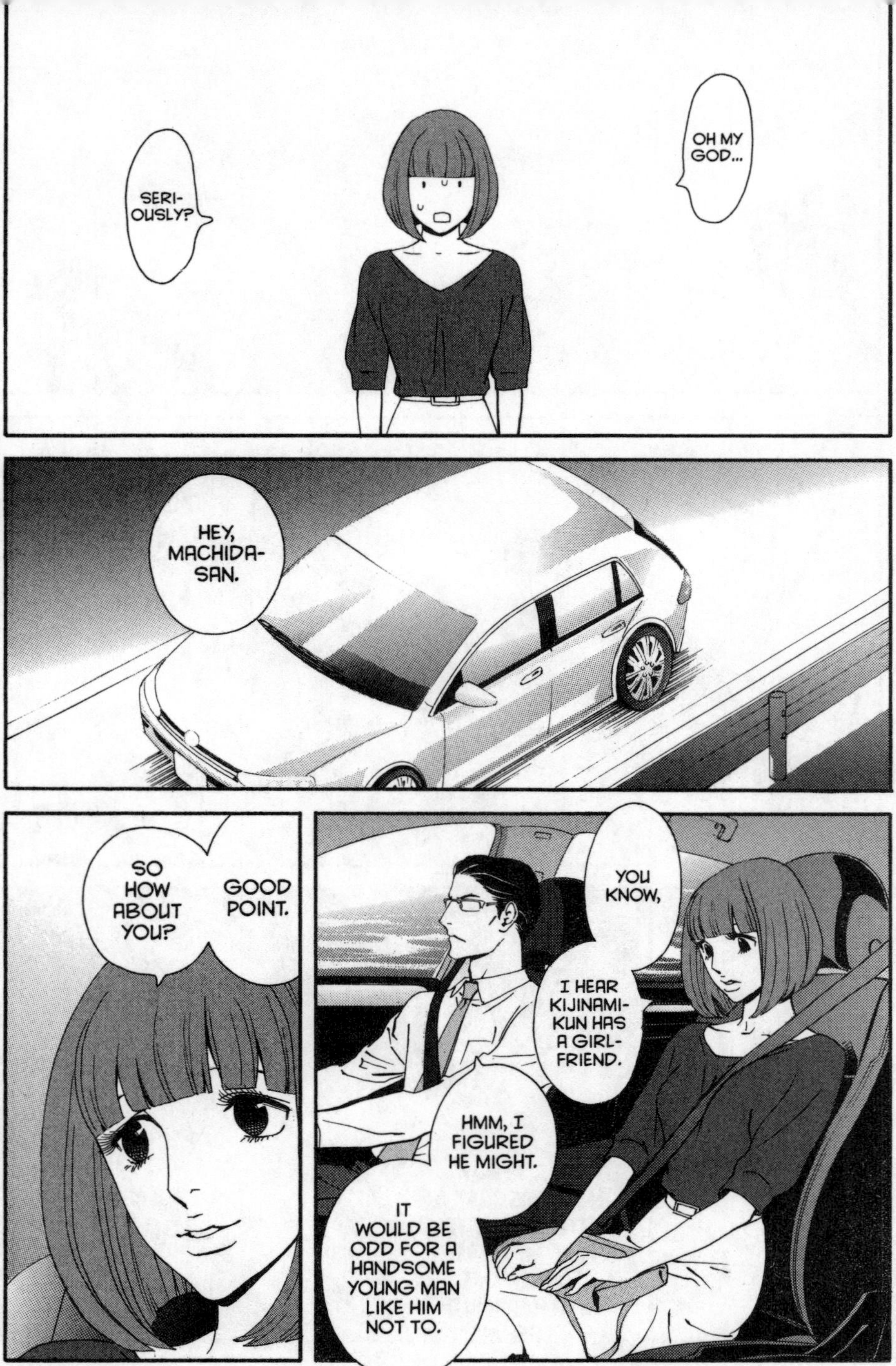
OH MY GOD...
SERI-OUSLY?
HEY, MACHIDA-SAN.
YOU KNOW,
I HEAR KIJINAMI-KUN HAS A GIRL-FRIEND.
HMM, I FIGURED HE MIGHT.
IT WOULD BE ODD FOR A HANDSOME YOUNG MAN LIKE HIM NOT TO.
GOOD POINT.
SO HOW ABOUT YOU?

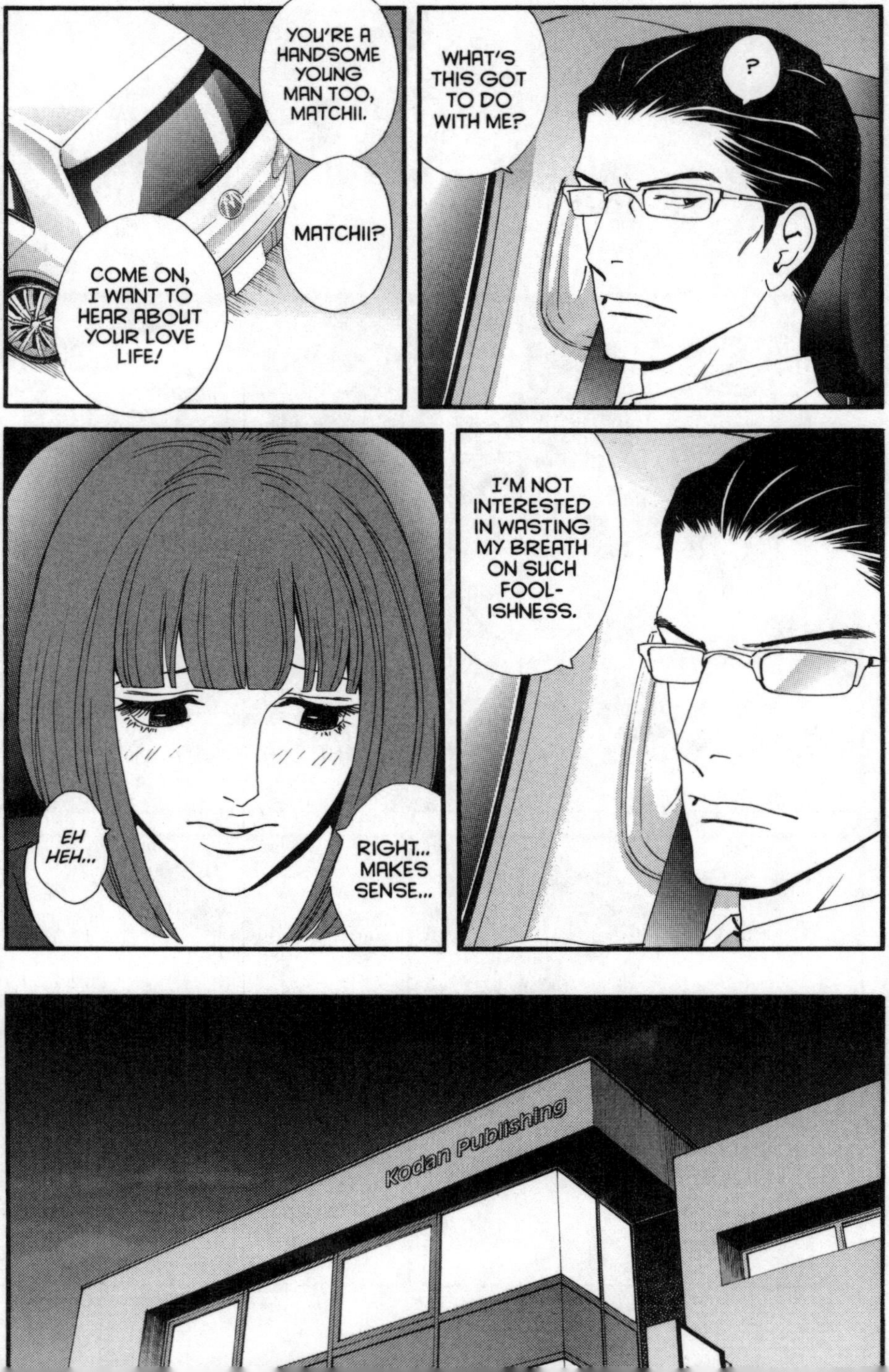
?
WHAT'S THIS GOT TO DO WITH ME?
YOU'RE A HANDSOME YOUNG MAN TOO, MATCHII.
MATCHII?
COME ON, I WANT TO HEAR ABOUT YOUR LOVE LIFE!
I'M NOT INTERESTED IN WASTING MY BREATH ON SUCH FOOLISHNESS.
RIGHT... MAKES SENSE...
EH HEH...
Kodan Publishing

*MATCHII IS A CUTESY ABBREVIATION OF MACHIDA.

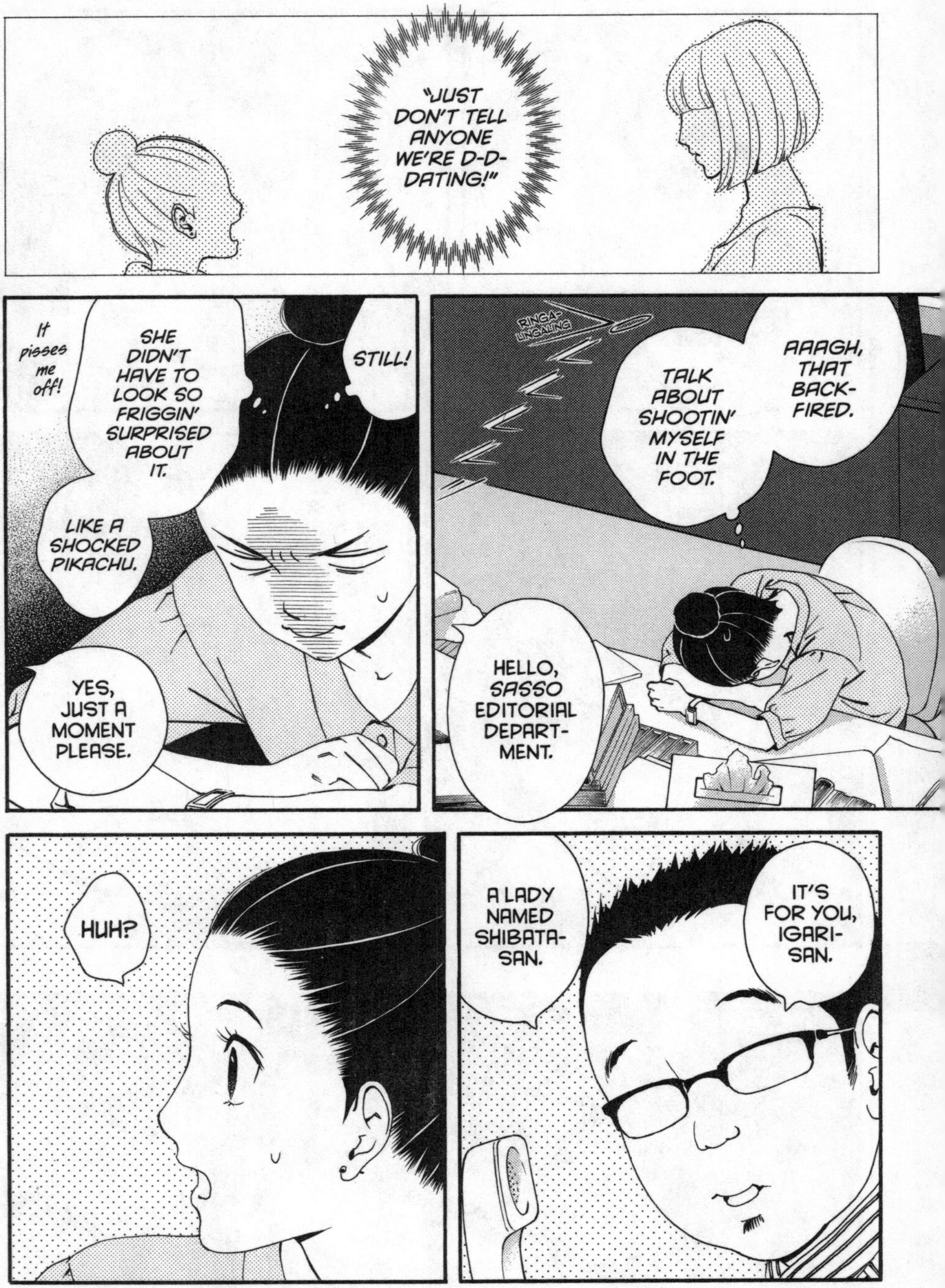

"JUST DON'T TELL ANYONE WE'RE D-D-DATING!"
RINGA-LINGALING
AAAGH, THAT BACK-FIRED.
TALK ABOUT SHOOTIN' MYSELF IN THE FOOT.
HELLO, SASSO EDITORIAL DEPARTMENT.
STILL!
SHE DIDN'T HAVE TO LOOK SO FRIGGIN' SURPRISED ABOUT IT.
It pisses me off!
LIKE A SHOCKED PIKACHU.
YES, JUST A MOMENT PLEASE.
IT'S FOR YOU, IGARI-SAN.
A LADY NAMED SHIBATA-SAN.
HUH?

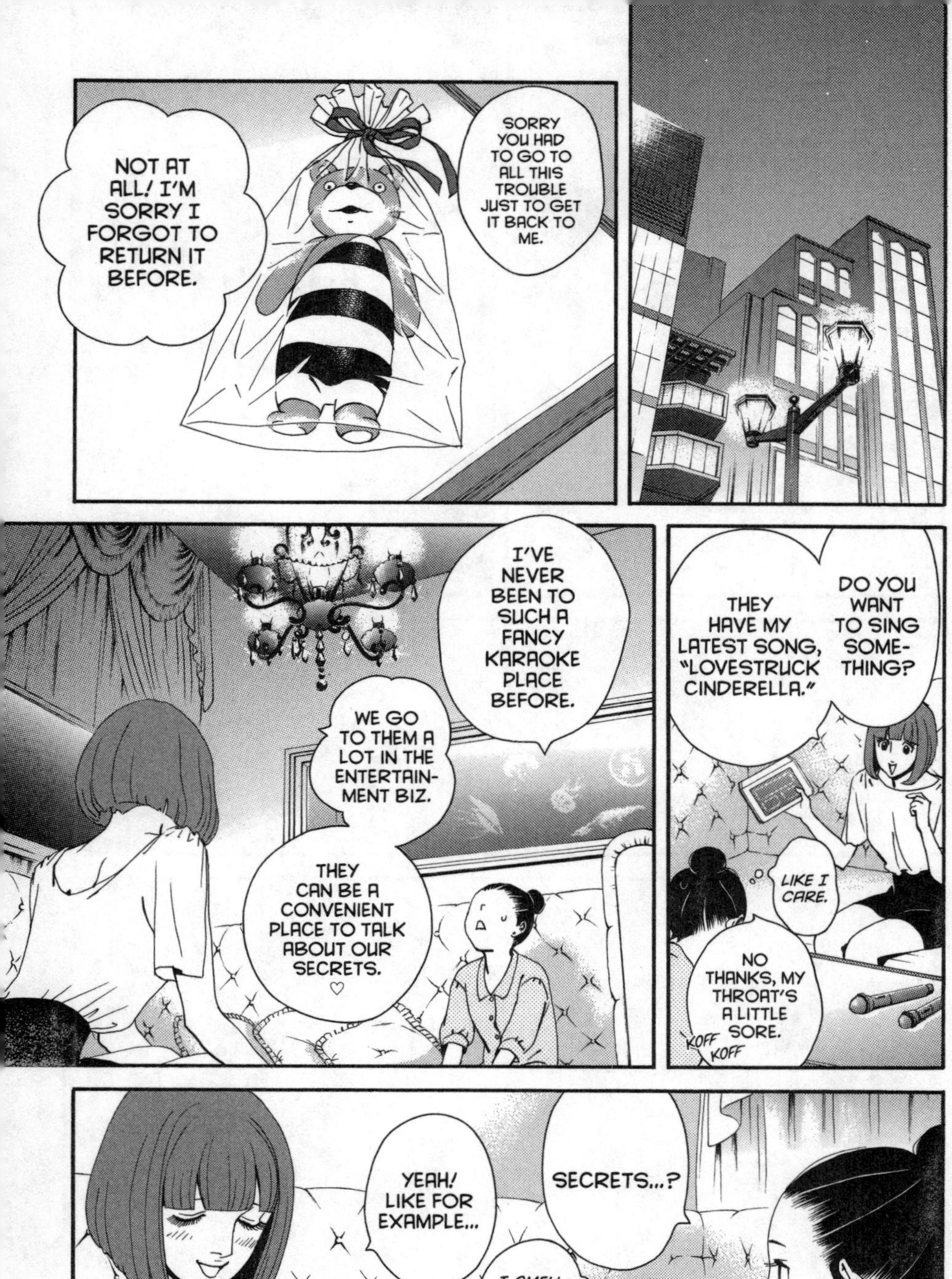
SORRY YOU HAD TO GO TO ALL THIS TROUBLE JUST TO GET IT BACK TO ME.
NOT AT ALL! I'M SORRY I FORGOT TO RETURN IT BEFORE.
DO YOU WANT TO SING SOME-THING?
THEY HAVE MY LATEST SONG, "LOVESTRUCK CINDERELLA."
LIKE I CARE.
NO THANKS, MY THROAT'S A LITTLE SORE.
KOFF KOFF
I'VE NEVER BEEN TO SUCH A FANCY KARAOKE PLACE BEFORE.
WE GO TO THEM A LOT IN THE ENTERTAIN-MENT BIZ.
THEY CAN BE A CONVENIENT PLACE TO TALK ABOUT OUR SECRETS. ♡
SECRETS...?
YEAH! LIKE FOR EXAMPLE...
I SMELL ALCOHOL ON HER BREATH.

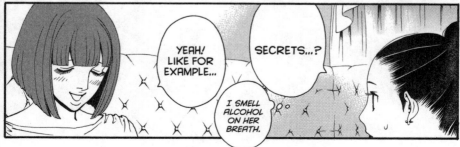

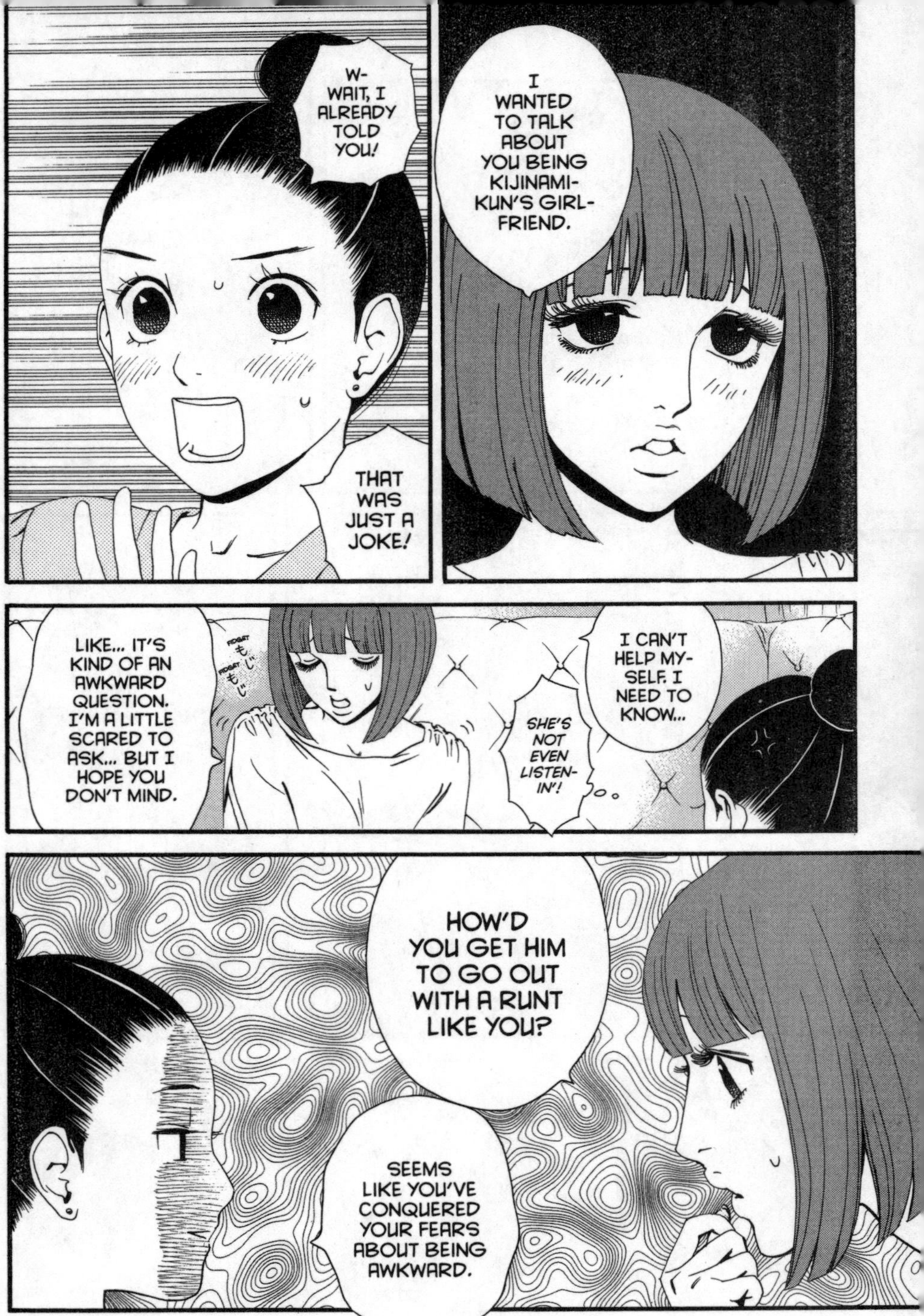
I WANTED TO TALK ABOUT YOU BEING KIJINAMI-KUN'S GIRL-FRIEND.
W-WAIT, I ALREADY TOLD YOU!
THAT WAS JUST A JOKE!
I CAN'T HELP MY-SELF. I NEED TO KNOW...
SHE'S NOT EVEN LISTEN-IN'!
FIDGET もじ
FIDGET もじ
LIKE... IT'S KIND OF AN AWKWARD QUESTION. I'M A LITTLE SCARED TO ASK... BUT I HOPE YOU DON'T MIND.
HOW'D YOU GET HIM TO GO OUT WITH A RUNT LIKE YOU?
SEEMS LIKE YOU'VE CONQUERED YOUR FEARS ABOUT BEING AWKWARD.

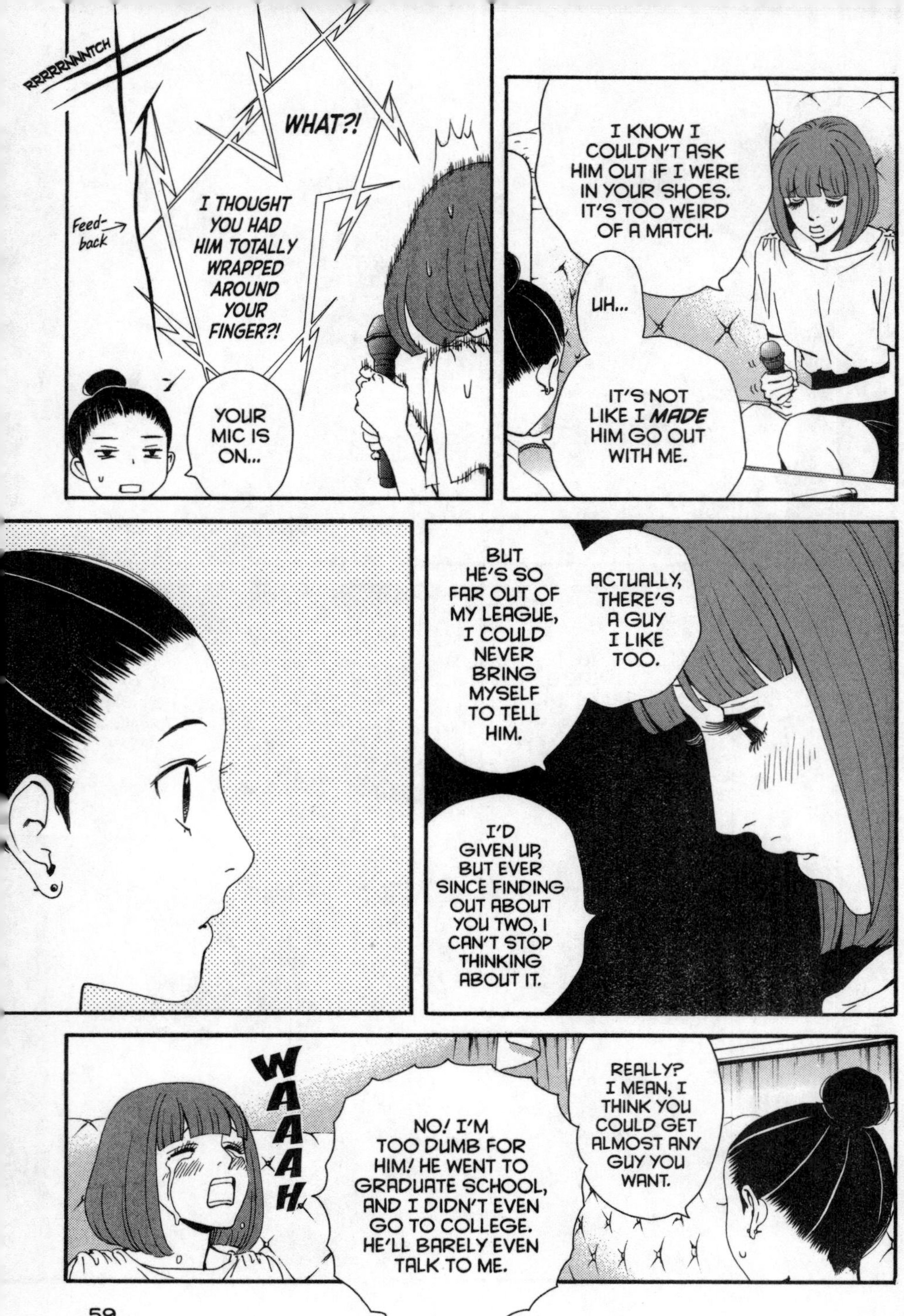
I KNOW I COULDN'T ASK HIM OUT IF I WERE IN YOUR SHOES. IT'S TOO WEIRD OF A MATCH.
UH...
IT'S NOT LIKE I *MADE* HIM GO OUT WITH ME.
RRRRRNNNNTCH
WHAT?!
I THOUGHT YOU HAD HIM TOTALLY WRAPPED AROUND YOUR FINGER?!
Feed-back
YOUR MIC IS ON...
ACTUALLY, THERE'S A GUY I LIKE TOO.
BUT HE'S SO FAR OUT OF MY LEAGUE, I COULD NEVER BRING MYSELF TO TELL HIM.
I'D GIVEN UP, BUT EVER SINCE FINDING OUT ABOUT YOU TWO, I CAN'T STOP THINKING ABOUT IT.
REALLY? I MEAN, I THINK YOU COULD GET ALMOST ANY GUY YOU WANT.
NO! I'M TOO DUMB FOR HIM! HE WENT TO GRADUATE SCHOOL, AND I DIDN'T EVEN GO TO COLLEGE. HE'LL BARELY EVEN TALK TO ME.
WAAAAH

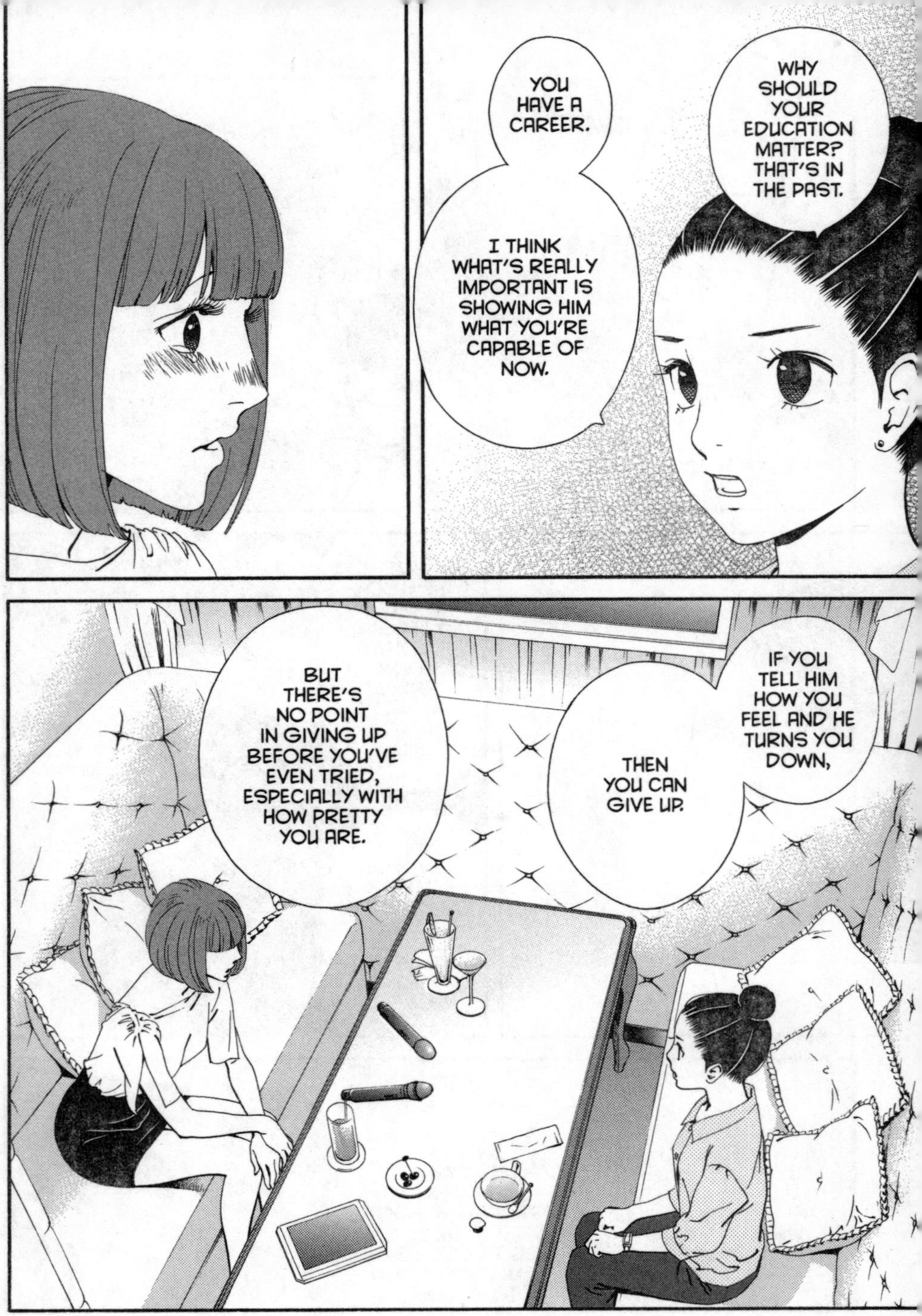
WHY SHOULD YOUR EDUCATION MATTER? THAT'S IN THE PAST.
YOU HAVE A CAREER.
I THINK WHAT'S REALLY IMPORTANT IS SHOWING HIM WHAT YOU'RE CAPABLE OF NOW.
IF YOU TELL HIM HOW YOU FEEL AND HE TURNS YOU DOWN,
THEN YOU CAN GIVE UP.
BUT THERE'S NO POINT IN GIVING UP BEFORE YOU'VE EVEN TRIED, ESPECIALLY WITH HOW PRETTY YOU ARE.

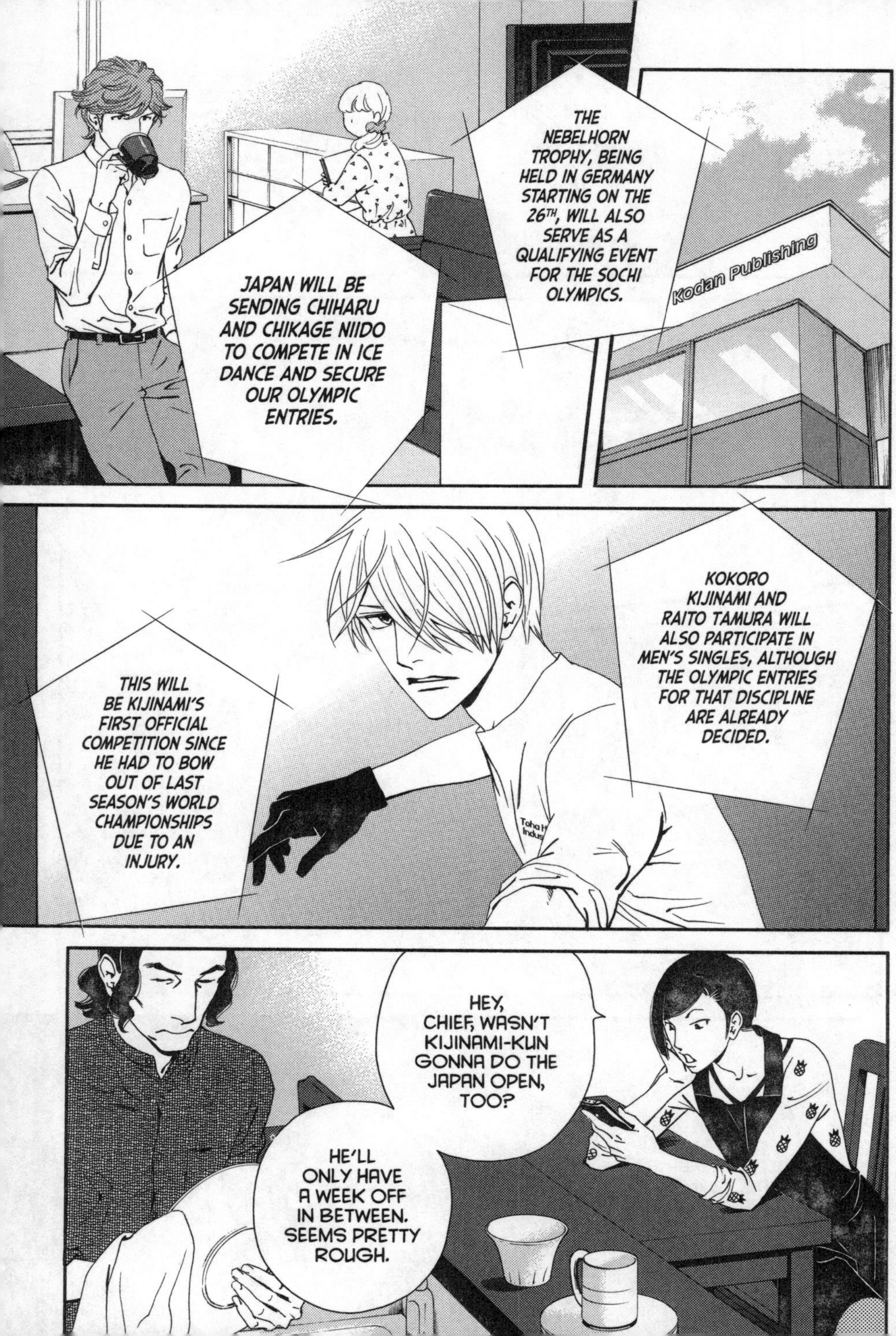

THE NEBELHORN TROPHY, BEING HELD IN GERMANY STARTING ON THE 26TH, WILL ALSO SERVE AS A QUALIFYING EVENT FOR THE SOCHI OLYMPICS.
Kodan Publishing
JAPAN WILL BE SENDING CHIHARU AND CHIKAGE NIIDO TO COMPETE IN ICE DANCE AND SECURE OUR OLYMPIC ENTRIES.
KOKORO KIJINAMI AND RAITO TAMURA WILL ALSO PARTICIPATE IN MEN'S SINGLES, ALTHOUGH THE OLYMPIC ENTRIES FOR THAT DISCIPLINE ARE ALREADY DECIDED.
THIS WILL BE KIJINAMI'S FIRST OFFICIAL COMPETITION SINCE HE HAD TO BOW OUT OF LAST SEASON'S WORLD CHAMPIONSHIPS DUE TO AN INJURY.
HEY, CHIEF, WASN'T KIJINAMI-KUN GONNA DO THE JAPAN OPEN, TOO?
HE'LL ONLY HAVE A WEEK OFF IN BETWEEN. SEEMS PRETTY ROUGH.

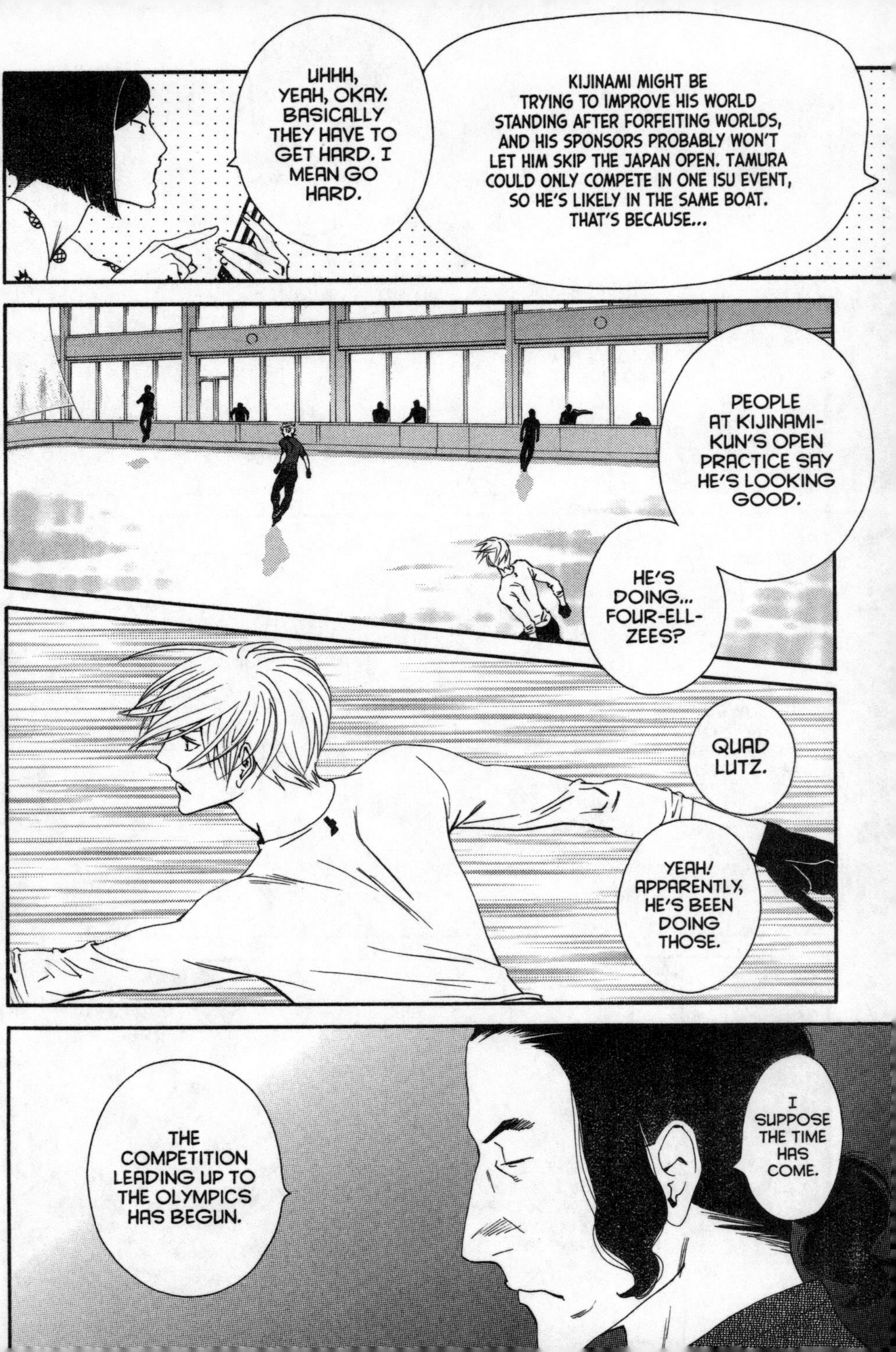
KIJINAMI MIGHT BE TRYING TO IMPROVE HIS WORLD STANDING AFTER FORFEITING WORLDS, AND HIS SPONSORS PROBABLY WON'T LET HIM SKIP THE JAPAN OPEN. TAMURA COULD ONLY COMPETE IN ONE ISU EVENT, SO HE'S LIKELY IN THE SAME BOAT. THAT'S BECAUSE...
UHHH, YEAH, OKAY. BASICALLY THEY HAVE TO GET HARD. I MEAN GO HARD.
PEOPLE AT KIJINAMI-KUN'S OPEN PRACTICE SAY HE'S LOOKING GOOD.
HE'S DOING... FOUR-ELL-ZEES?
QUAD LUTZ.
YEAH! APPARENTLY, HE'S BEEN DOING THOSE.
I SUPPOSE THE TIME HAS COME.
THE COMPETITION LEADING UP TO THE OLYMPICS HAS BEGUN.

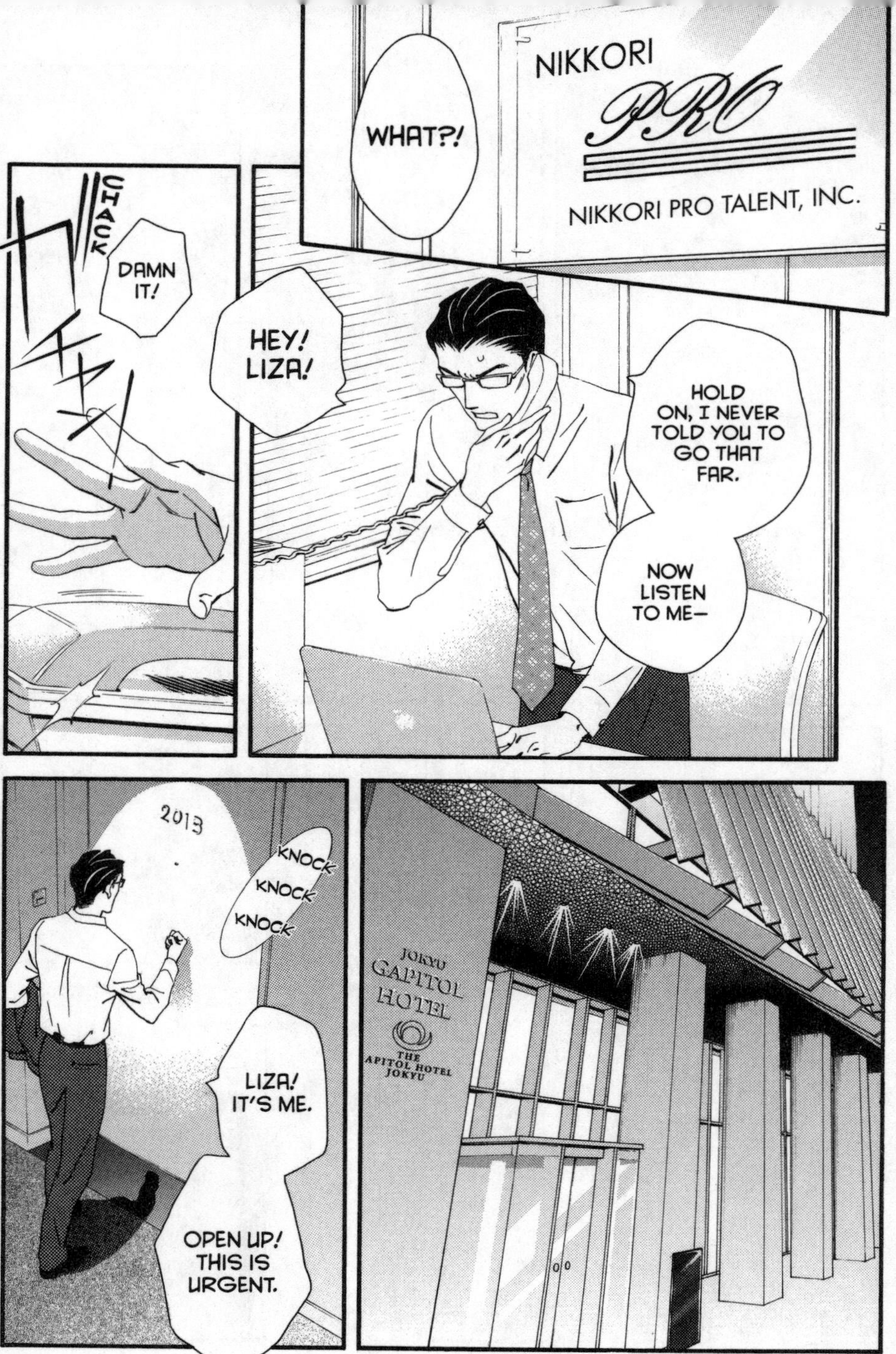
NIKKORI PRO
NIKKORI PRO TALENT, INC.
WHAT?!
HOLD ON, I NEVER TOLD YOU TO GO THAT FAR.
NOW LISTEN TO ME—
HEY! LIZA!
CHACK
DAMN IT!
JOKYU GAPITOL HOTEL
THE APITOL HOTEL JOKYU
2013
KNOCK KNOCK KNOCK
LIZA! IT'S ME.
OPEN UP! THIS IS URGENT.

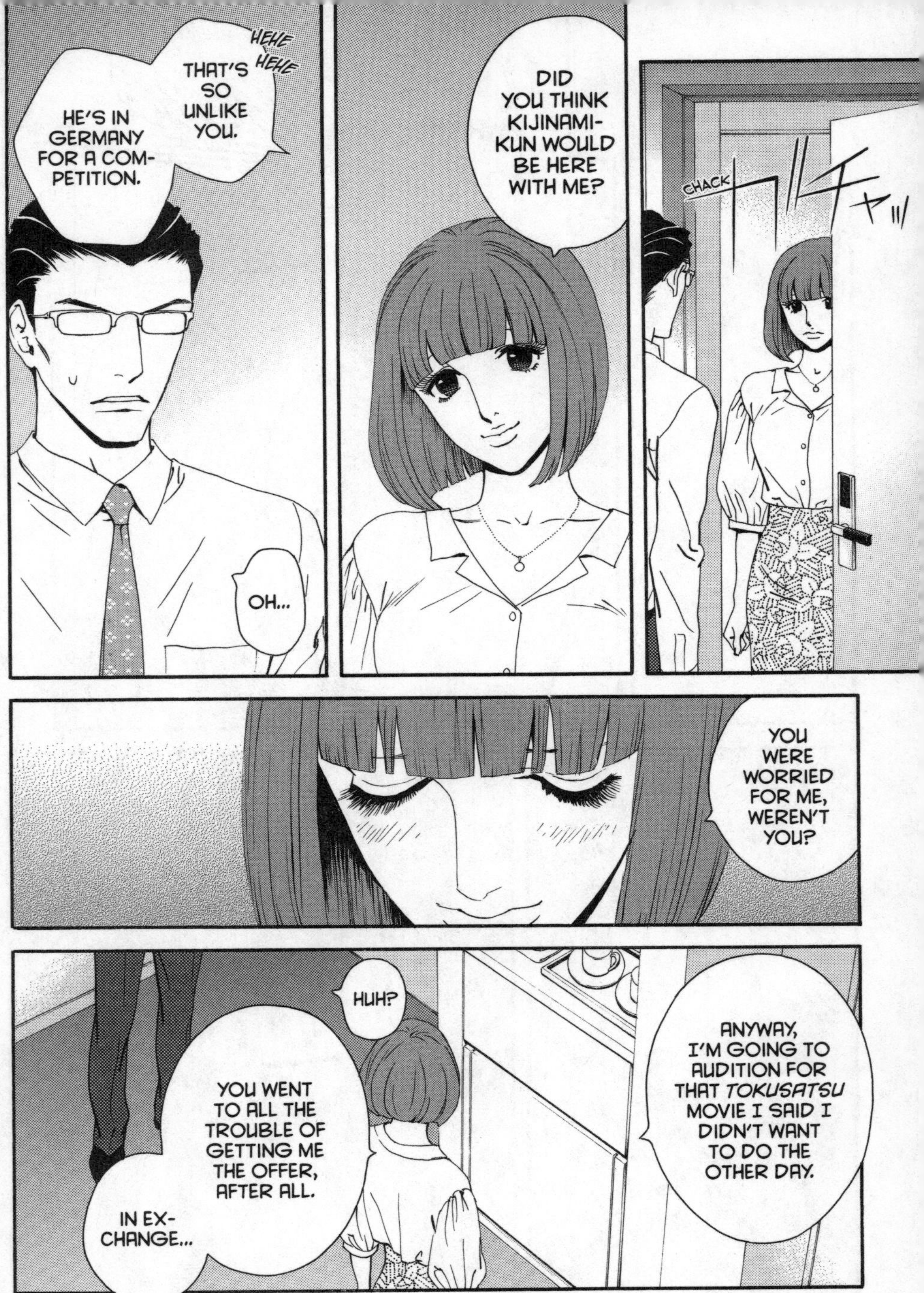
CHACK
ガチャッ
DID YOU THINK KIJINAMI-KUN WOULD BE HERE WITH ME?
HEHE HEHE
THAT'S SO UNLIKE YOU.
HE'S IN GERMANY FOR A COMPETITION.
OH...
YOU WERE WORRIED FOR ME, WEREN'T YOU?
ANYWAY, I'M GOING TO AUDITION FOR THAT *TOKUSATSU* MOVIE I SAID I DIDN'T WANT TO DO THE OTHER DAY.
HUH?
YOU WENT TO ALL THE TROUBLE OF GETTING ME THE OFFER, AFTER ALL.
IN EX-CHANGE...

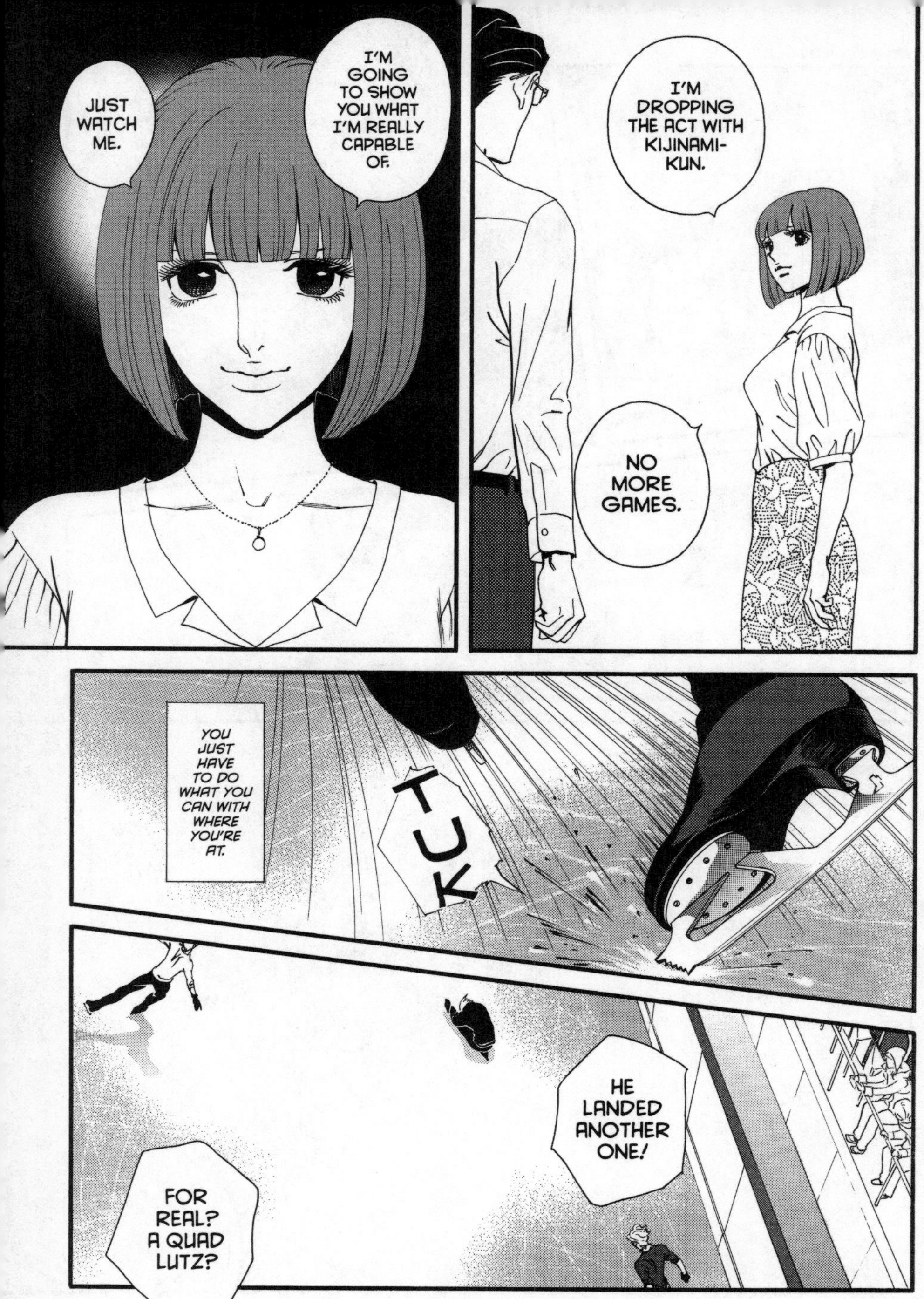
I'M DROPPING THE ACT WITH KIJINAMI-KUN.
NO MORE GAMES.
I'M GOING TO SHOW YOU WHAT I'M REALLY CAPABLE OF.
JUST WATCH ME.
YOU JUST HAVE TO DO WHAT YOU CAN WITH WHERE YOU'RE AT.
TUK
HE LANDED ANOTHER ONE!
FOR REAL? A QUAD LUTZ?

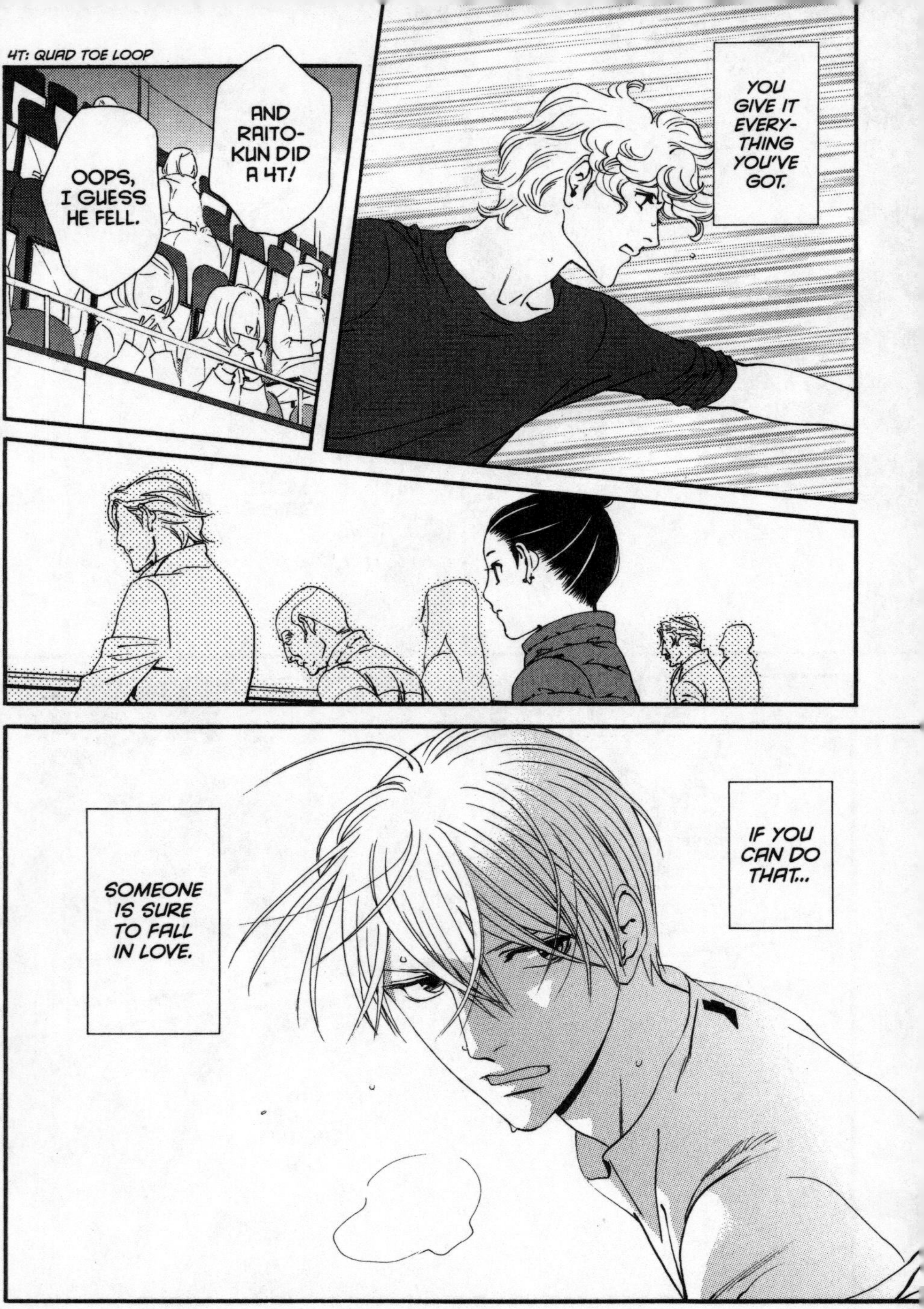
YOU GIVE IT EVERY-THING YOU'VE GOT.
AND RAITO-KUN DID A 4T!
OOPS, I GUESS HE FELL.
IF YOU CAN DO THAT...
SOMEONE IS SURE TO FALL IN LOVE.

4T: QUAD TOE LOOP

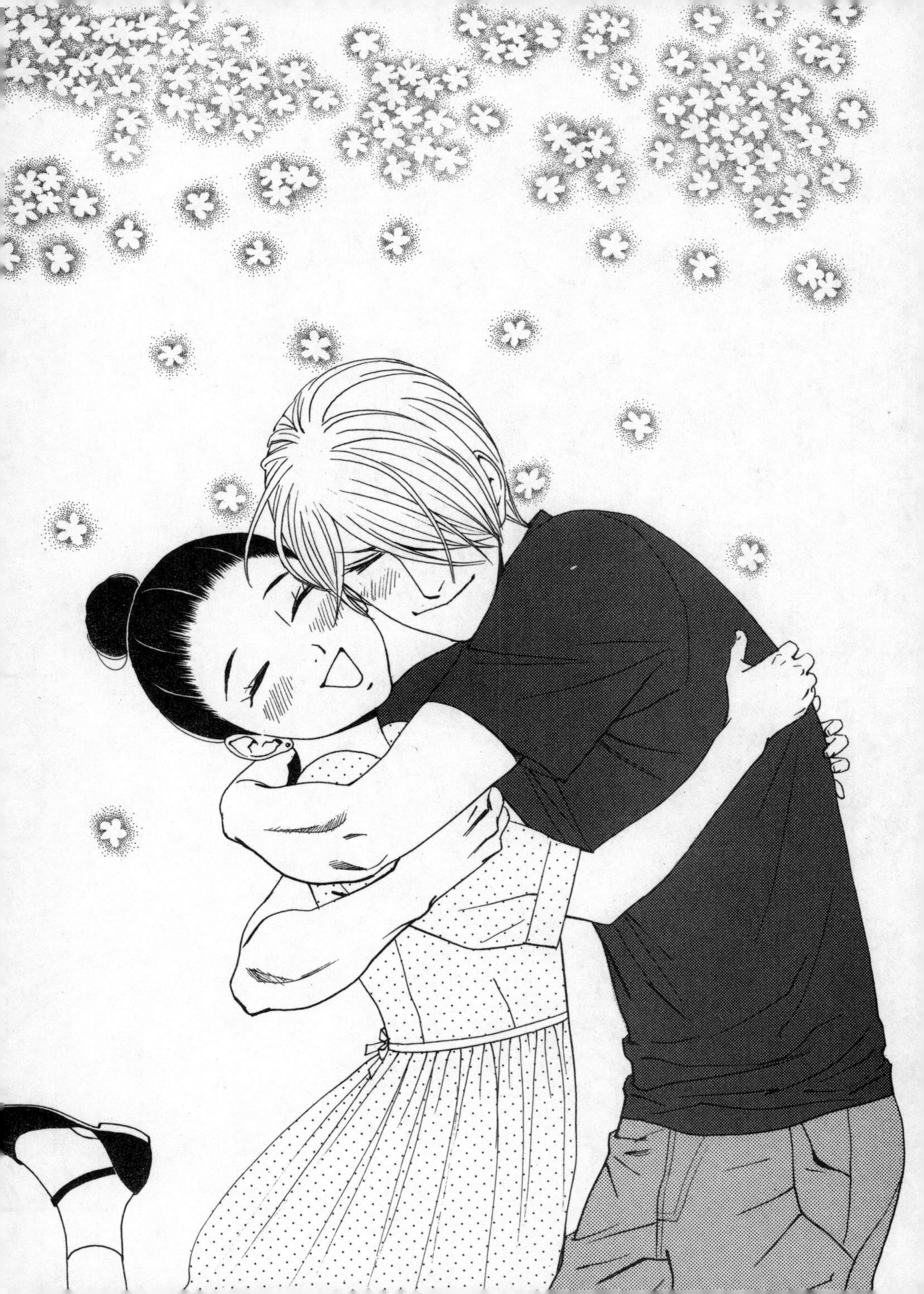

Spell 34
Her Secret

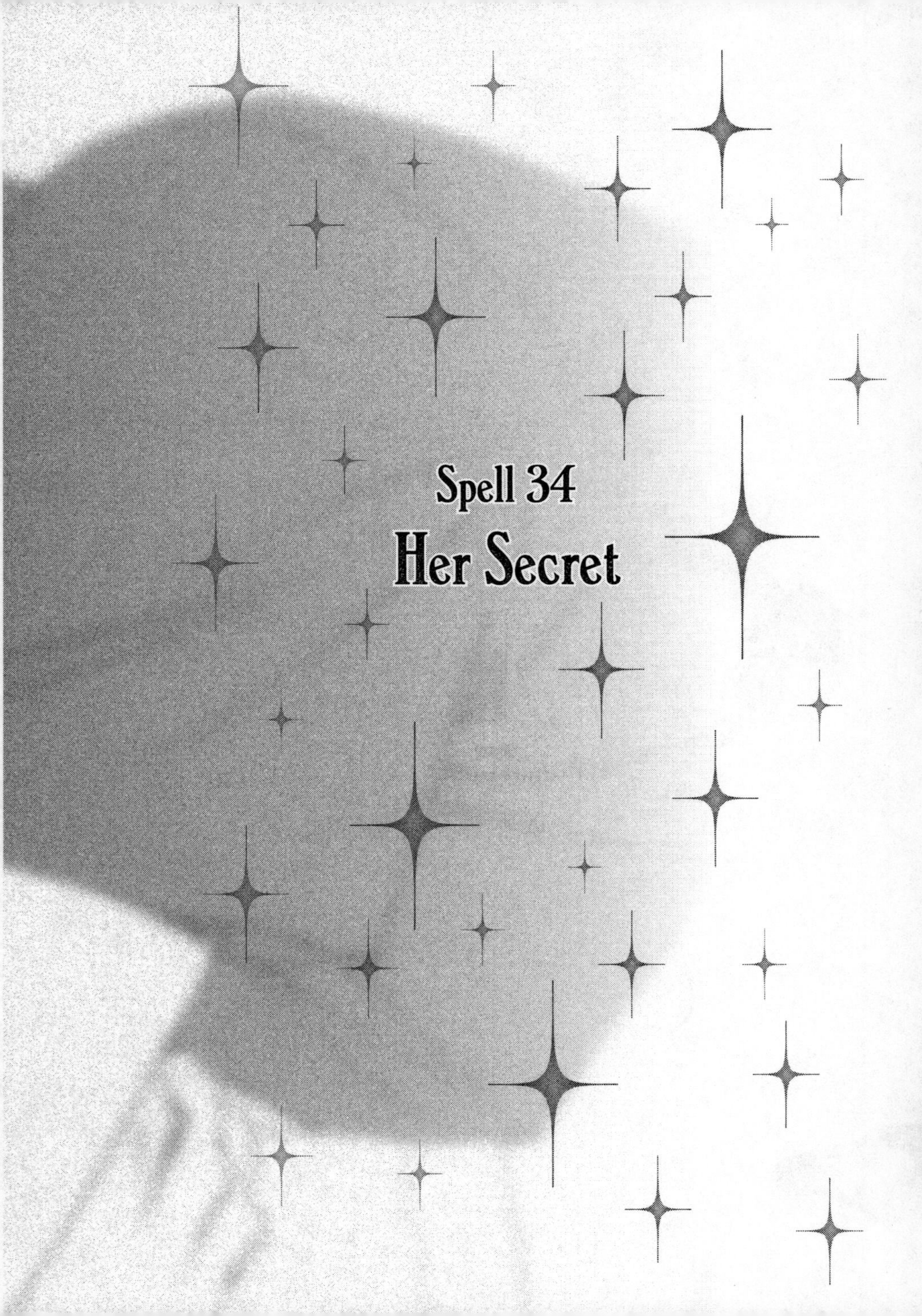

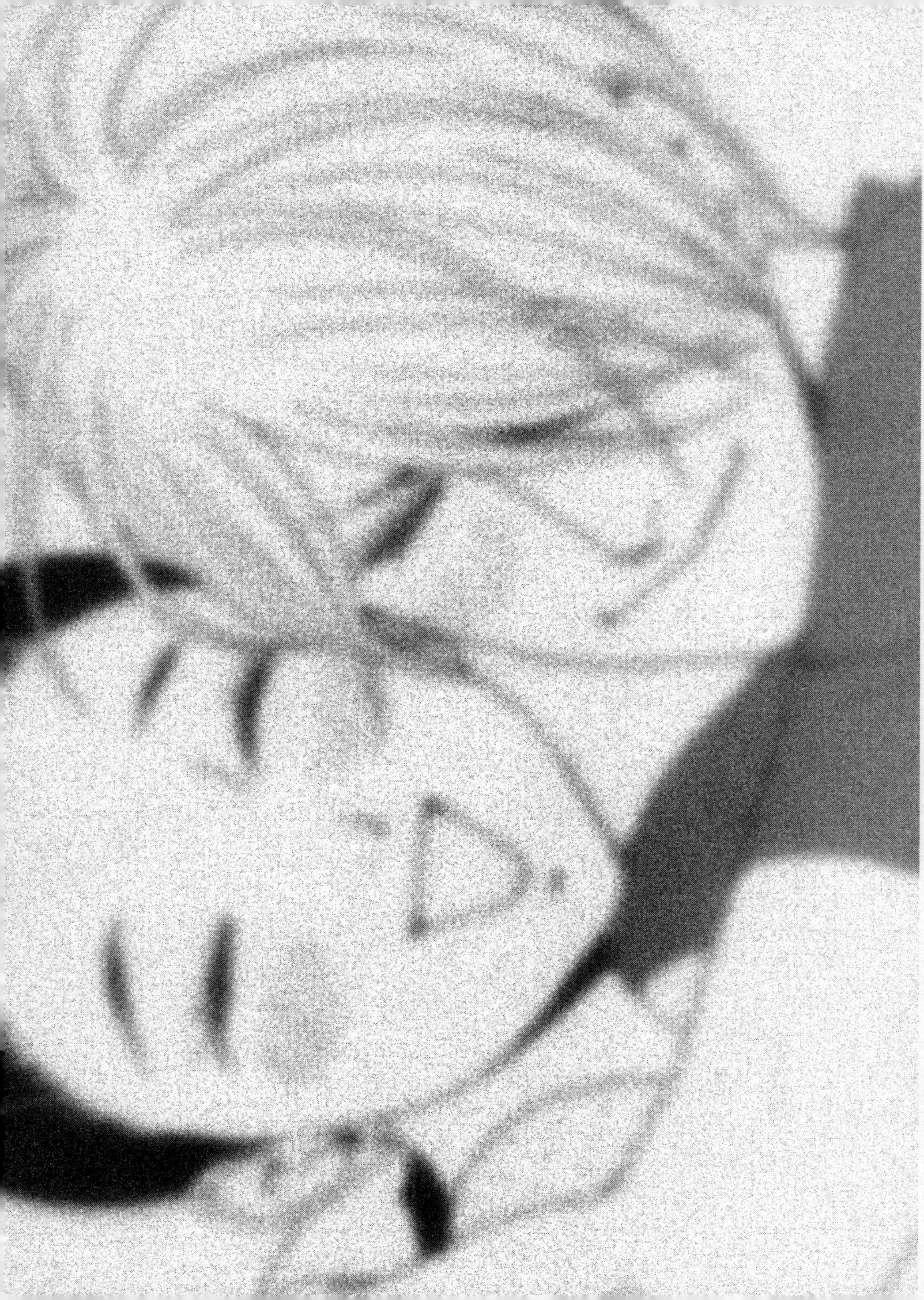

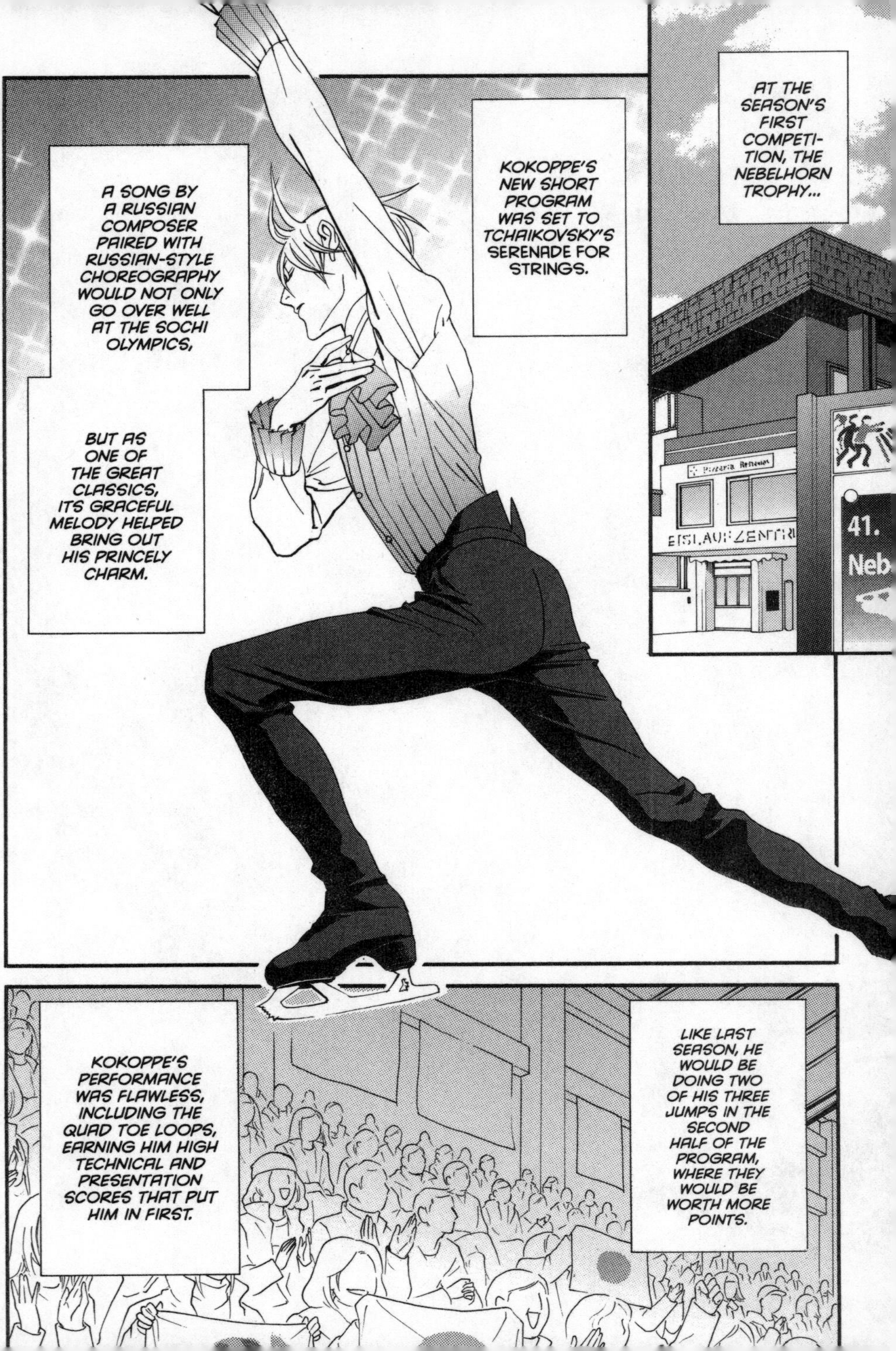
AT THE SEASON'S FIRST COMPETITION, THE NEBELHORN TROPHY...
KOKOPPE'S NEW SHORT PROGRAM WAS SET TO TCHAIKOVSKY'S SERENADE FOR STRINGS.
A SONG BY A RUSSIAN COMPOSER PAIRED WITH RUSSIAN-STYLE CHOREOGRAPHY WOULD NOT ONLY GO OVER WELL AT THE SOCHI OLYMPICS,
BUT AS ONE OF THE GREAT CLASSICS, ITS GRACEFUL MELODY HELPED BRING OUT HIS PRINCELY CHARM.
LIKE LAST SEASON, HE WOULD BE DOING TWO OF HIS THREE JUMPS IN THE SECOND HALF OF THE PROGRAM, WHERE THEY WOULD BE WORTH MORE POINTS.
KOKOPPE'S PERFORMANCE WAS FLAWLESS, INCLUDING THE QUAD TOE LOOPS, EARNING HIM HIGH TECHNICAL AND PRESENTATION SCORES THAT PUT HIM IN FIRST.

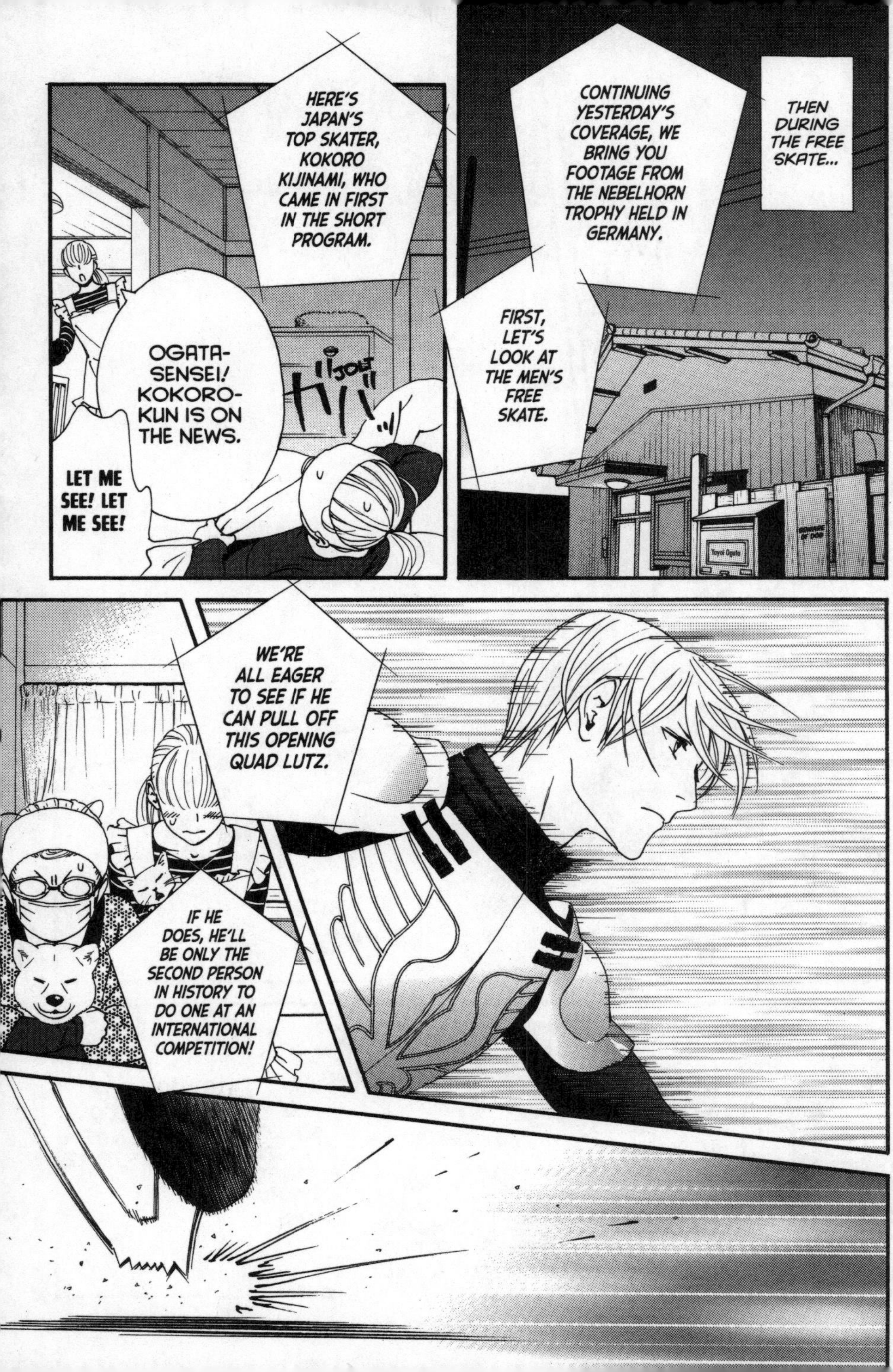
THEN DURING THE FREE SKATE...
CONTINUING YESTERDAY'S COVERAGE, WE BRING YOU FOOTAGE FROM THE NEBELHORN TROPHY HELD IN GERMANY.
FIRST, LET'S LOOK AT THE MEN'S FREE SKATE.
Yayoi Ogata
HERE'S JAPAN'S TOP SKATER, KOKORO KIJINAMI, WHO CAME IN FIRST IN THE SHORT PROGRAM.
JOLT
OGATA-SENSEI! KOKORO-KUN IS ON THE NEWS.
LET ME SEE! LET ME SEE!
WE'RE ALL EAGER TO SEE IF HE CAN PULL OFF THIS OPENING QUAD LUTZ.
IF HE DOES, HE'LL BE ONLY THE SECOND PERSON IN HISTORY TO DO ONE AT AN INTERNATIONAL COMPETITION!

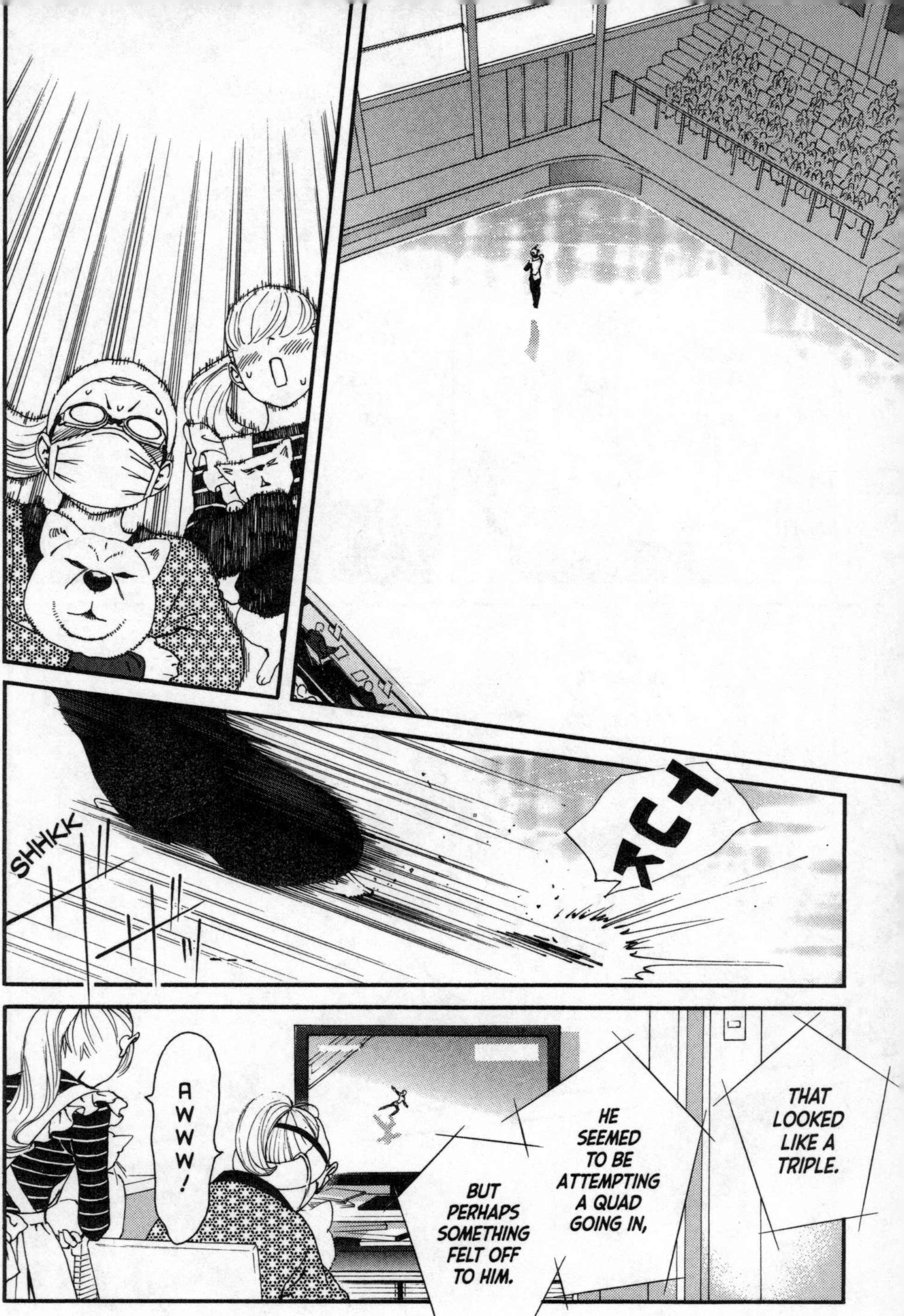
TUK
SHHKK
THAT LOOKED LIKE A TRIPLE.
HE SEEMED TO BE ATTEMPTING A QUAD GOING IN,
BUT PERHAPS SOMETHING FELT OFF TO HIM.
AWWW!

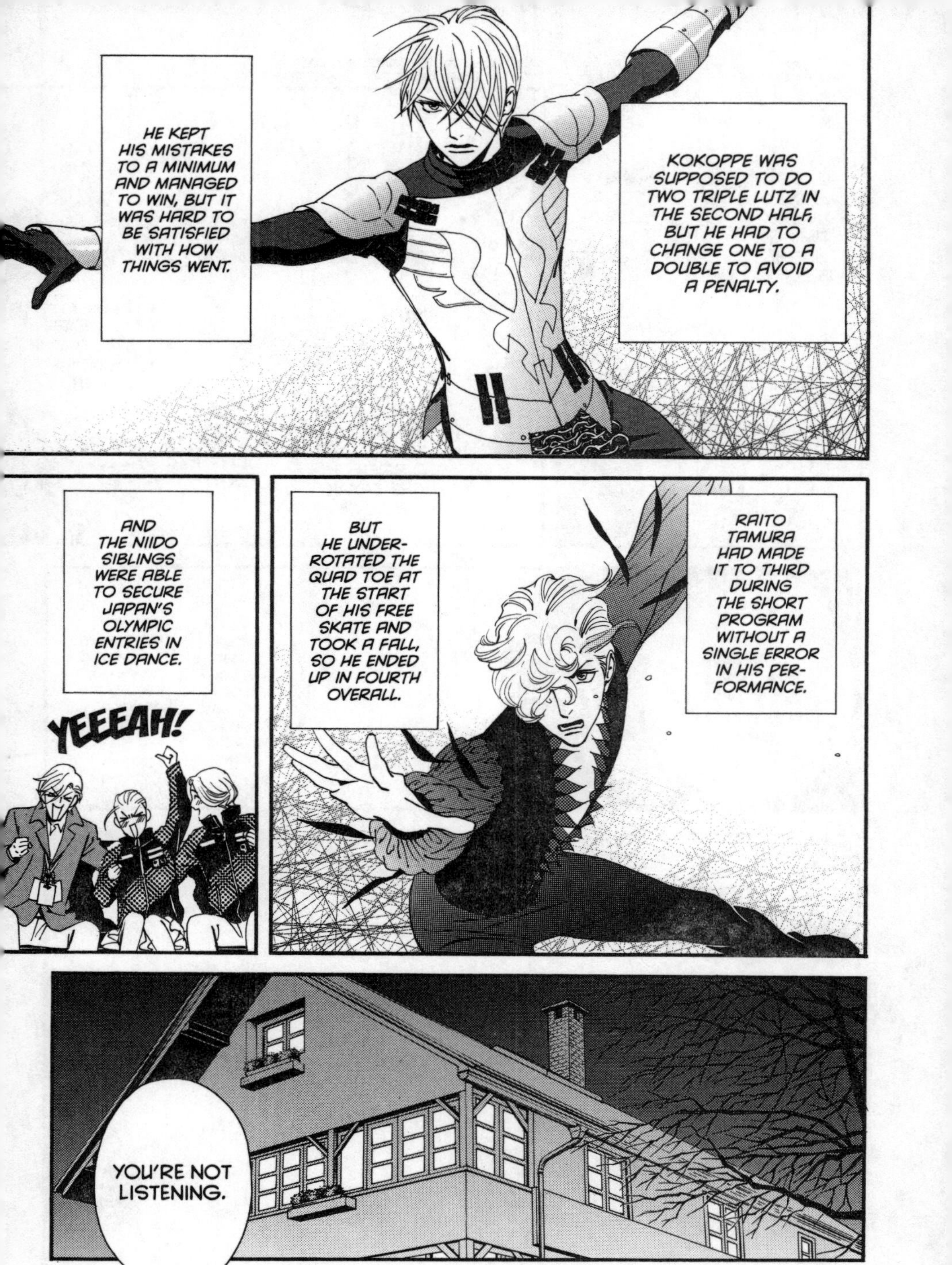
KOKOPPE WAS SUPPOSED TO DO TWO TRIPLE LUTZ IN THE SECOND HALF, BUT HE HAD TO CHANGE ONE TO A DOUBLE TO AVOID A PENALTY.
HE KEPT HIS MISTAKES TO A MINIMUM AND MANAGED TO WIN, BUT IT WAS HARD TO BE SATISFIED WITH HOW THINGS WENT.
RAITO TAMURA HAD MADE IT TO THIRD DURING THE SHORT PROGRAM WITHOUT A SINGLE ERROR IN HIS PER-FORMANCE.
BUT HE UNDER-ROTATED THE QUAD TOE AT THE START OF HIS FREE SKATE AND TOOK A FALL, SO HE ENDED UP IN FOURTH OVERALL.
AND THE NIIDO SIBLINGS WERE ABLE TO SECURE JAPAN'S OLYMPIC ENTRIES IN ICE DANCE.
YEEEAH!
YOU'RE NOT LISTENING.

*POP: TO STOP ROTATING MID-JUMP
**ZAYAK RULE: A RULE THAT LIMITS REPEATED JUMPS

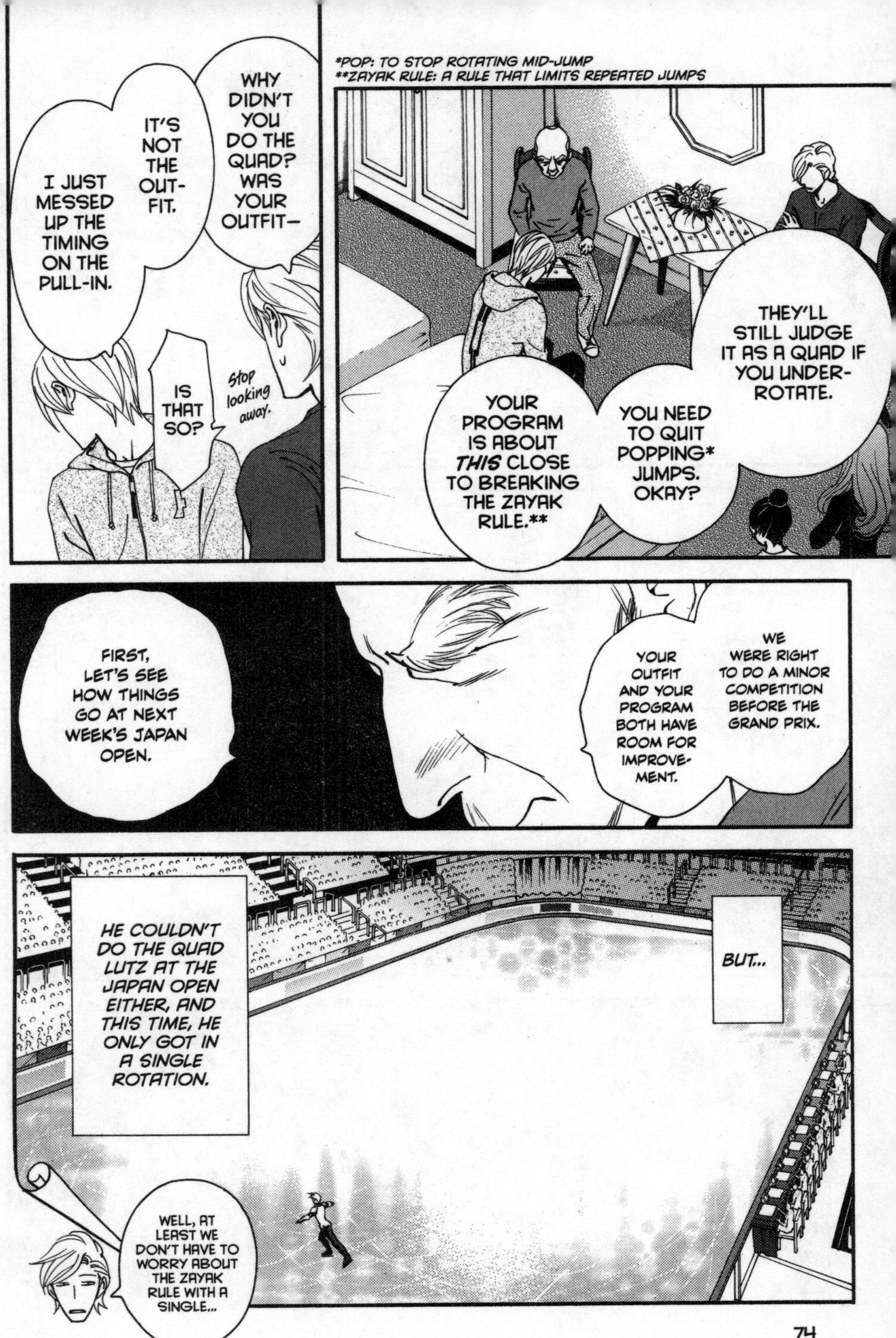

THEY'LL STILL JUDGE IT AS A QUAD IF YOU UNDER-ROTATE.
YOU NEED TO QUIT POPPING* JUMPS. OKAY?
YOUR PROGRAM IS ABOUT *THIS* CLOSE TO BREAKING THE ZAYAK RULE.**
WHY DIDN'T YOU DO THE QUAD? WAS YOUR OUTFIT—
IT'S NOT THE OUTFIT.
I JUST MESSED UP THE TIMING ON THE PULL-IN.
Stop looking away.
IS THAT SO?
WE WERE RIGHT TO DO A MINOR COMPETITION BEFORE THE GRAND PRIX.
YOUR OUTFIT AND YOUR PROGRAM BOTH HAVE ROOM FOR IMPROVE-MENT.
FIRST, LET'S SEE HOW THINGS GO AT NEXT WEEK'S JAPAN OPEN.
BUT...
HE COULDN'T DO THE QUAD LUTZ AT THE JAPAN OPEN EITHER, AND THIS TIME, HE ONLY GOT IN A SINGLE ROTATION.
WELL, AT LEAST WE DON'T HAVE TO WORRY ABOUT THE ZAYAK RULE WITH A SINGLE...

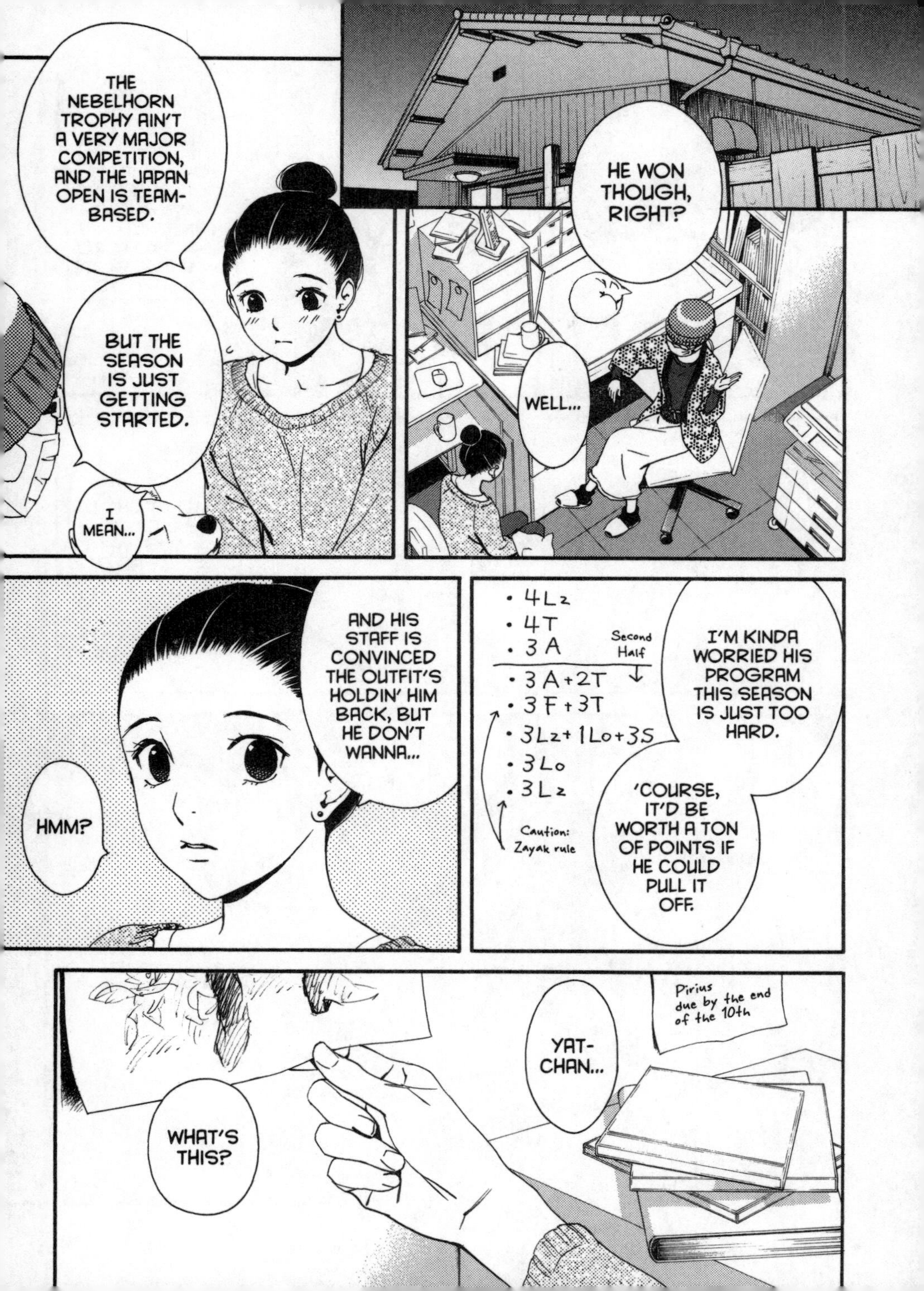
HE WON THOUGH, RIGHT?
WELL...
THE NEBELHORN TROPHY AIN'T A VERY MAJOR COMPETITION, AND THE JAPAN OPEN IS TEAM-BASED.
BUT THE SEASON IS JUST GETTING STARTED.
I MEAN...
• 4Lz
• 4T
• 3A
Second Half
• 3A+2T
• 3F+3T
• 3Lz+1Lo+3S
• 3Lo
• 3Lz
Caution: Zayak rule
I'M KINDA WORRIED HIS PROGRAM THIS SEASON IS JUST TOO HARD.
'COURSE, IT'D BE WORTH A TON OF POINTS IF HE COULD PULL IT OFF.
AND HIS STAFF IS CONVINCED THE OUTFIT'S HOLDIN' HIM BACK, BUT HE DON'T WANNA...
HMM?
Pirius due by the end of the 10th
YAT-CHAN...
WHAT'S THIS?

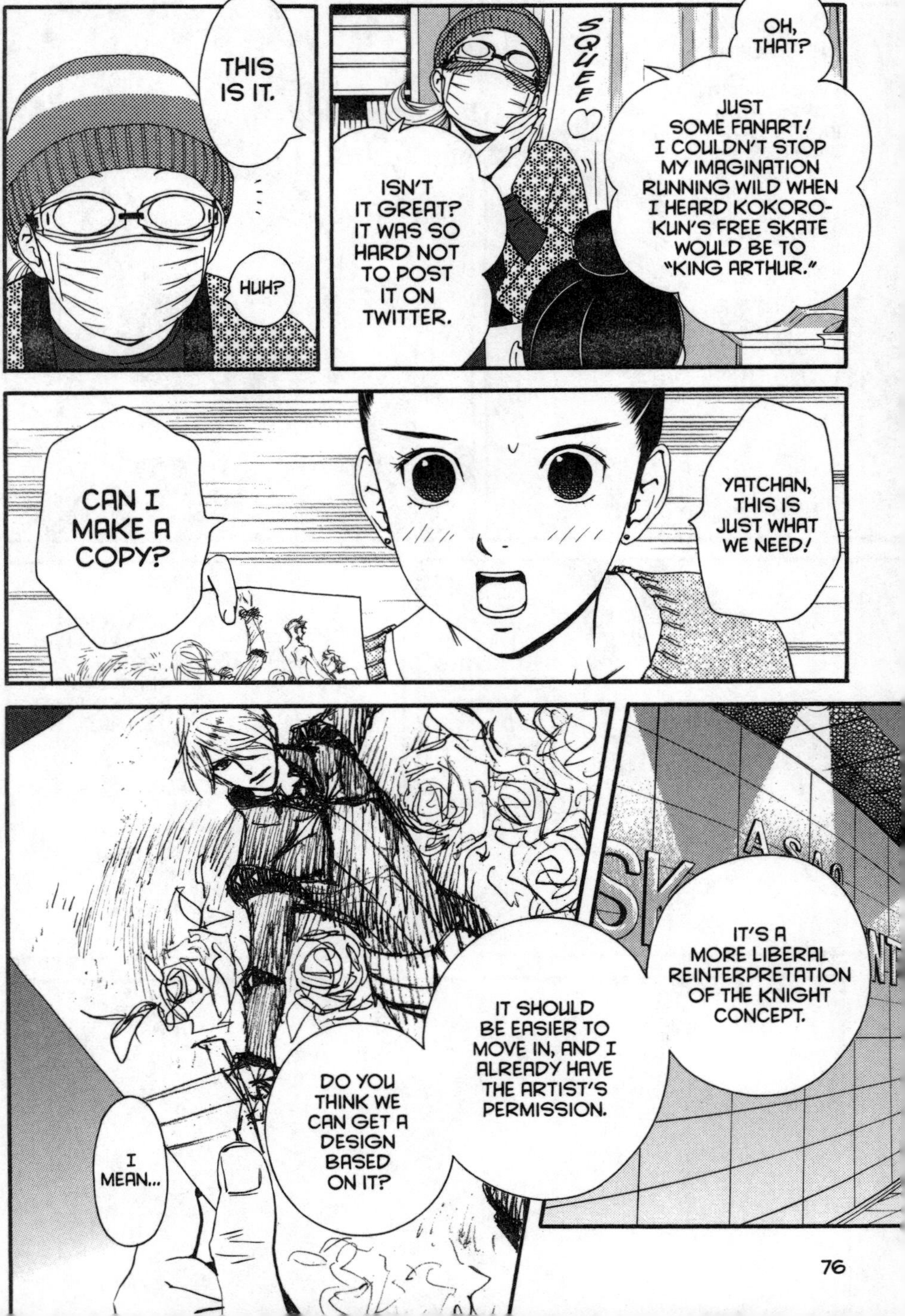
OH, THAT?
SQUEEE
JUST SOME FANART! I COULDN'T STOP MY IMAGINATION RUNNING WILD WHEN I HEARD KOKORO-KUN'S FREE SKATE WOULD BE TO "KING ARTHUR."
ISN'T IT GREAT? IT WAS SO HARD NOT TO POST IT ON TWITTER.
THIS IS IT.
HUH?
YATCHAN, THIS IS JUST WHAT WE NEED!
CAN I MAKE A COPY?
IT'S A MORE LIBERAL REINTERPRETATION OF THE KNIGHT CONCEPT.
IT SHOULD BE EASIER TO MOVE IN, AND I ALREADY HAVE THE ARTIST'S PERMISSION.
DO YOU THINK WE CAN GET A DESIGN BASED ON IT?
I MEAN...

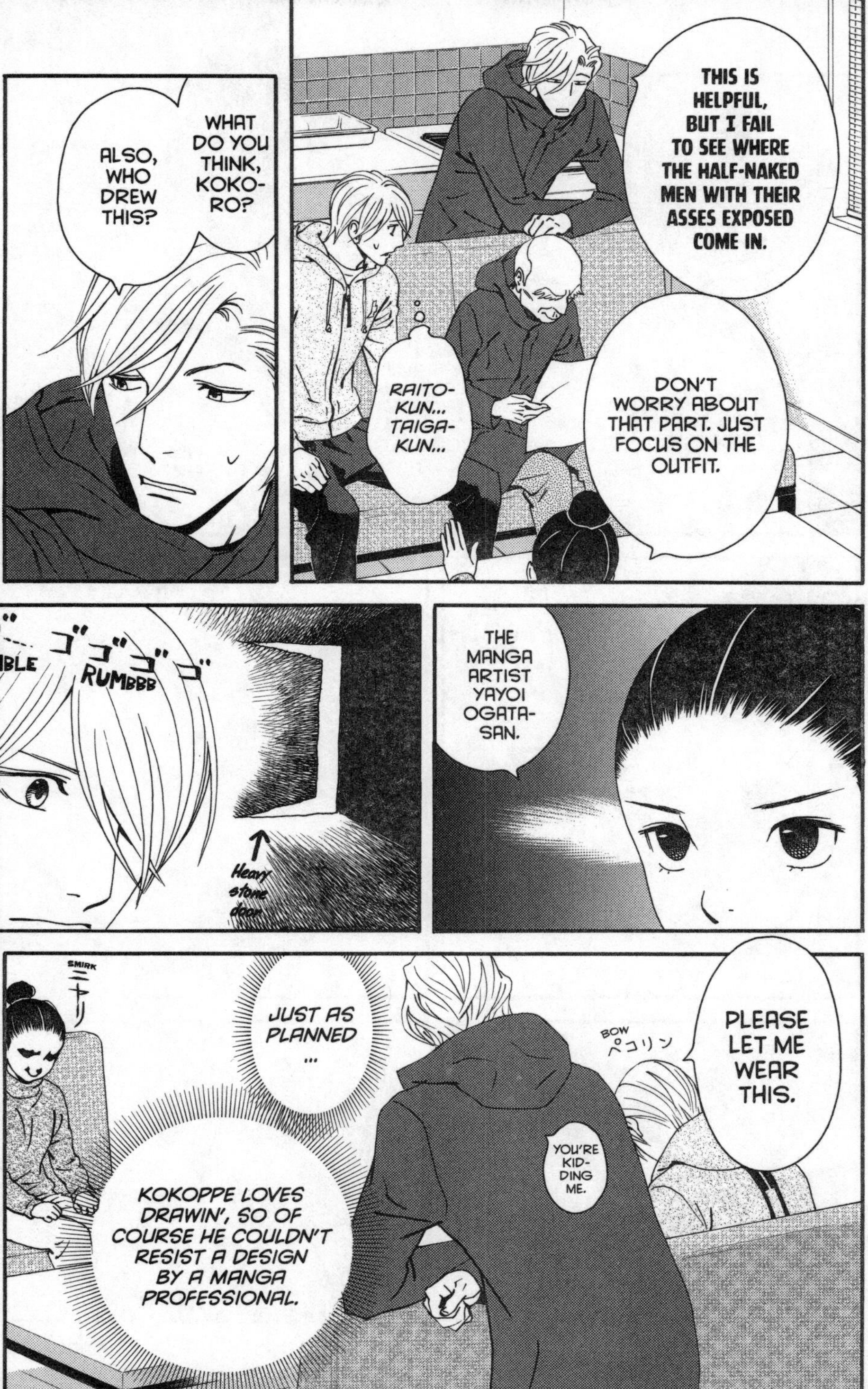
THIS IS HELPFUL, BUT I FAIL TO SEE WHERE THE HALF-NAKED MEN WITH THEIR ASSES EXPOSED COME IN.
DON'T WORRY ABOUT THAT PART. JUST FOCUS ON THE OUTFIT.
RAITO-KUN... TAIGA-KUN...
WHAT DO YOU THINK, KOKORO?
ALSO, WHO DREW THIS?
THE MANGA ARTIST YAYOI OGATA-SAN.
ゴ RUMBLE
ゴゴゴゴ RUMBBB
Heavy stone door
PLEASE LET ME WEAR THIS.
BOW ペコリン
JUST AS PLANNED...
SMIRK ニヤリ
YOU'RE KIDDING ME.
KOKOPPE LOVES DRAWIN', SO OF COURSE HE COULDN'T RESIST A DESIGN BY A MANGA PROFESSIONAL.

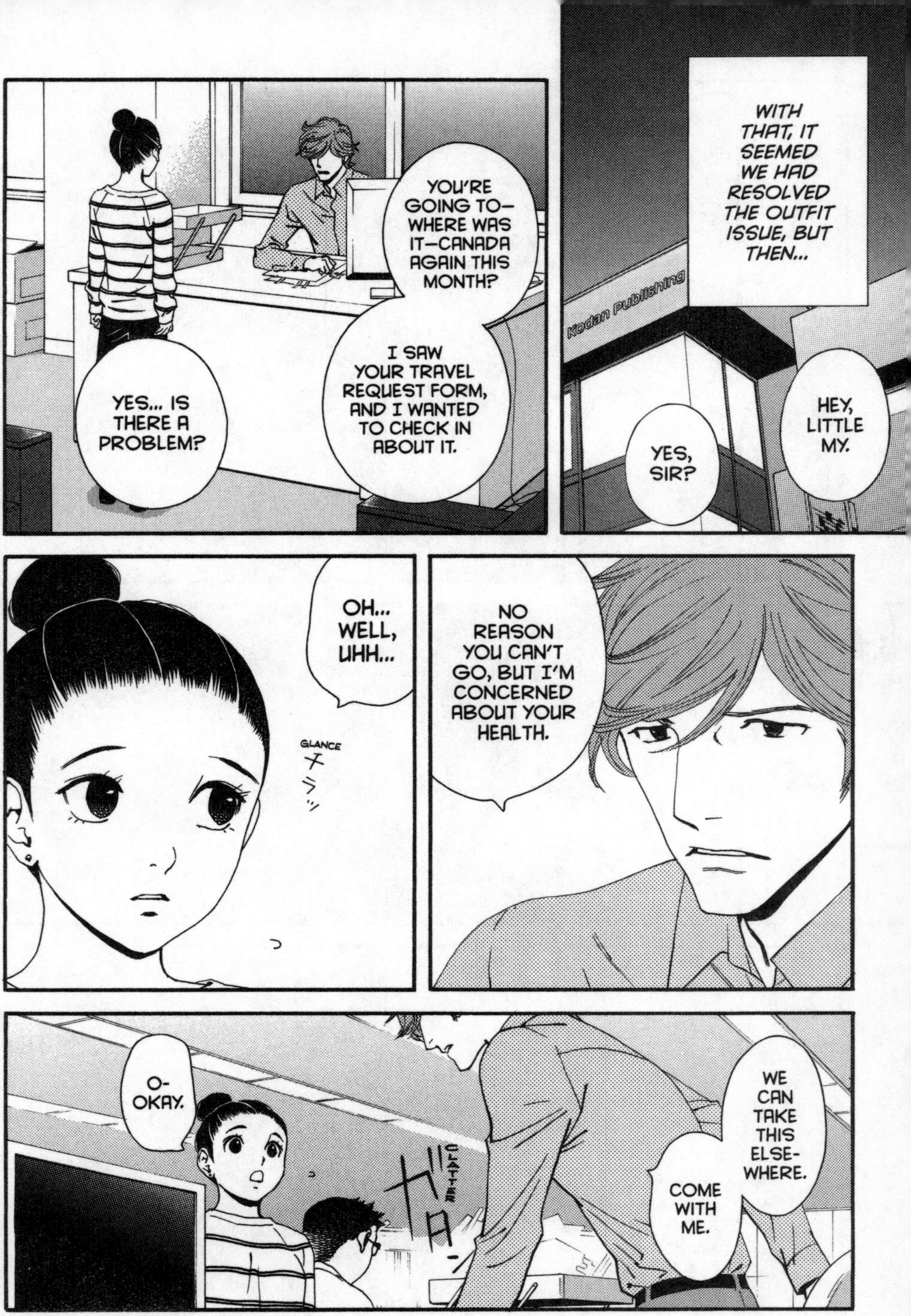
WITH THAT, IT SEEMED WE HAD RESOLVED THE OUTFIT ISSUE, BUT THEN...
Kodan Publishing
HEY, LITTLE MY.
YES, SIR?
YOU'RE GOING TO—WHERE WAS IT—CANADA AGAIN THIS MONTH?
I SAW YOUR TRAVEL REQUEST FORM, AND I WANTED TO CHECK IN ABOUT IT.
YES... IS THERE A PROBLEM?
NO REASON YOU CAN'T GO, BUT I'M CONCERNED ABOUT YOUR HEALTH.
OH... WELL, UHH...
GLANCE
WE CAN TAKE THIS ELSE-WHERE.
COME WITH ME.
CLATTER
O-OKAY.

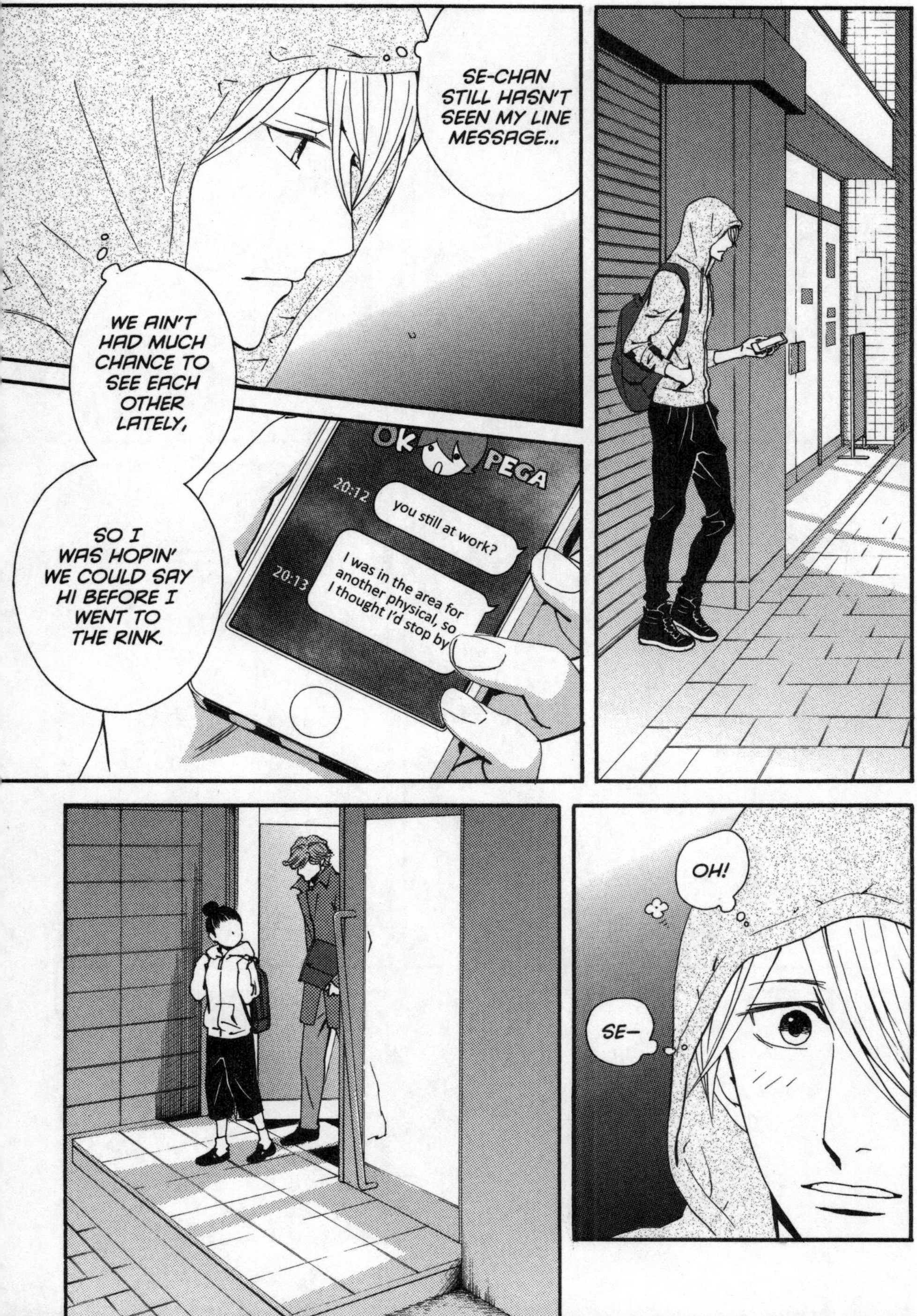
SE-CHAN STILL HASN'T SEEN MY LINE MESSAGE...
WE AIN'T HAD MUCH CHANCE TO SEE EACH OTHER LATELY,
SO I WAS HOPIN' WE COULD SAY HI BEFORE I WENT TO THE RINK.
OK PEGA
20:12
you still at work?
20:13
I was in the area for another physical, so I thought I'd stop by
OH!
SE–

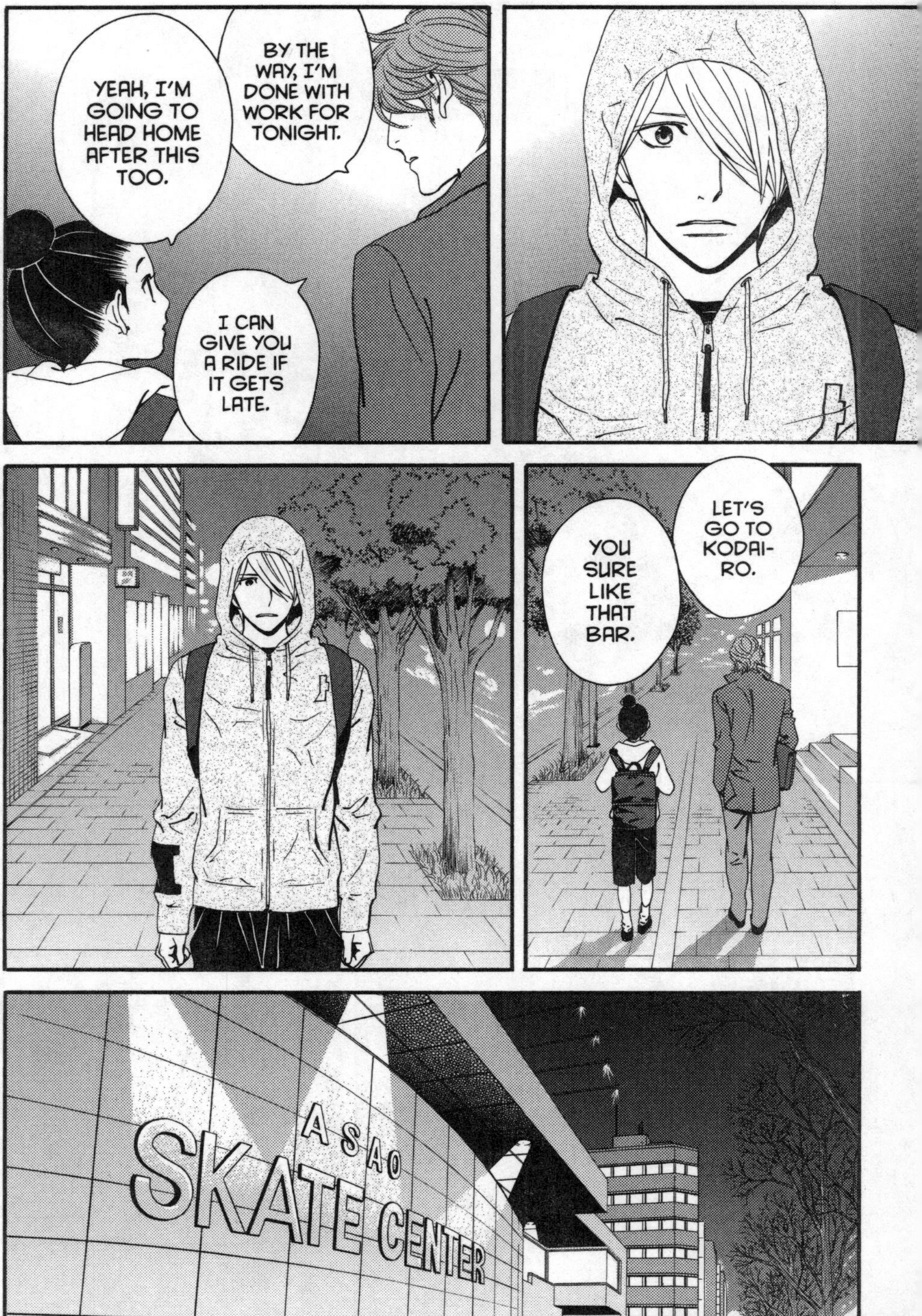
BY THE WAY, I'M DONE WITH WORK FOR TONIGHT.
YEAH, I'M GOING TO HEAD HOME AFTER THIS TOO.
I CAN GIVE YOU A RIDE IF IT GETS LATE.
LET'S GO TO KODAI-RO.
YOU SURE LIKE THAT BAR.
ASAO
SKATE CENTER

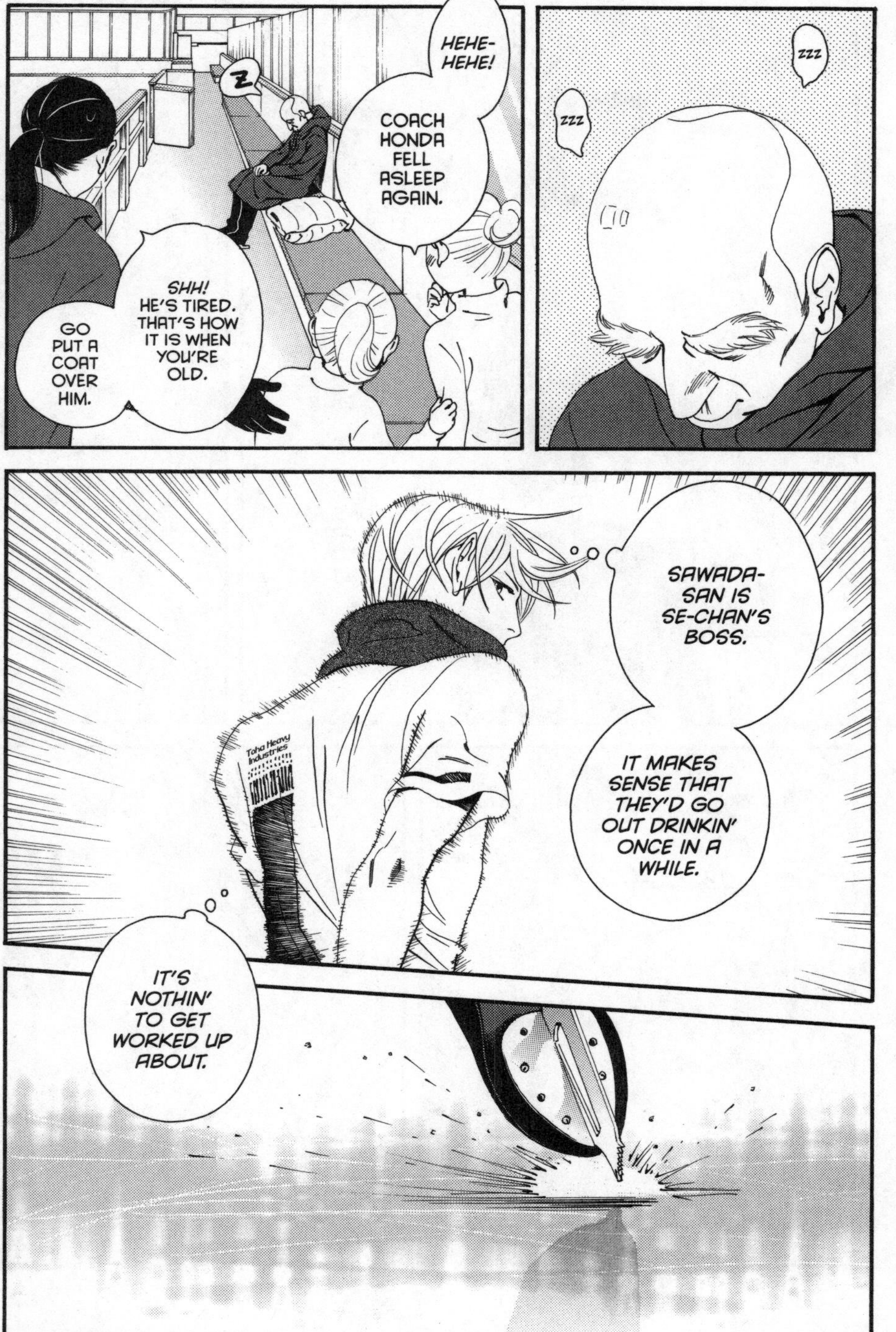
ZZZ
ZZZ
HEHE-HEHE!
COACH HONDA FELL ASLEEP AGAIN.
SHH! HE'S TIRED. THAT'S HOW IT IS WHEN YOU'RE OLD.
GO PUT A COAT OVER HIM.
SAWADA-SAN IS SE-CHAN'S BOSS.
IT MAKES SENSE THAT THEY'D GO OUT DRINKIN' ONCE IN A WHILE.
Toha Heavy Industries
IT'S NOTHIN' TO GET WORKED UP ABOUT.

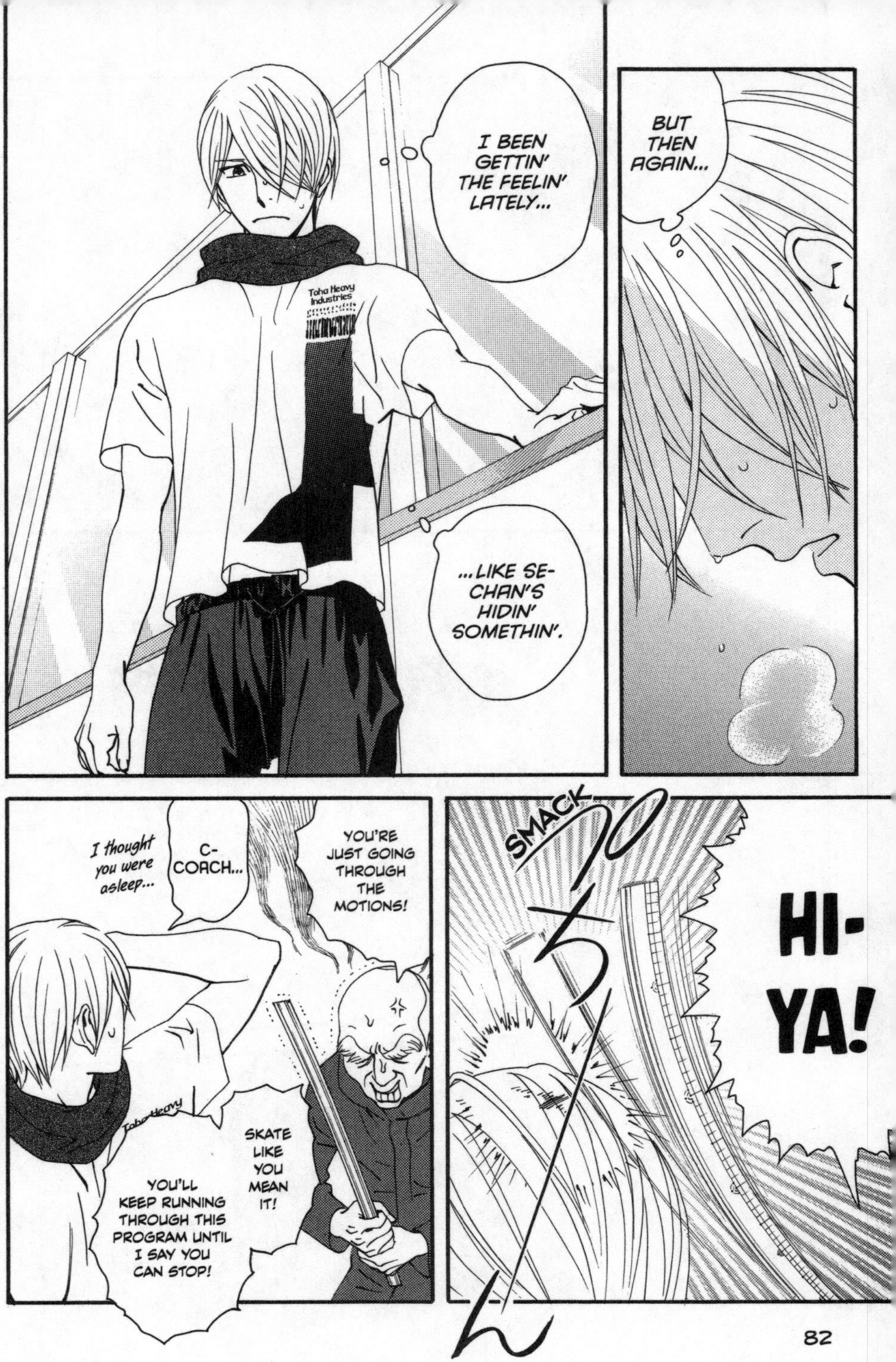
BUT THEN AGAIN...
I BEEN GETTIN' THE FEELIN' LATELY...
Toha Heavy Industries
...LIKE SE-CHAN'S HIDIN' SOMETHIN'.
SMACK
HI-YA!
YOU'RE JUST GOING THROUGH THE MOTIONS!
C-COACH...
I thought you were asleep...
Toha Heavy
SKATE LIKE YOU MEAN IT!
YOU'LL KEEP RUNNING THROUGH THIS PROGRAM UNTIL I SAY YOU CAN STOP!

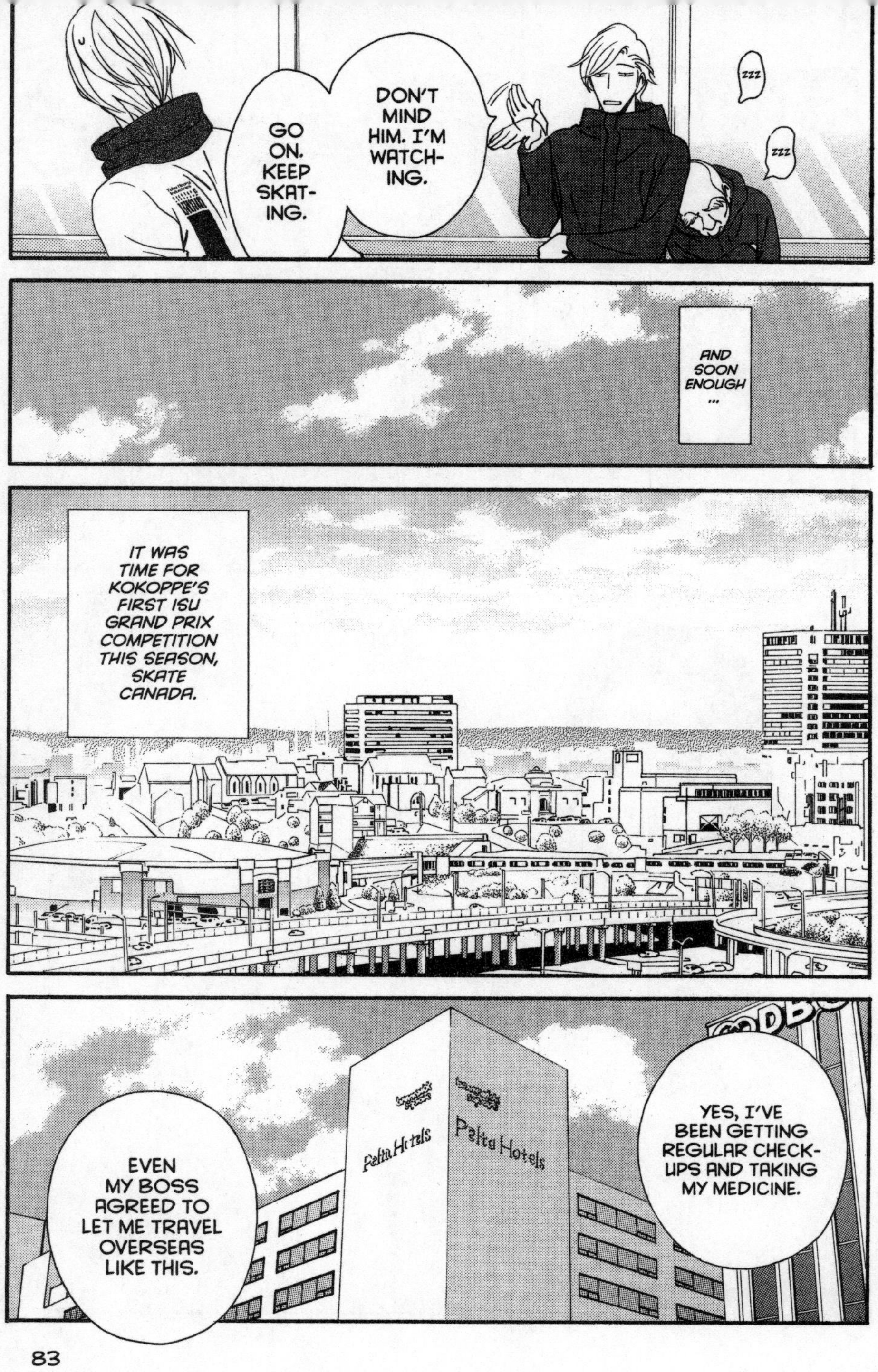
ZZZ
ZZZ
DON'T MIND HIM. I'M WATCH-ING.
GO ON. KEEP SKAT-ING.
AND SOON ENOUGH ...
IT WAS TIME FOR KOKOPPE'S FIRST ISU GRAND PRIX COMPETITION THIS SEASON, SKATE CANADA.
Pelta Hotels
Pelta Hotels
YES, I'VE BEEN GETTING REGULAR CHECK-UPS AND TAKING MY MEDICINE.
EVEN MY BOSS AGREED TO LET ME TRAVEL OVERSEAS LIKE THIS.

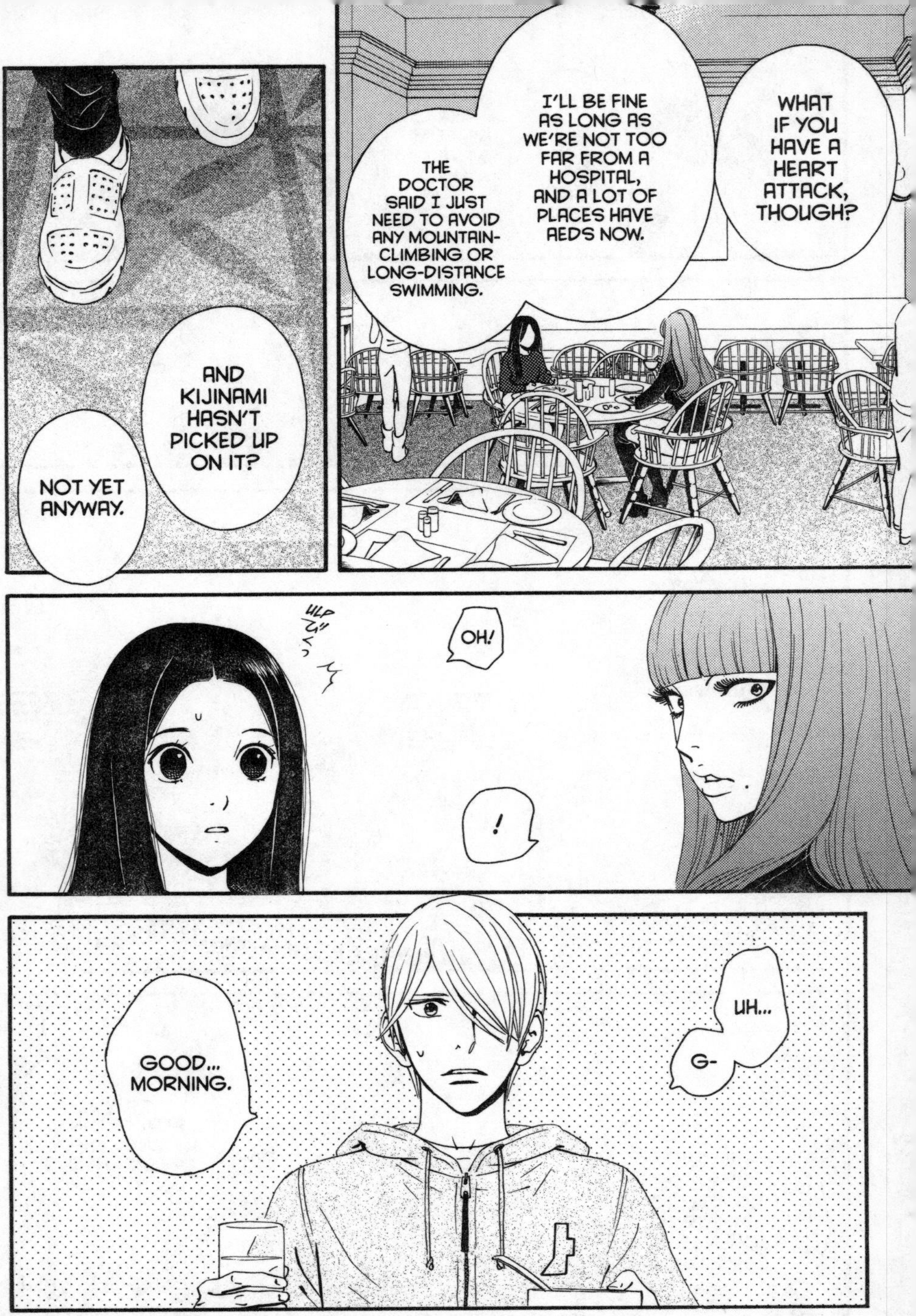
WHAT IF YOU HAVE A HEART ATTACK, THOUGH?
I'LL BE FINE AS LONG AS WE'RE NOT TOO FAR FROM A HOSPITAL, AND A LOT OF PLACES HAVE AEDS NOW.
THE DOCTOR SAID I JUST NEED TO AVOID ANY MOUNTAIN-CLIMBING OR LONG-DISTANCE SWIMMING.
AND KIJINAMI HASN'T PICKED UP ON IT?
NOT YET ANYWAY.
OH!
ULP
!
UH...
G-
GOOD... MORNING.

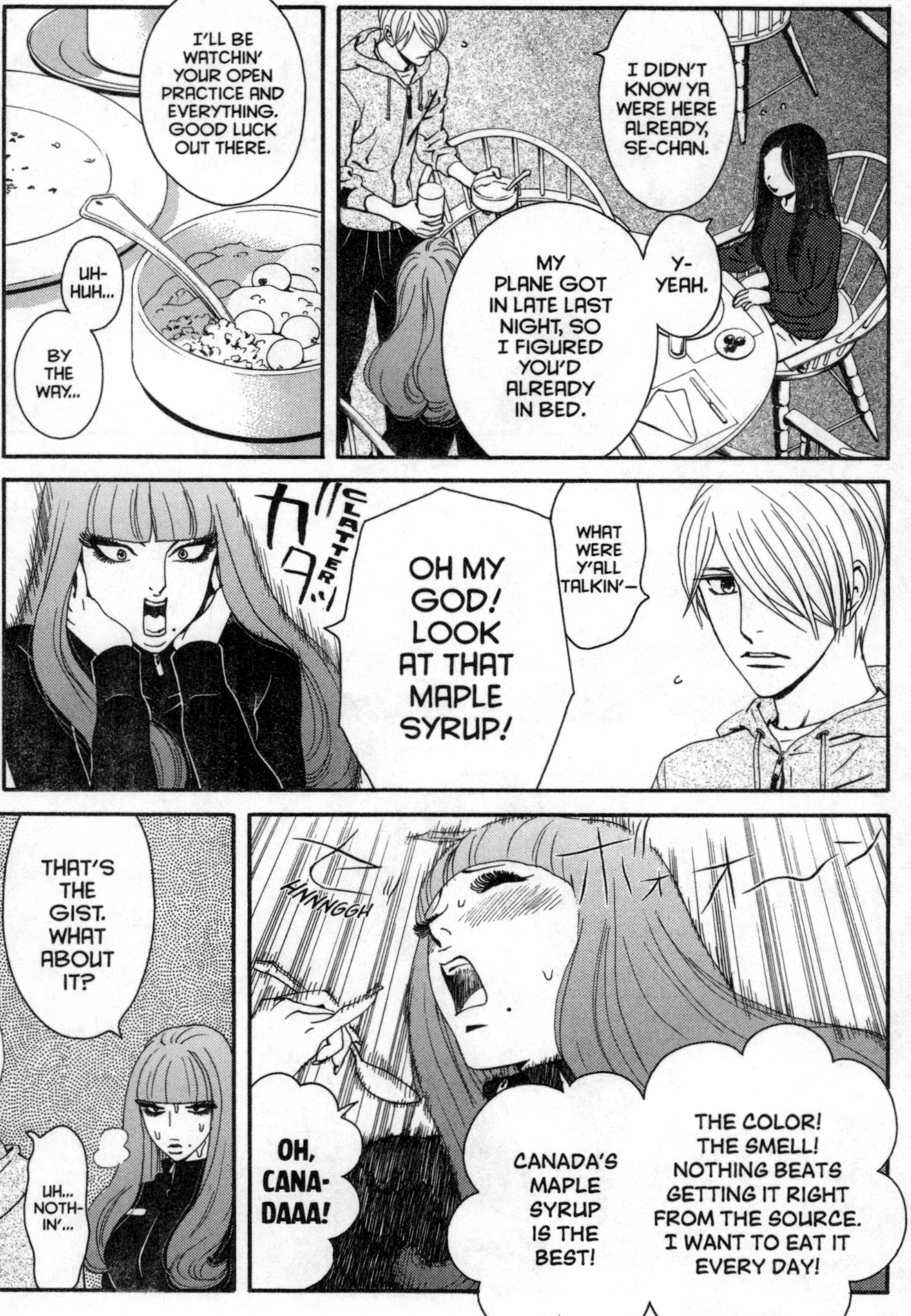
I DIDN'T KNOW YA WERE HERE ALREADY, SE-CHAN.
Y-YEAH.
MY PLANE GOT IN LATE LAST NIGHT, SO I FIGURED YOU'D ALREADY IN BED.
I'LL BE WATCHIN' YOUR OPEN PRACTICE AND EVERYTHING. GOOD LUCK OUT THERE.
UH-HUH...
BY THE WAY...
WHAT WERE Y'ALL TALKIN'—
CLATTER
OH MY GOD! LOOK AT THAT MAPLE SYRUP!
HNNNGGH
THE COLOR! THE SMELL! NOTHING BEATS GETTING IT RIGHT FROM THE SOURCE. I WANT TO EAT IT EVERY DAY!
CANADA'S MAPLE SYRUP IS THE BEST!
OH, CANA-DAAA!
THAT'S THE GIST. WHAT ABOUT IT?
UH... NOTH-IN'...

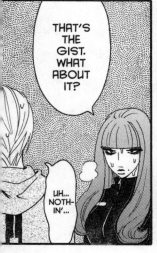

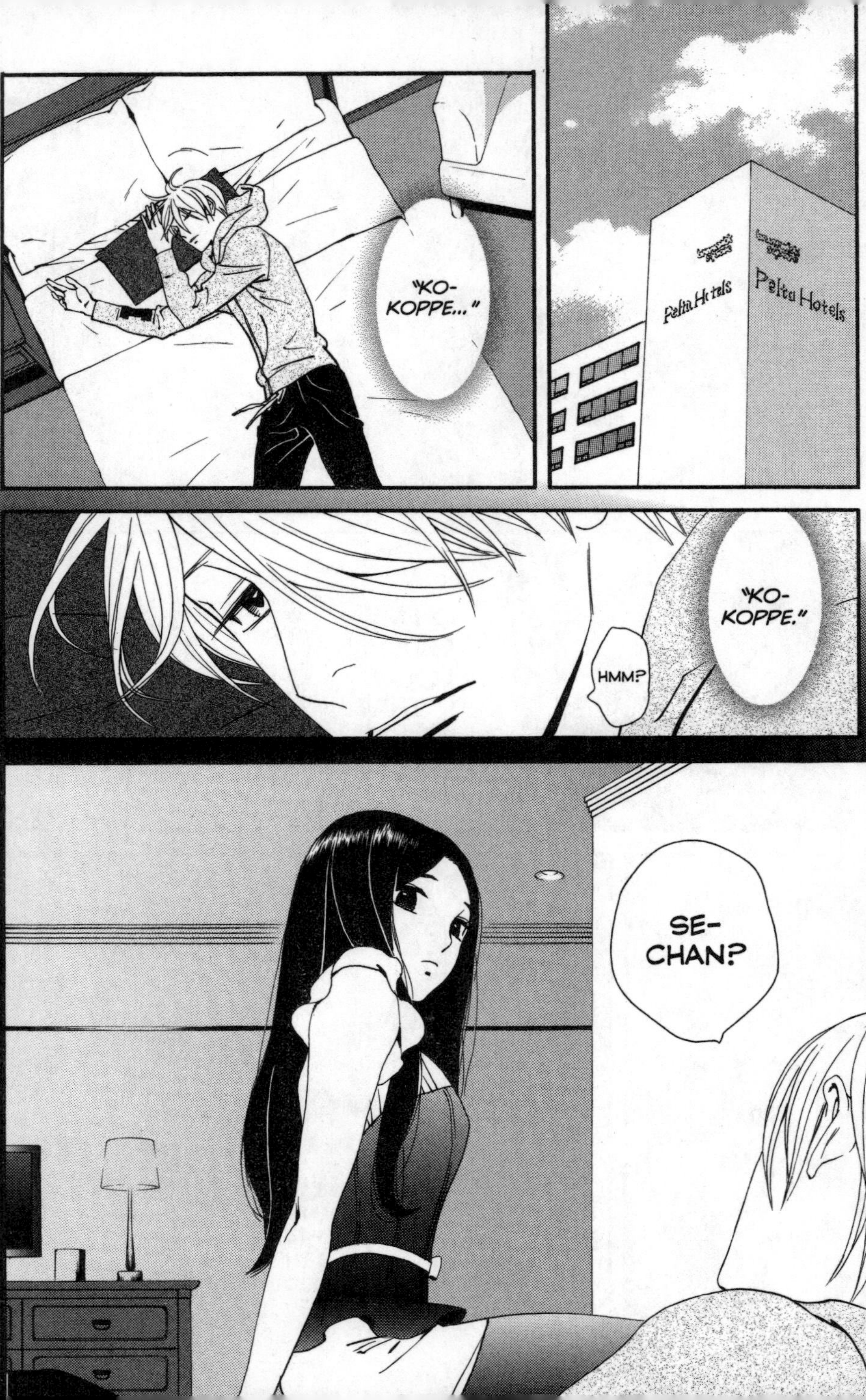
Pelta Hotels
Pelta Hotels
"KO-KOPPE..."
"KO-KOPPE."
HMM?
SE-CHAN?

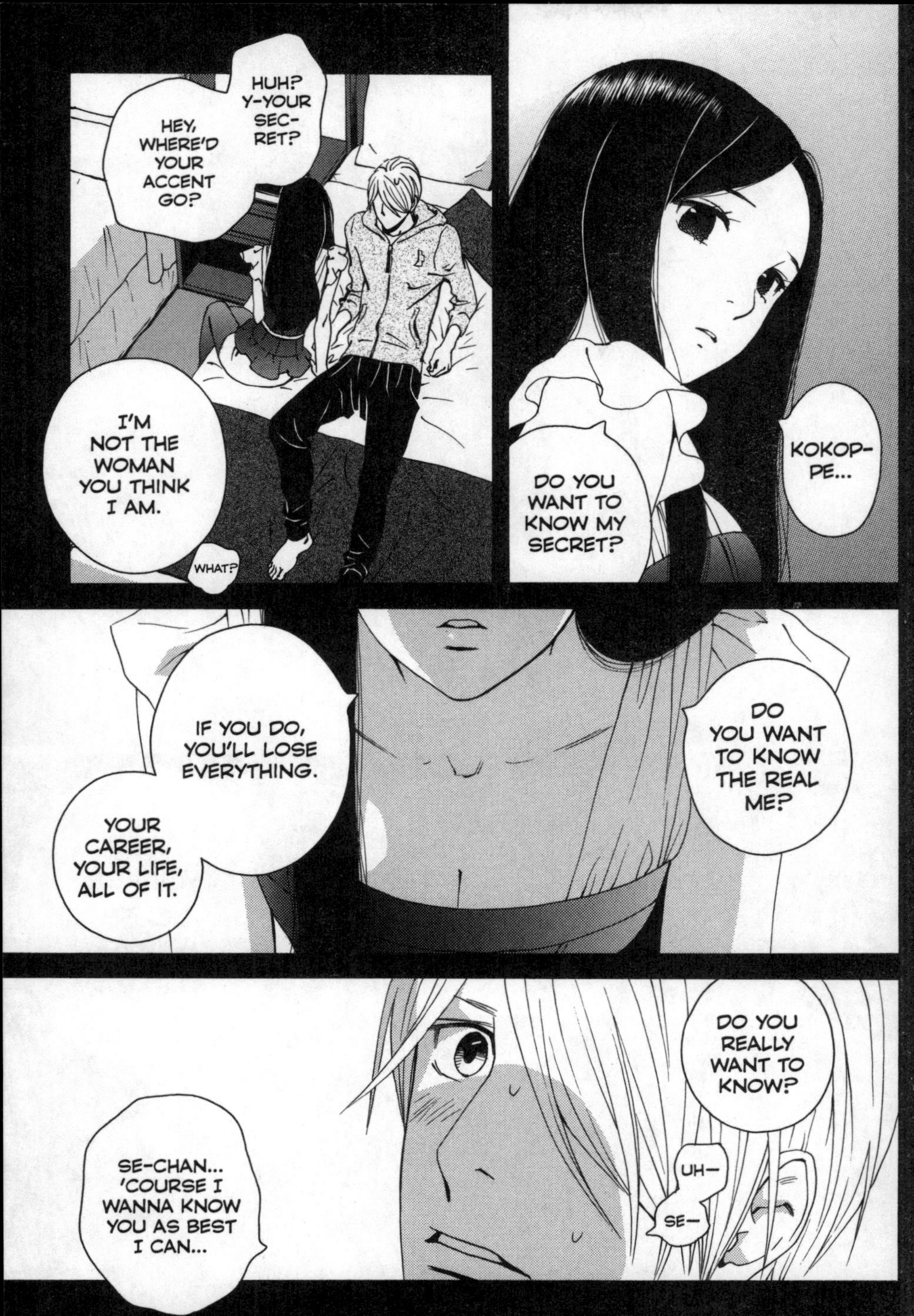
KOKOP-PE...
DO YOU WANT TO KNOW MY SECRET?
HUH? Y-YOUR SEC-RET?
HEY, WHERE'D YOUR ACCENT GO?
I'M NOT THE WOMAN YOU THINK I AM.
WHAT?
DO YOU WANT TO KNOW THE REAL ME?
IF YOU DO, YOU'LL LOSE EVERYTHING.
YOUR CAREER, YOUR LIFE, ALL OF IT.
DO YOU REALLY WANT TO KNOW?
UH—
SE—
SE-CHAN... 'COURSE I WANNA KNOW YOU AS BEST I CAN...

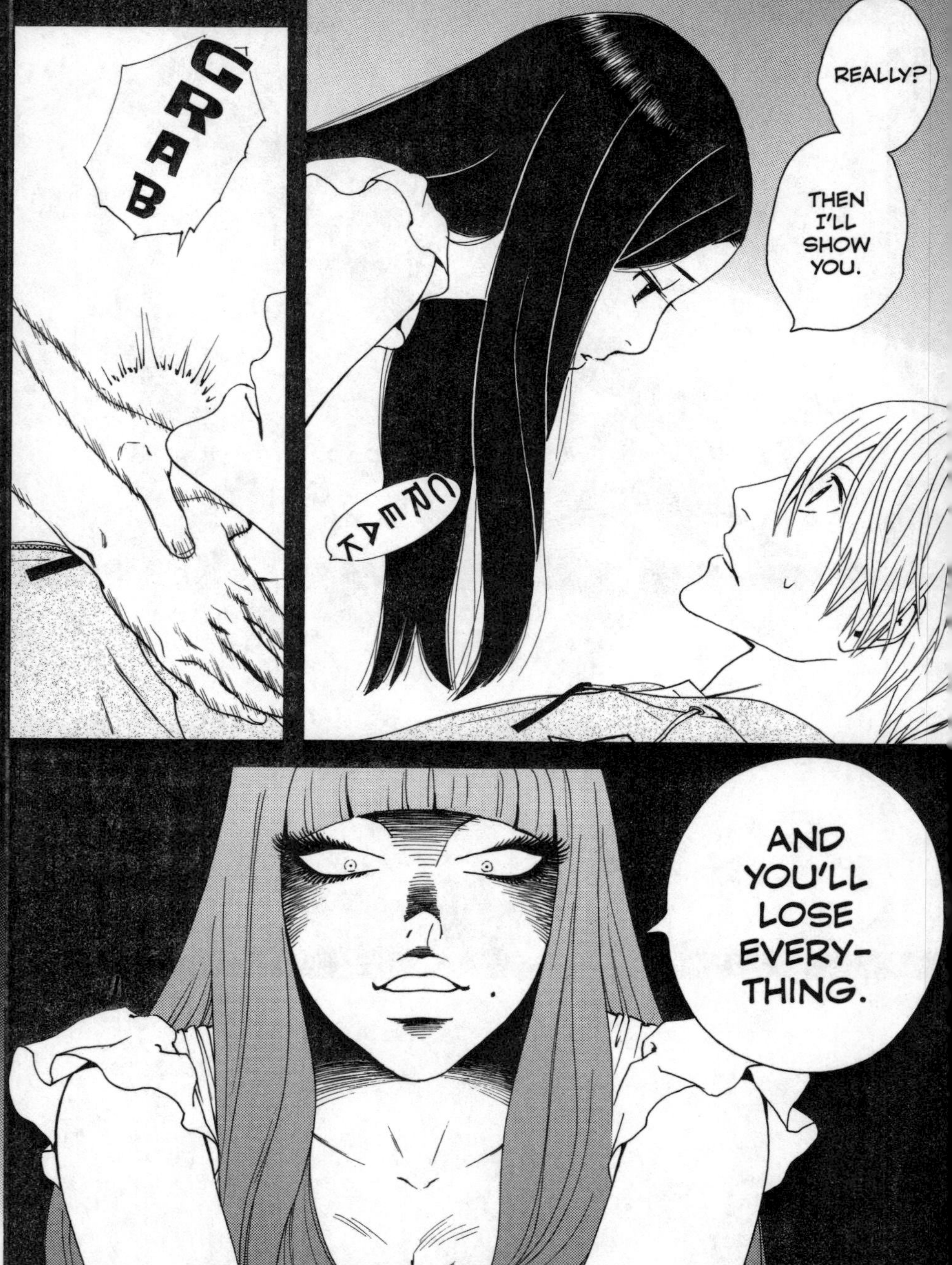
REALLY?
THEN I'LL SHOW YOU.
CREAK
GRAB
AND YOU'LL LOSE EVERY-THING.

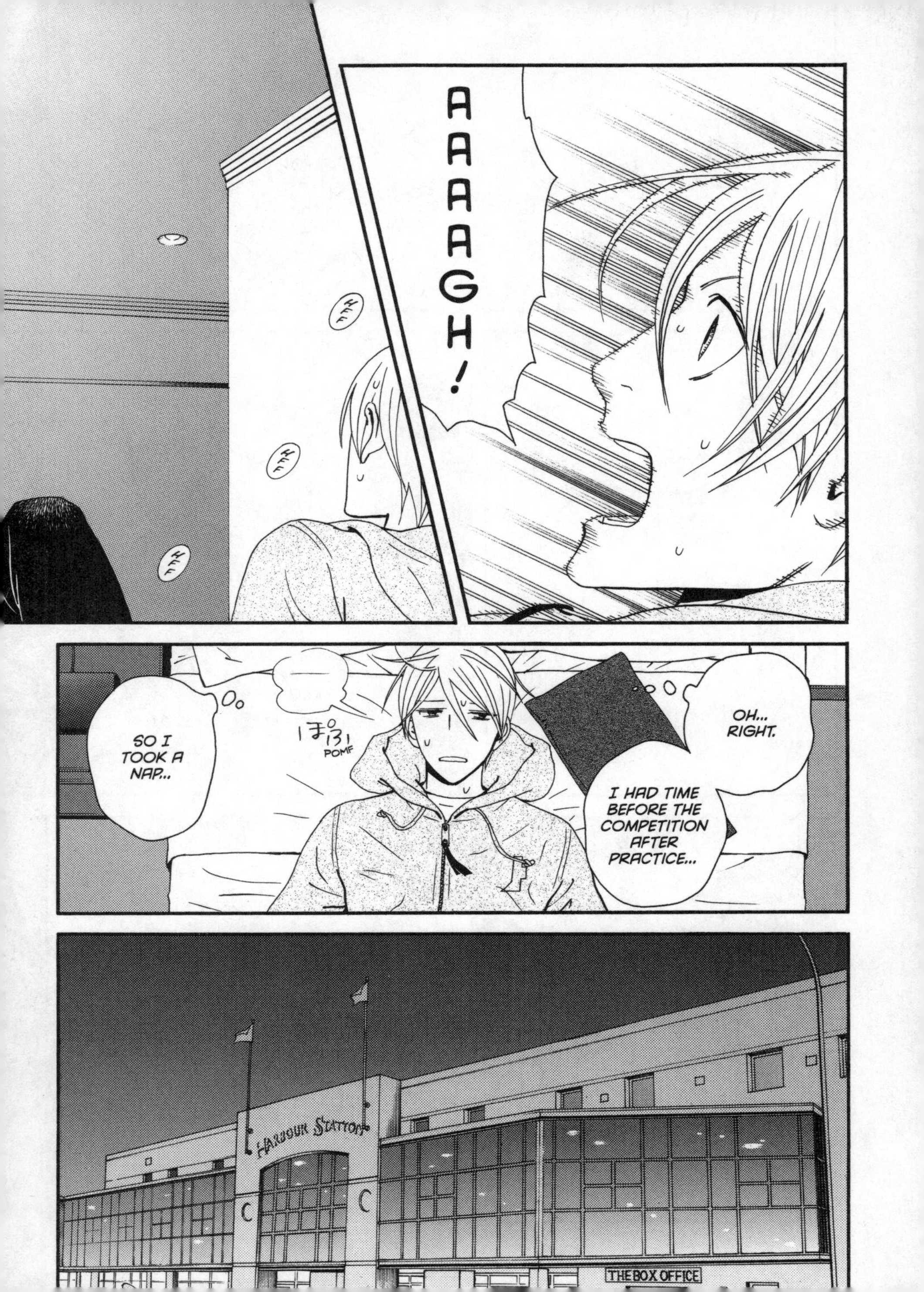
AAAAAGH!
HFF
HFF
HFF
OH... RIGHT.
I HAD TIME BEFORE THE COMPETITION AFTER PRACTICE...
ぽふ
POMF
SO I TOOK A NAP...
HARBOUR STATION
THE BOX OFFICE

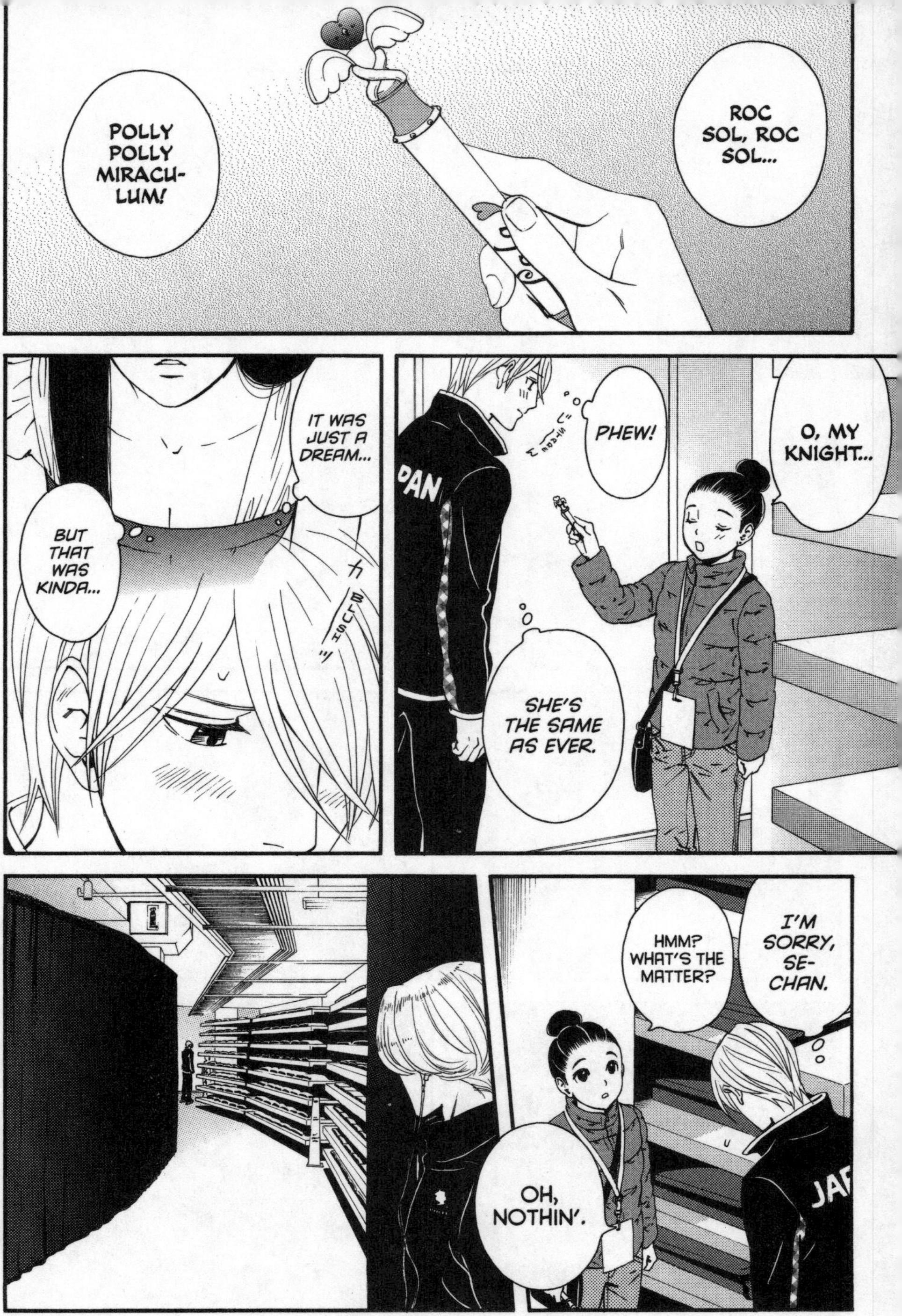
ROC SOL, ROC SOL...
POLLY POLLY MIRACULUM!
O, MY KNIGHT...
PHEW!
SHE'S THE SAME AS EVER.
IT WAS JUST A DREAM...
BUT THAT WAS KINDA...
BLUSH
I'M SORRY, SE-CHAN.
HMM? WHAT'S THE MATTER?
OH, NOTHIN'.

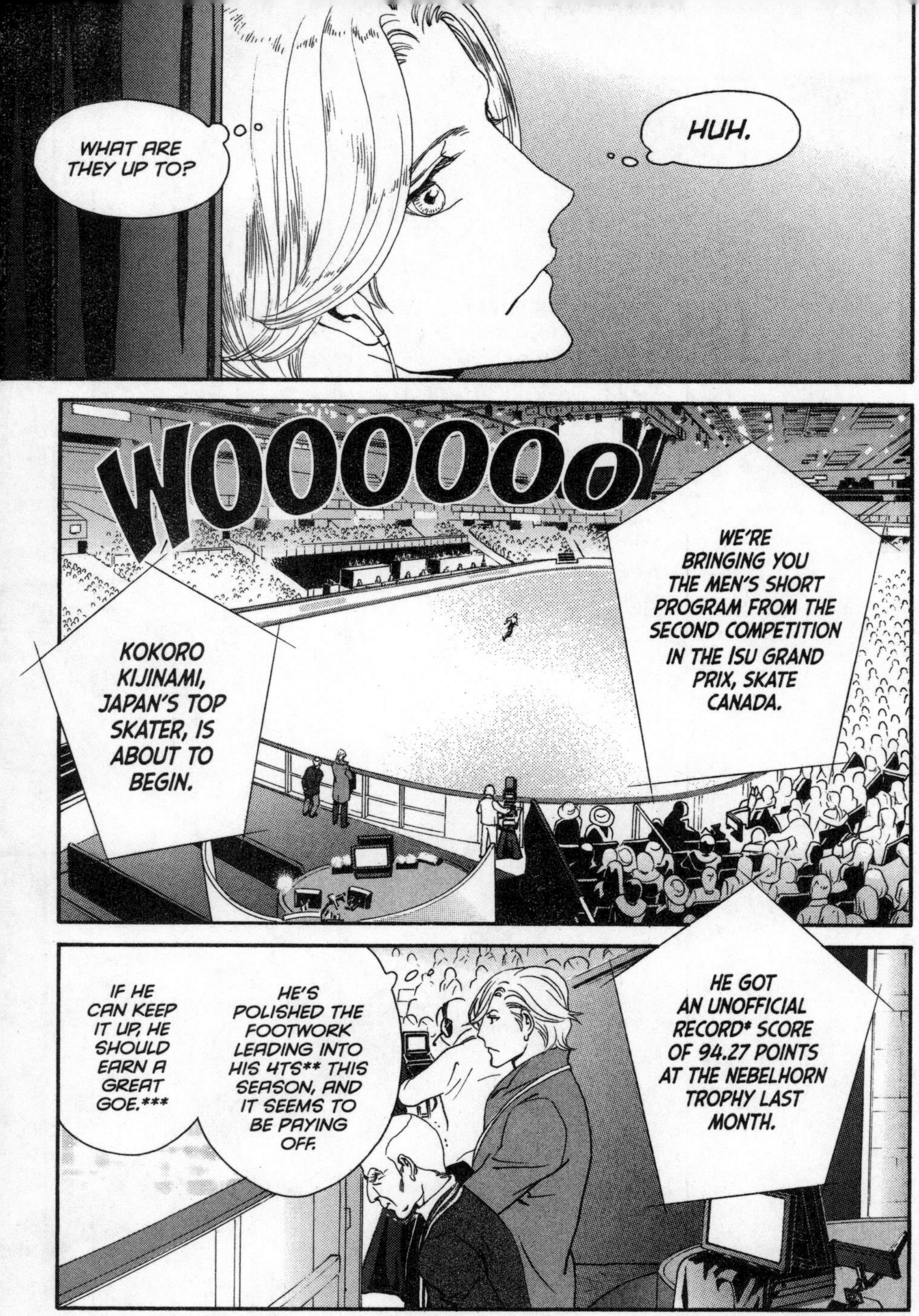
HUH.
WHAT ARE THEY UP TO?
WOOOOOO
WE'RE BRINGING YOU THE MEN'S SHORT PROGRAM FROM THE SECOND COMPETITION IN THE ISU GRAND PRIX, SKATE CANADA.
KOKORO KIJINAMI, JAPAN'S TOP SKATER, IS ABOUT TO BEGIN.
HE GOT AN UNOFFICIAL RECORD* SCORE OF 94.27 POINTS AT THE NEBELHORN TROPHY LAST MONTH.
HE'S POLISHED THE FOOTWORK LEADING INTO HIS 4TS** THIS SEASON, AND IT SEEMS TO BE PAYING OFF.
IF HE CAN KEEP IT UP, HE SHOULD EARN A GREAT GOE.***

*BECAUSE IT WAS NOT AN ISU COMPETITION. **4T: QUAD TOE LOOP ***GOE: GRADE OF EXECUTION

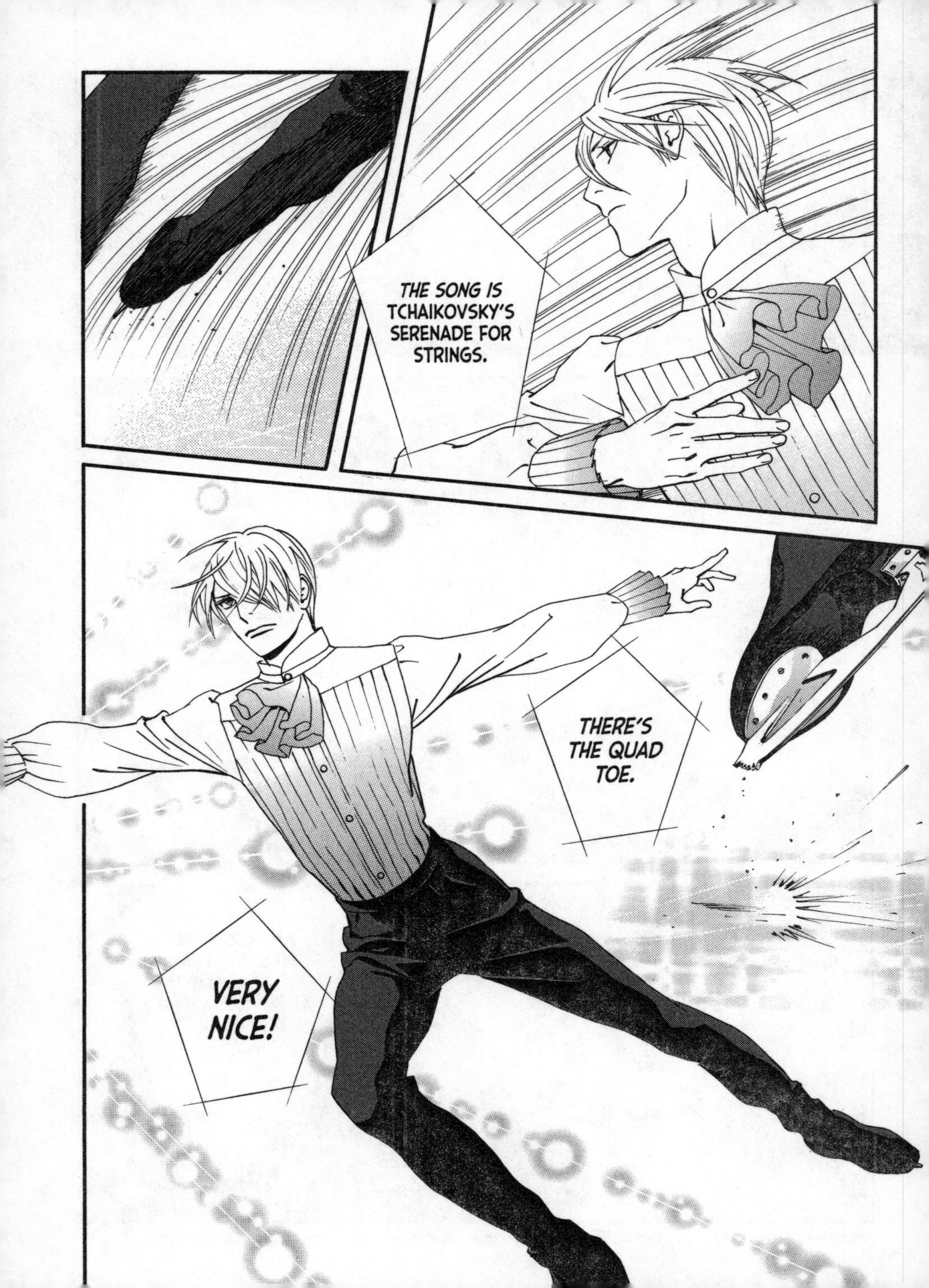
THE SONG IS TCHAIKOVSKY'S SERENADE FOR STRINGS.
THERE'S THE QUAD TOE.
VERY NICE!

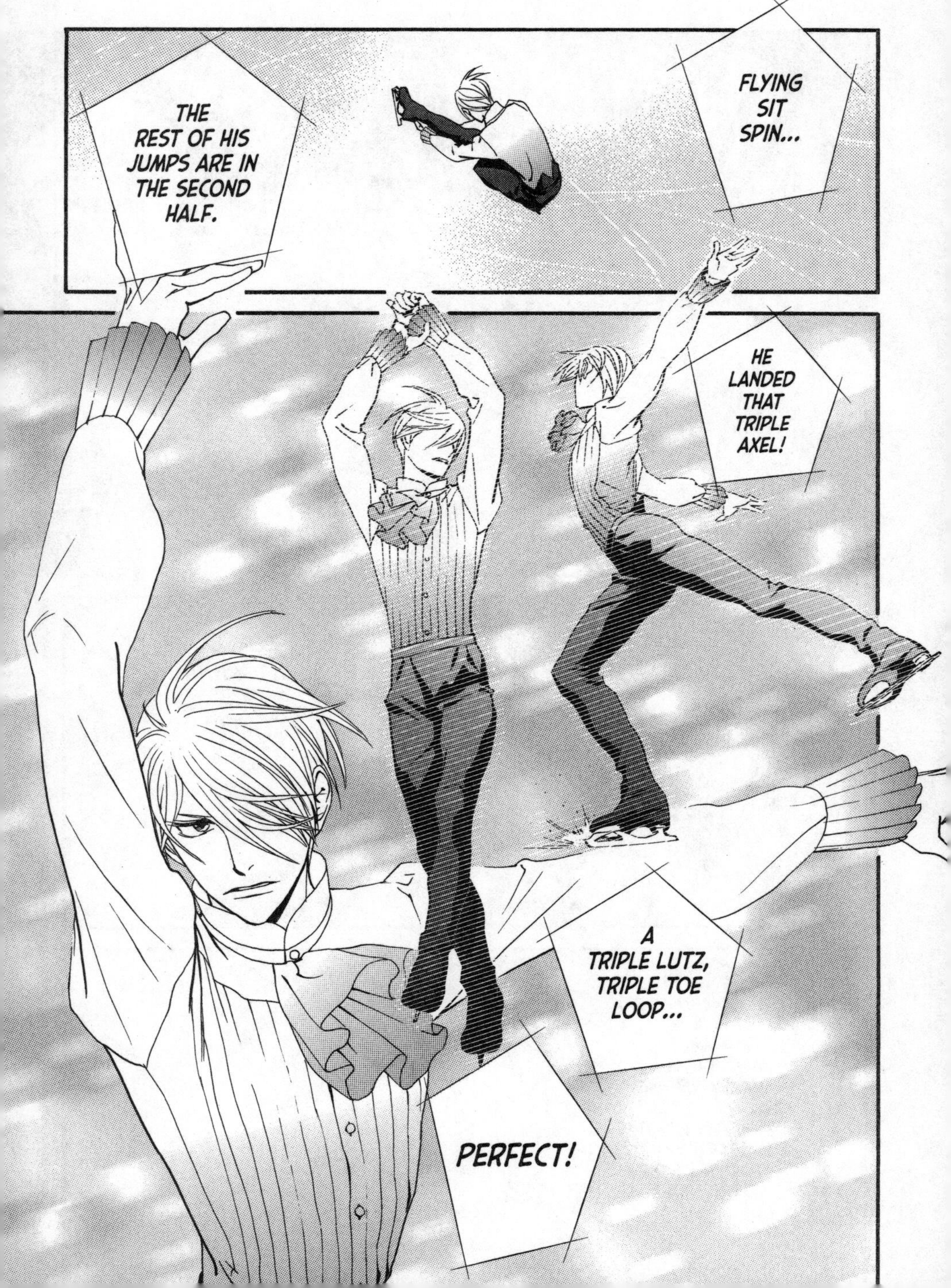
FLYING SIT SPIN...
THE REST OF HIS JUMPS ARE IN THE SECOND HALF.
HE LANDED THAT TRIPLE AXEL!
A TRIPLE LUTZ, TRIPLE TOE LOOP...
PERFECT!

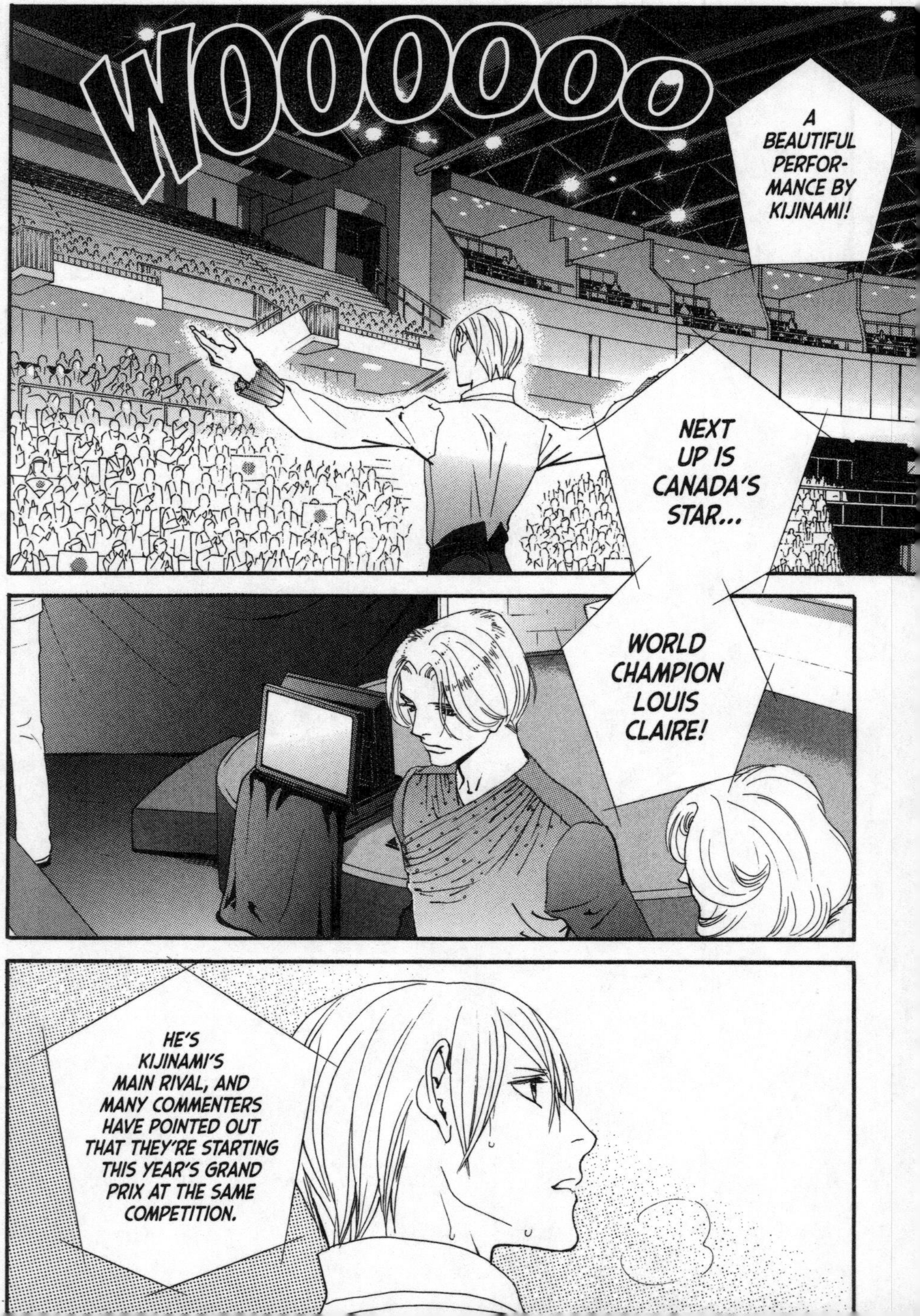
WOOOOOO
A BEAUTIFUL PERFORMANCE BY KIJINAMI!
NEXT UP IS CANADA'S STAR...
WORLD CHAMPION LOUIS CLAIRE!
HE'S KIJINAMI'S MAIN RIVAL, AND MANY COMMENTERS HAVE POINTED OUT THAT THEY'RE STARTING THIS YEAR'S GRAND PRIX AT THE SAME COMPETITION.

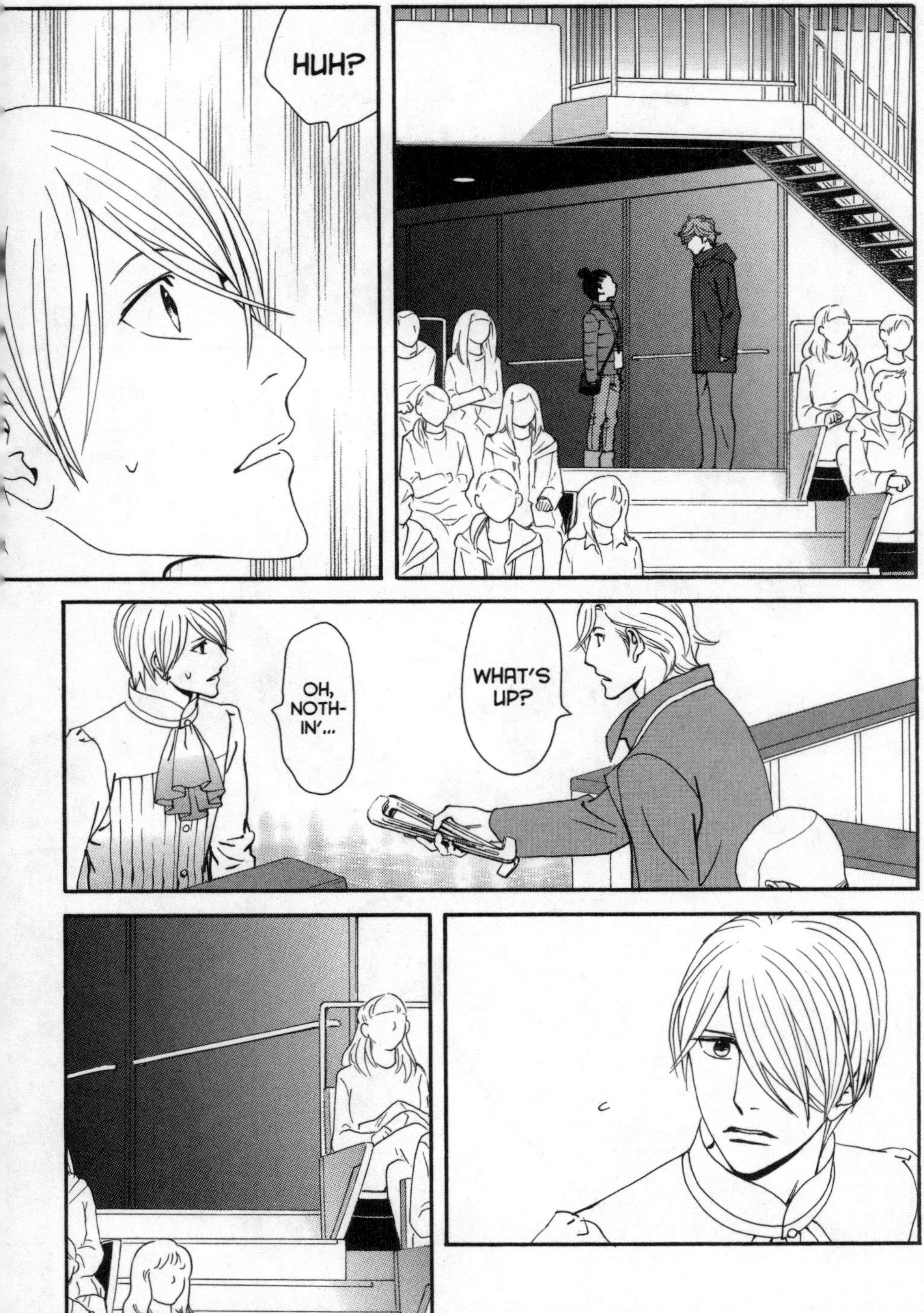
HUH?
WHAT'S UP?
OH, NOTH-IN'...

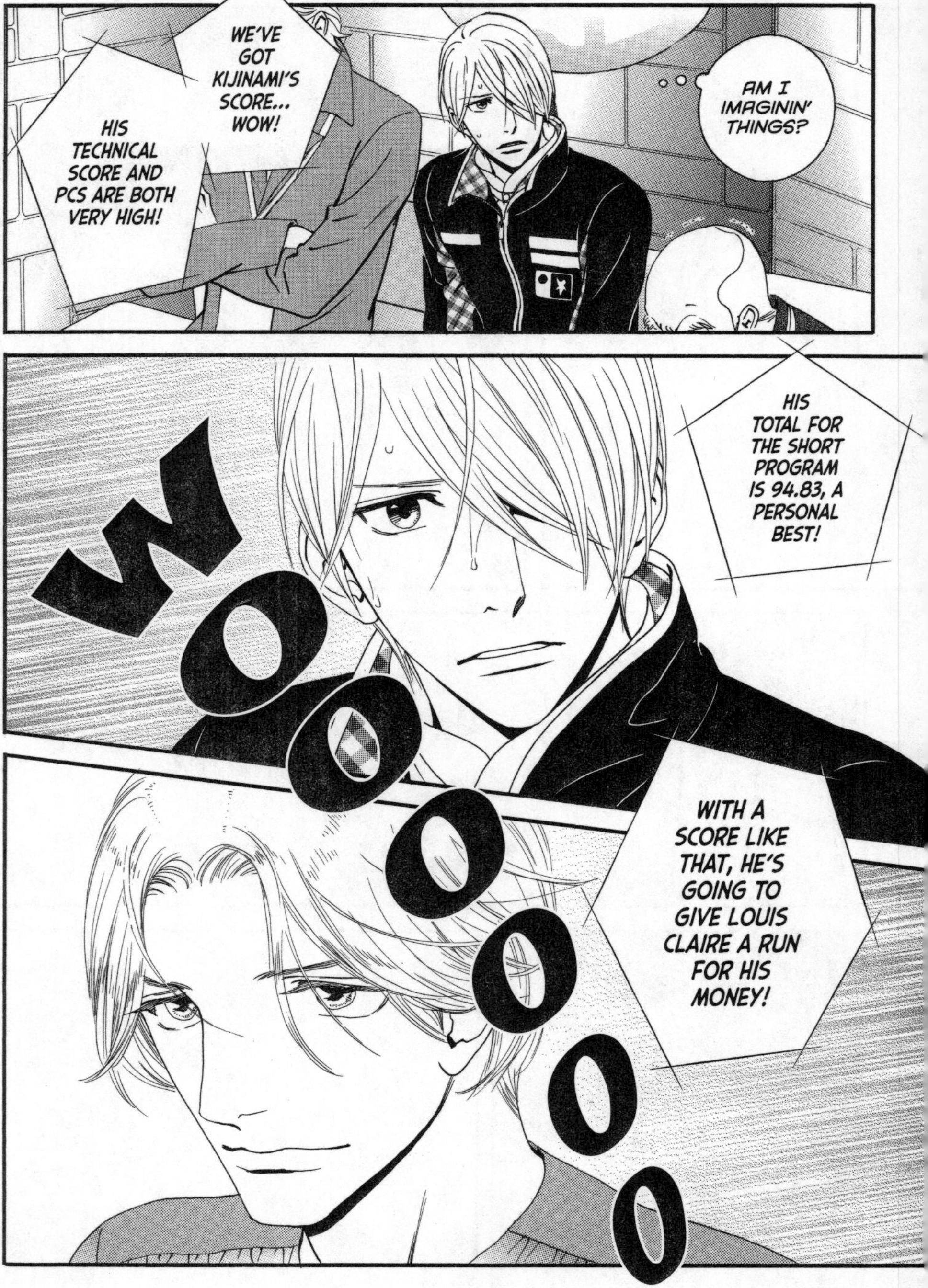
AM I IMAGININ' THINGS?
WE'VE GOT KIJINAMI'S SCORE... WOW!
HIS TECHNICAL SCORE AND PCS ARE BOTH VERY HIGH!
HIS TOTAL FOR THE SHORT PROGRAM IS 94.83, A PERSONAL BEST!
WOOOOOO
WITH A SCORE LIKE THAT, HE'S GOING TO GIVE LOUIS CLAIRE A RUN FOR HIS MONEY!

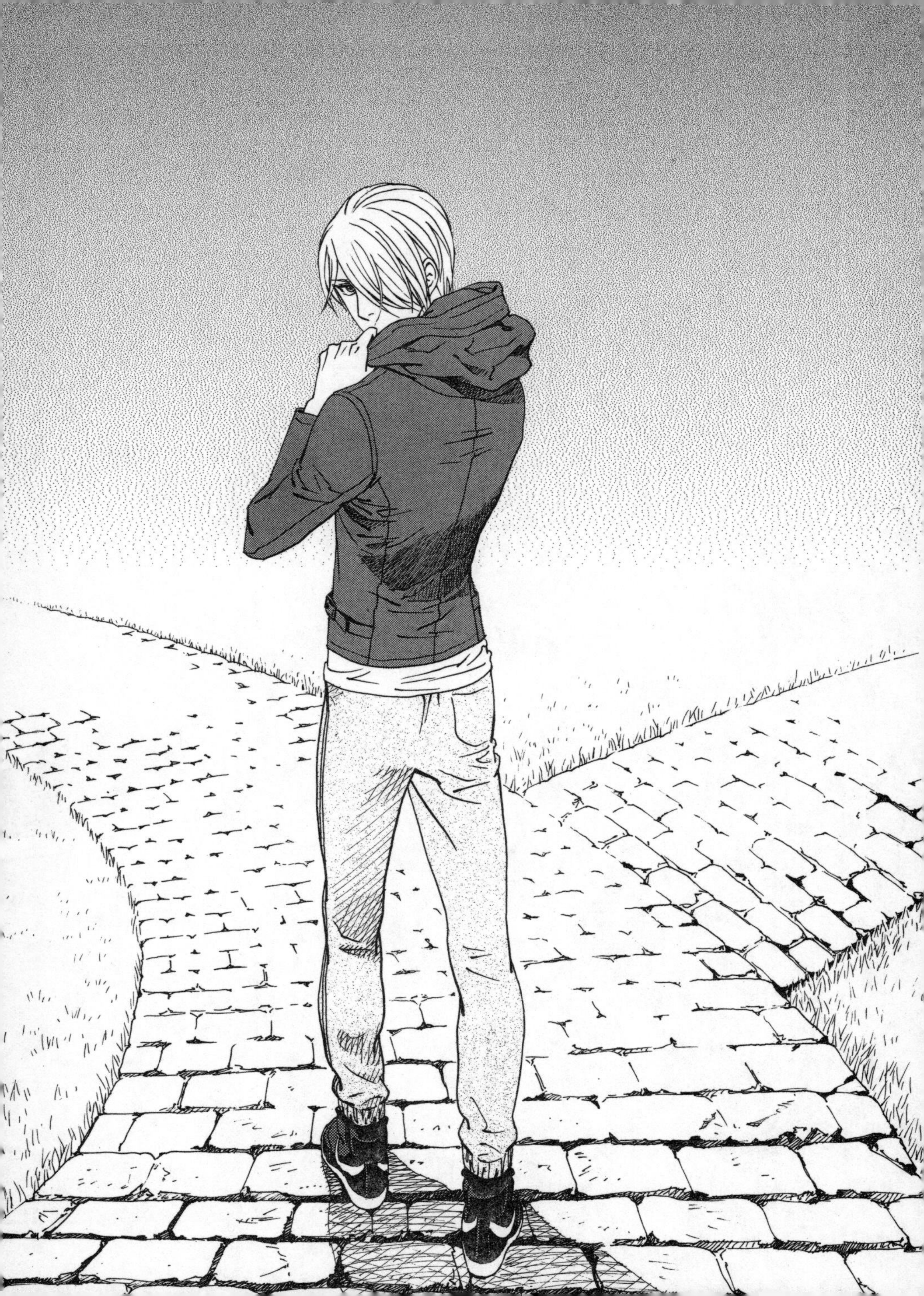

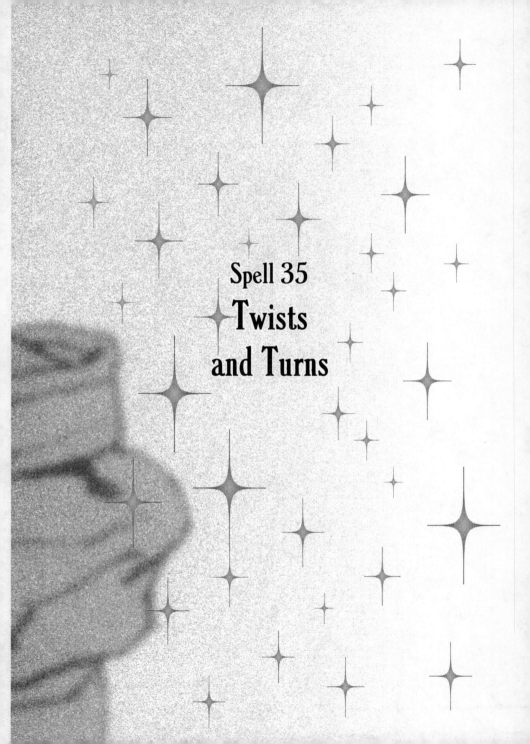

Spell 35
Twists
and Turns

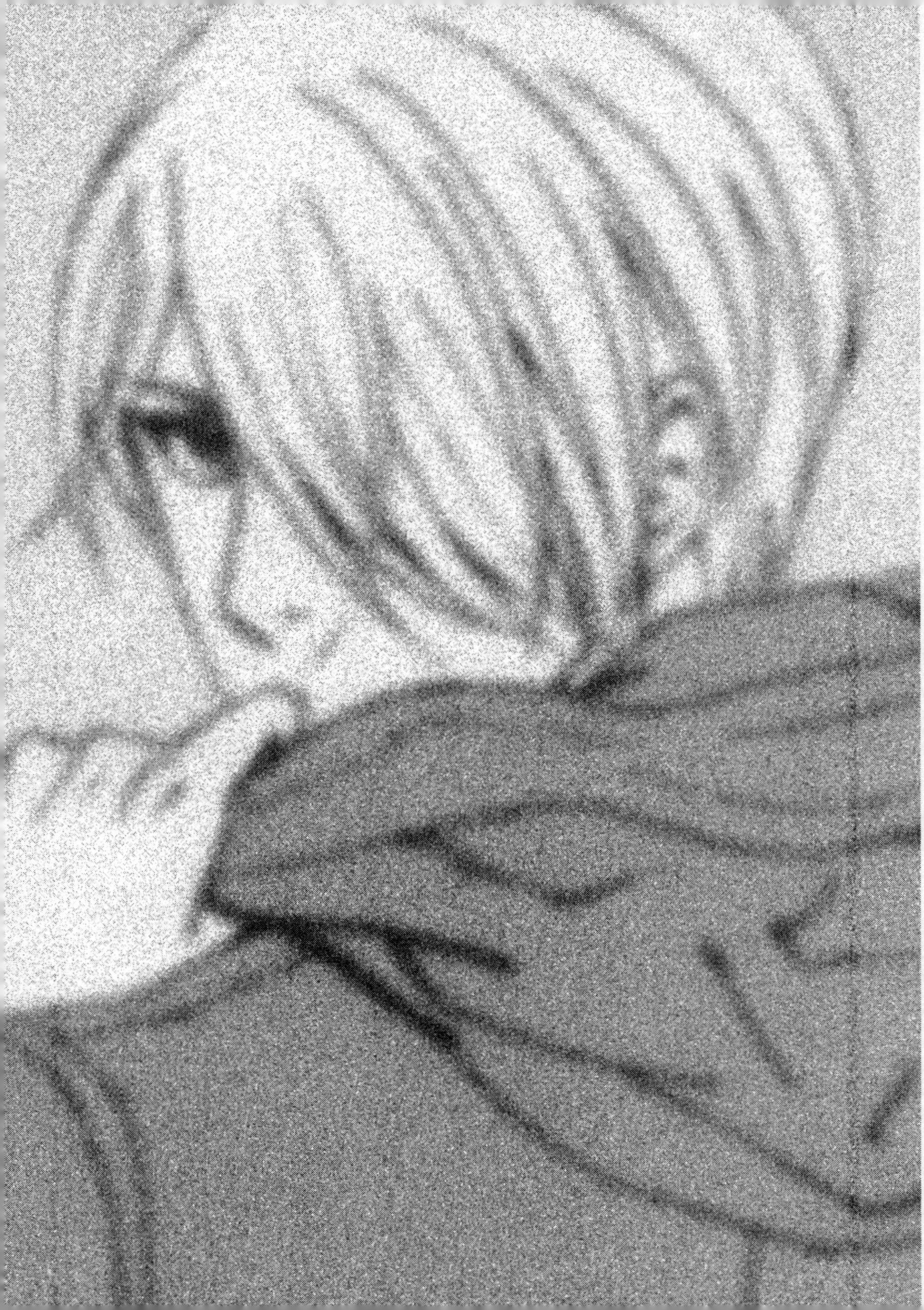

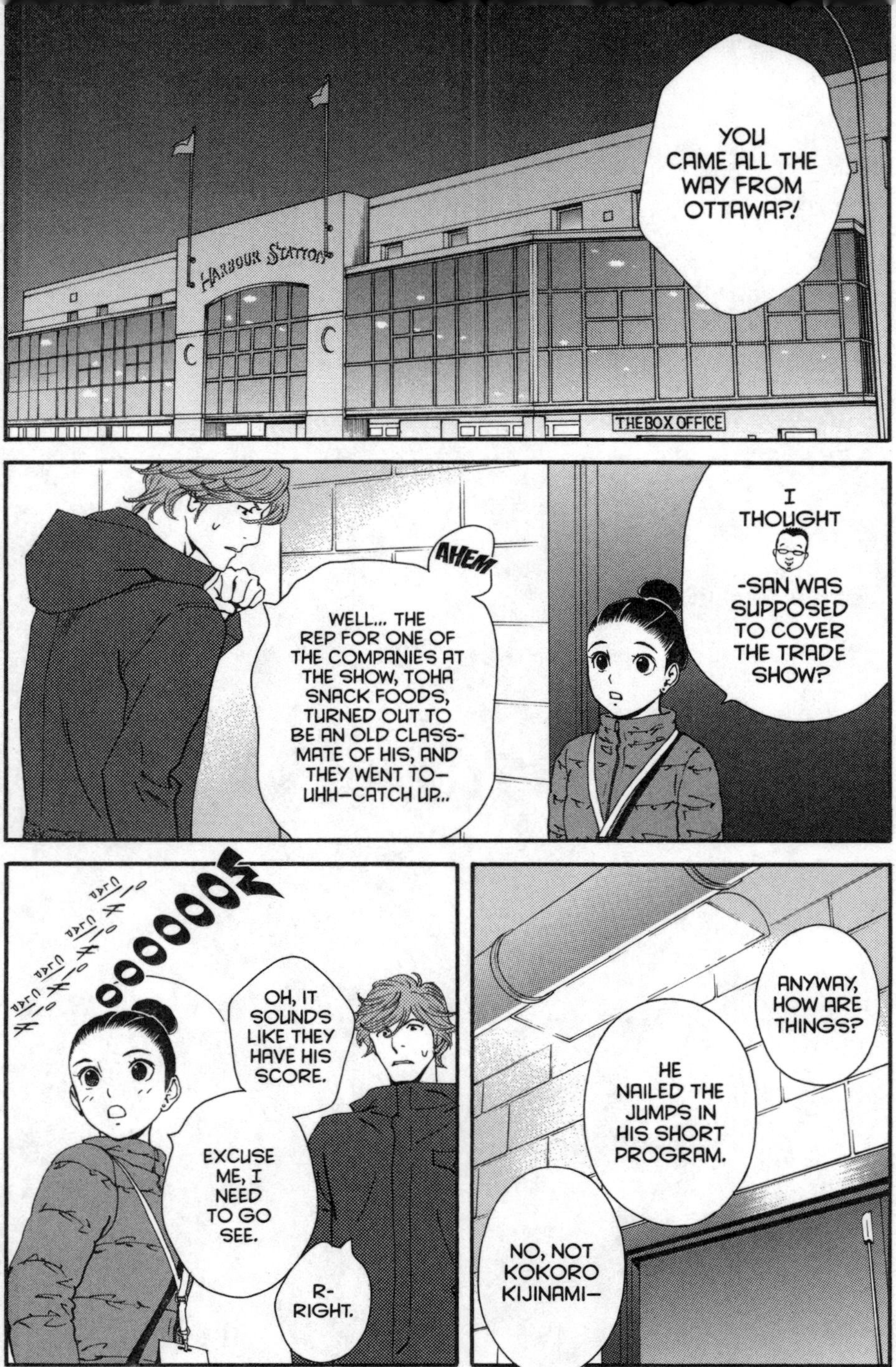
HARBOUR STATION
THE BOX OFFICE
YOU CAME ALL THE WAY FROM OTTAWA?!
I THOUGHT -SAN WAS SUPPOSED TO COVER THE TRADE SHOW?
AHEM
WELL... THE REP FOR ONE OF THE COMPANIES AT THE SHOW, TOHA SNACK FOODS, TURNED OUT TO BE AN OLD CLASS-MATE OF HIS, AND THEY WENT TO—UHH—CATCH UP...
ANYWAY, HOW ARE THINGS?
HE NAILED THE JUMPS IN HIS SHORT PROGRAM.
NO, NOT KOKORO KIJINAMI—
O-OOOOOO
OH, IT SOUNDS LIKE THEY HAVE HIS SCORE.
EXCUSE ME, I NEED TO GO SEE.
R-RIGHT.

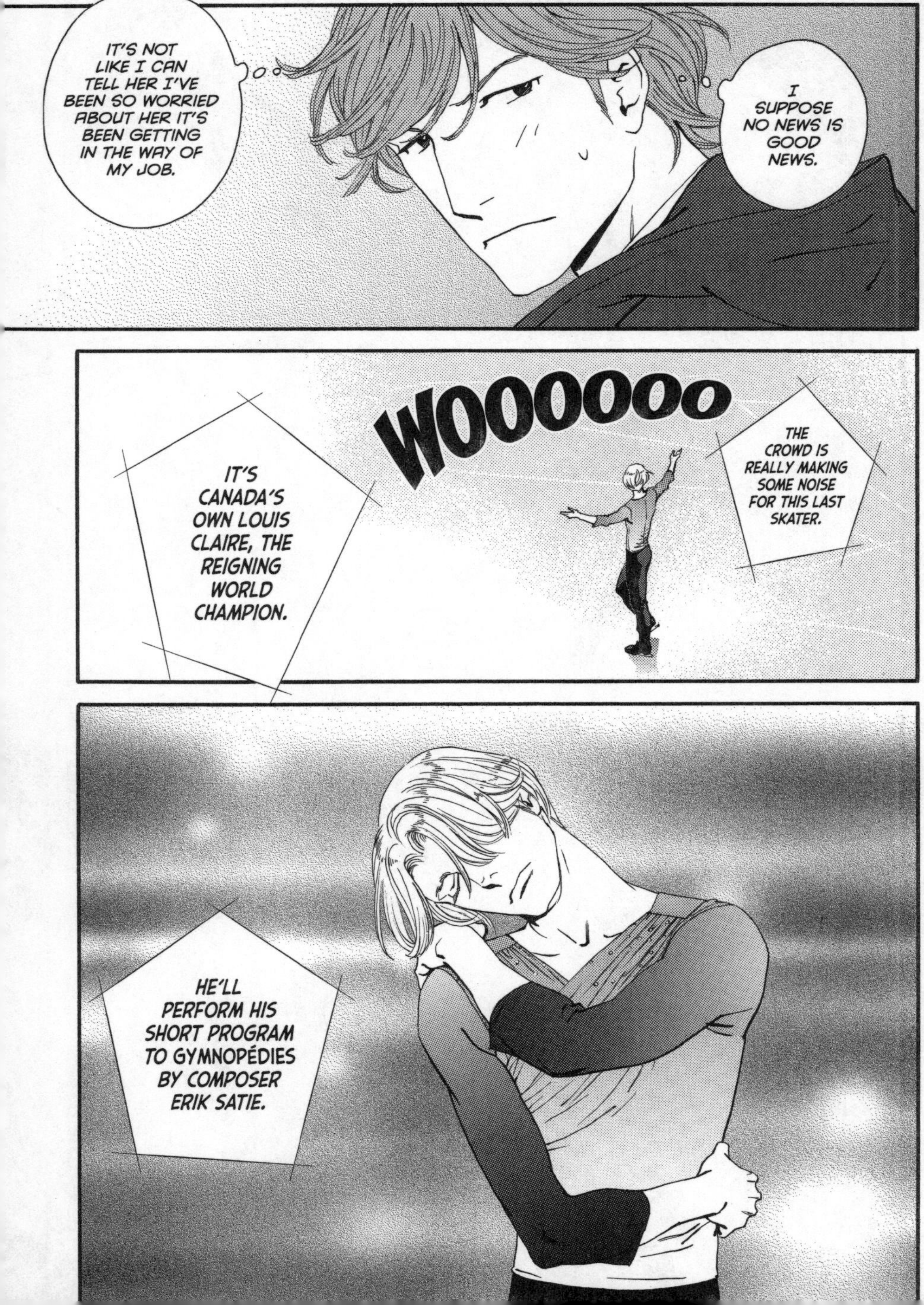
I SUPPOSE NO NEWS IS GOOD NEWS.
IT'S NOT LIKE I CAN TELL HER I'VE BEEN SO WORRIED ABOUT HER IT'S BEEN GETTING IN THE WAY OF MY JOB.
THE CROWD IS REALLY MAKING SOME NOISE FOR THIS LAST SKATER.
WOOOOOO
IT'S CANADA'S OWN LOUIS CLAIRE, THE REIGNING WORLD CHAMPION.
HE'LL PERFORM HIS SHORT PROGRAM TO GYMNOPÉDIES BY COMPOSER ERIK SATIE.

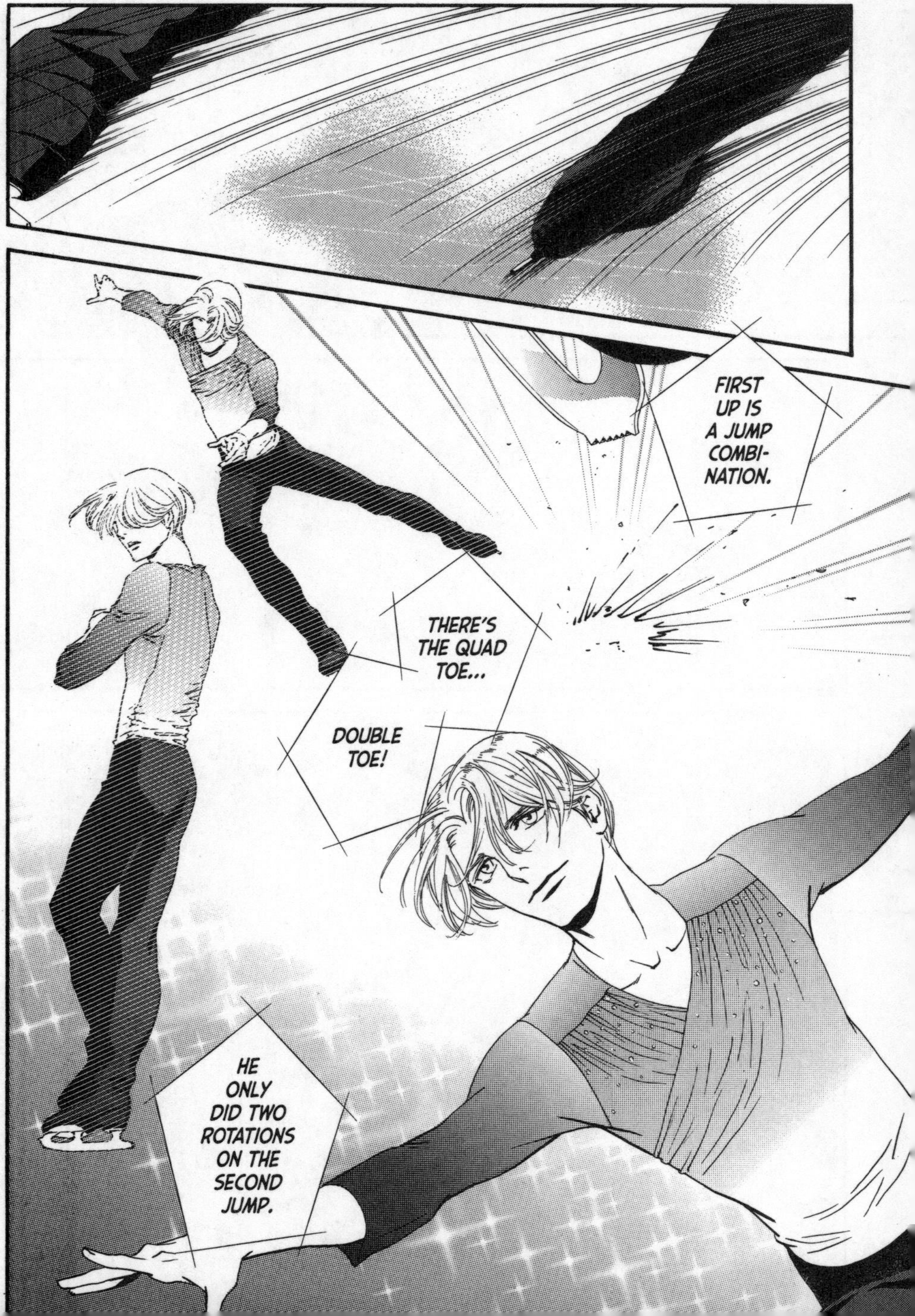
FIRST UP IS A JUMP COMBI-NATION.
THERE'S THE QUAD TOE...
DOUBLE TOE!
HE ONLY DID TWO ROTATIONS ON THE SECOND JUMP.

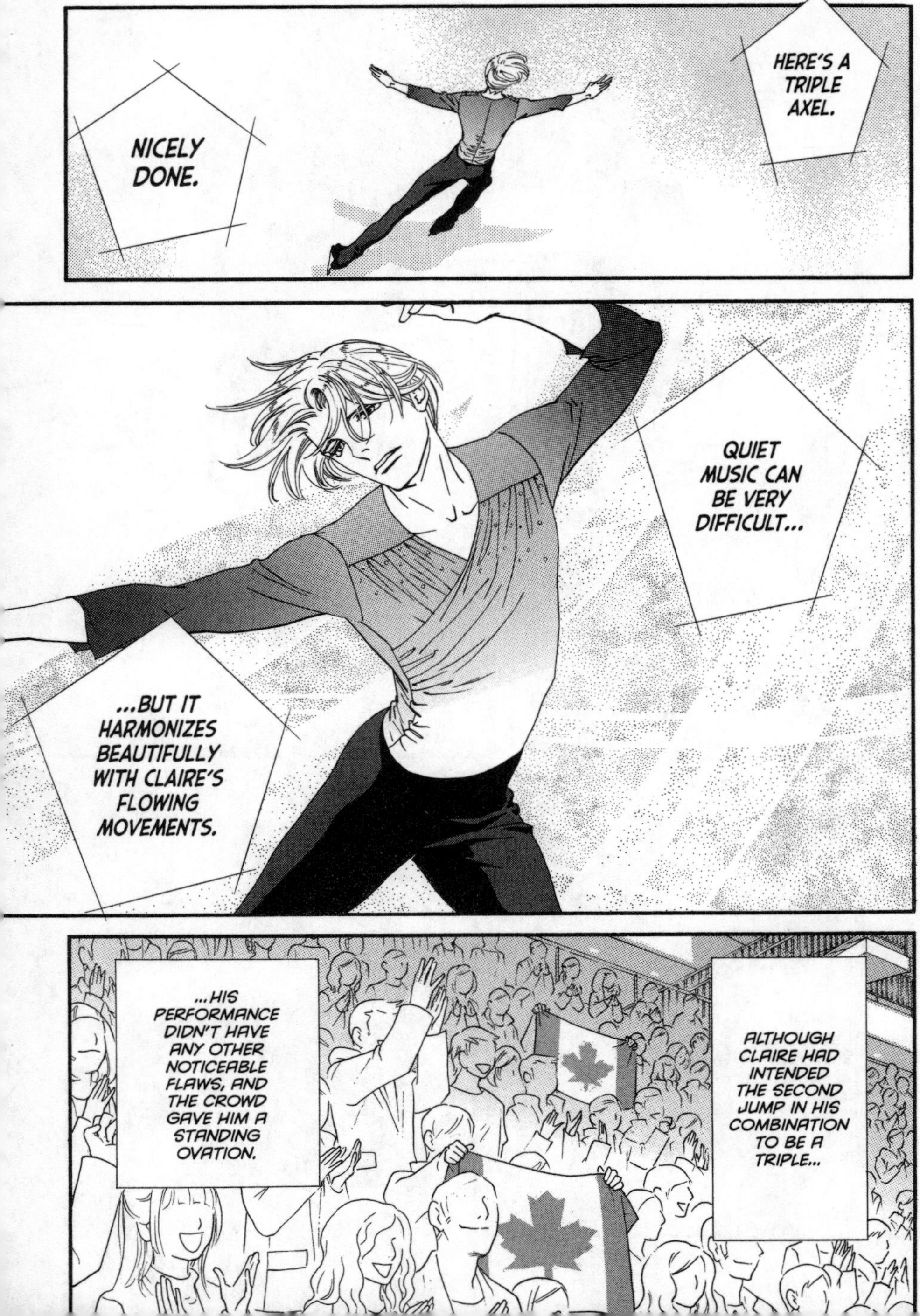
HERE'S A TRIPLE AXEL.
NICELY DONE.
QUIET MUSIC CAN BE VERY DIFFICULT...
...BUT IT HARMONIZES BEAUTIFULLY WITH CLAIRE'S FLOWING MOVEMENTS.
ALTHOUGH CLAIRE HAD INTENDED THE SECOND JUMP IN HIS COMBINATION TO BE A TRIPLE...
...HIS PERFORMANCE DIDN'T HAVE ANY OTHER NOTICEABLE FLAWS, AND THE CROWD GAVE HIM A STANDING OVATION.

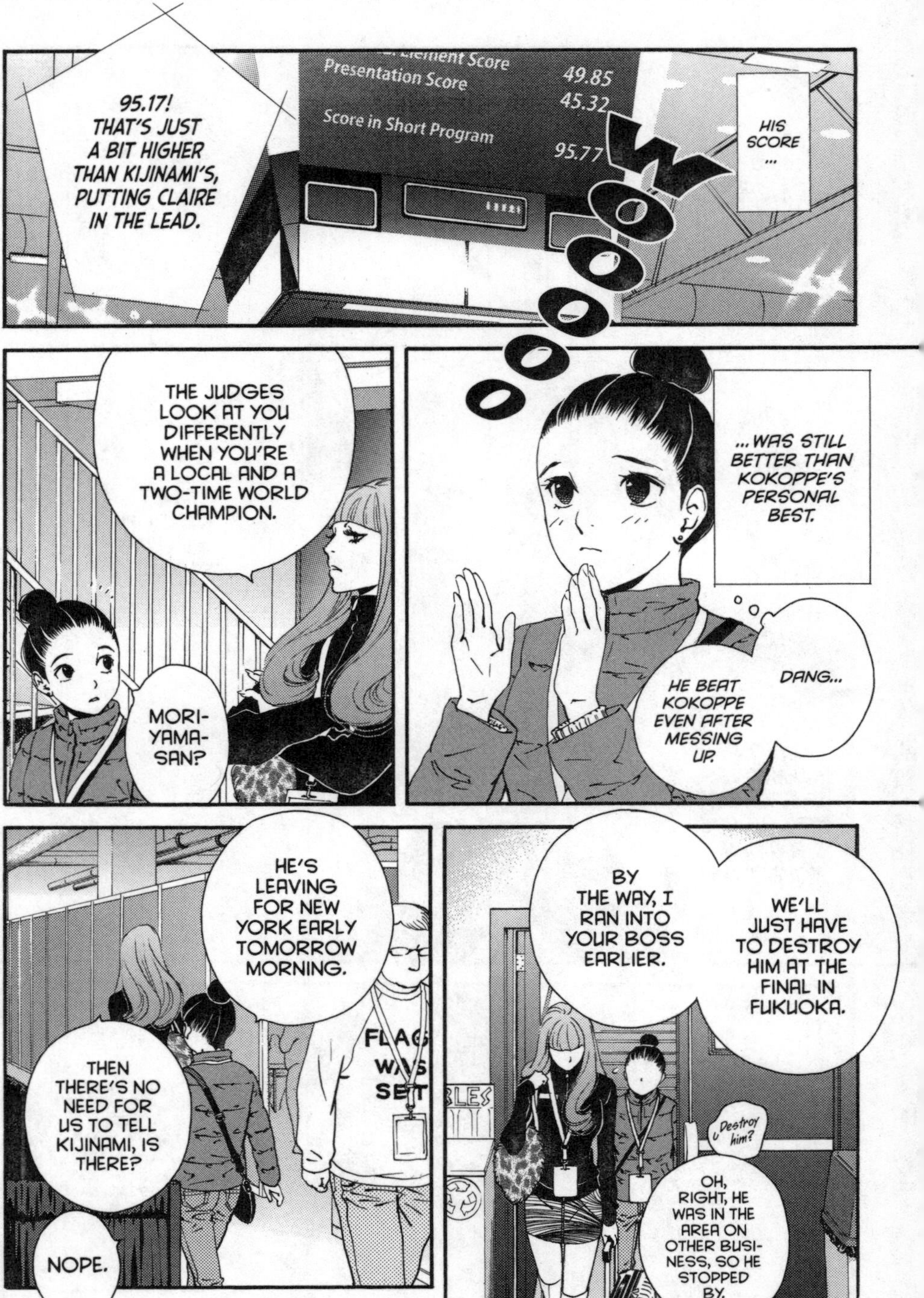
HIS SCORE ...
WOOOOOOO
Element Score
Presentation Score
49.85
45.32
Score in Short Program
95.77
95.17! THAT'S JUST A BIT HIGHER THAN KIJINAMI'S, PUTTING CLAIRE IN THE LEAD.
...WAS STILL BETTER THAN KOKOPPE'S PERSONAL BEST.
DANG...
HE BEAT KOKOPPE EVEN AFTER MESSING UP.
THE JUDGES LOOK AT YOU DIFFERENTLY WHEN YOU'RE A LOCAL AND A TWO-TIME WORLD CHAMPION.
MORI-YAMA-SAN?
WE'LL JUST HAVE TO DESTROY HIM AT THE FINAL IN FUKUOKA.
BY THE WAY, I RAN INTO YOUR BOSS EARLIER.
Destroy him?
OH, RIGHT, HE WAS IN THE AREA ON OTHER BUSINESS, SO HE STOPPED BY.
HE'S LEAVING FOR NEW YORK EARLY TOMORROW MORNING.
FLAG WAS SET
THEN THERE'S NO NEED FOR US TO TELL KIJINAMI, IS THERE?
NOPE.

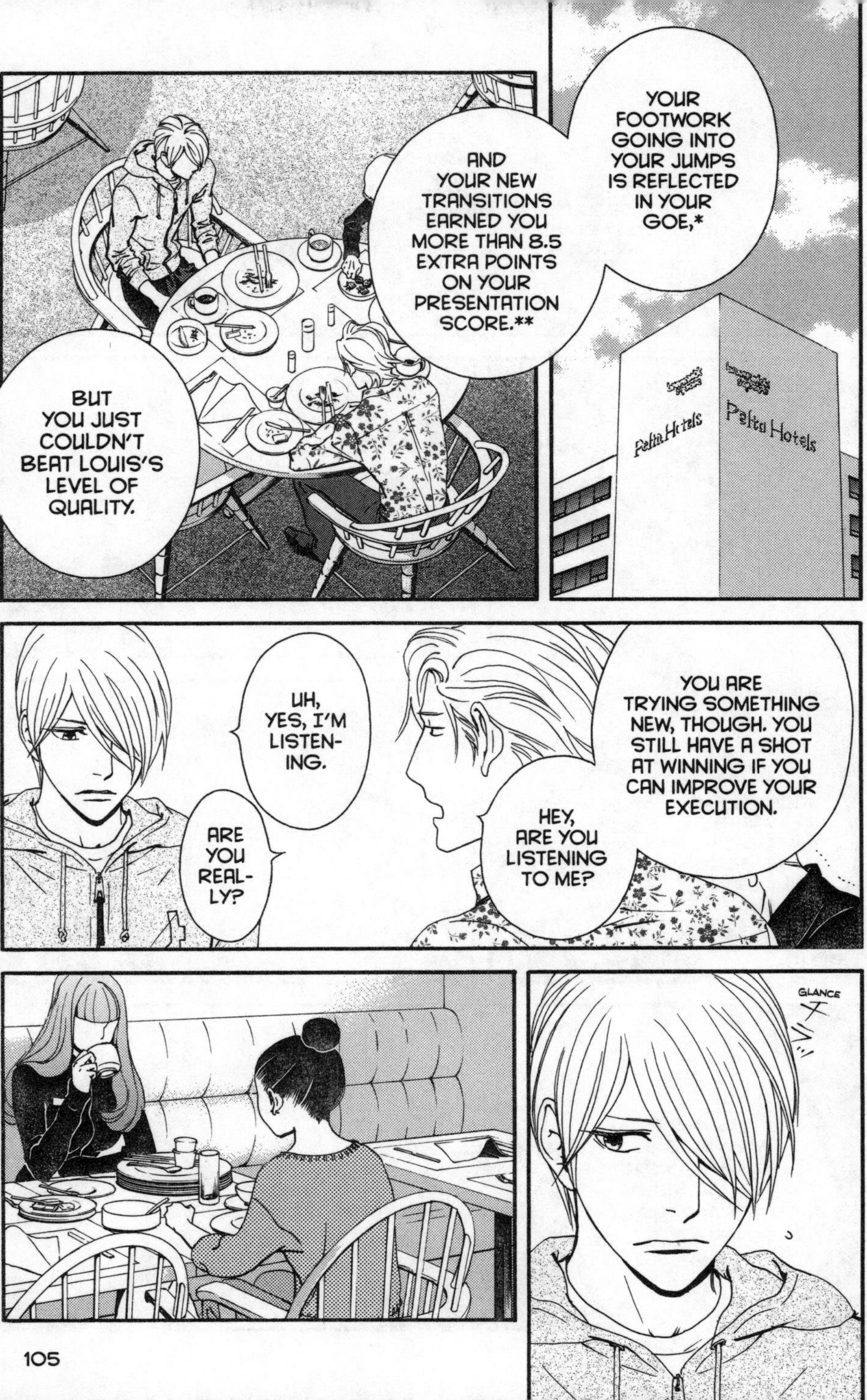
Pelta Hotels
YOUR FOOTWORK GOING INTO YOUR JUMPS IS REFLECTED IN YOUR GOE,*
AND YOUR NEW TRANSITIONS EARNED YOU MORE THAN 8.5 EXTRA POINTS ON YOUR PRESENTATION SCORE.**
BUT YOU JUST COULDN'T BEAT LOUIS'S LEVEL OF QUALITY.
YOU ARE TRYING SOMETHING NEW, THOUGH. YOU STILL HAVE A SHOT AT WINNING IF YOU CAN IMPROVE YOUR EXECUTION.
HEY, ARE YOU LISTENING TO ME?
UH, YES, I'M LISTEN-ING.
ARE YOU REAL-LY?
GLANCE

*GOE: GRADE OF EXECUTION
**SCORE FOR THE PROGRAM COMPONENTS OF SKATING SKILLS, TRANSITIONS, PERFORMANCE, COMPOSITION, AND INTERPRETATION

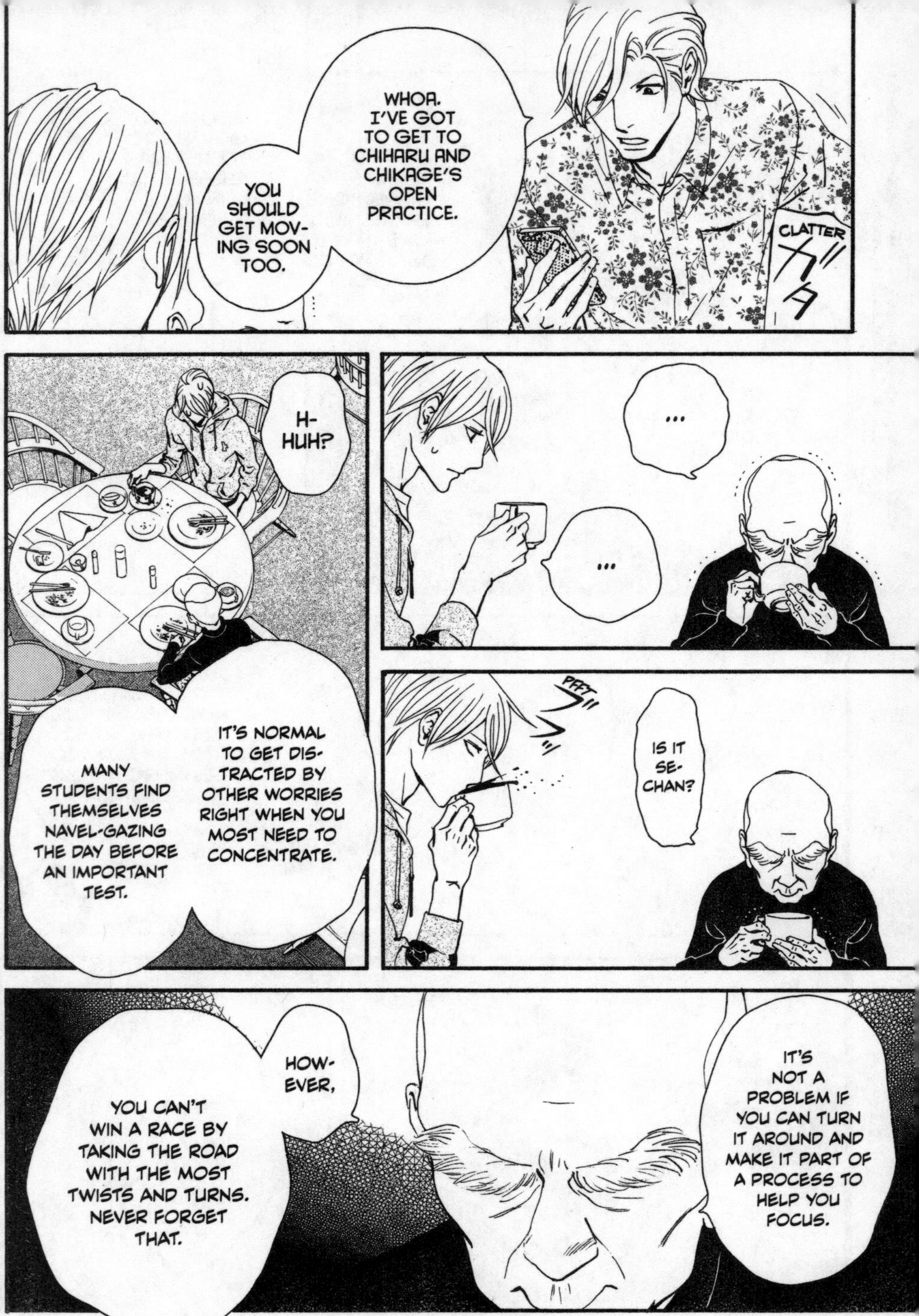
WHOA. I'VE GOT TO GET TO CHIHARU AND CHIKAGE'S OPEN PRACTICE.
CLATTER
YOU SHOULD GET MOV-ING SOON TOO.
...
...
...
PFFT
IS IT SE-CHAN?
H-HUH?
IT'S NORMAL TO GET DIS-TRACTED BY OTHER WORRIES RIGHT WHEN YOU MOST NEED TO CONCENTRATE.
MANY STUDENTS FIND THEMSELVES NAVEL-GAZING THE DAY BEFORE AN IMPORTANT TEST.
IT'S NOT A PROBLEM IF YOU CAN TURN IT AROUND AND MAKE IT PART OF A PROCESS TO HELP YOU FOCUS.
HOW-EVER,
YOU CAN'T WIN A RACE BY TAKING THE ROAD WITH THE MOST TWISTS AND TURNS. NEVER FORGET THAT.

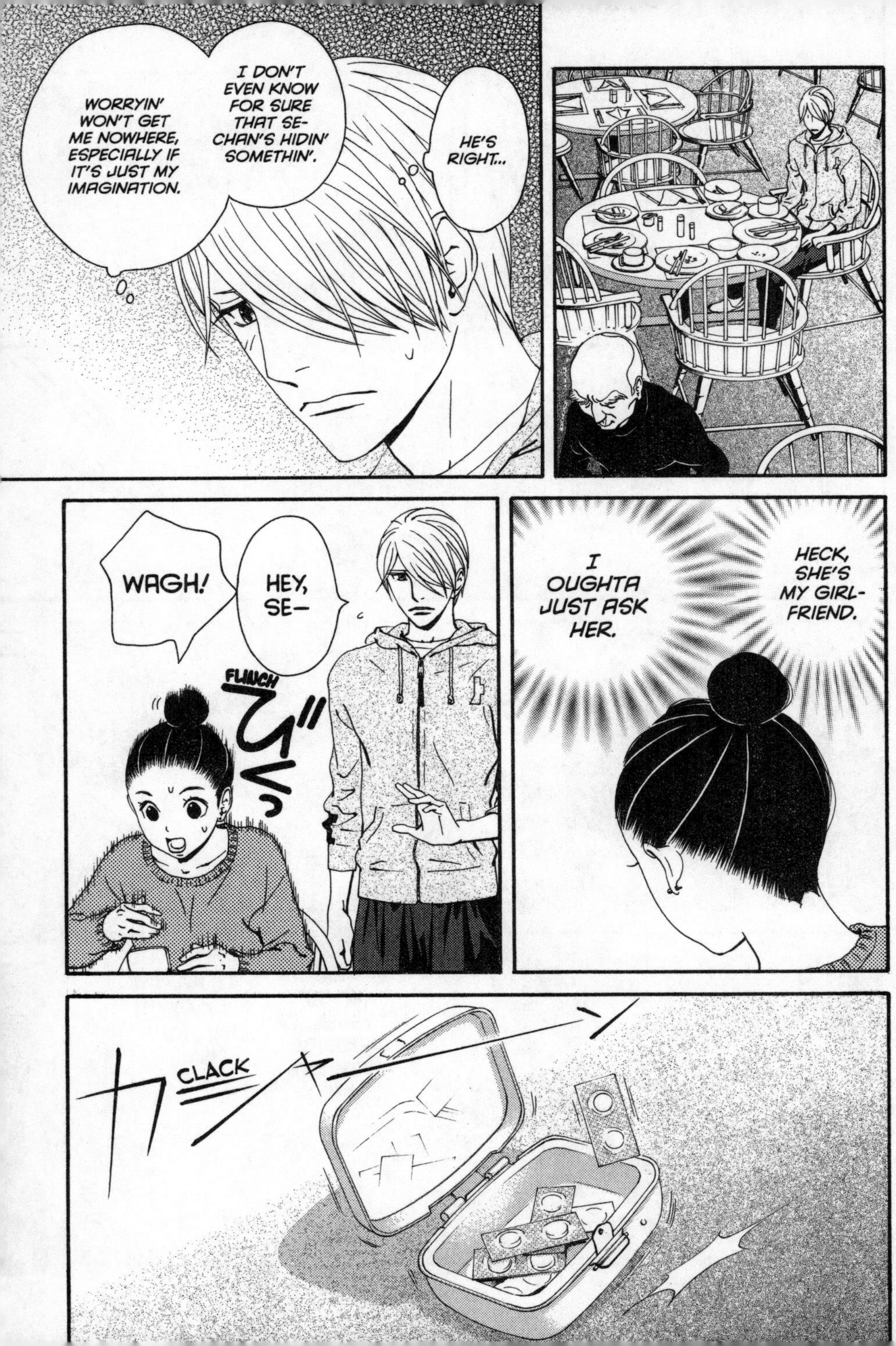
HE'S RIGHT...
I DON'T EVEN KNOW FOR SURE THAT SE-CHAN'S HIDIN' SOMETHIN'.
WORRYIN' WON'T GET ME NOWHERE, ESPECIALLY IF IT'S JUST MY IMAGINATION.
HECK, SHE'S MY GIRL-FRIEND.
I OUGHTA JUST ASK HER.
HEY, SE—
WAGH!
FLINCH
CLACK

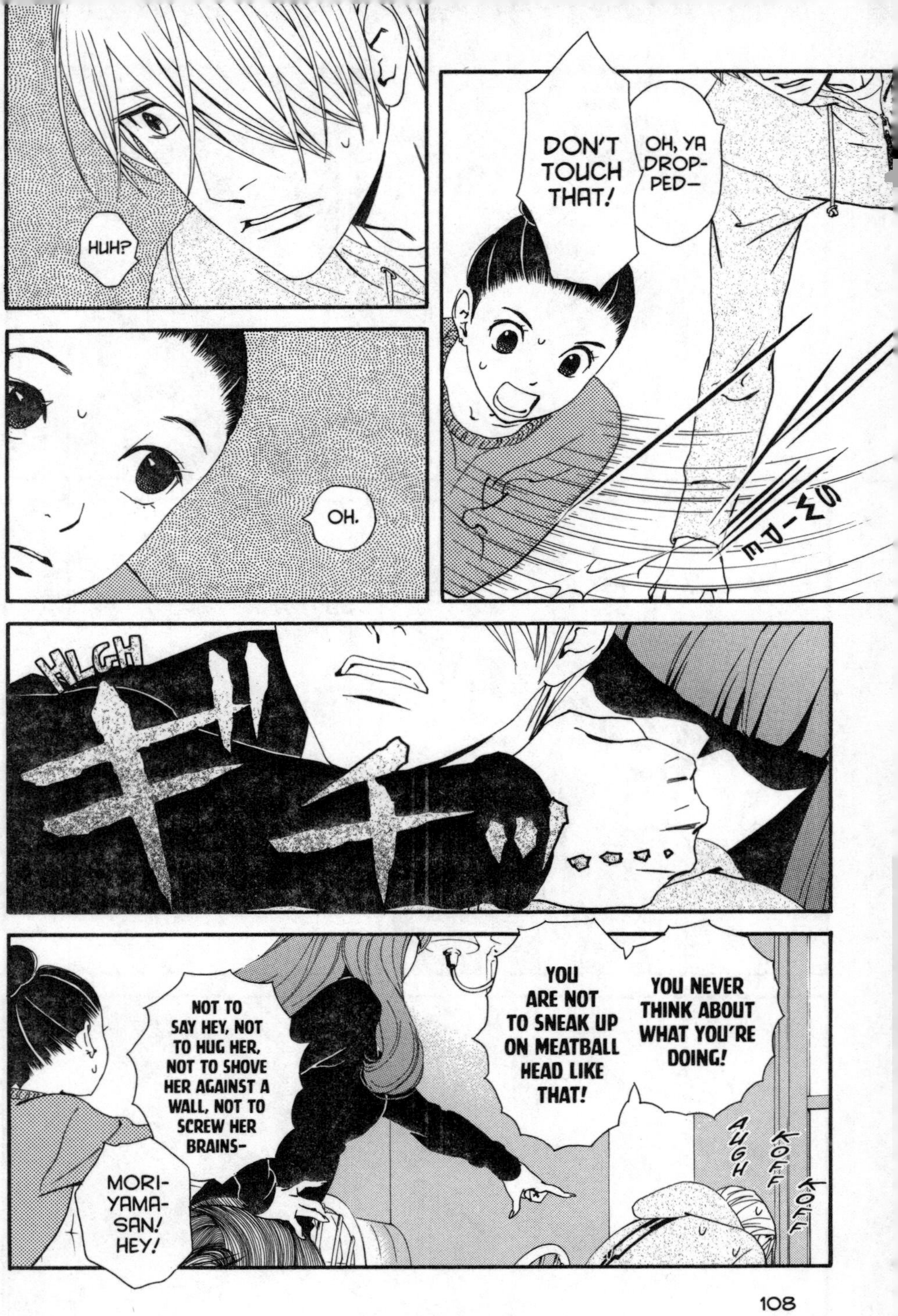
OH, YA DROPPED—
DON'T TOUCH THAT!
SWIPE
HUH?
OH.
HLGH
YOU NEVER THINK ABOUT WHAT YOU'RE DOING!
YOU ARE NOT TO SNEAK UP ON MEATBALL HEAD LIKE THAT!
NOT TO SAY HEY, NOT TO HUG HER, NOT TO SHOVE HER AGAINST A WALL, NOT TO SCREW HER BRAINS-
KOFF KOFF
AUGH
MORI-YAMA-SAN! HEY!

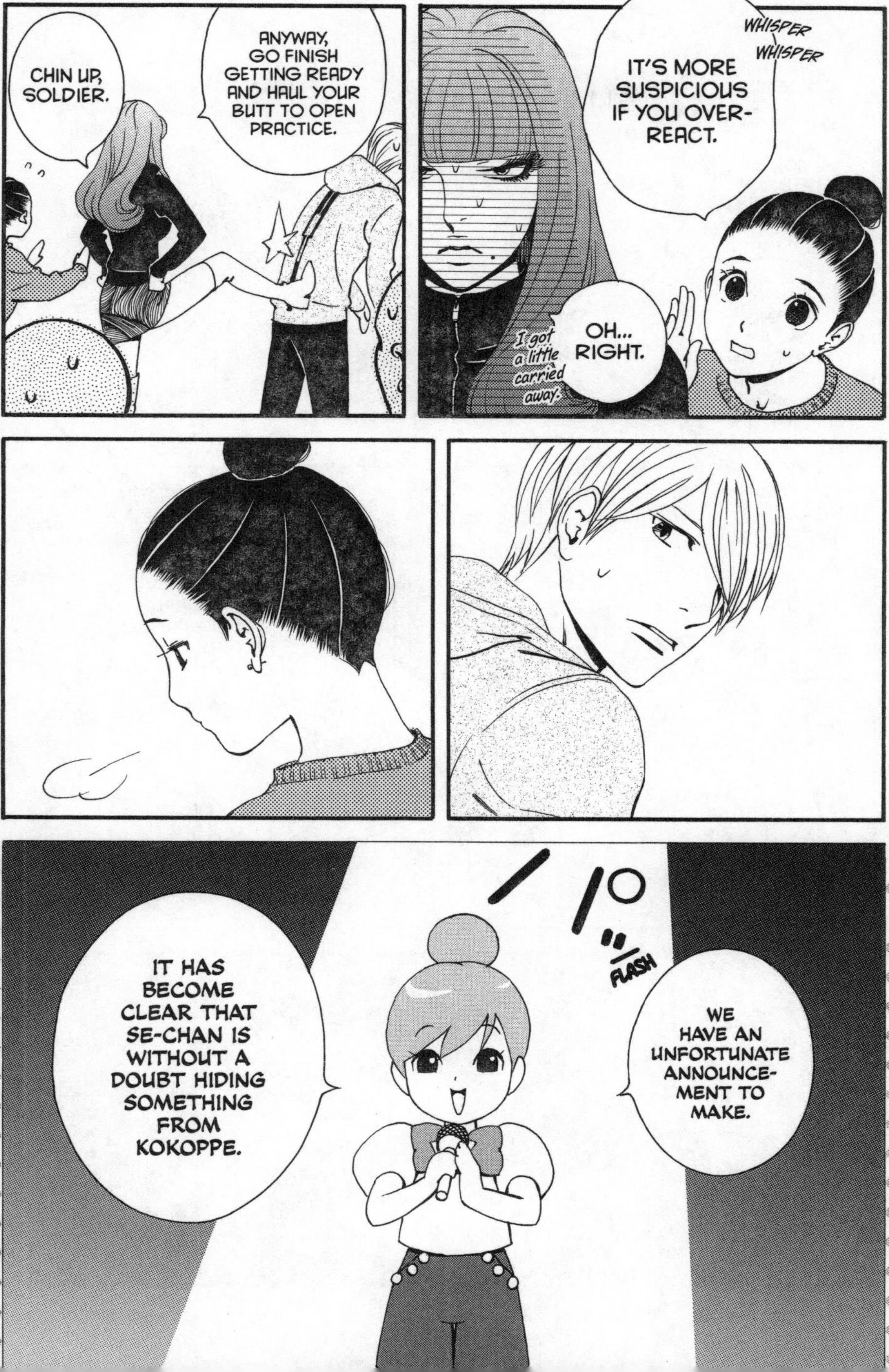
WHISPER WHISPER
IT'S MORE SUSPICIOUS IF YOU OVER-REACT.
OH... RIGHT.
I got a little carried away.
ANYWAY, GO FINISH GETTING READY AND HAUL YOUR BUTT TO OPEN PRACTICE.
CHIN UP, SOLDIER.
FLASH
WE HAVE AN UNFORTUNATE ANNOUNCE-MENT TO MAKE.
IT HAS BECOME CLEAR THAT SE-CHAN IS WITHOUT A DOUBT HIDING SOMETHING FROM KOKOPPE.

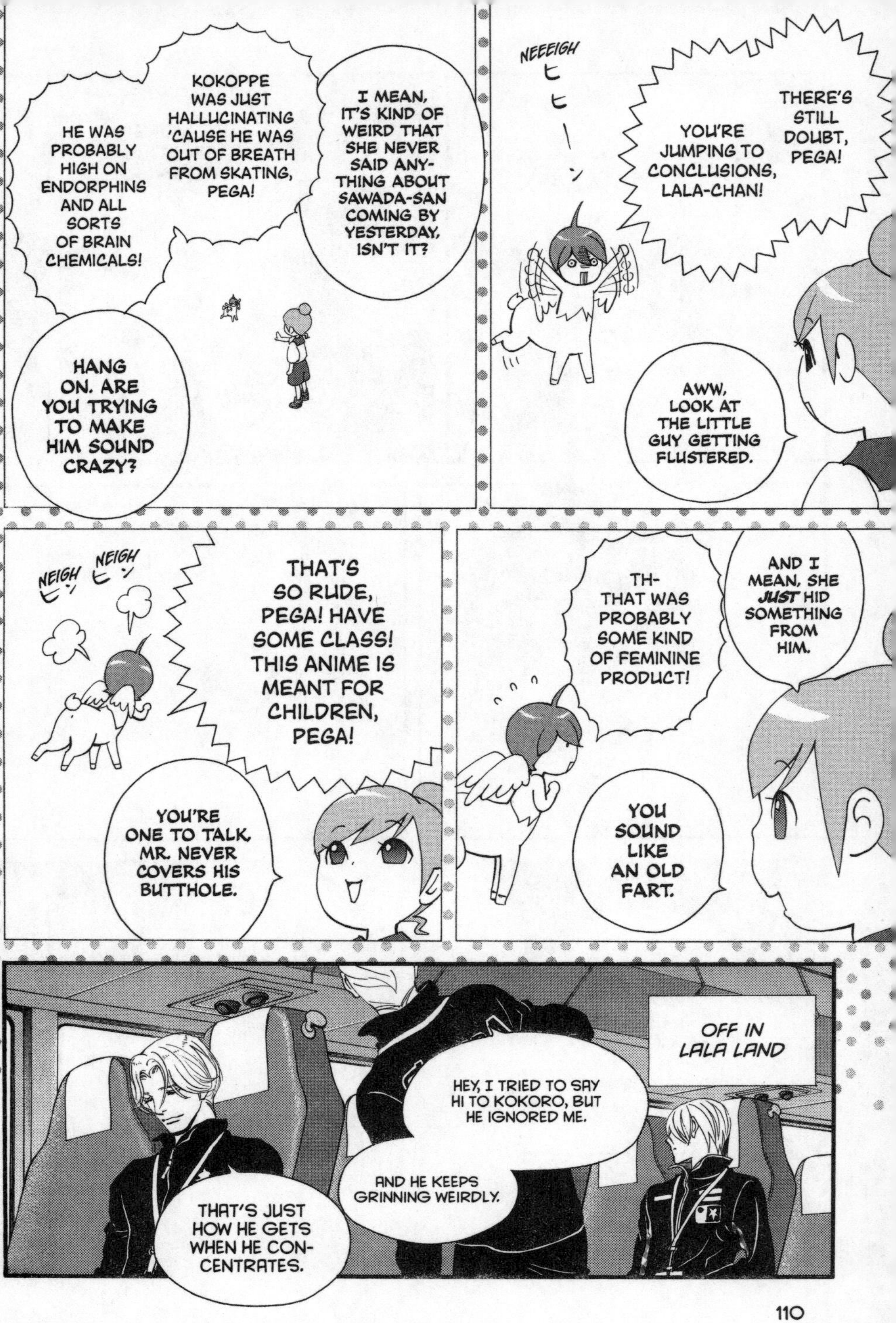

THERE'S STILL DOUBT, PEGA!
YOU'RE JUMPING TO CONCLUSIONS, LALA-CHAN!
NEEEIGH ヒヒーン
AWW, LOOK AT THE LITTLE GUY GETTING FLUSTERED.
I MEAN, IT'S KIND OF WEIRD THAT SHE NEVER SAID ANYTHING ABOUT SAWADA-SAN COMING BY YESTERDAY, ISN'T IT?
KOKOPPE WAS JUST HALLUCINATING 'CAUSE HE WAS OUT OF BREATH FROM SKATING, PEGA!
HE WAS PROBABLY HIGH ON ENDORPHINS AND ALL SORTS OF BRAIN CHEMICALS!
HANG ON. ARE YOU TRYING TO MAKE HIM SOUND CRAZY?
AND I MEAN, SHE *JUST* HID SOMETHING FROM HIM.
TH- THAT WAS PROBABLY SOME KIND OF FEMININE PRODUCT!
YOU SOUND LIKE AN OLD FART.
THAT'S SO RUDE, PEGA! HAVE SOME CLASS! THIS ANIME IS MEANT FOR CHILDREN, PEGA!
NEIGH ヒン
NEIGH ヒン
YOU'RE ONE TO TALK, MR. NEVER COVERS HIS BUTTHOLE.
OFF IN LALA LAND
HEY, I TRIED TO SAY HI TO KOKORO, BUT HE IGNORED ME.
AND HE KEEPS GRINNING WEIRDLY.
THAT'S JUST HOW HE GETS WHEN HE CONCENTRATES.

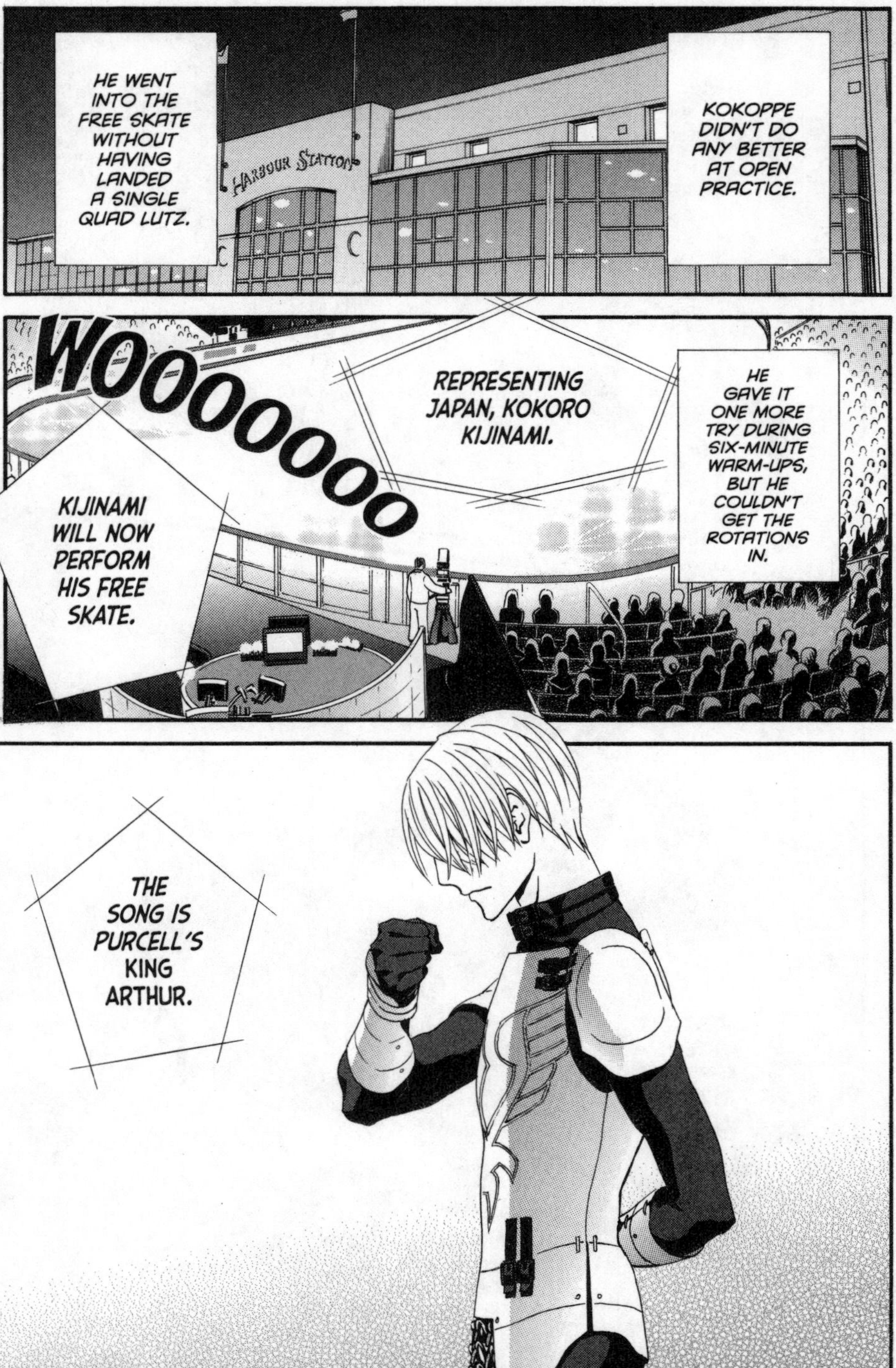
KOKOPPE DIDN'T DO ANY BETTER AT OPEN PRACTICE.
HE WENT INTO THE FREE SKATE WITHOUT HAVING LANDED A SINGLE QUAD LUTZ.
HARBOUR STATION
HE GAVE IT ONE MORE TRY DURING SIX-MINUTE WARM-UPS, BUT HE COULDN'T GET THE ROTATIONS IN.
REPRESENTING JAPAN, KOKORO KIJINAMI.
WOOOOOOO
KIJINAMI WILL NOW PERFORM HIS FREE SKATE.
THE SONG IS PURCELL'S KING ARTHUR.

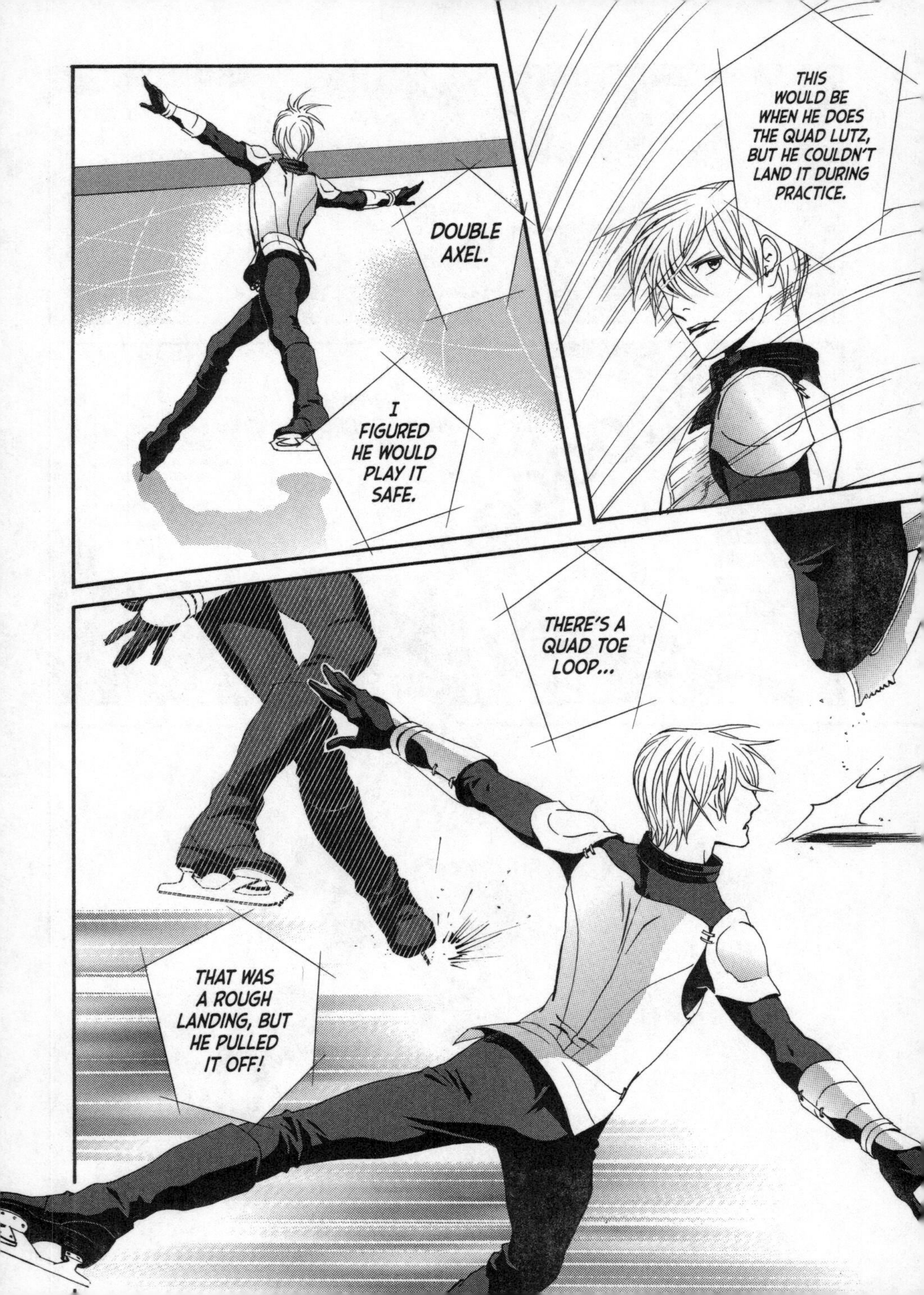
THIS WOULD BE WHEN HE DOES THE QUAD LUTZ, BUT HE COULDN'T LAND IT DURING PRACTICE.
DOUBLE AXEL.
I FIGURED HE WOULD PLAY IT SAFE.
THERE'S A QUAD TOE LOOP...
THAT WAS A ROUGH LANDING, BUT HE PULLED IT OFF!

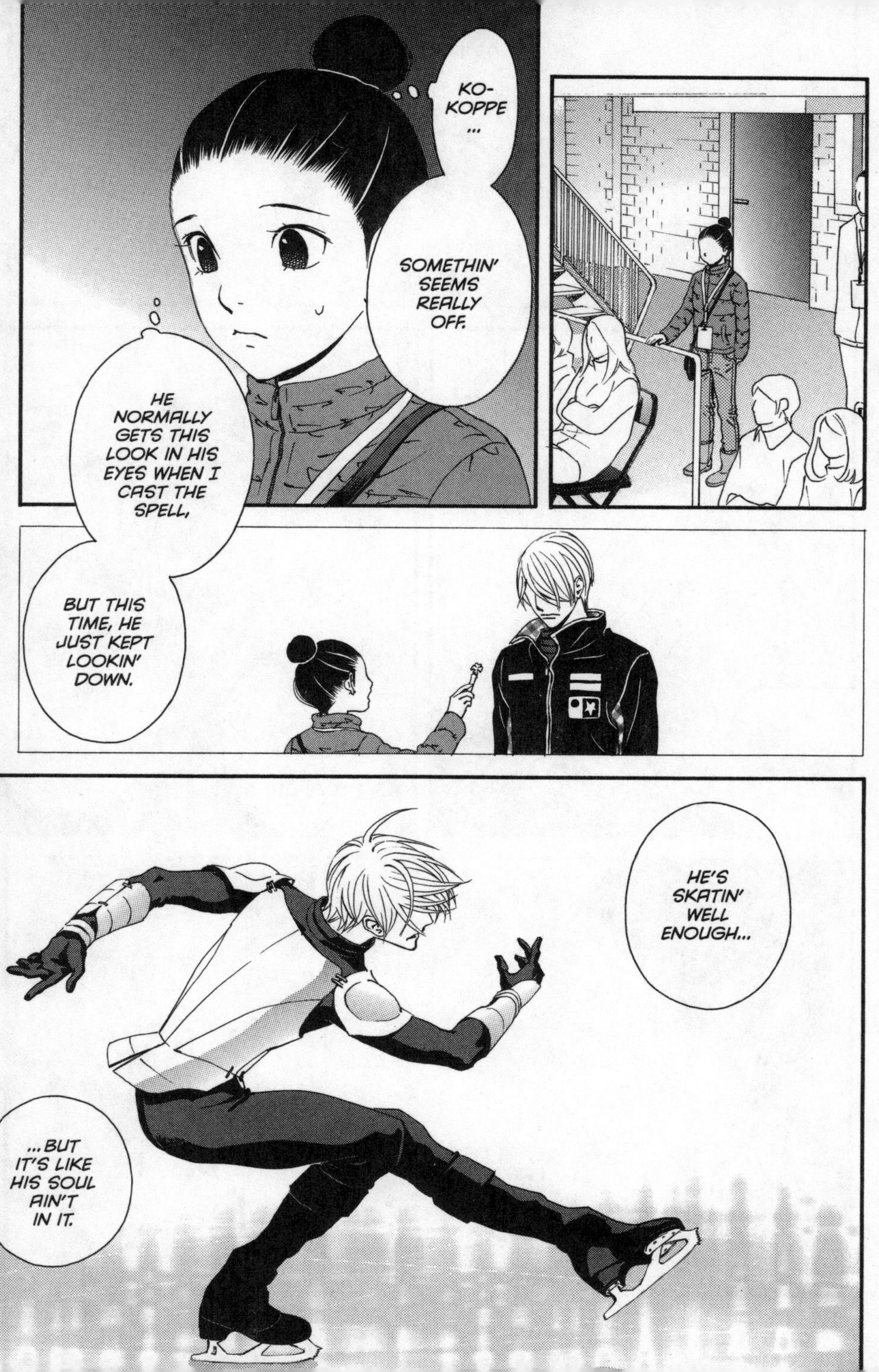
KO-KOPPE ...
SOMETHIN' SEEMS REALLY OFF.
HE NORMALLY GETS THIS LOOK IN HIS EYES WHEN I CAST THE SPELL,
BUT THIS TIME, HE JUST KEPT LOOKIN' DOWN.
HE'S SKATIN' WELL ENOUGH...
...BUT IT'S LIKE HIS SOUL AIN'T IN IT.

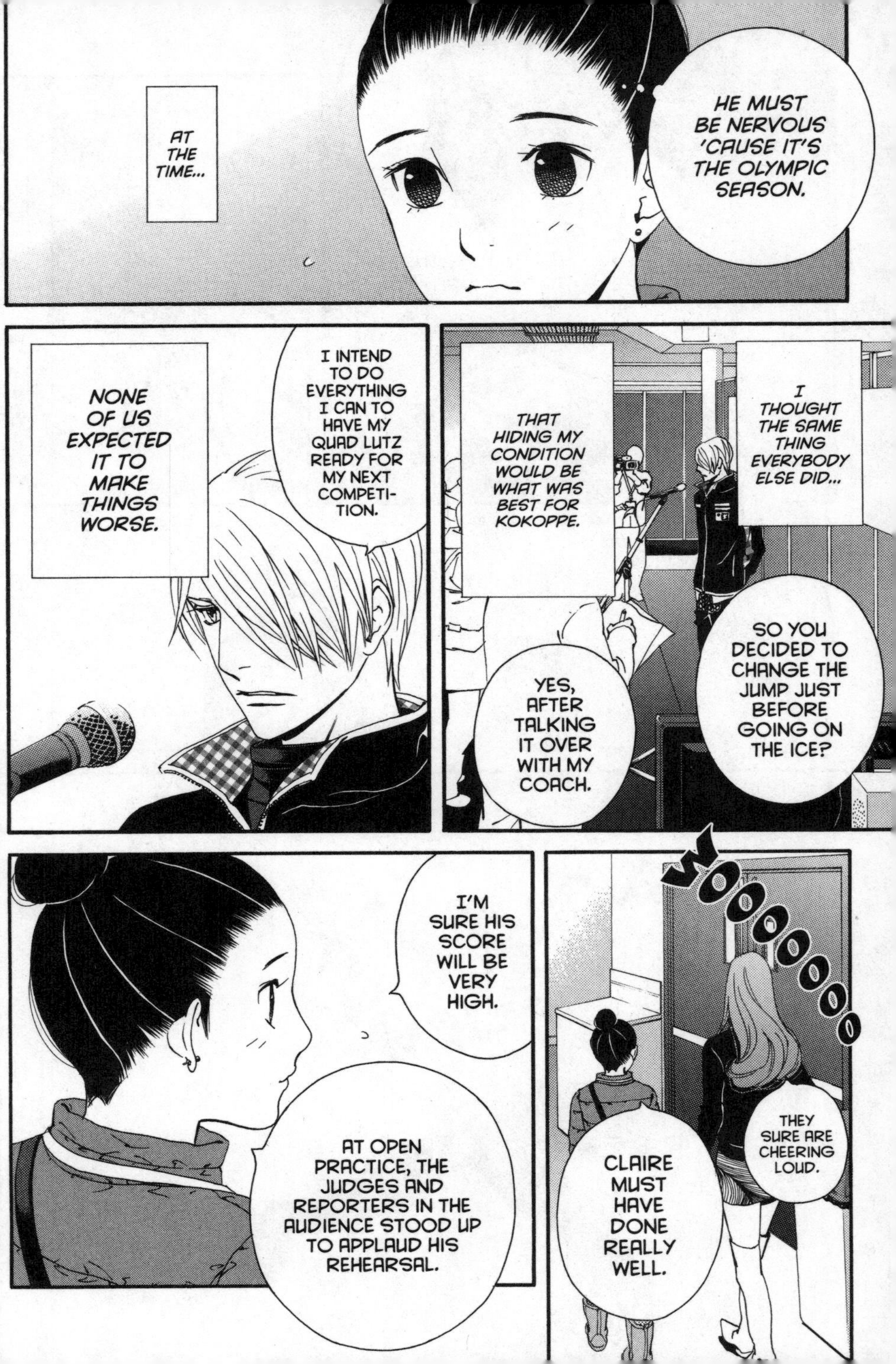
HE MUST BE NERVOUS 'CAUSE IT'S THE OLYMPIC SEASON.
AT THE TIME...
I THOUGHT THE SAME THING EVERYBODY ELSE DID...
THAT HIDING MY CONDITION WOULD BE WHAT WAS BEST FOR KOKOPPE.
SO YOU DECIDED TO CHANGE THE JUMP JUST BEFORE GOING ON THE ICE?
YES, AFTER TALKING IT OVER WITH MY COACH.
I INTEND TO DO EVERYTHING I CAN TO HAVE MY QUAD LUTZ READY FOR MY NEXT COMPETITION.
NONE OF US EXPECTED IT TO MAKE THINGS WORSE.
WOOOOOOOO
THEY SURE ARE CHEERING LOUD.
CLAIRE MUST HAVE DONE REALLY WELL.
I'M SURE HIS SCORE WILL BE VERY HIGH.
AT OPEN PRACTICE, THE JUDGES AND REPORTERS IN THE AUDIENCE STOOD UP TO APPLAUD HIS REHEARSAL.

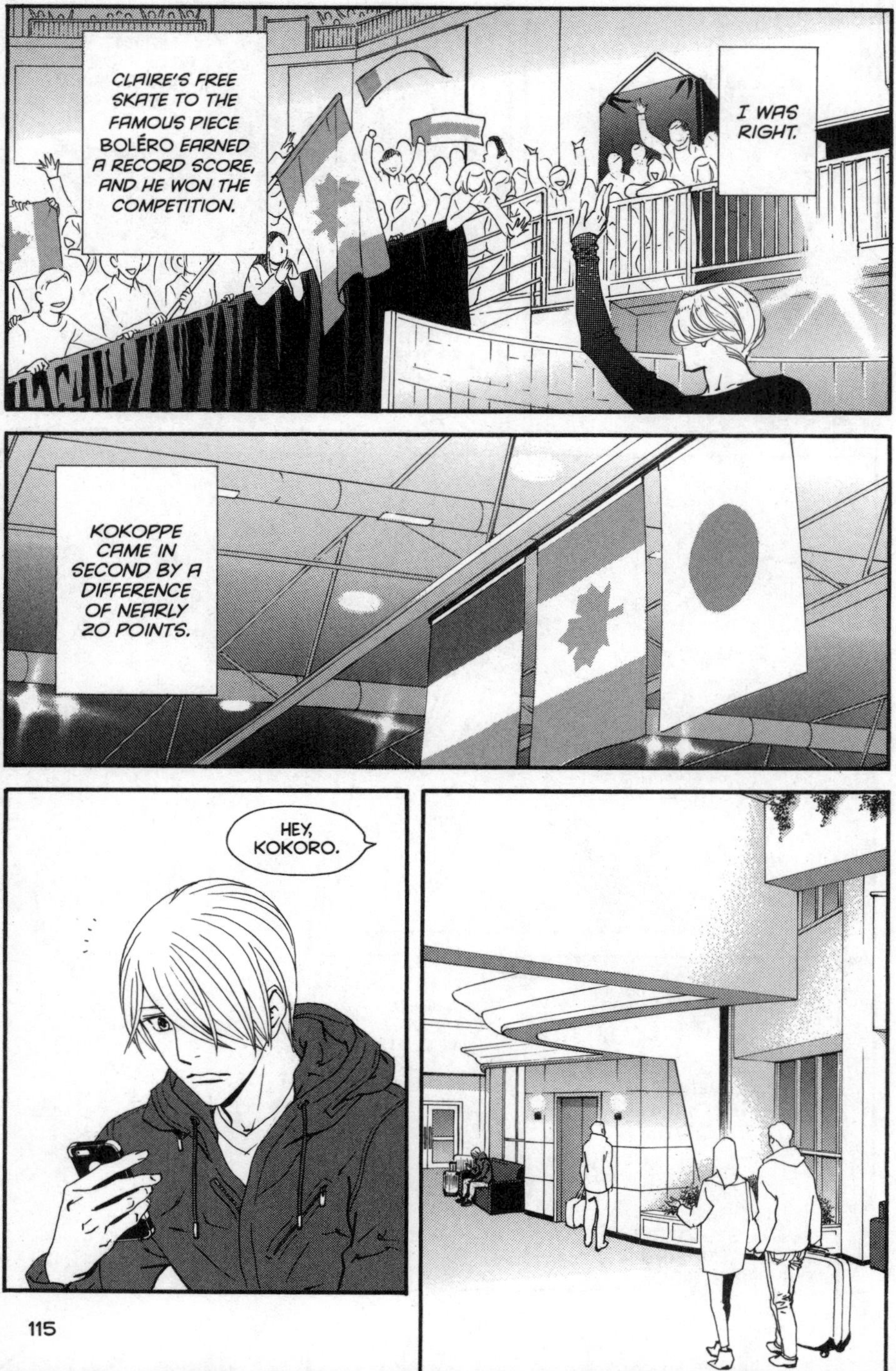
I WAS RIGHT.
CLAIRE'S FREE SKATE TO THE FAMOUS PIECE BOLÉRO EARNED A RECORD SCORE, AND HE WON THE COMPETITION.
KOKOPPE CAME IN SECOND BY A DIFFERENCE OF NEARLY 20 POINTS.
HEY, KOKORO.

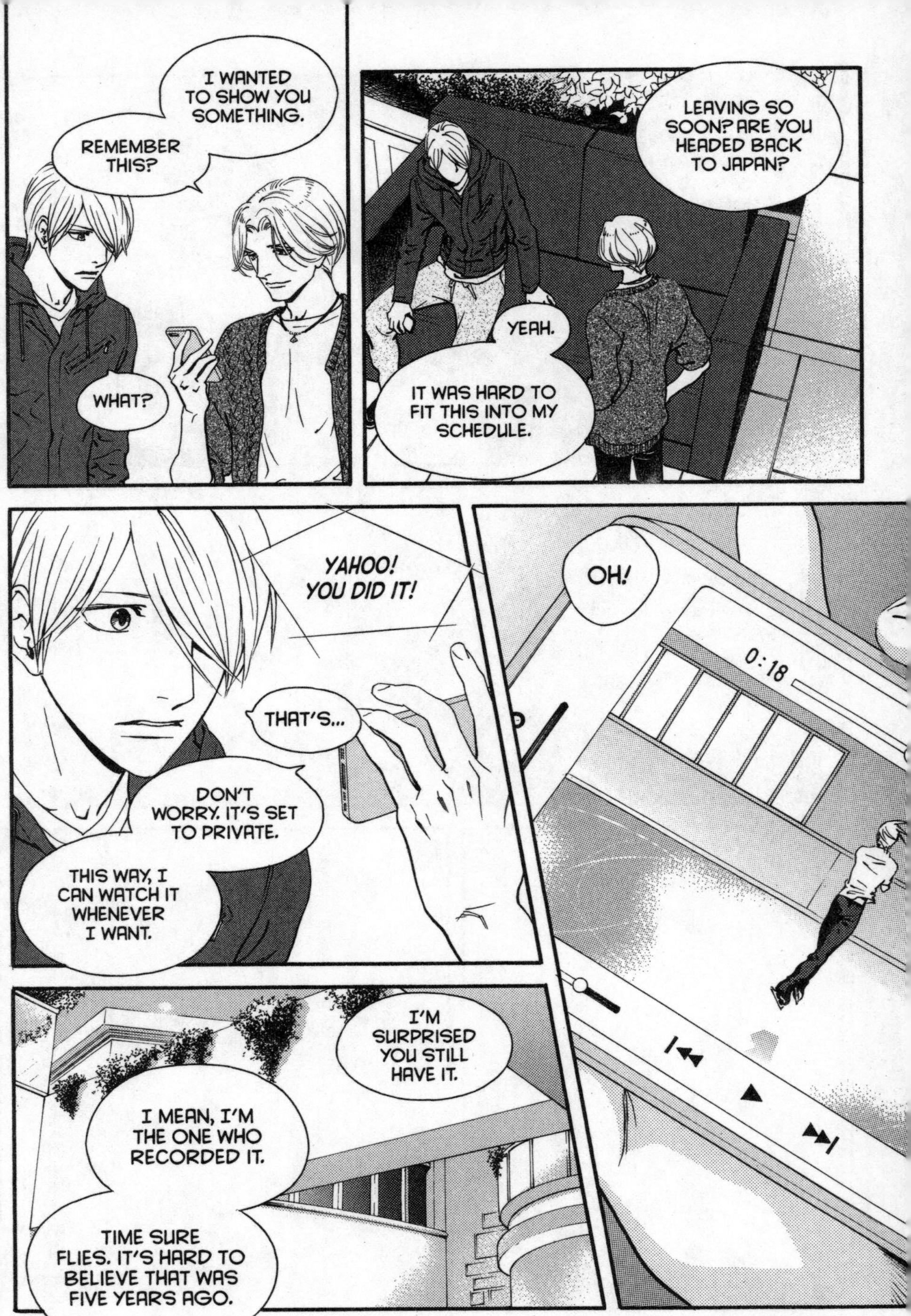
LEAVING SO SOON? ARE YOU HEADED BACK TO JAPAN?
YEAH.
IT WAS HARD TO FIT THIS INTO MY SCHEDULE.
I WANTED TO SHOW YOU SOMETHING.
REMEMBER THIS?
WHAT?
OH!
0:18
YAHOO! YOU DID IT!
THAT'S...
DON'T WORRY. IT'S SET TO PRIVATE.
THIS WAY, I CAN WATCH IT WHENEVER I WANT.
I'M SURPRISED YOU STILL HAVE IT.
I MEAN, I'M THE ONE WHO RECORDED IT.
TIME SURE FLIES. IT'S HARD TO BELIEVE THAT WAS FIVE YEARS AGO.

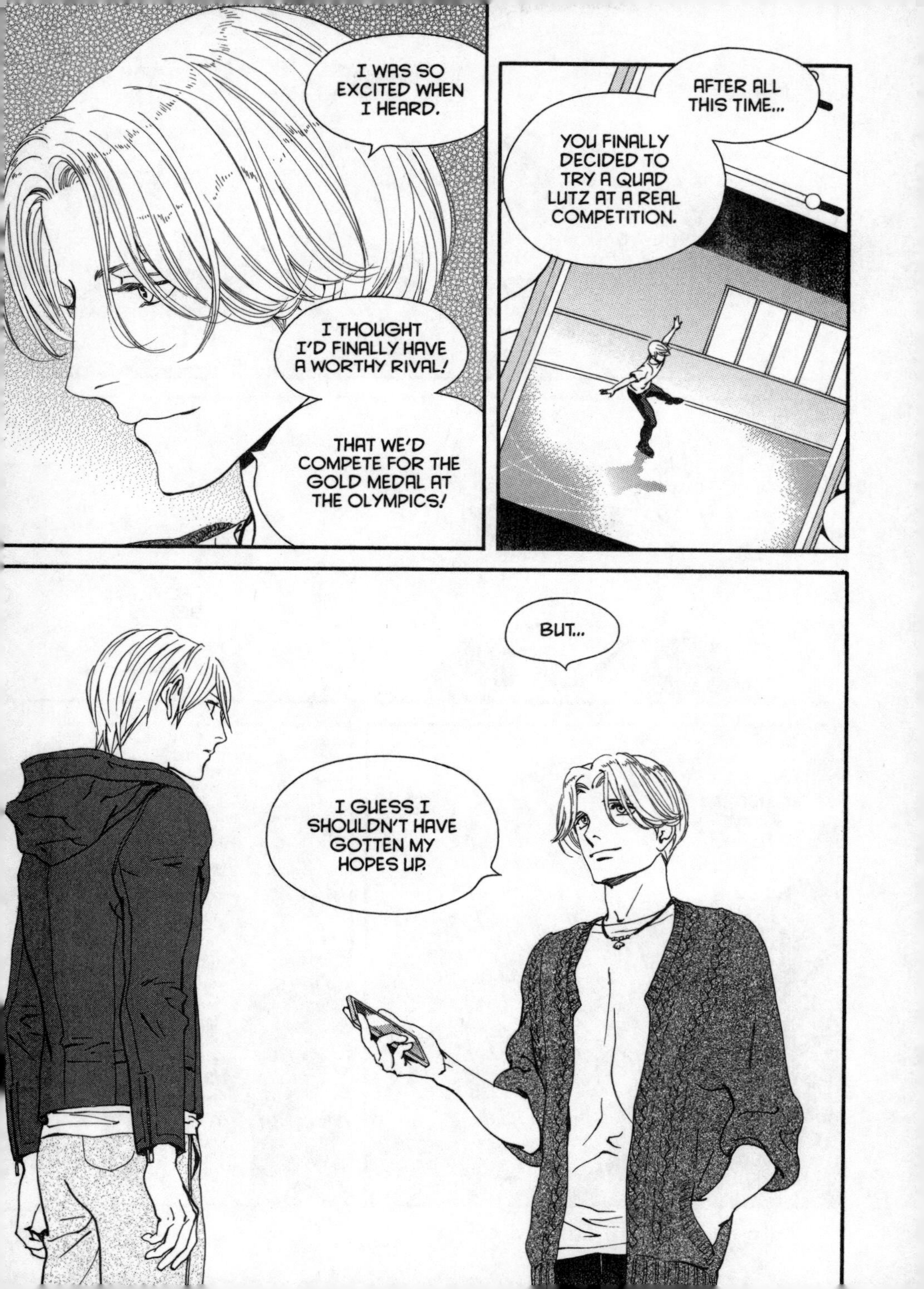
AFTER ALL THIS TIME...
YOU FINALLY DECIDED TO TRY A QUAD LUTZ AT A REAL COMPETITION.
I WAS SO EXCITED WHEN I HEARD.
I THOUGHT I'D FINALLY HAVE A WORTHY RIVAL!
THAT WE'D COMPETE FOR THE GOLD MEDAL AT THE OLYMPICS!
BUT...
I GUESS I SHOULDN'T HAVE GOTTEN MY HOPES UP.

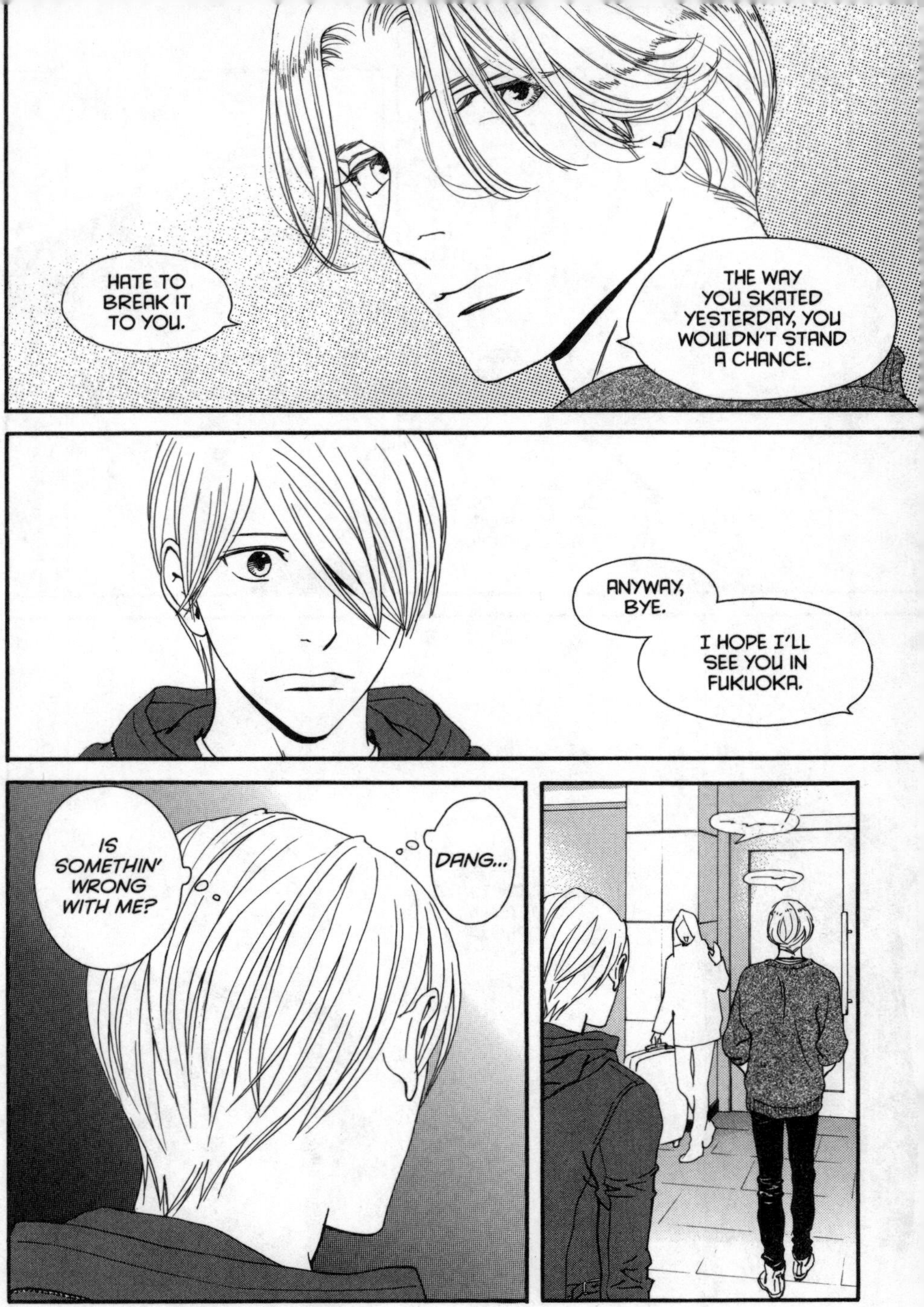
THE WAY YOU SKATED YESTERDAY, YOU WOULDN'T STAND A CHANCE.
HATE TO BREAK IT TO YOU.
ANYWAY, BYE.
I HOPE I'LL SEE YOU IN FUKUOKA.
DANG...
IS SOMETHIN' WRONG WITH ME?

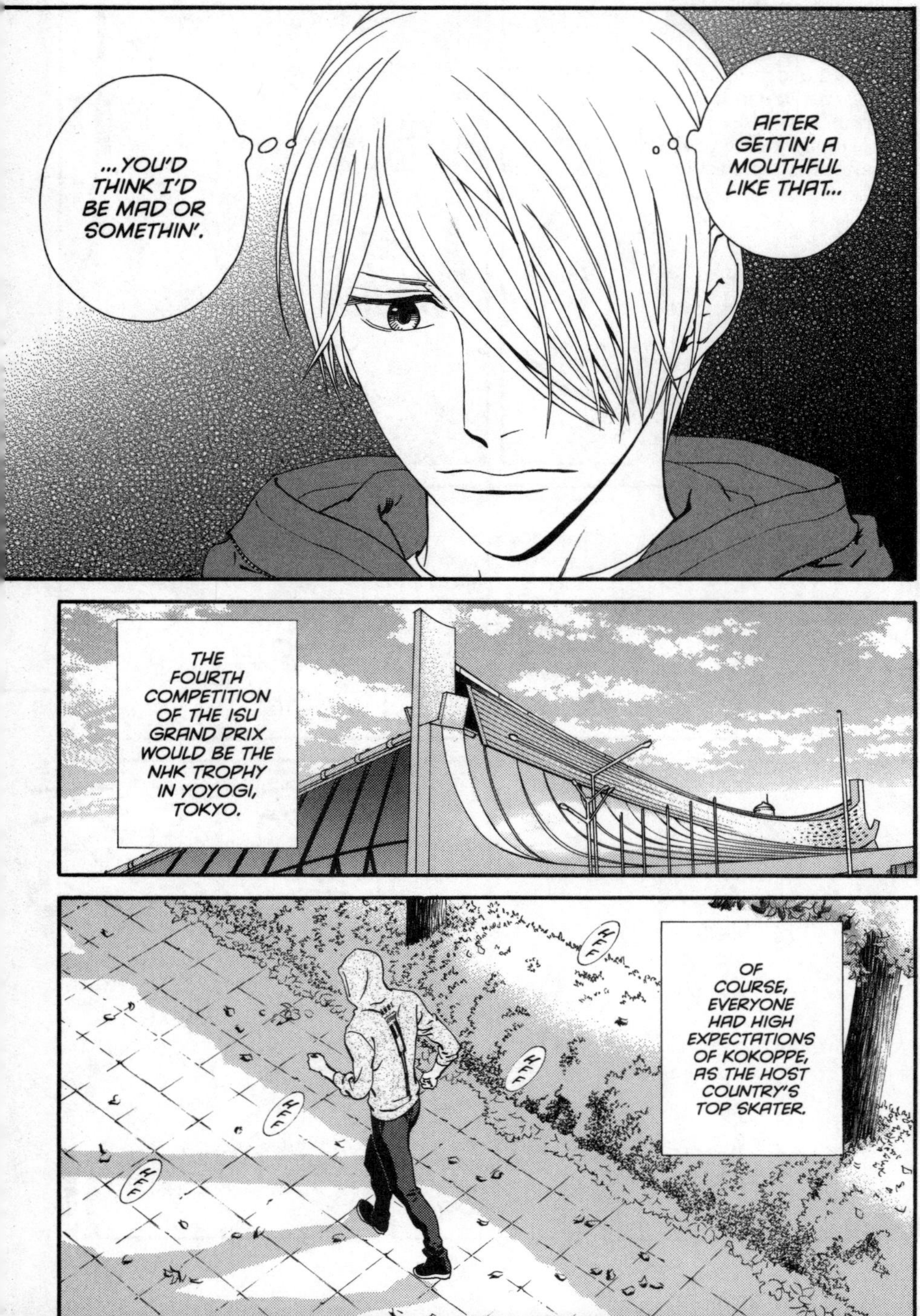
AFTER GETTIN' A MOUTHFUL LIKE THAT...
...YOU'D THINK I'D BE MAD OR SOMETHIN'.
THE FOURTH COMPETITION OF THE ISU GRAND PRIX WOULD BE THE NHK TROPHY IN YOYOGI, TOKYO.
OF COURSE, EVERYONE HAD HIGH EXPECTATIONS OF KOKOPPE, AS THE HOST COUNTRY'S TOP SKATER.
HFF
HFF
HFF
HFF

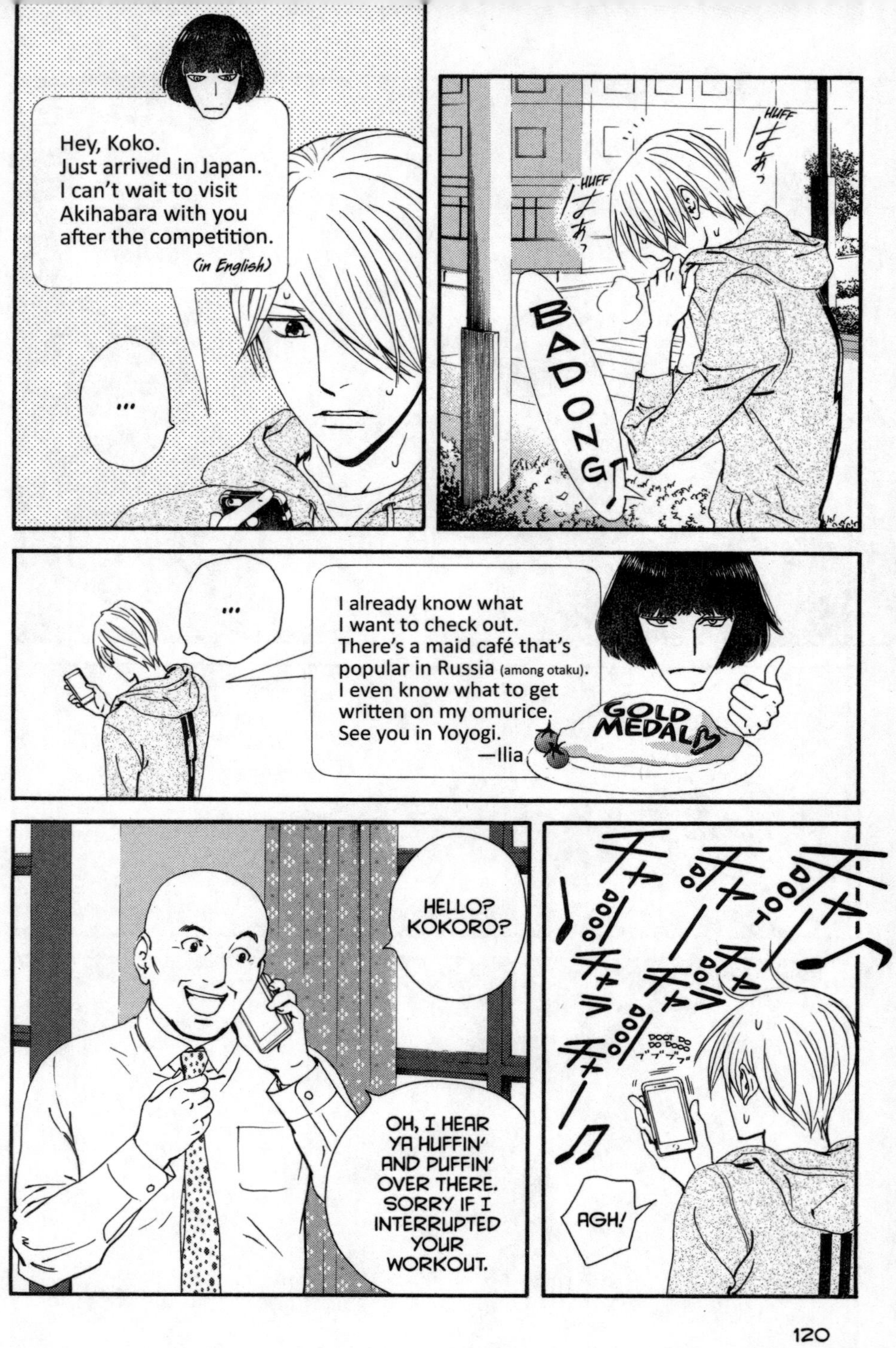
HUFF
はあっ
HUFF
はあっ
BADONG!
Hey, Koko. Just arrived in Japan. I can't wait to visit Akihabara with you after the competition. (in English)
...
I already know what I want to check out. There's a maid café that's popular in Russia (among otaku). I even know what to get written on my omurice. See you in Yoyogi. —Ilia
GOLD MEDAL
...
DOOT DO DO DOOO
ブブブブ
AGH!
HELLO? KOKORO?
OH, I HEAR YA HUFFIN' AND PUFFIN' OVER THERE. SORRY IF I INTERRUPTED YOUR WORKOUT.

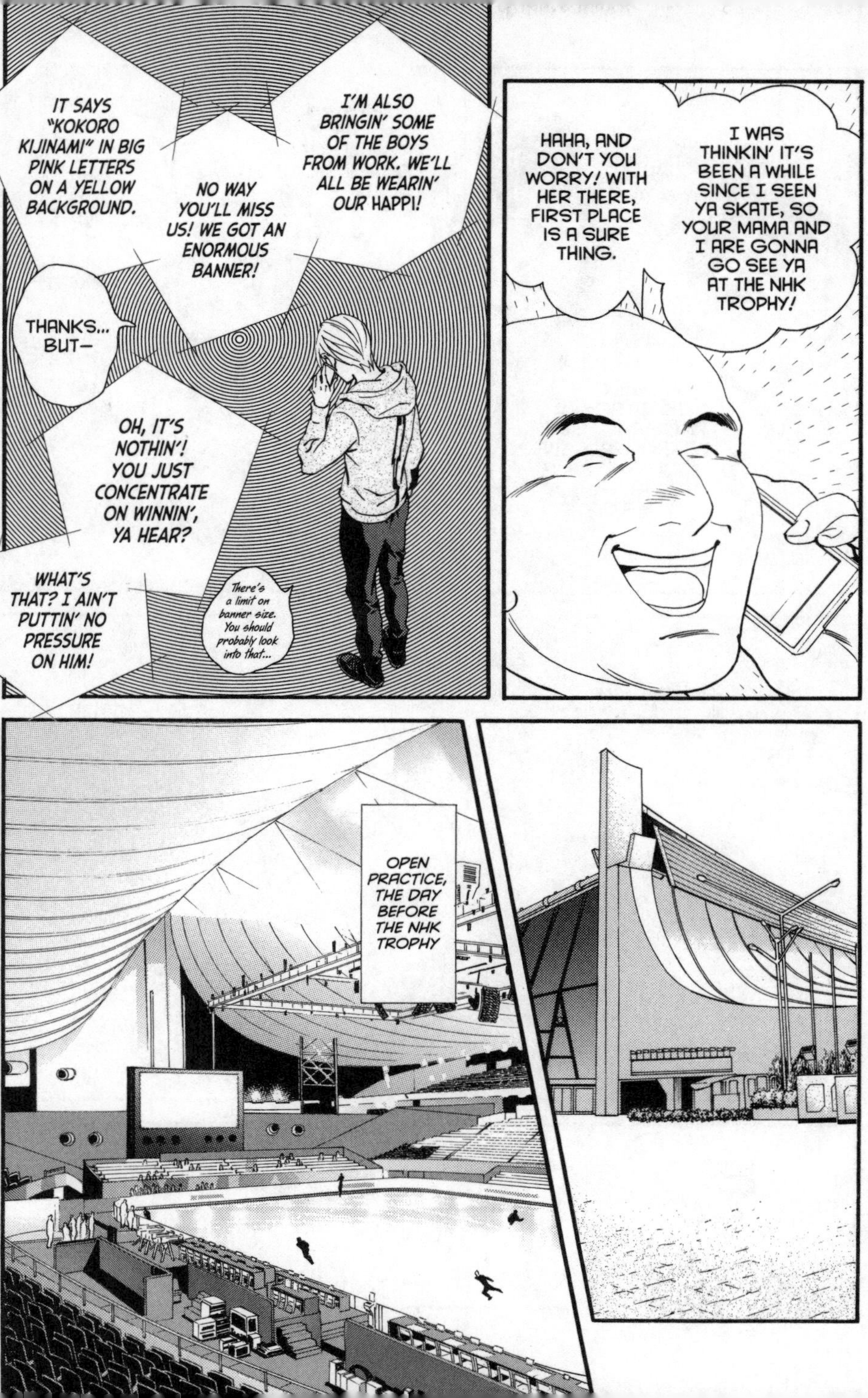
I WAS THINKIN' IT'S BEEN A WHILE SINCE I SEEN YA SKATE, SO YOUR MAMA AND I ARE GONNA GO SEE YA AT THE NHK TROPHY!
HAHA, AND DON'T YOU WORRY! WITH HER THERE, FIRST PLACE IS A SURE THING.
I'M ALSO BRINGIN' SOME OF THE BOYS FROM WORK. WE'LL ALL BE WEARIN' OUR HAPPI!
IT SAYS "KOKORO KIJINAMI" IN BIG PINK LETTERS ON A YELLOW BACKGROUND.
NO WAY YOU'LL MISS US! WE GOT AN ENORMOUS BANNER!
THANKS... BUT—
OH, IT'S NOTHIN'! YOU JUST CONCENTRATE ON WINNIN', YA HEAR?
There's a limit on banner size. You should probably look into that...
WHAT'S THAT? I AIN'T PUTTIN' NO PRESSURE ON HIM!
OPEN PRACTICE, THE DAY BEFORE THE NHK TROPHY

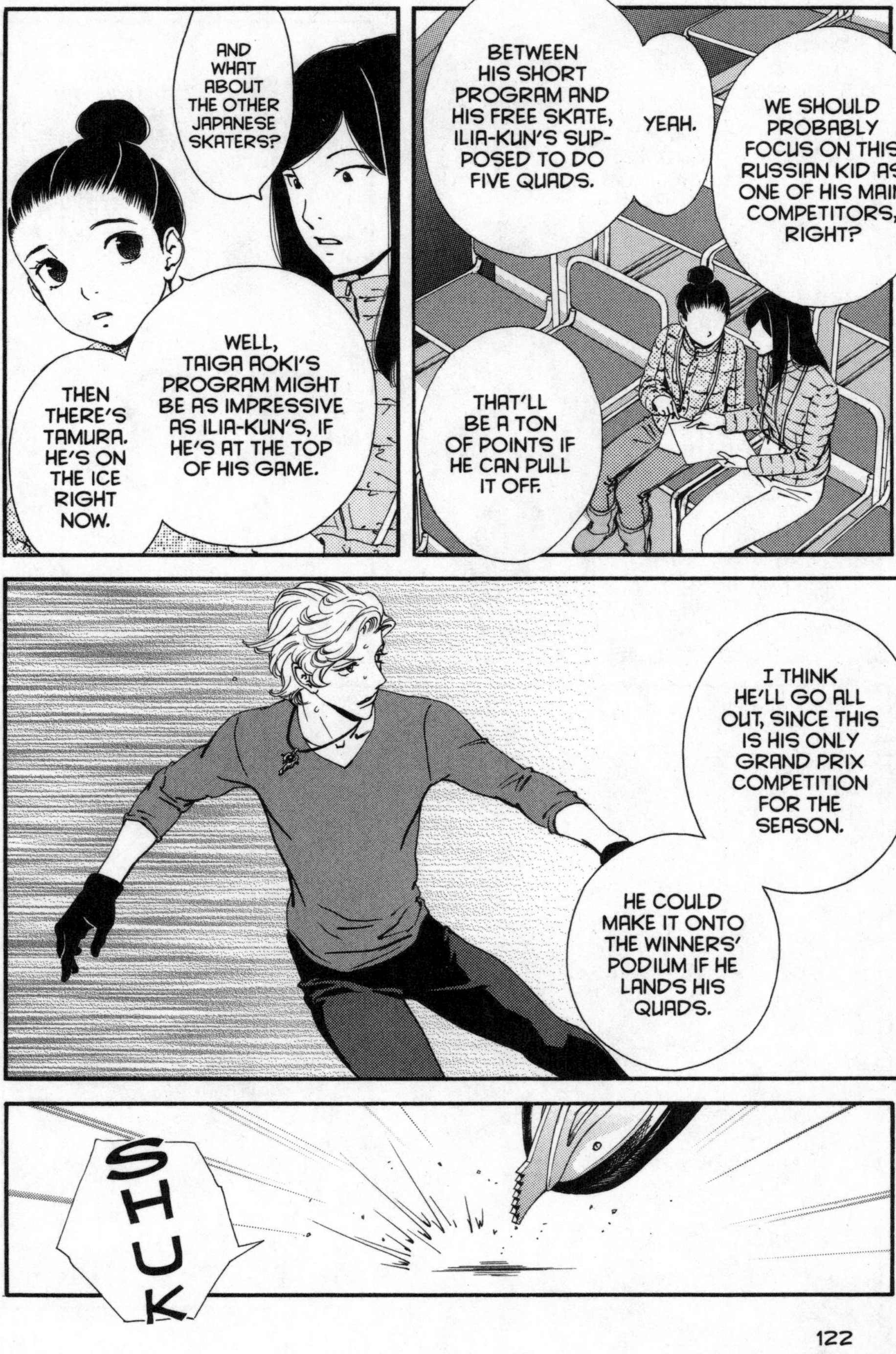

WE SHOULD PROBABLY FOCUS ON THIS RUSSIAN KID AS ONE OF HIS MAIN COMPETITORS, RIGHT?
YEAH.
BETWEEN HIS SHORT PROGRAM AND HIS FREE SKATE, ILIA-KUN'S SUP-POSED TO DO FIVE QUADS.
THAT'LL BE A TON OF POINTS IF HE CAN PULL IT OFF.
AND WHAT ABOUT THE OTHER JAPANESE SKATERS?
WELL, TAIGA AOKI'S PROGRAM MIGHT BE AS IMPRESSIVE AS ILIA-KUN'S, IF HE'S AT THE TOP OF HIS GAME.
THEN THERE'S TAMURA. HE'S ON THE ICE RIGHT NOW.
I THINK HE'LL GO ALL OUT, SINCE THIS IS HIS ONLY GRAND PRIX COMPETITION FOR THE SEASON.
HE COULD MAKE IT ONTO THE WINNERS' PODIUM IF HE LANDS HIS QUADS.
SHUK

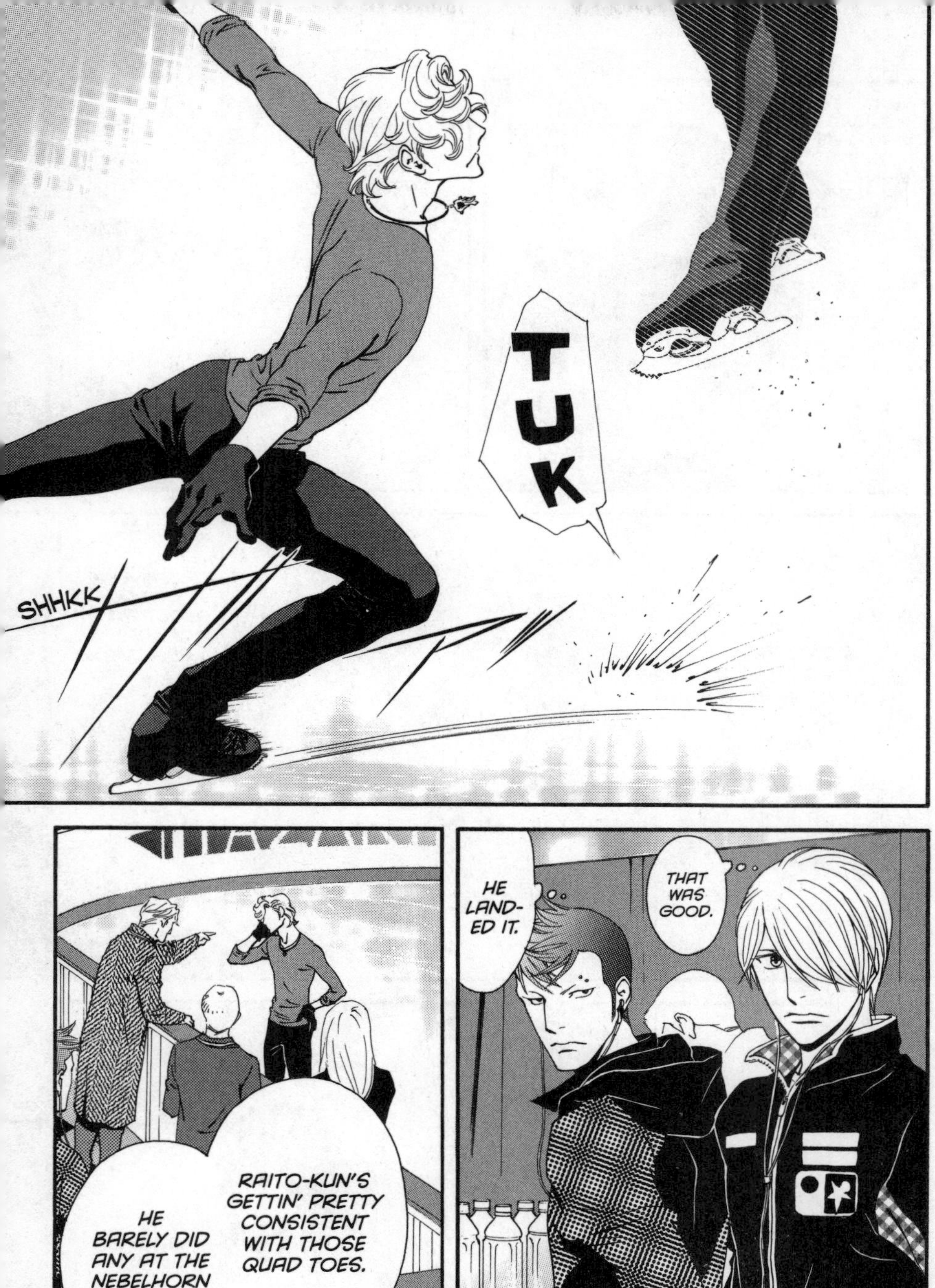
TUK
SHHKK
THAT WAS GOOD.
HE LAND-ED IT.
RAITO-KUN'S GETTIN' PRETTY CONSISTENT WITH THOSE QUAD TOES.
HE BARELY DID ANY AT THE NEBELHORN TROPHY.

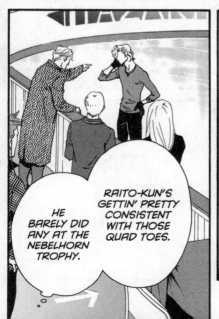

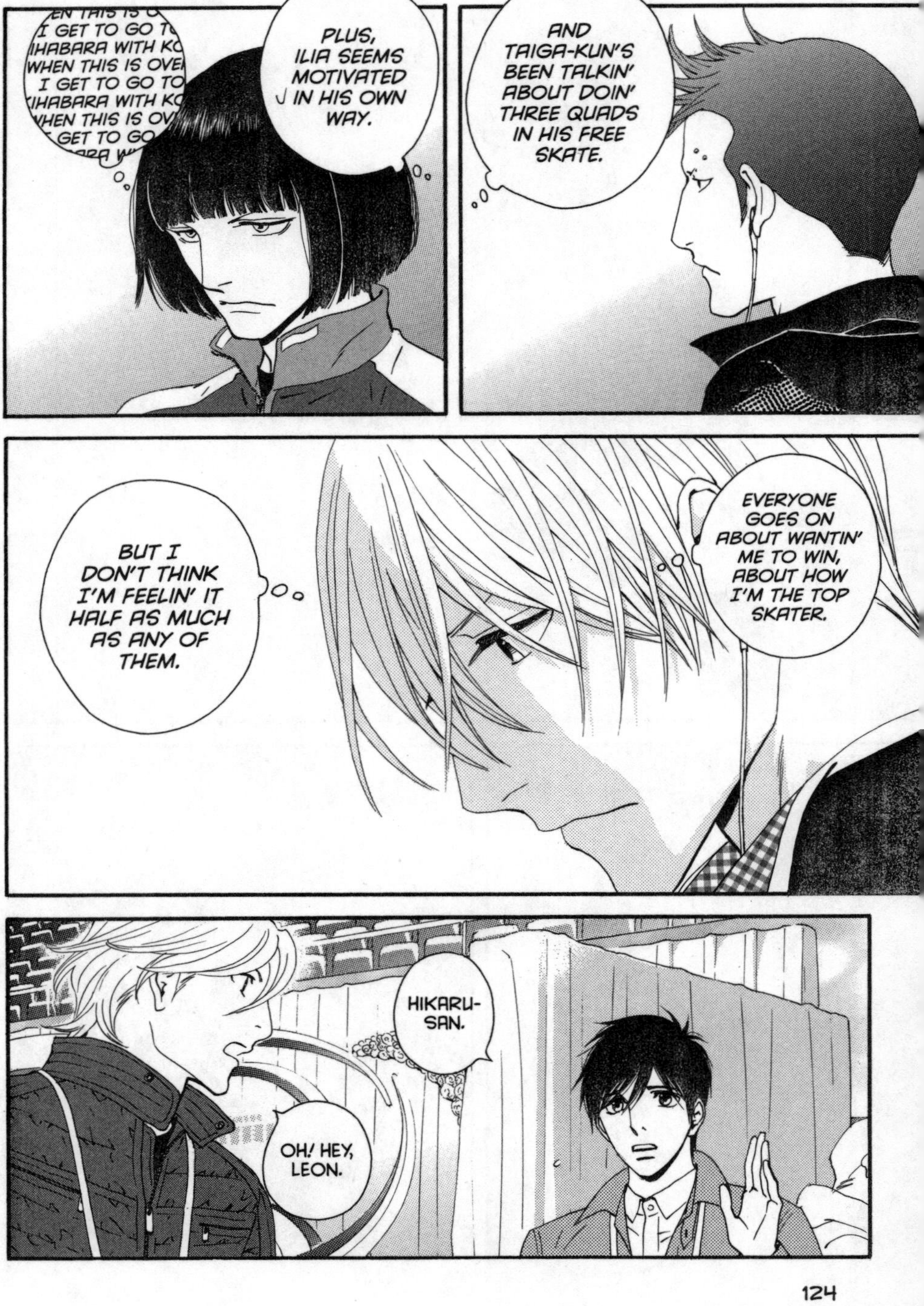
AND TAIGA-KUN'S BEEN TALKIN' ABOUT DOIN' THREE QUADS IN HIS FREE SKATE.
PLUS, ILIA SEEMS MOTIVATED IN HIS OWN WAY.
EN THIS IS O I GET TO GO T IHABARA WITH KO WHEN THIS IS OVE I GET TO GO T IHABARA WITH KO WHEN THIS IS OVE I GET TO GO
EVERYONE GOES ON ABOUT WANTIN' ME TO WIN, ABOUT HOW I'M THE TOP SKATER.
BUT I DON'T THINK I'M FEELIN' IT HALF AS MUCH AS ANY OF THEM.
HIKARU-SAN.
OH! HEY, LEON.

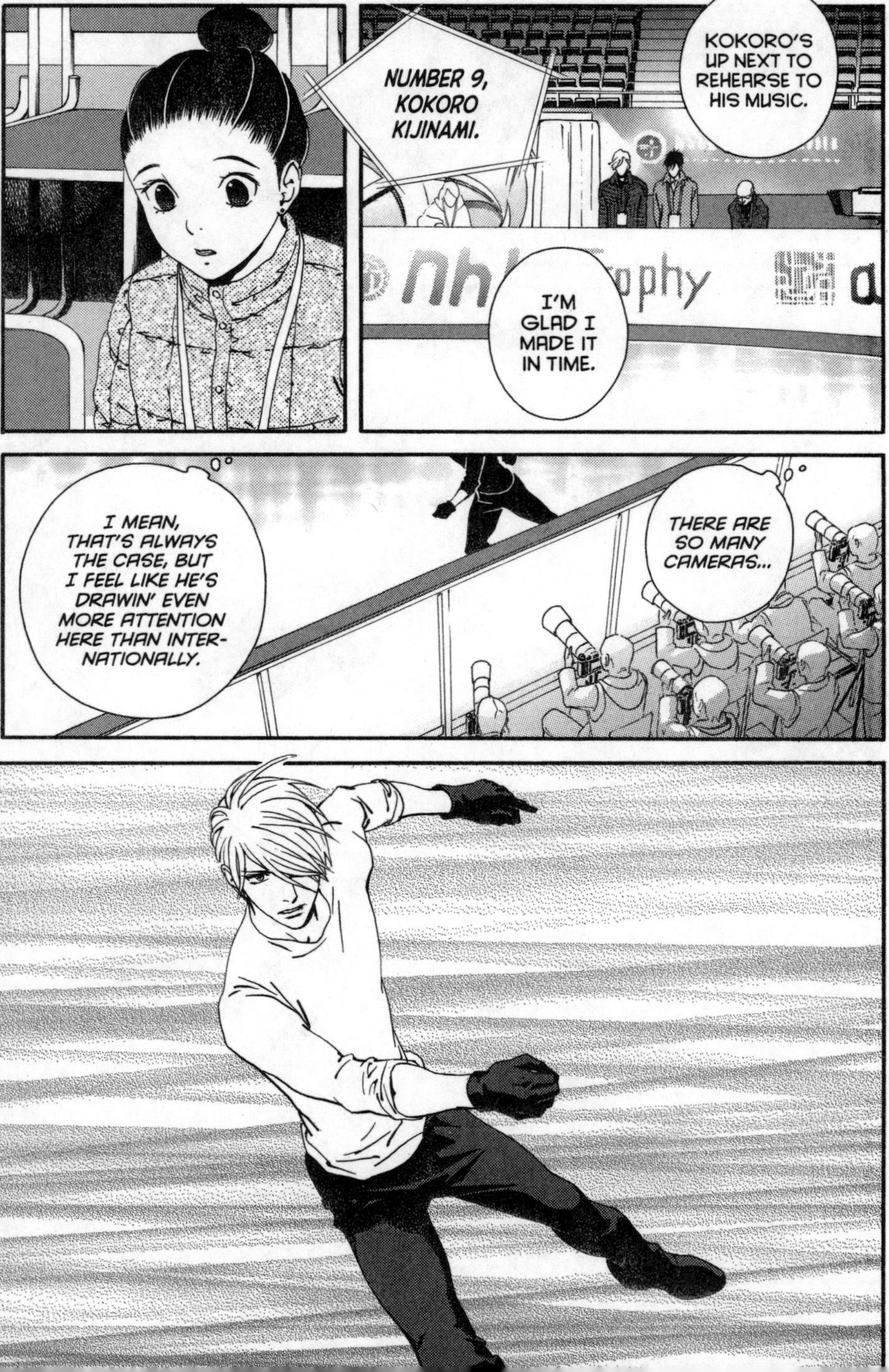
KOKORO'S UP NEXT TO REHEARSE TO HIS MUSIC.
NUMBER 9, KOKORO KIJINAMI.
I'M GLAD I MADE IT IN TIME.
THERE ARE SO MANY CAMERAS...
I MEAN, THAT'S ALWAYS THE CASE, BUT I FEEL LIKE HE'S DRAWIN' EVEN MORE ATTENTION HERE THAN INTER-NATIONALLY.

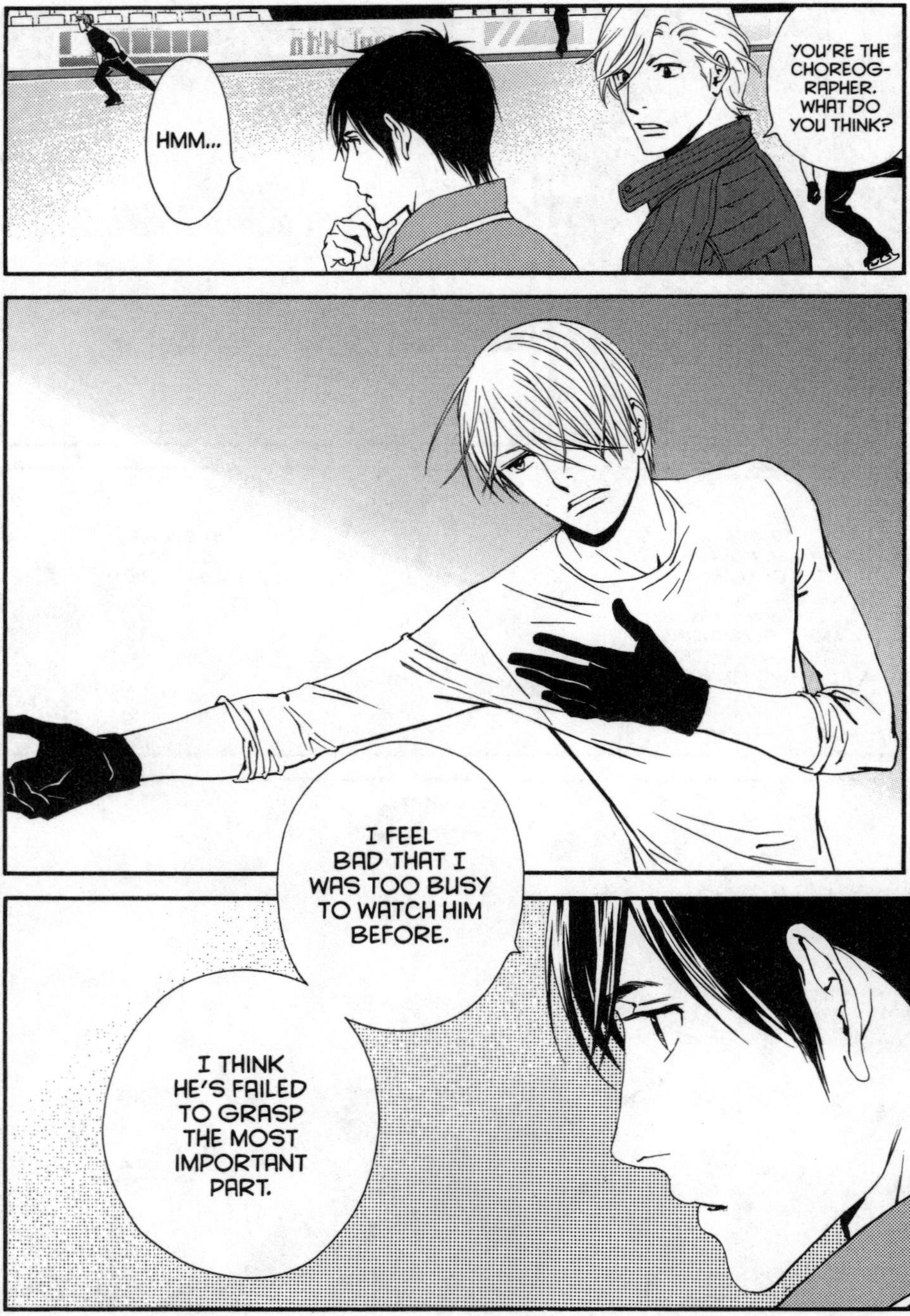
YOU'RE THE CHOREOG-RAPHER. WHAT DO YOU THINK?
HMM...
I FEEL BAD THAT I WAS TOO BUSY TO WATCH HIM BEFORE.
I THINK HE'S FAILED TO GRASP THE MOST IMPORTANT PART.

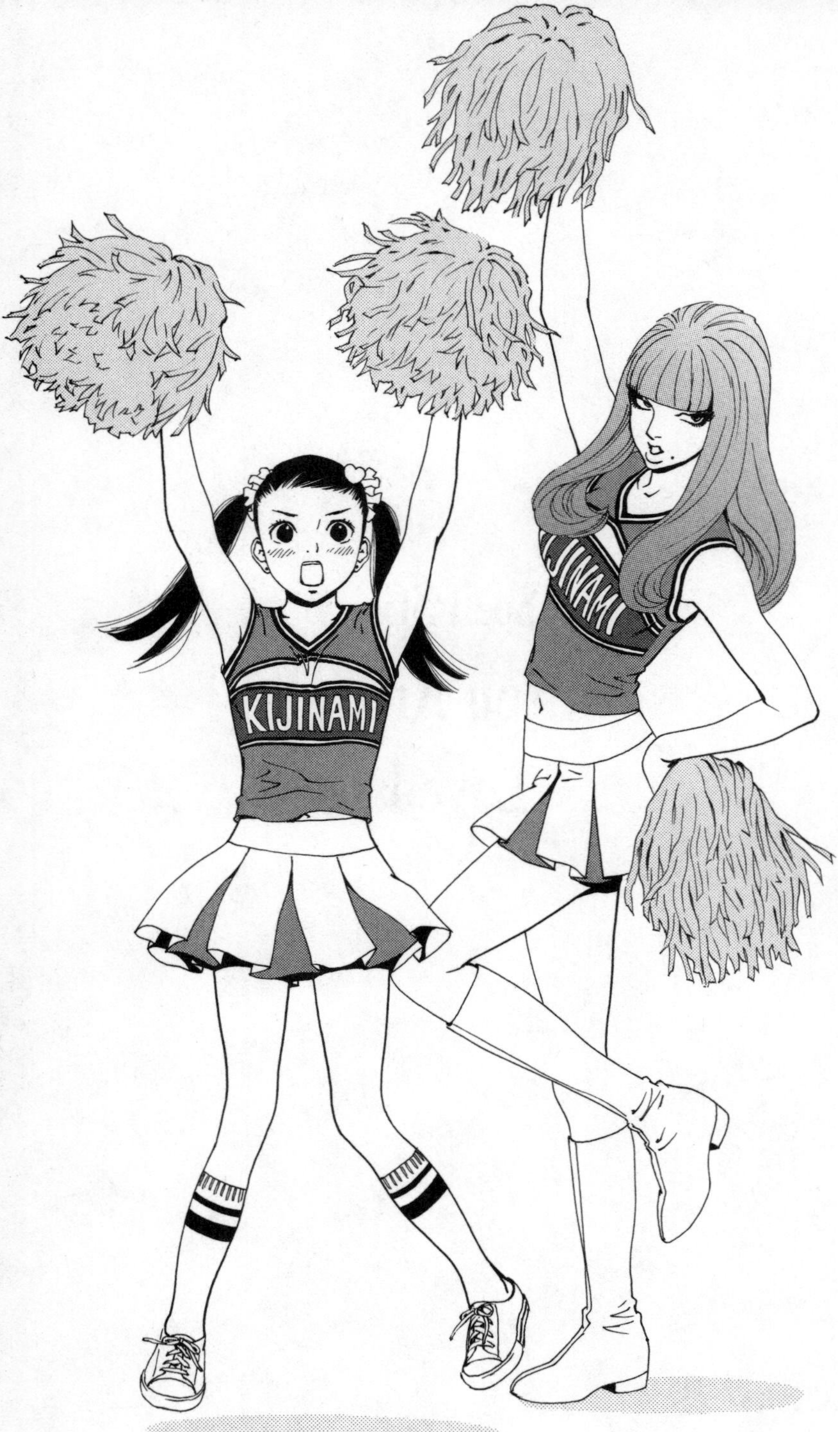
KIJINAMI
KIJINAMI

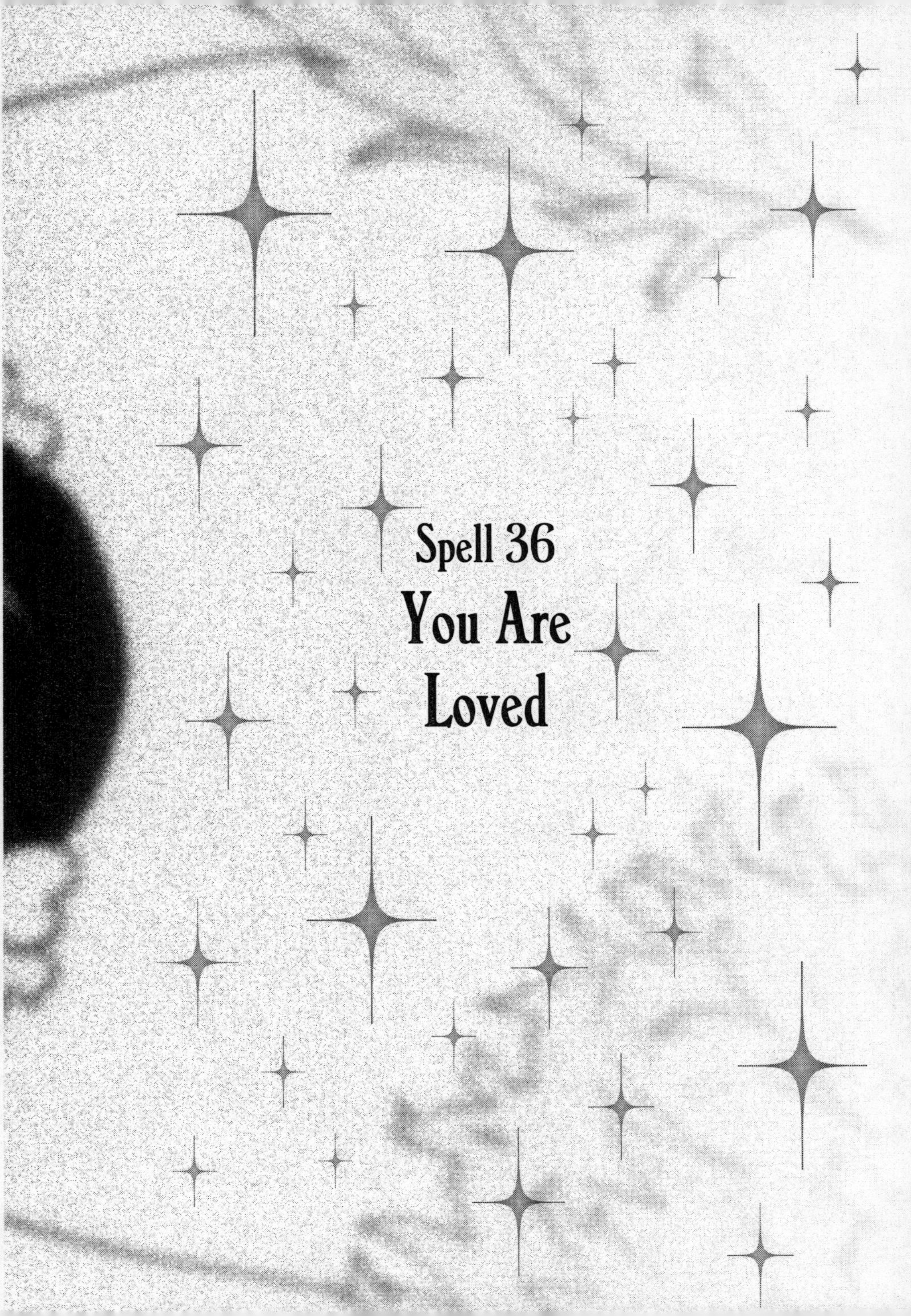

Spell 36
You Are Loved

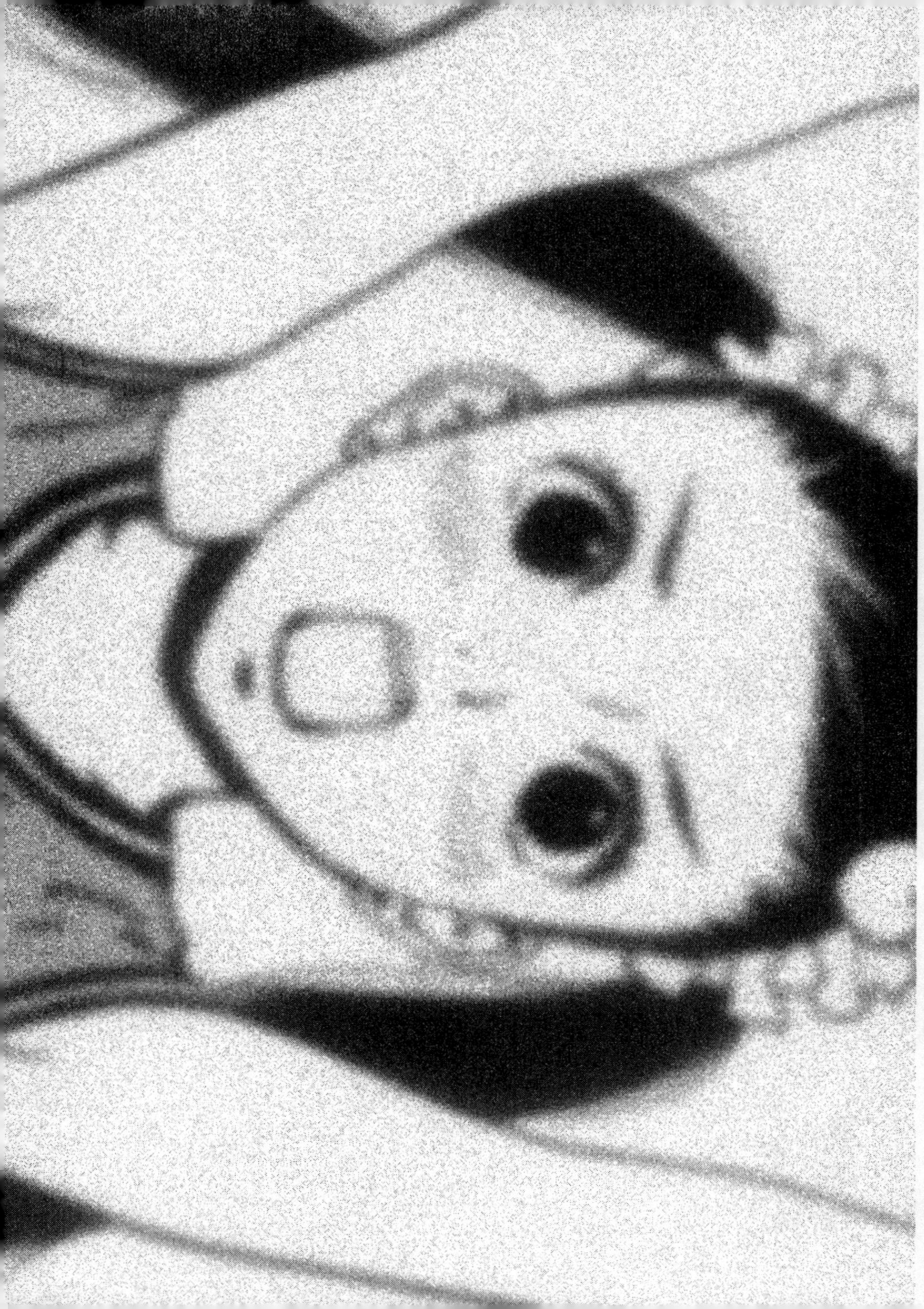

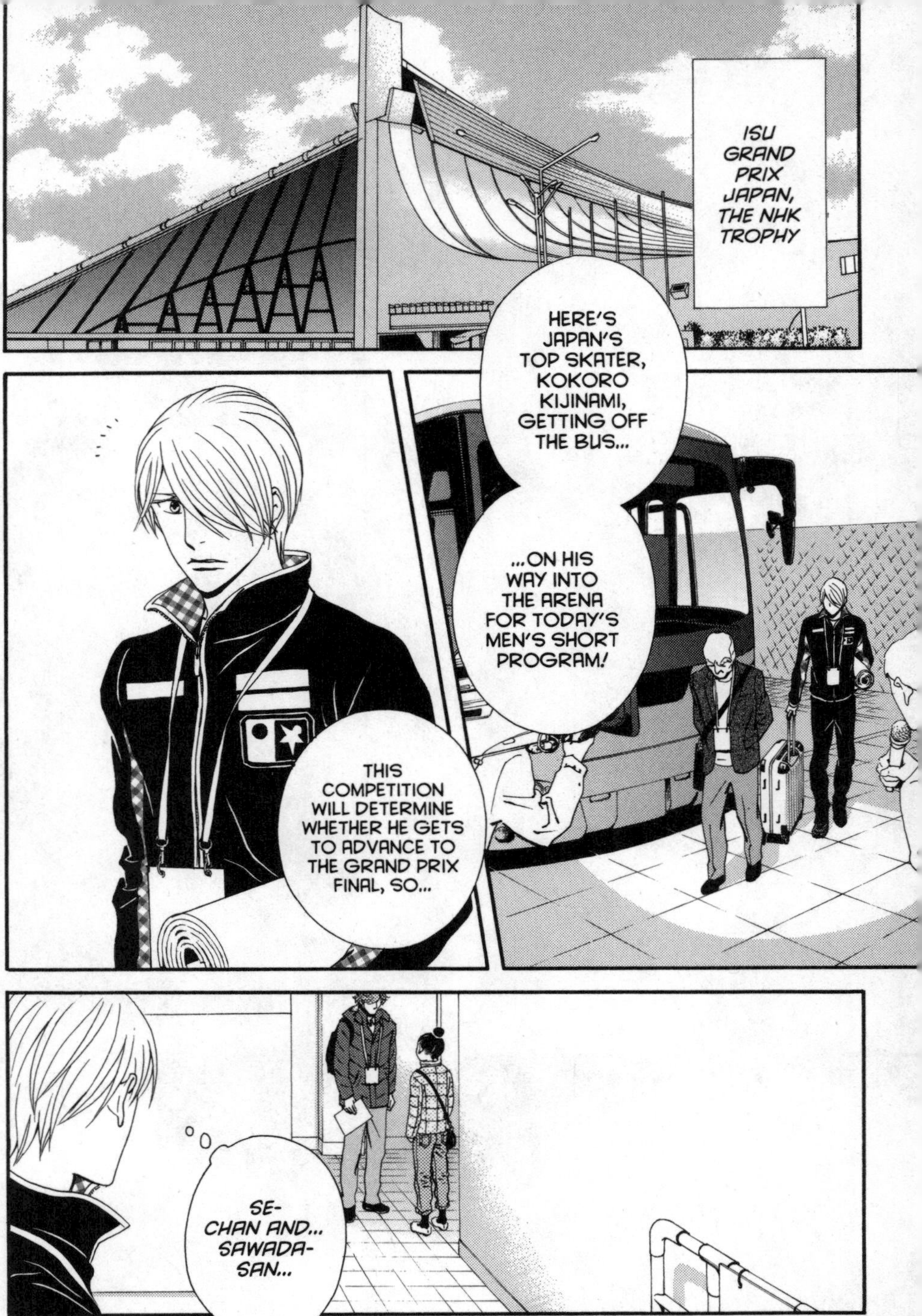
ISU GRAND PRIX JAPAN, THE NHK TROPHY
HERE'S JAPAN'S TOP SKATER, KOKORO KIJINAMI, GETTING OFF THE BUS...
...ON HIS WAY INTO THE ARENA FOR TODAY'S MEN'S SHORT PROGRAM!
THIS COMPETITION WILL DETERMINE WHETHER HE GETS TO ADVANCE TO THE GRAND PRIX FINAL, SO...
SE-CHAN AND... SAWADA-SAN...

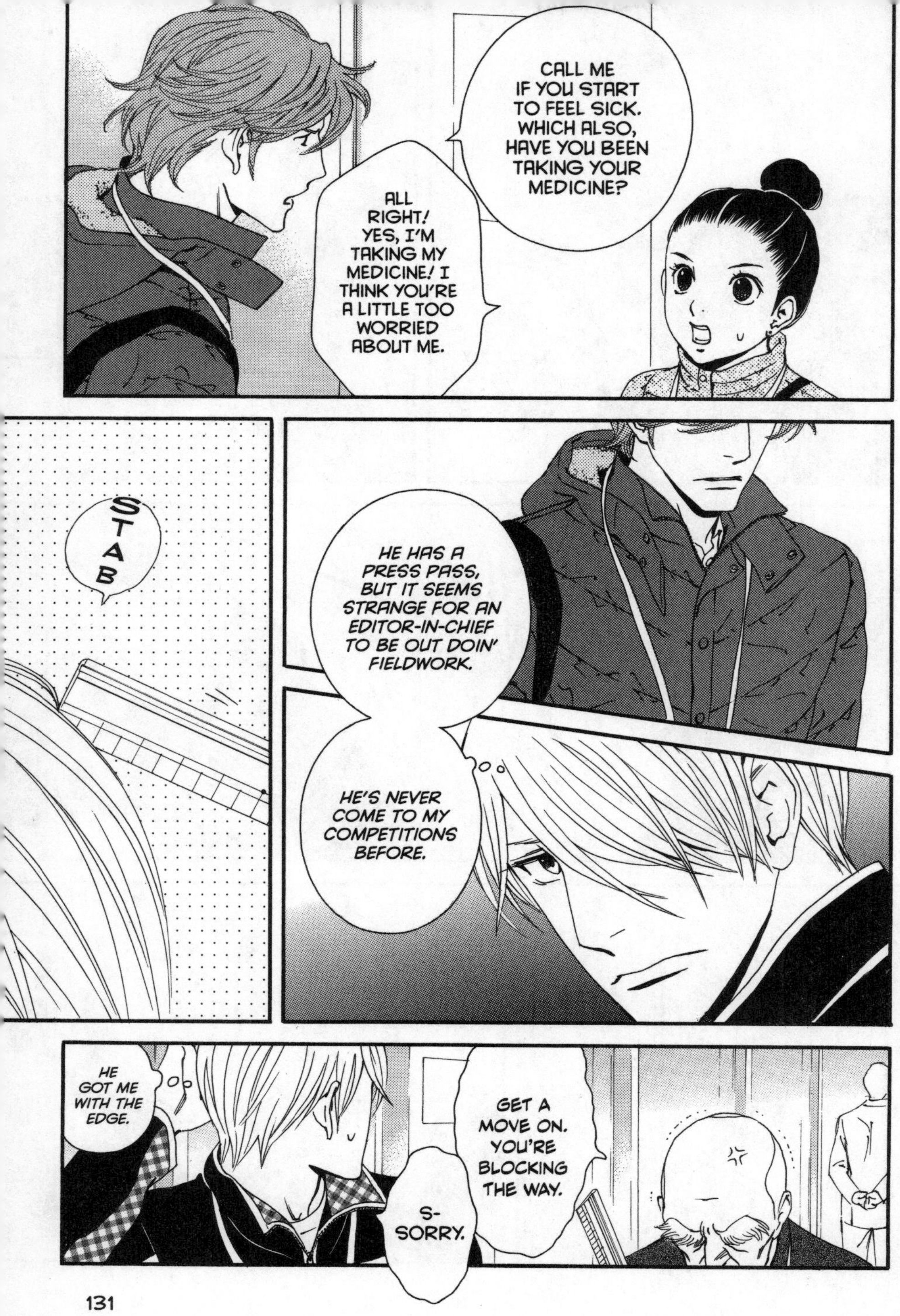
CALL ME IF YOU START TO FEEL SICK. WHICH ALSO, HAVE YOU BEEN TAKING YOUR MEDICINE?
ALL RIGHT! YES, I'M TAKING MY MEDICINE! I THINK YOU'RE A LITTLE TOO WORRIED ABOUT ME.
HE HAS A PRESS PASS, BUT IT SEEMS STRANGE FOR AN EDITOR-IN-CHIEF TO BE OUT DOIN' FIELDWORK.
HE'S NEVER COME TO MY COMPETITIONS BEFORE.
STAB
GET A MOVE ON. YOU'RE BLOCKING THE WAY.
HE GOT ME WITH THE EDGE.
S-SORRY.

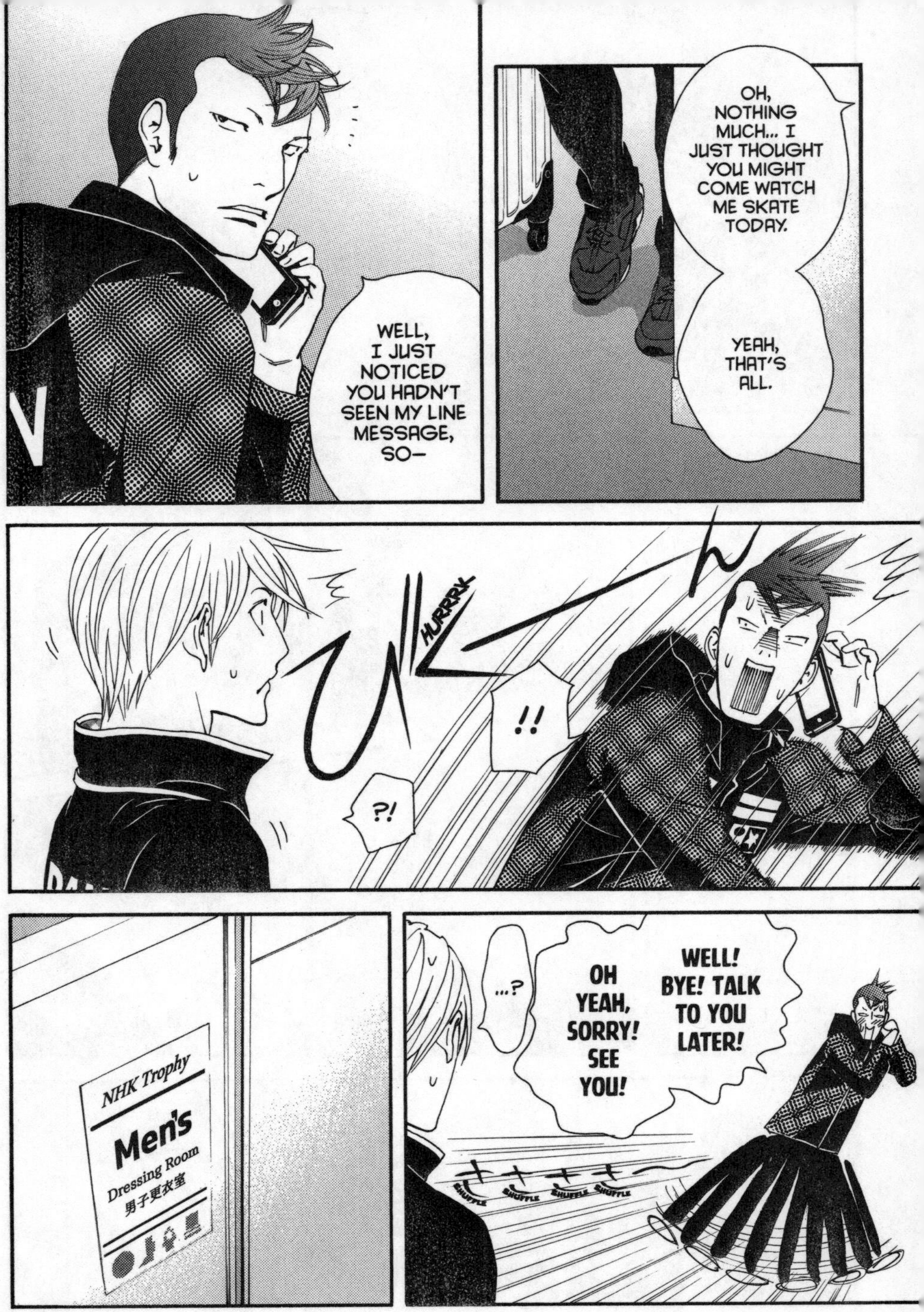
OH, NOTHING MUCH... I JUST THOUGHT YOU MIGHT COME WATCH ME SKATE TODAY.
YEAH, THAT'S ALL.
WELL, I JUST NOTICED YOU HADN'T SEEN MY LINE MESSAGE, SO—
HURRRK
!!
?!
WELL! BYE! TALK TO YOU LATER!
OH YEAH, SORRY! SEE YOU!
...?
SHUFFLE
SHUFFLE
SHUFFLE
SHUFFLE
NHK Trophy
Men's
Dressing Room
男子更衣室

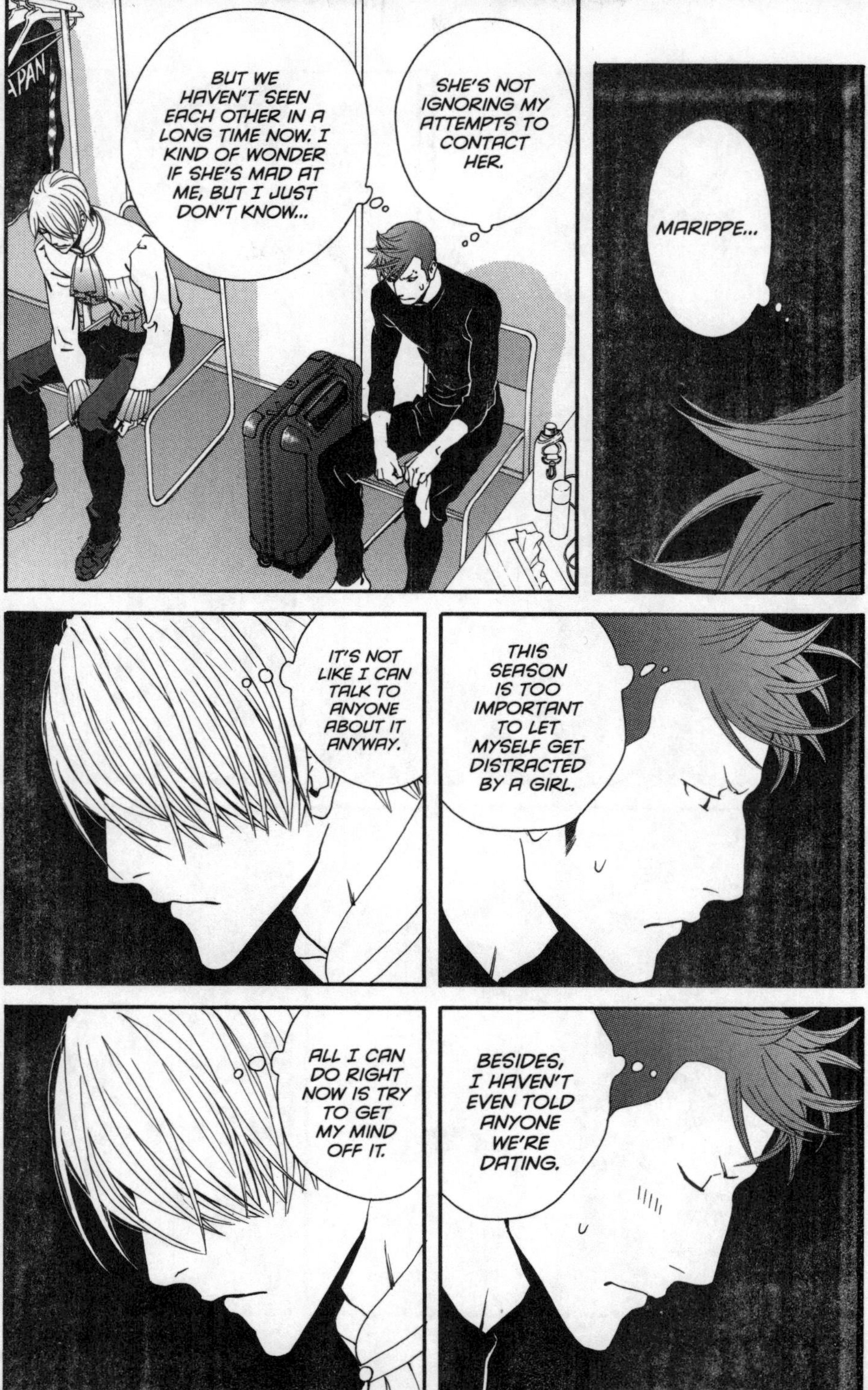
MARIPPE...
SHE'S NOT IGNORING MY ATTEMPTS TO CONTACT HER.
BUT WE HAVEN'T SEEN EACH OTHER IN A LONG TIME NOW. I KIND OF WONDER IF SHE'S MAD AT ME, BUT I JUST DON'T KNOW...
THIS SEASON IS TOO IMPORTANT TO LET MYSELF GET DISTRACTED BY A GIRL.
IT'S NOT LIKE I CAN TALK TO ANYONE ABOUT IT ANYWAY.
BESIDES, I HAVEN'T EVEN TOLD ANYONE WE'RE DATING.
ALL I CAN DO RIGHT NOW IS TRY TO GET MY MIND OFF IT.

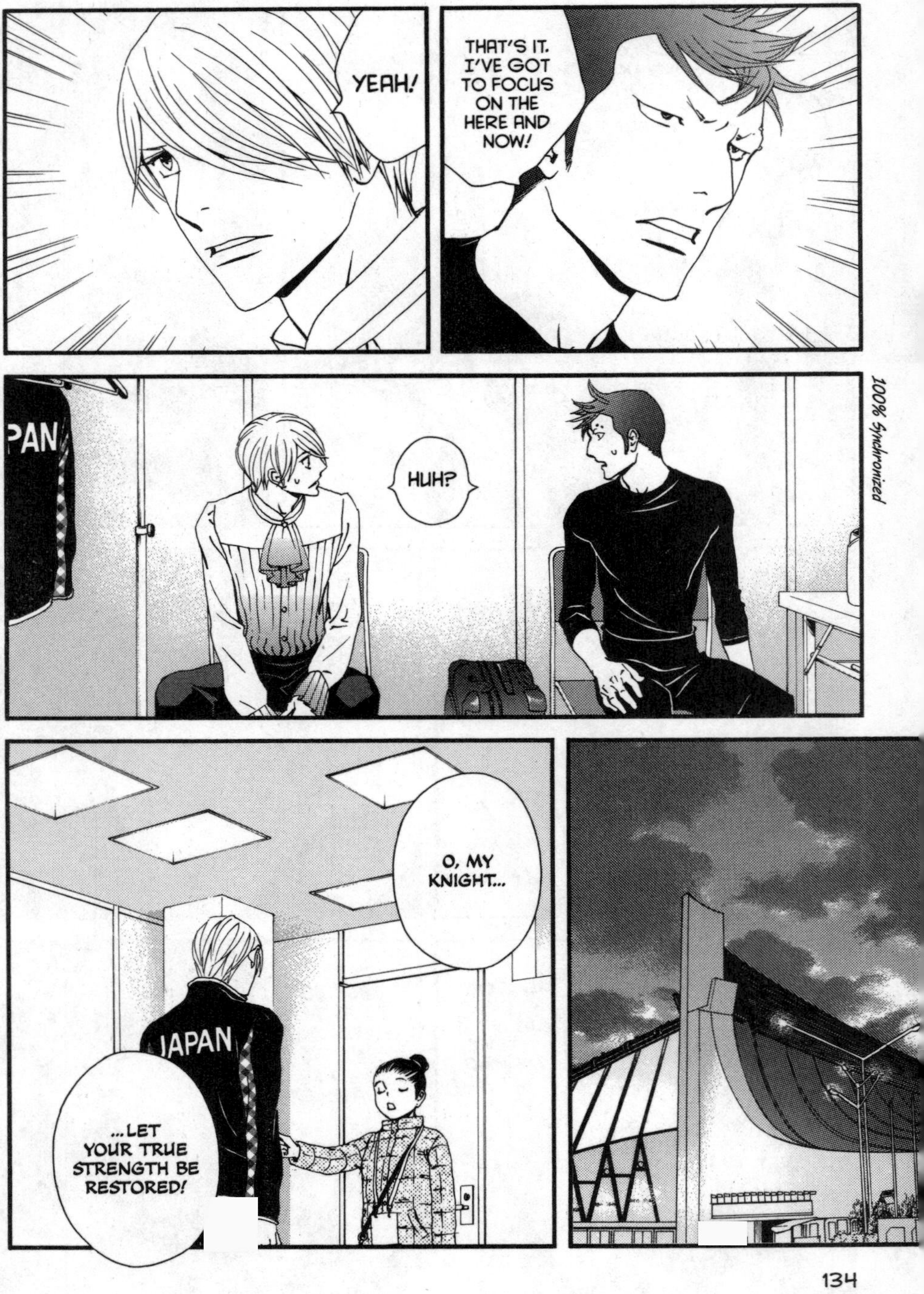
THAT'S IT. I'VE GOT TO FOCUS ON THE HERE AND NOW!
YEAH!
HUH?
100% Synchronized
O, MY KNIGHT...
...LET YOUR TRUE STRENGTH BE RESTORED!

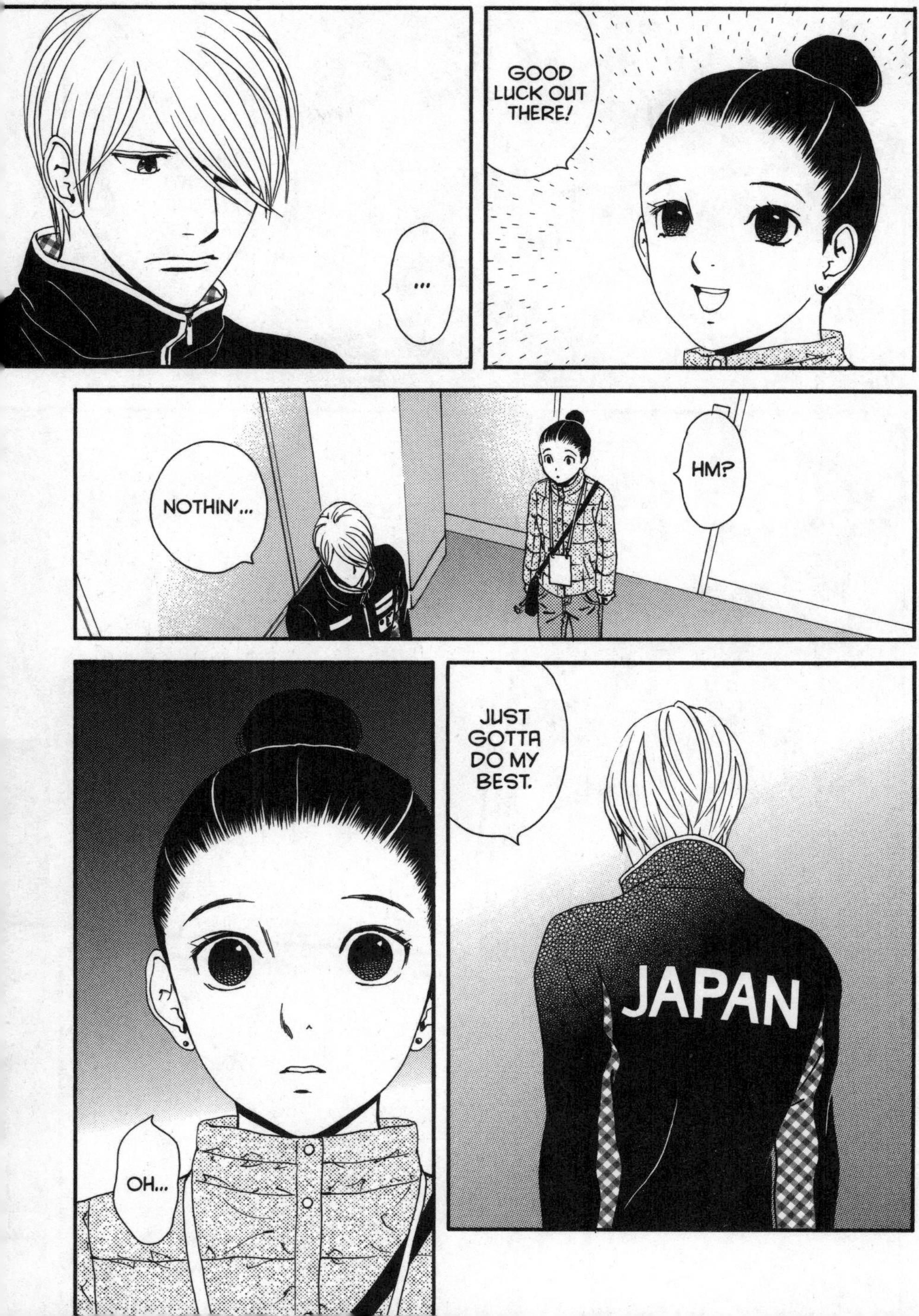
GOOD LUCK OUT THERE!
...
HM?
NOTHIN'...
JUST GOTTA DO MY BEST.
JAPAN
OH...

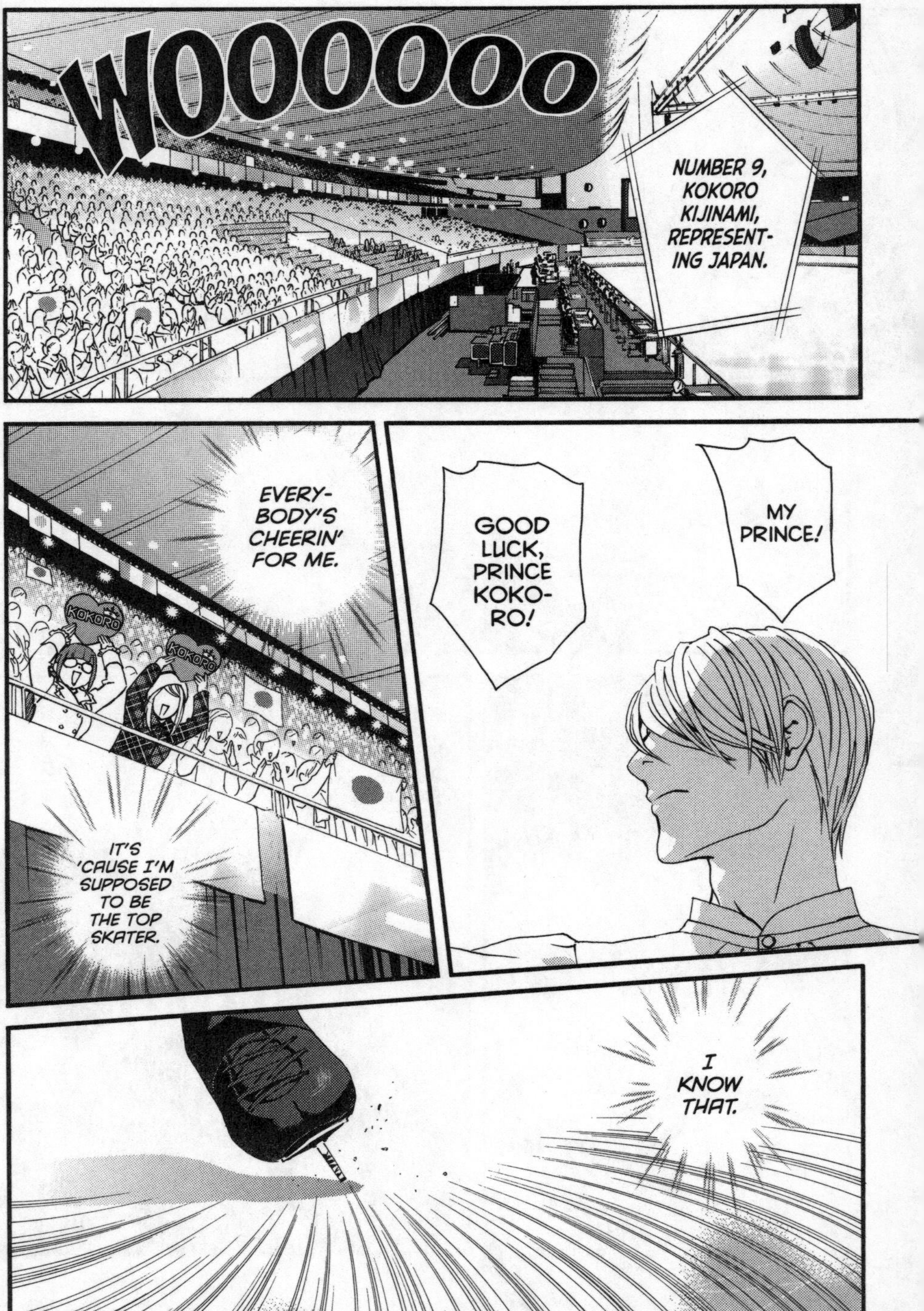
WOOOOOO
NUMBER 9, KOKORO KIJINAMI, REPRESENT-ING JAPAN.
MY PRINCE!
GOOD LUCK, PRINCE KOKO-RO!
EVERY-BODY'S CHEERIN' FOR ME.
KOKORO
KOKORO
IT'S 'CAUSE I'M SUPPOSED TO BE THE TOP SKATER.
I KNOW THAT.

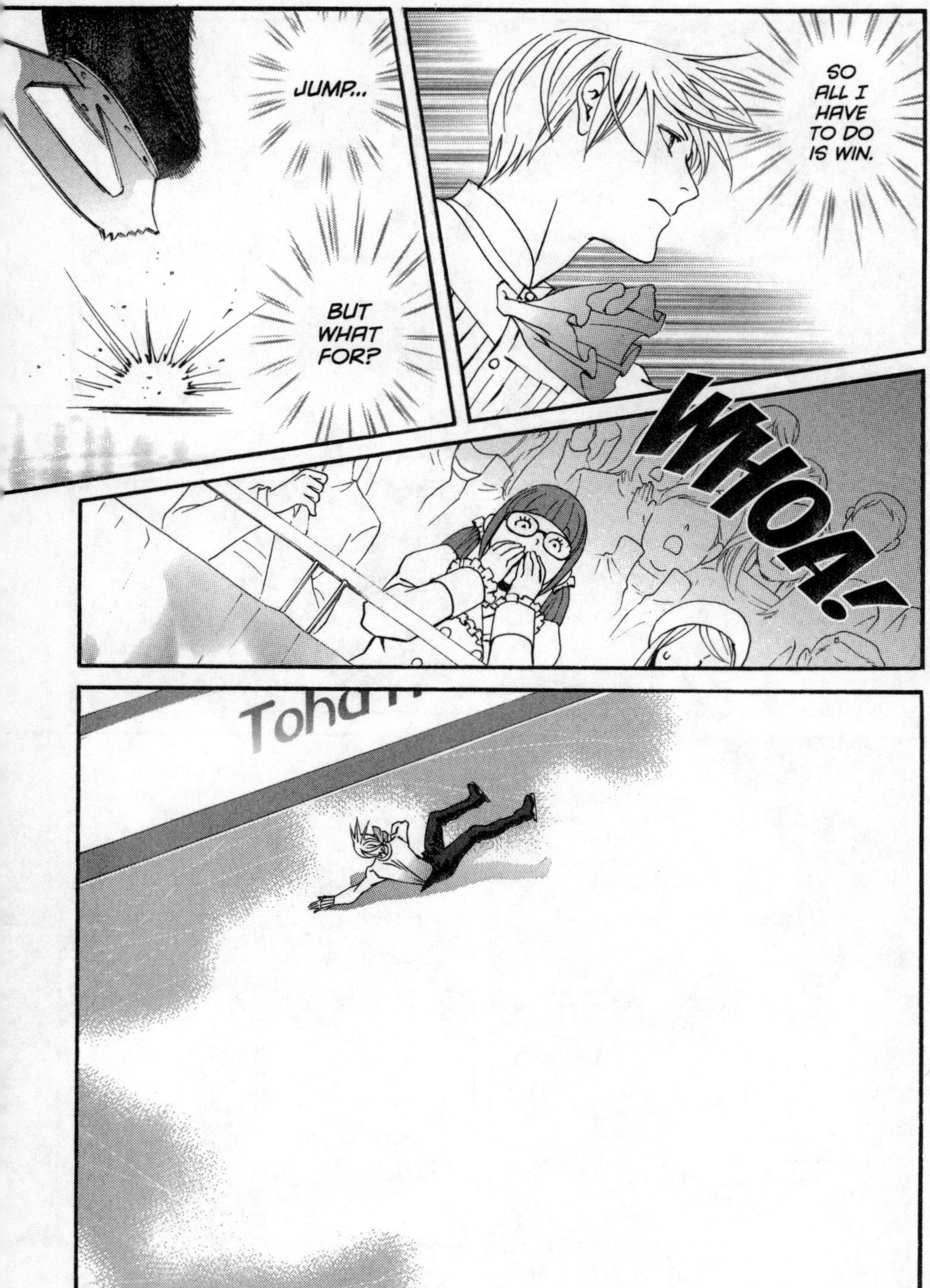
SO ALL I HAVE TO DO IS WIN.
JUMP...
BUT WHAT FOR?
WHOA!
Toha

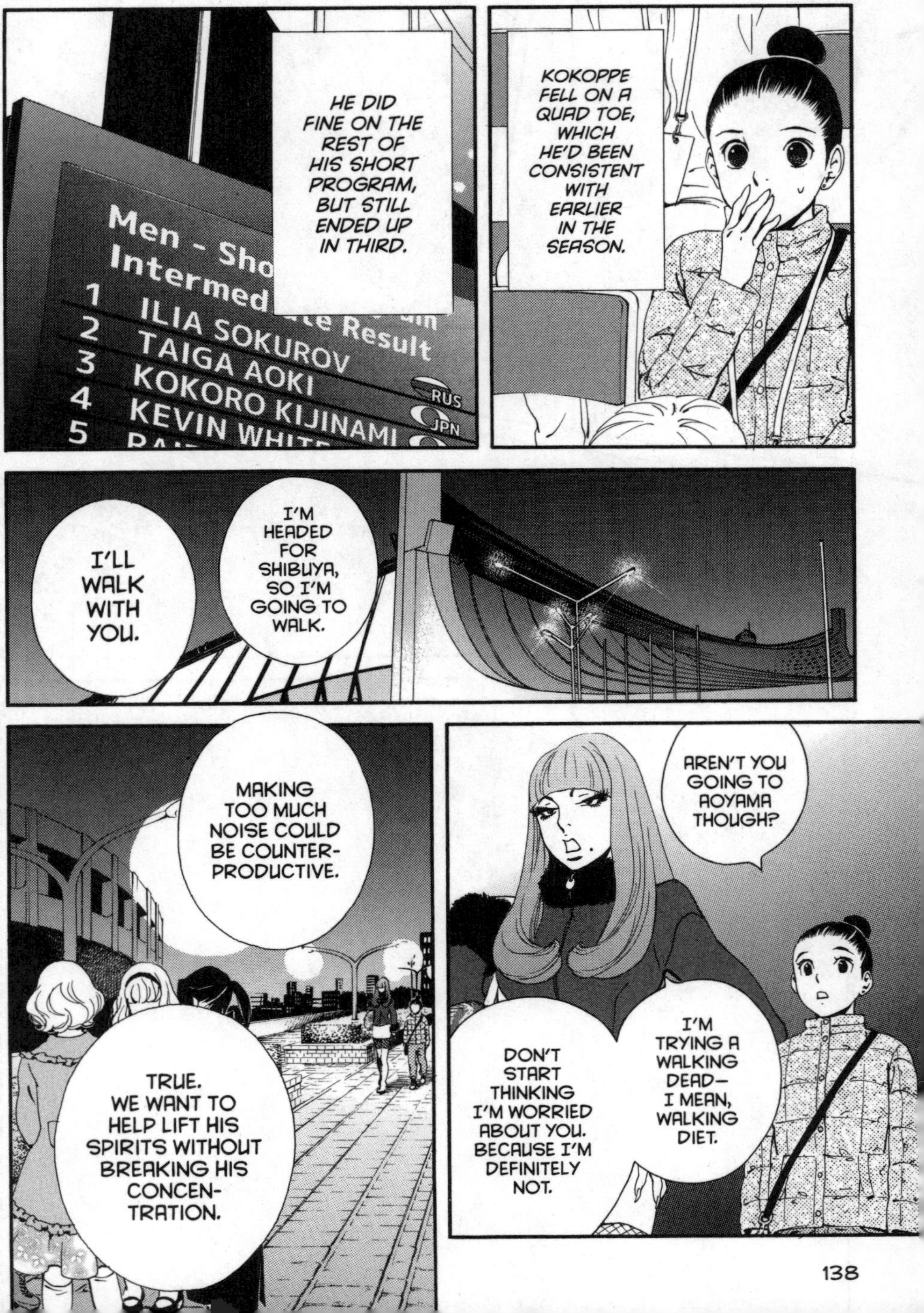
KOKOPPE FELL ON A QUAD TOE, WHICH HE'D BEEN CONSISTENT WITH EARLIER IN THE SEASON.
HE DID FINE ON THE REST OF HIS SHORT PROGRAM, BUT STILL ENDED UP IN THIRD.
1 ILIA SOKUROV
2 TAIGA AOKI
3 KOKORO KIJINAMI
RUS
JPN
I'M HEADED FOR SHIBUYA, SO I'M GOING TO WALK.
I'LL WALK WITH YOU.
AREN'T YOU GOING TO AOYAMA THOUGH?
I'M TRYING A WALKING DEAD— I MEAN, WALKING DIET.
DON'T START THINKING I'M WORRIED ABOUT YOU. BECAUSE I'M DEFINITELY NOT.
MAKING TOO MUCH NOISE COULD BE COUNTER-PRODUCTIVE.
TRUE. WE WANT TO HELP LIFT HIS SPIRITS WITHOUT BREAKING HIS CONCEN-TRATION.

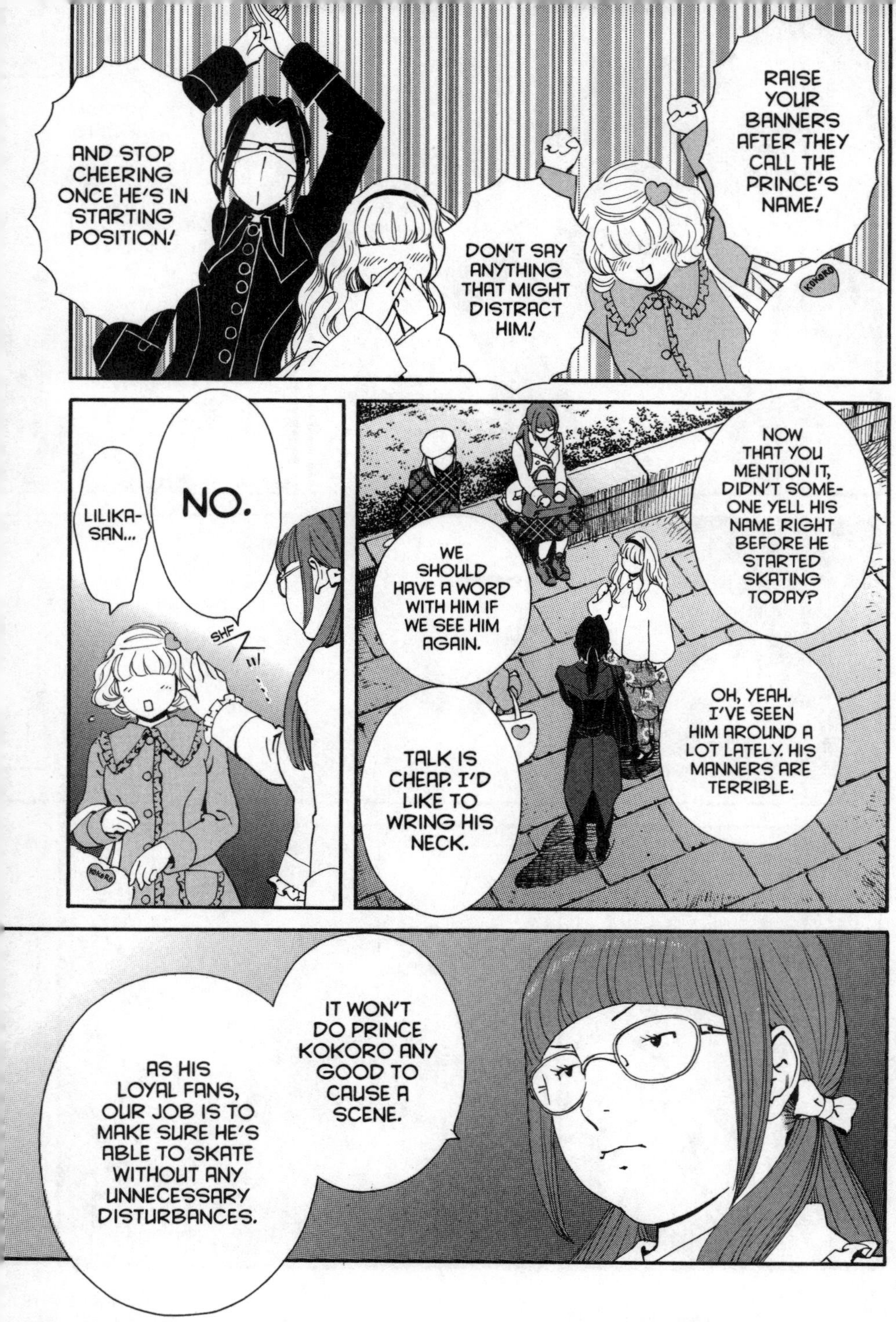
RAISE YOUR BANNERS AFTER THEY CALL THE PRINCE'S NAME!
KOKORO
DON'T SAY ANYTHING THAT MIGHT DISTRACT HIM!
AND STOP CHEERING ONCE HE'S IN STARTING POSITION!
NOW THAT YOU MENTION IT, DIDN'T SOME-ONE YELL HIS NAME RIGHT BEFORE HE STARTED SKATING TODAY?
WE SHOULD HAVE A WORD WITH HIM IF WE SEE HIM AGAIN.
OH, YEAH. I'VE SEEN HIM AROUND A LOT LATELY. HIS MANNERS ARE TERRIBLE.
TALK IS CHEAP. I'D LIKE TO WRING HIS NECK.
NO.
LILIKA-SAN...
SHF
KOKORO
IT WON'T DO PRINCE KOKORO ANY GOOD TO CAUSE A SCENE.
AS HIS LOYAL FANS, OUR JOB IS TO MAKE SURE HE'S ABLE TO SKATE WITHOUT ANY UNNECESSARY DISTURBANCES.

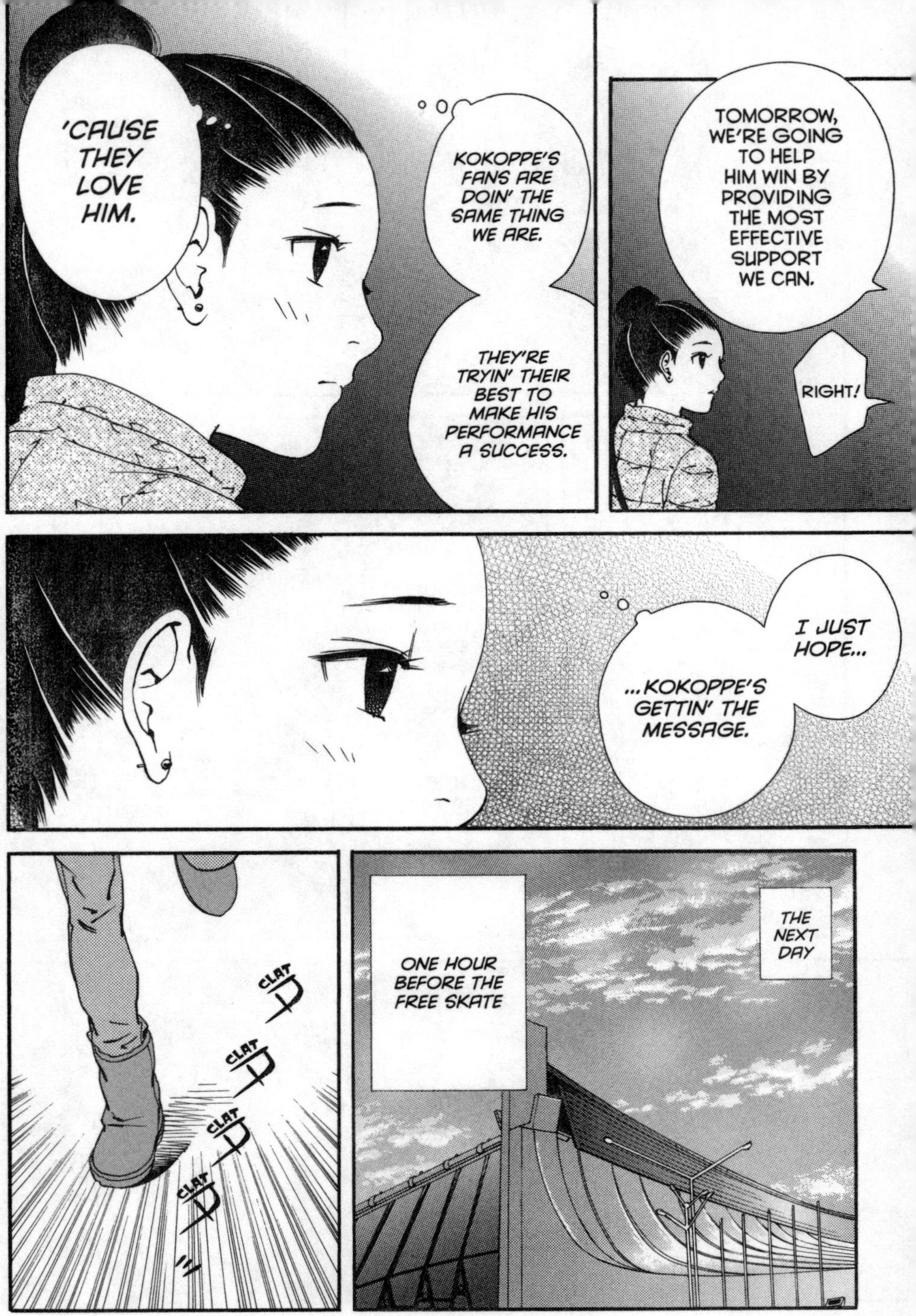
TOMORROW, WE'RE GOING TO HELP HIM WIN BY PROVIDING THE MOST EFFECTIVE SUPPORT WE CAN.
RIGHT!
KOKOPPE'S FANS ARE DOIN' THE SAME THING WE ARE.
THEY'RE TRYIN' THEIR BEST TO MAKE HIS PERFORMANCE A SUCCESS.
'CAUSE THEY LOVE HIM.
I JUST HOPE...
...KOKOPPE'S GETTIN' THE MESSAGE.
THE NEXT DAY
ONE HOUR BEFORE THE FREE SKATE
CLAT
CLAT
CLAT
CLAT

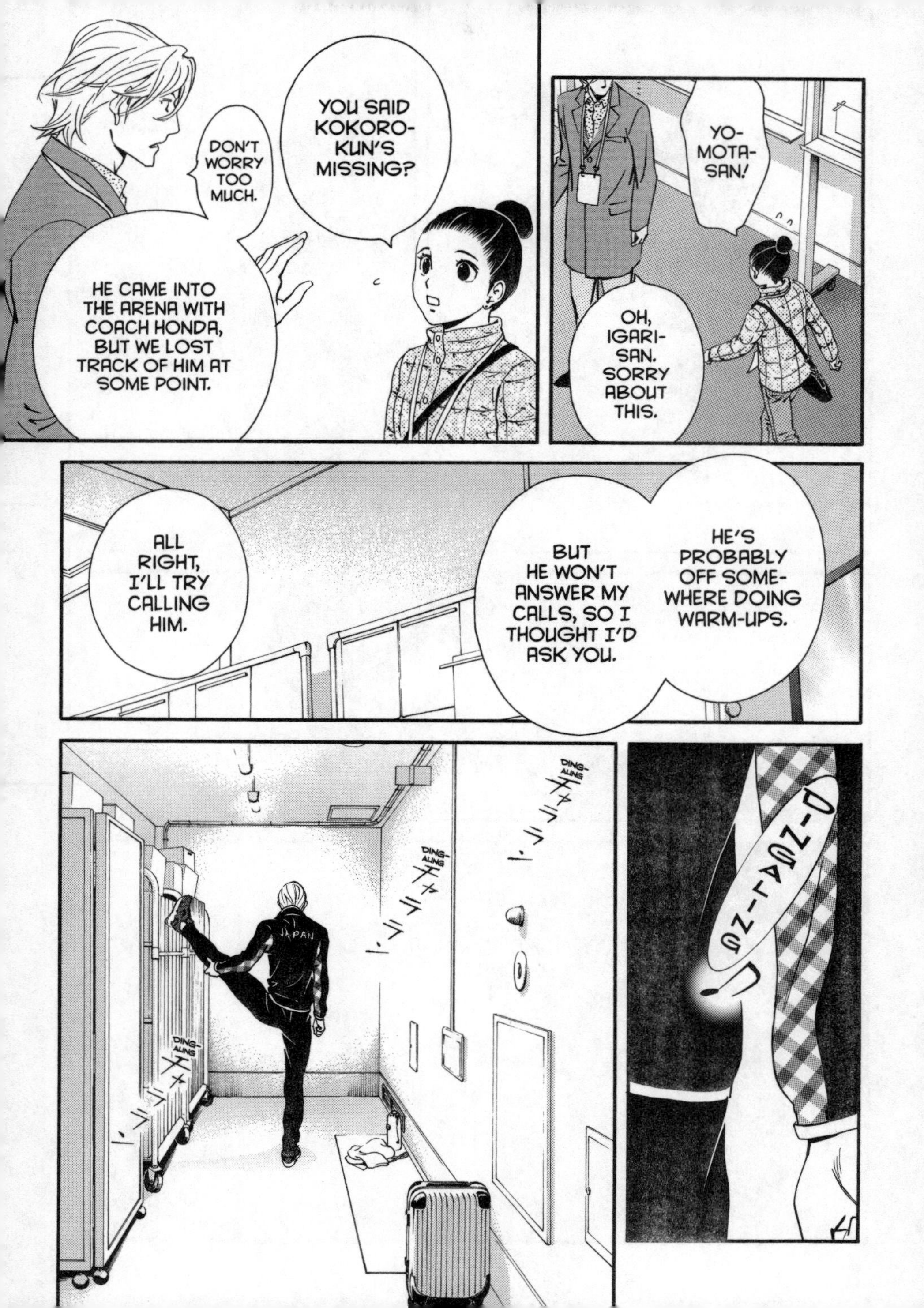
YO-MOTA-SAN!
OH, IGARI-SAN. SORRY ABOUT THIS.
YOU SAID KOKORO-KUN'S MISSING?
DON'T WORRY TOO MUCH.
HE CAME INTO THE ARENA WITH COACH HONDA, BUT WE LOST TRACK OF HIM AT SOME POINT.
HE'S PROBABLY OFF SOME-WHERE DOING WARM-UPS.
BUT HE WON'T ANSWER MY CALLS, SO I THOUGHT I'D ASK YOU.
ALL RIGHT, I'LL TRY CALLING HIM.
D-DING-A-LING
DING-ALING
DING-ALING
DING-ALING

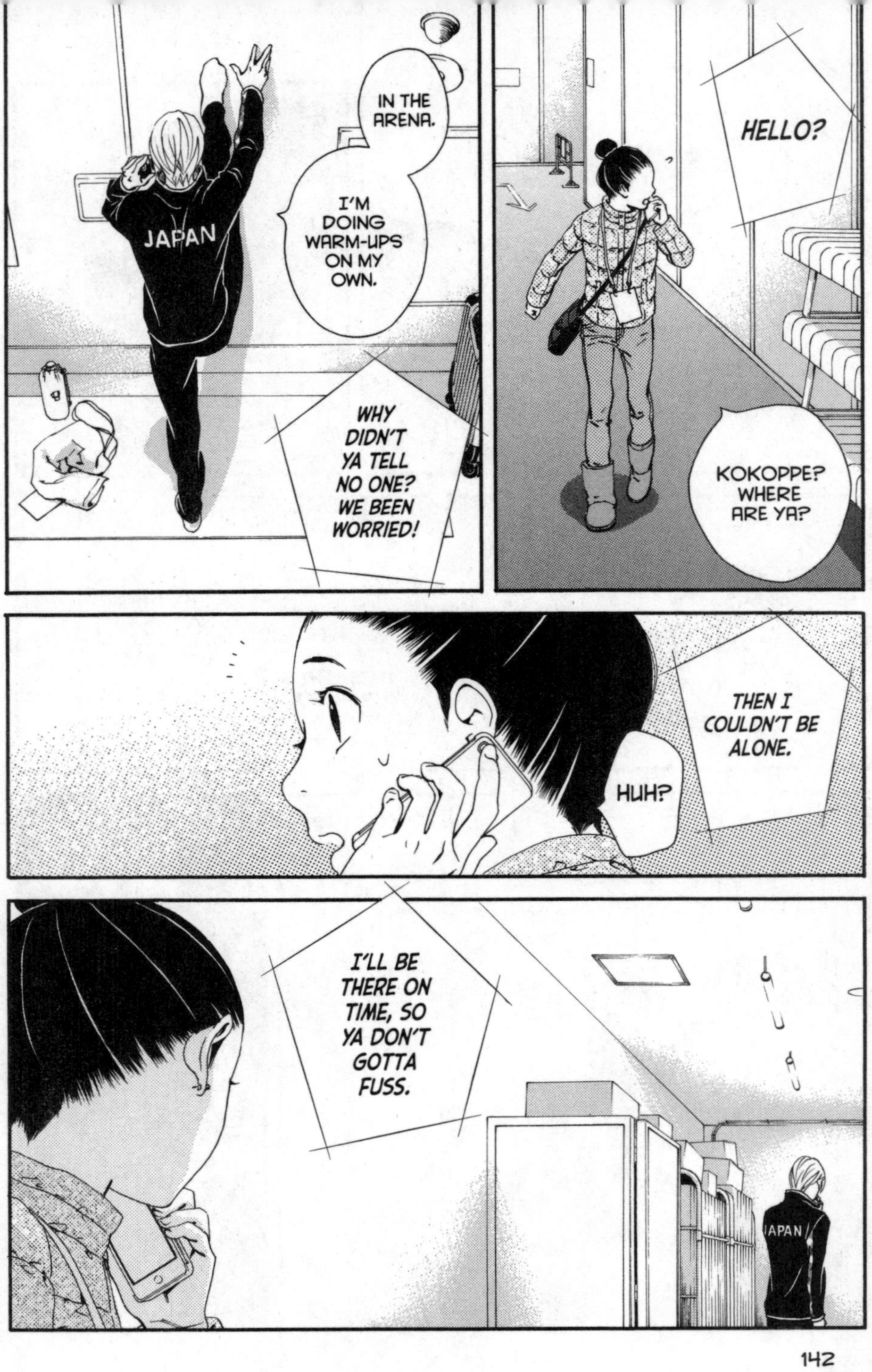
HELLO?
KOKOPPE? WHERE ARE YA?
IN THE ARENA.
I'M DOING WARM-UPS ON MY OWN.
WHY DIDN'T YA TELL NO ONE? WE BEEN WORRIED!
THEN I COULDN'T BE ALONE.
HUH?
I'LL BE THERE ON TIME, SO YA DON'T GOTTA FUSS.
JAPAN

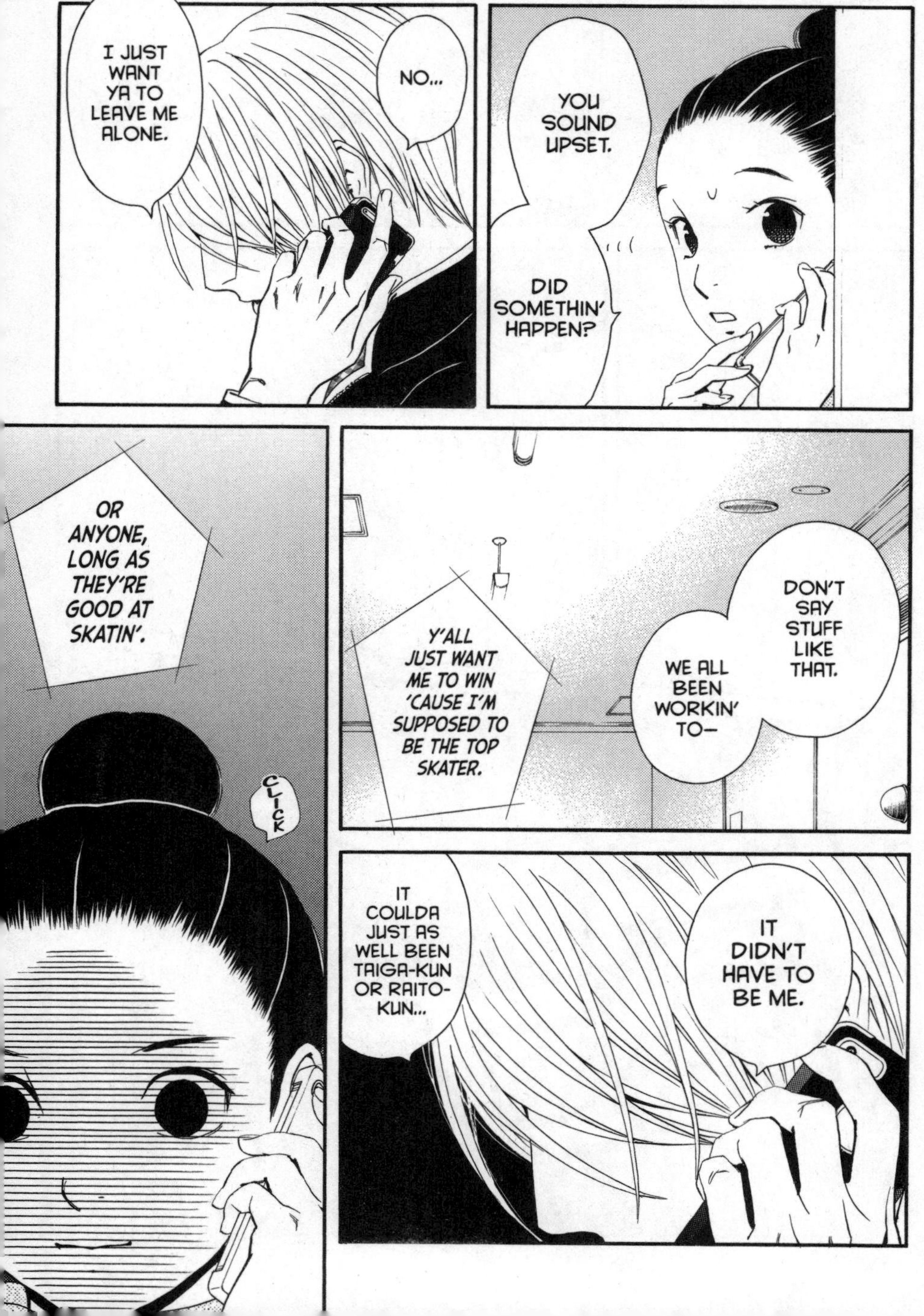
YOU SOUND UPSET.
DID SOMETHIN' HAPPEN?
NO...
I JUST WANT YA TO LEAVE ME ALONE.
DON'T SAY STUFF LIKE THAT.
WE ALL BEEN WORKIN' TO—
Y'ALL JUST WANT ME TO WIN 'CAUSE I'M SUPPOSED TO BE THE TOP SKATER.
IT DIDN'T HAVE TO BE ME.
IT COULDA JUST AS WELL BEEN TAIGA-KUN OR RAITO-KUN...
OR ANYONE, LONG AS THEY'RE GOOD AT SKATIN'.
CLICK

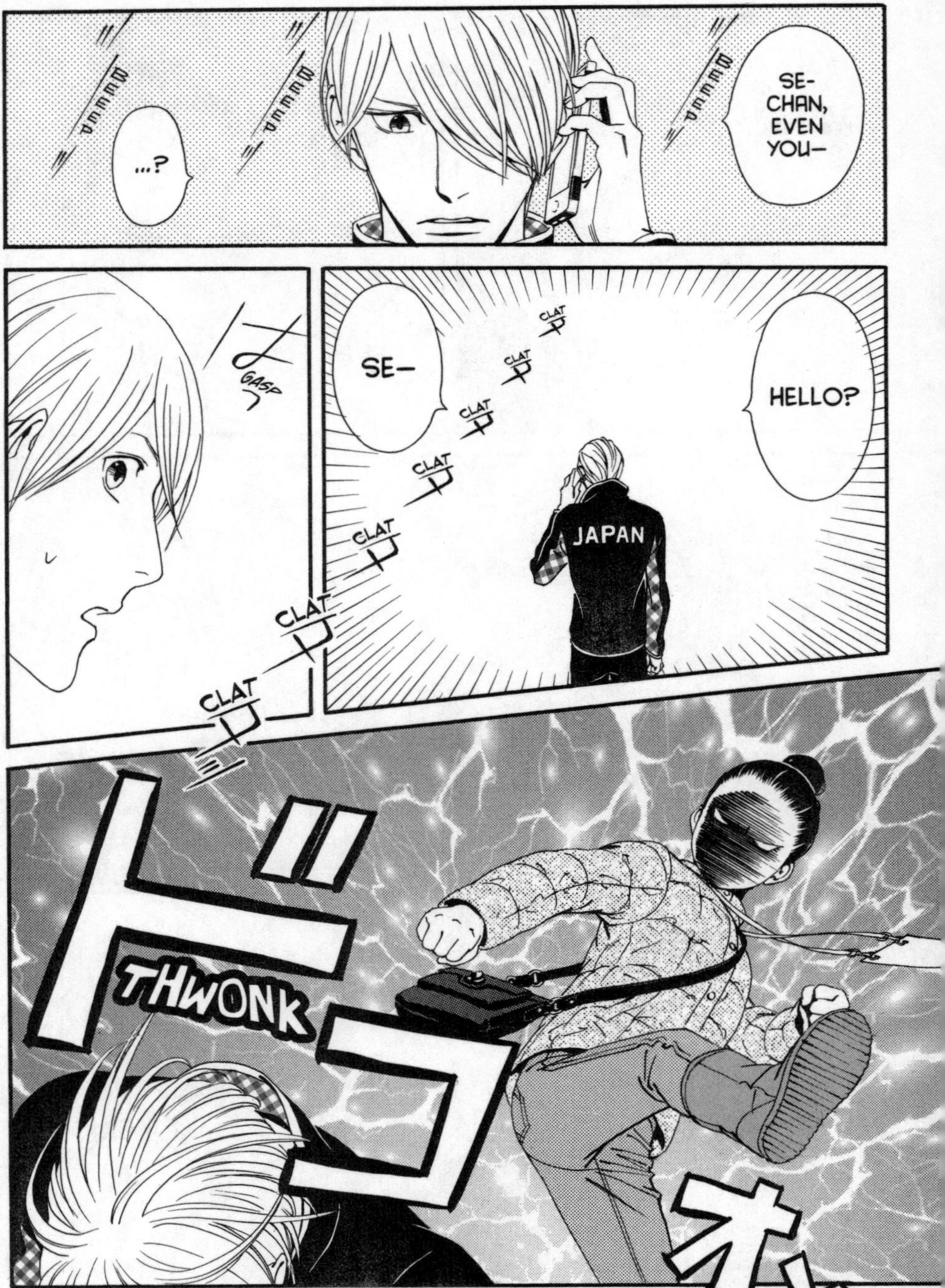
SE-CHAN, EVEN YOU–
BWWWA
BWWWA
...?
BWWWA
HELLO?
SE–
CLAT
CLAT
CLAT
CLAT
CLAT
CLAT
CLAT
GASP
THWONK

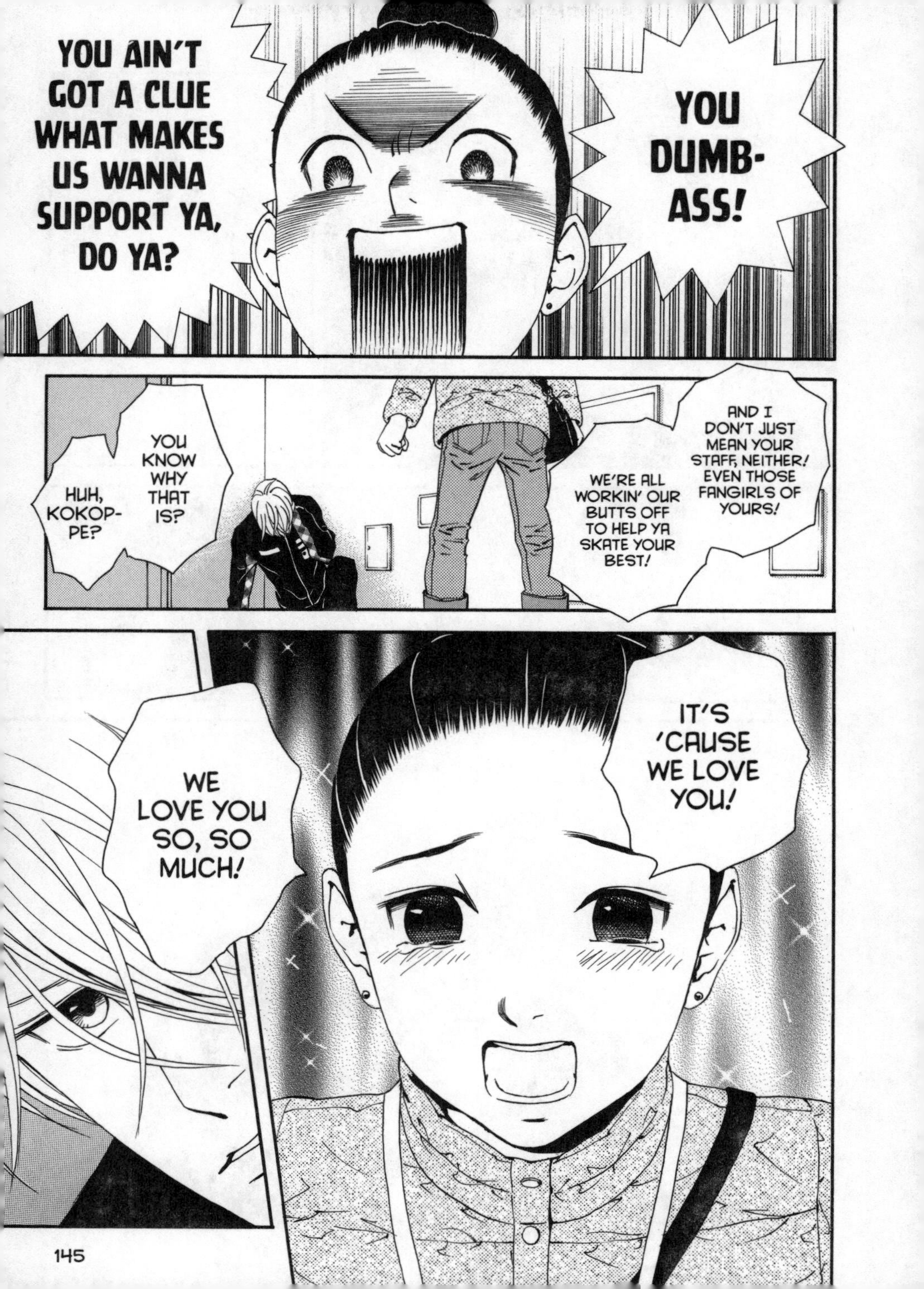
YOU DUMB-ASS!
YOU AIN'T GOT A CLUE WHAT MAKES US WANNA SUPPORT YA, DO YA?
AND I DON'T JUST MEAN YOUR STAFF, NEITHER! EVEN THOSE FANGIRLS OF YOURS!
WE'RE ALL WORKIN' OUR BUTTS OFF TO HELP YA SKATE YOUR BEST!
YOU KNOW WHY THAT IS?
HUH, KOKOP-PE?
IT'S 'CAUSE WE LOVE YOU!
WE LOVE YOU SO, SO MUCH!

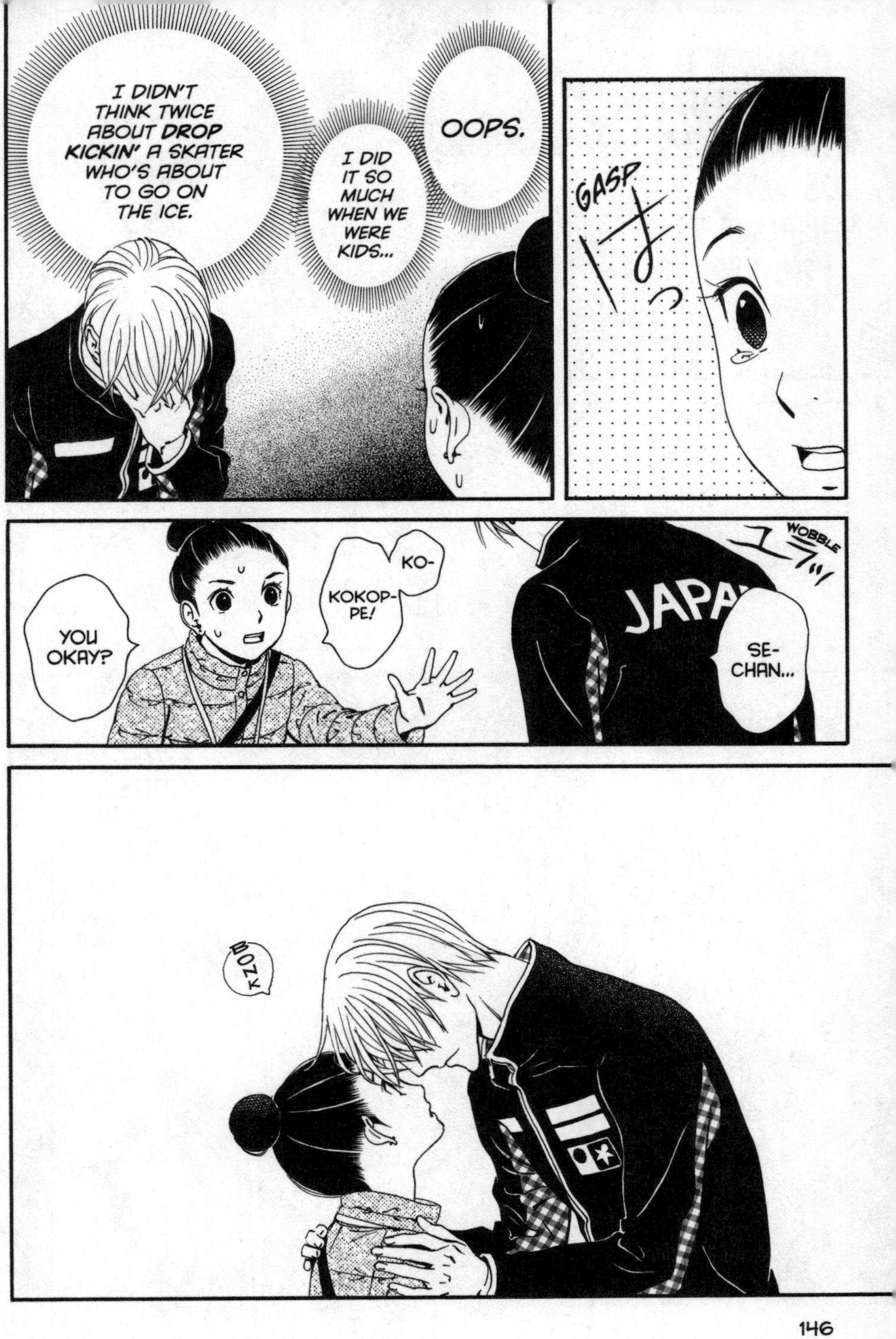
GASP
OOPS.
I DID IT SO MUCH WHEN WE WERE KIDS...
I DIDN'T THINK TWICE ABOUT **DROP KICKIN'** A SKATER WHO'S ABOUT TO GO ON THE ICE.
WOBBLE
JAPA
SE-CHAN...
KO- KOKOPPE!
YOU OKAY?
BONK

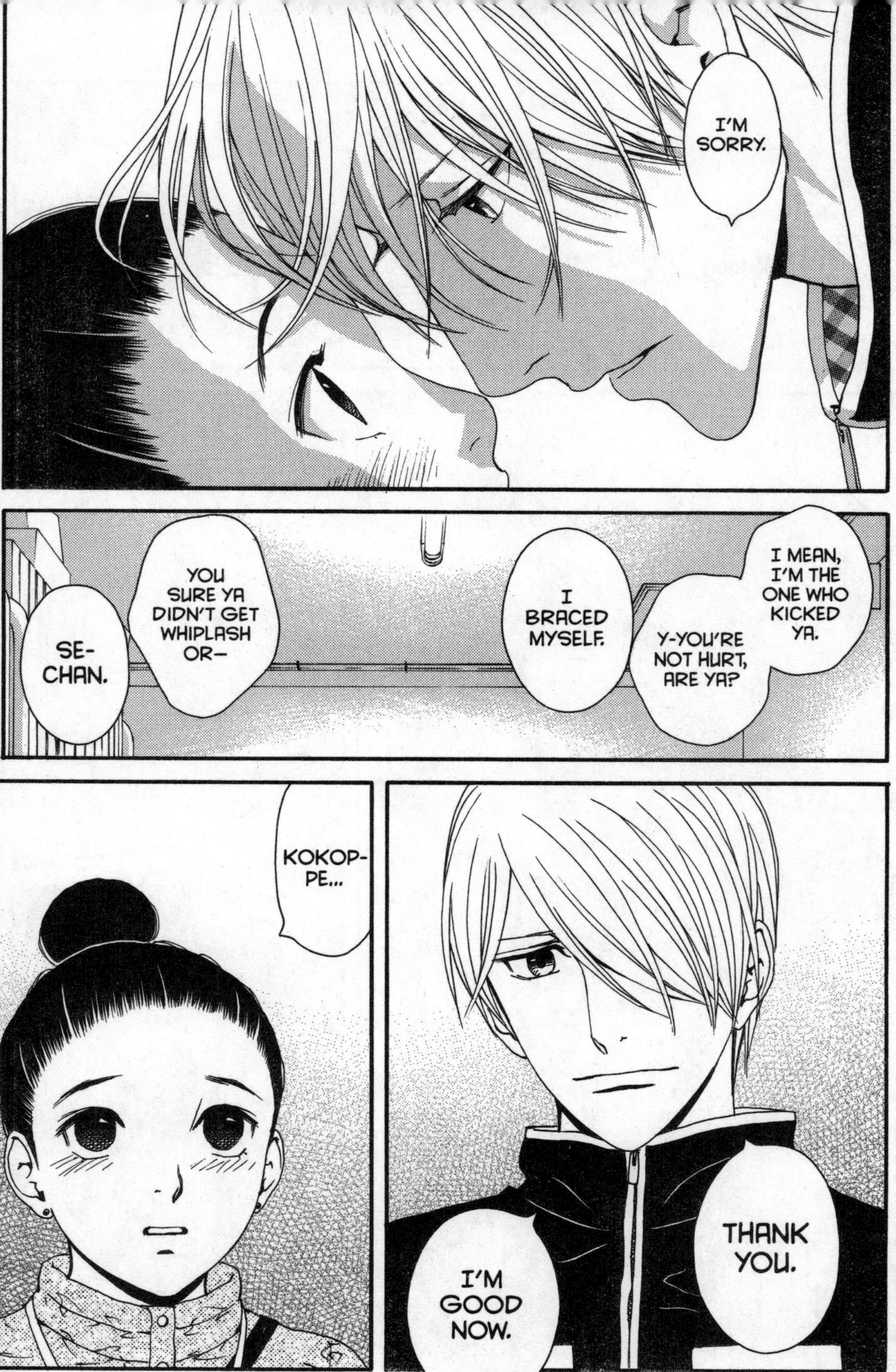
I'M SORRY.
I MEAN, I'M THE ONE WHO KICKED YA.
Y-YOU'RE NOT HURT, ARE YA?
I BRACED MYSELF.
YOU SURE YA DIDN'T GET WHIPLASH OR—
SE-CHAN.
THANK YOU.
I'M GOOD NOW.
KOKOP-PE...

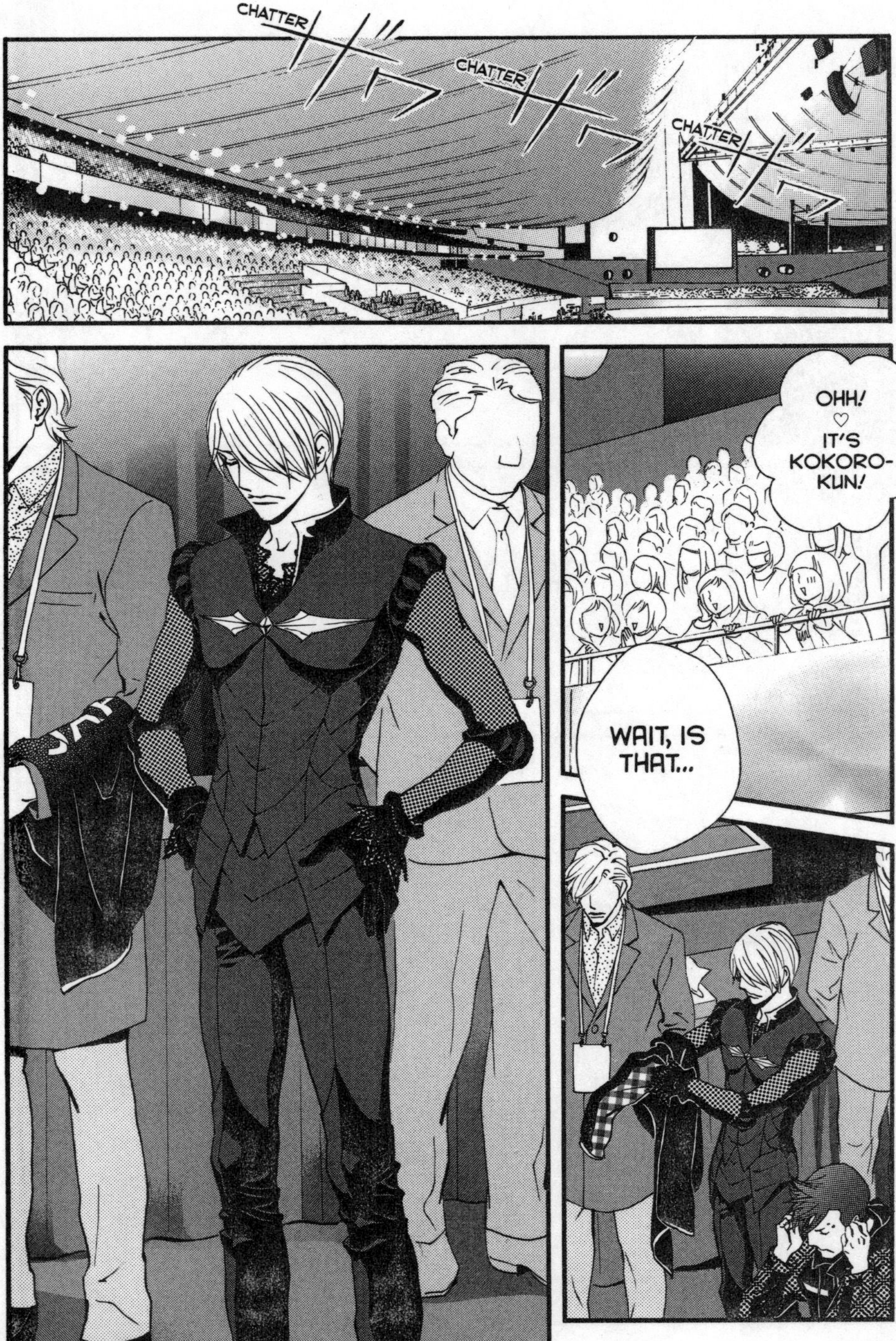
CHATTER
CHATTER
CHATTER
OHH! ♡ IT'S KOKORO-KUN!
WAIT, IS THAT...

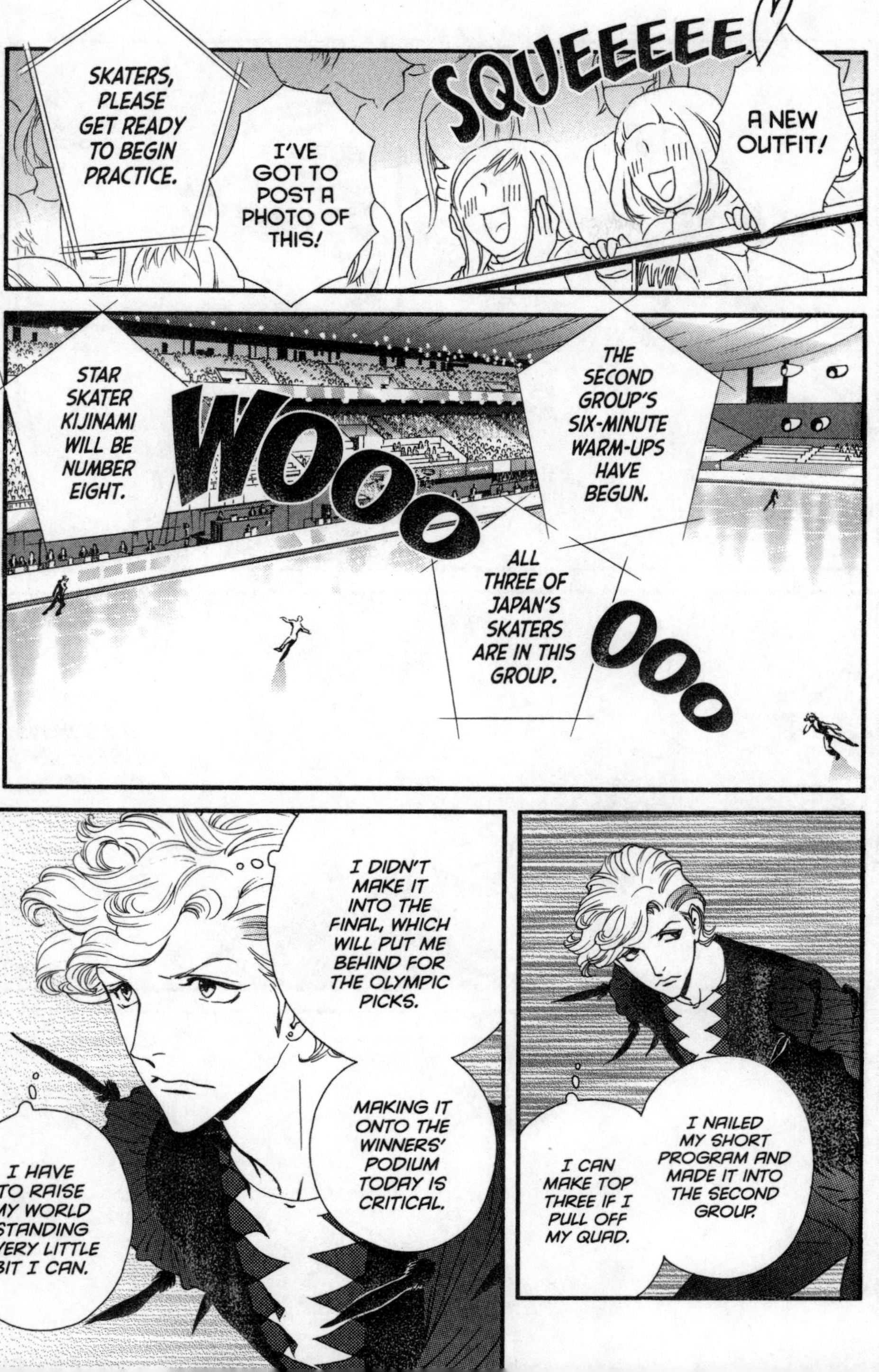
A NEW OUTFIT!
SQUEEEEEEE
I'VE GOT TO POST A PHOTO OF THIS!
SKATERS, PLEASE GET READY TO BEGIN PRACTICE.
THE SECOND GROUP'S SIX-MINUTE WARM-UPS HAVE BEGUN.
ALL THREE OF JAPAN'S SKATERS ARE IN THIS GROUP.
WOOOOOOO
STAR SKATER KIJINAMI WILL BE NUMBER EIGHT.
I NAILED MY SHORT PROGRAM AND MADE IT INTO THE SECOND GROUP.
I CAN MAKE TOP THREE IF I PULL OFF MY QUAD.
I DIDN'T MAKE IT INTO THE FINAL, WHICH WILL PUT ME BEHIND FOR THE OLYMPIC PICKS.
MAKING IT ONTO THE WINNERS' PODIUM TODAY IS CRITICAL.
I HAVE TO RAISE MY WORLD STANDING EVERY LITTLE BIT I CAN.

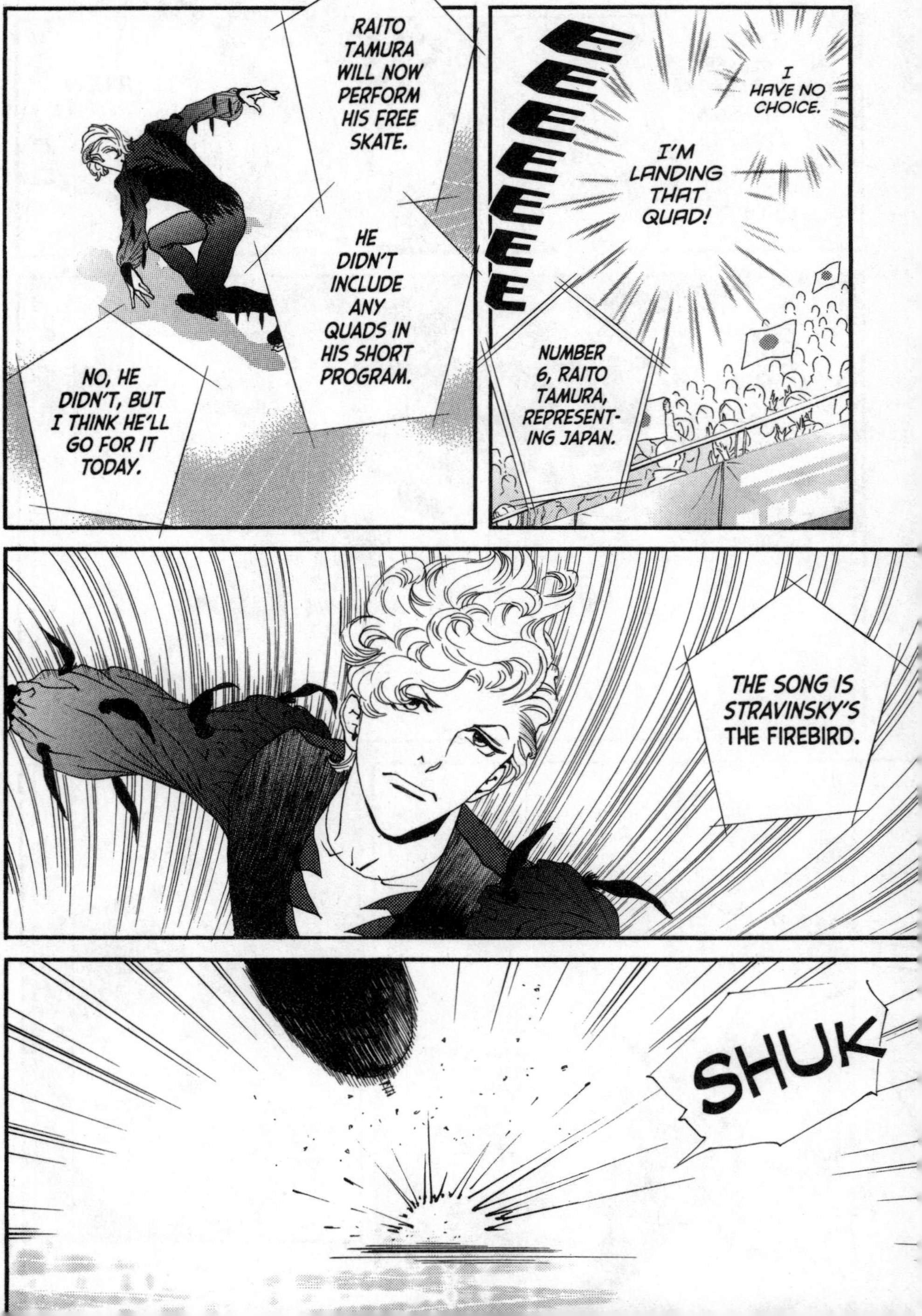
EEEEEEEE
I HAVE NO CHOICE.
I'M LANDING THAT QUAD!
NUMBER 6, RAITO TAMURA, REPRESENT-ING JAPAN.
RAITO TAMURA WILL NOW PERFORM HIS FREE SKATE.
HE DIDN'T INCLUDE ANY QUADS IN HIS SHORT PROGRAM.
NO, HE DIDN'T, BUT I THINK HE'LL GO FOR IT TODAY.
THE SONG IS STRAVINSKY'S THE FIREBIRD.
SHUK

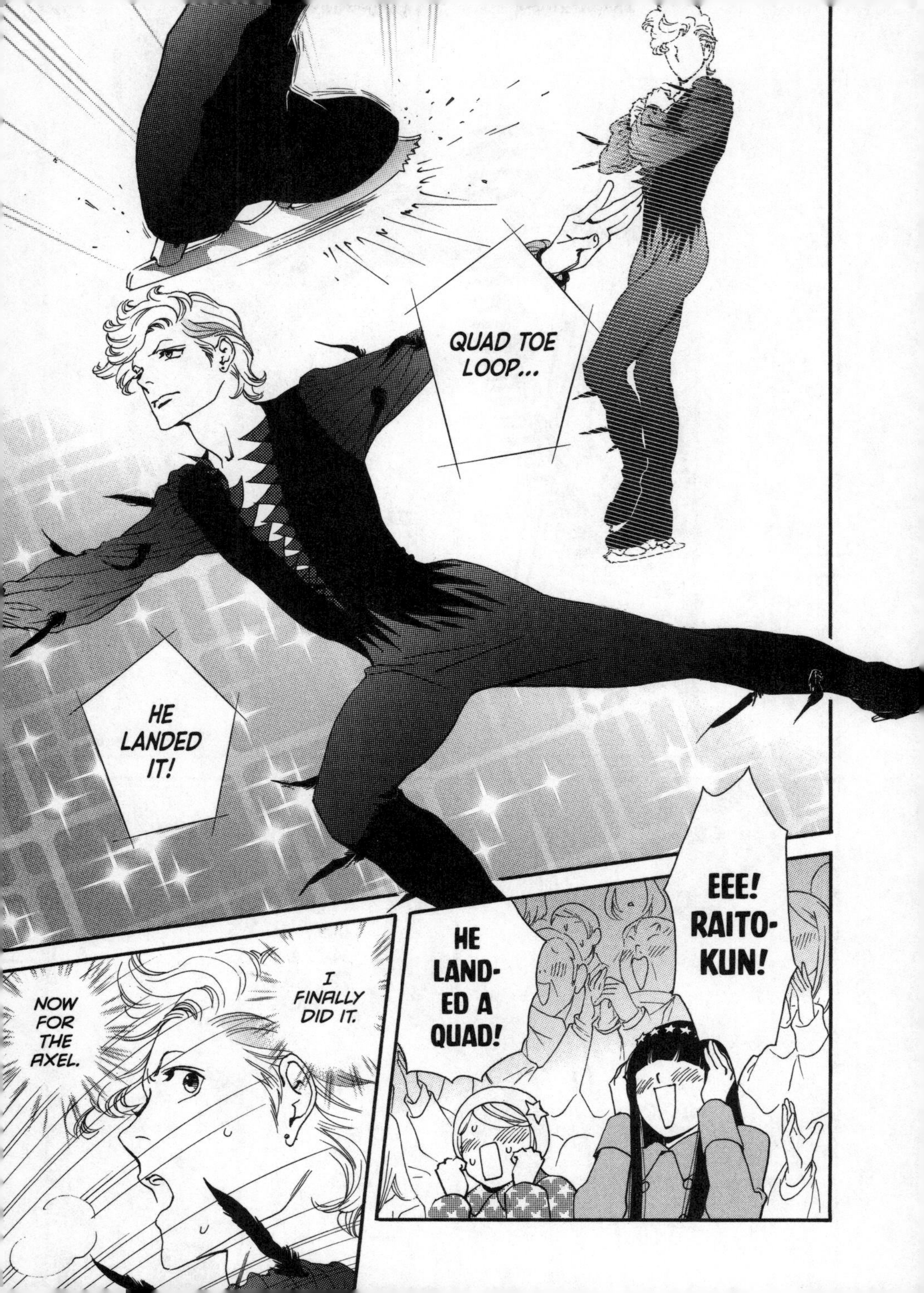
QUAD TOE LOOP...
HE LANDED IT!
EEE! RAITO-KUN!
HE LANDED A QUAD!
I FINALLY DID IT.
NOW FOR THE AXEL.

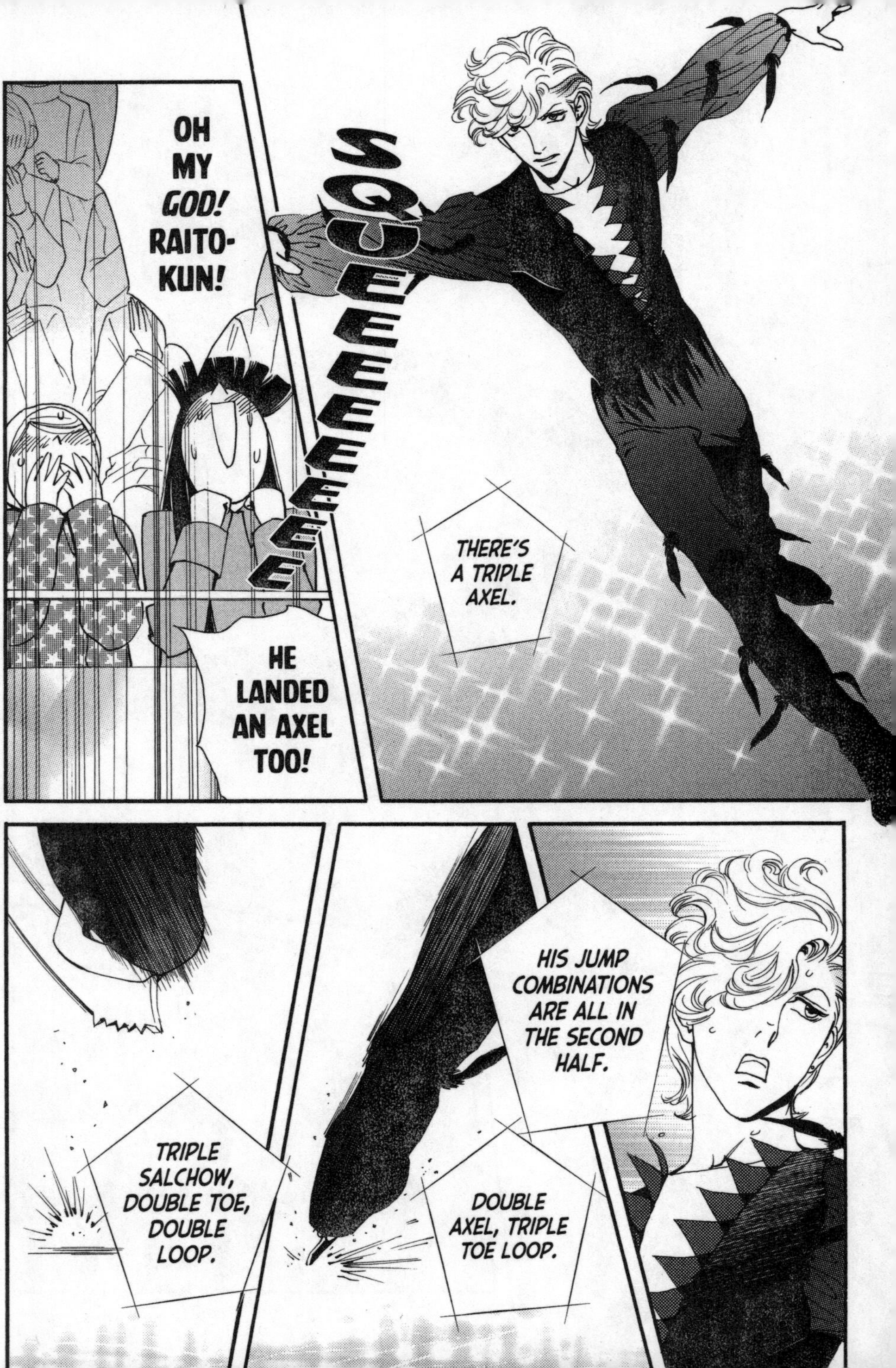
SQUEEEEEEEEEE
THERE'S A TRIPLE AXEL.
OH MY GOD! RAITO-KUN!
HE LANDED AN AXEL TOO!
HIS JUMP COMBINATIONS ARE ALL IN THE SECOND HALF.
DOUBLE AXEL, TRIPLE TOE LOOP.
TRIPLE SALCHOW, DOUBLE TOE, DOUBLE LOOP.

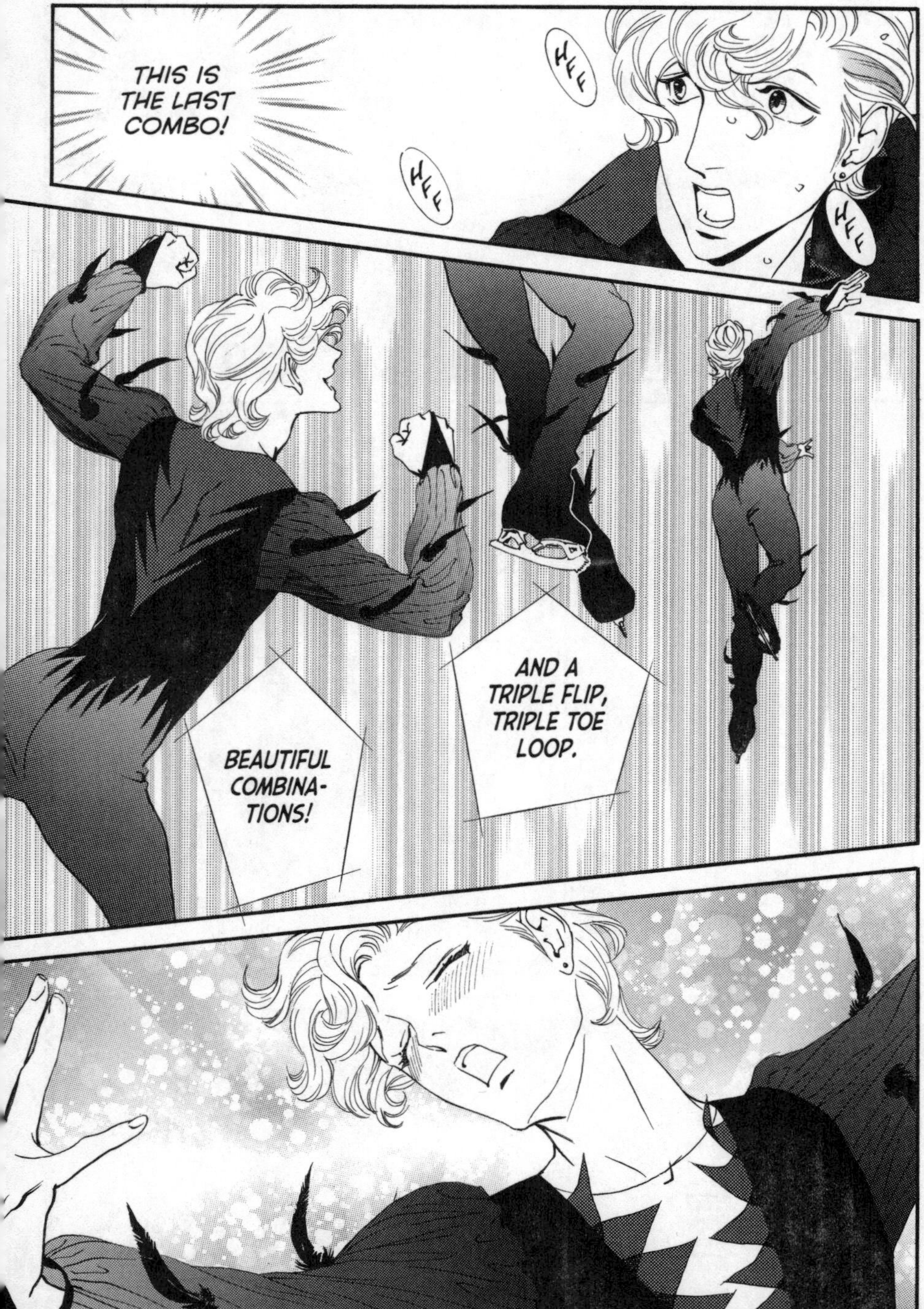
HFF
HFF
THIS IS THE LAST COMBO!
HFF
AND A TRIPLE FLIP, TRIPLE TOE LOOP.
BEAUTIFUL COMBINA-TIONS!

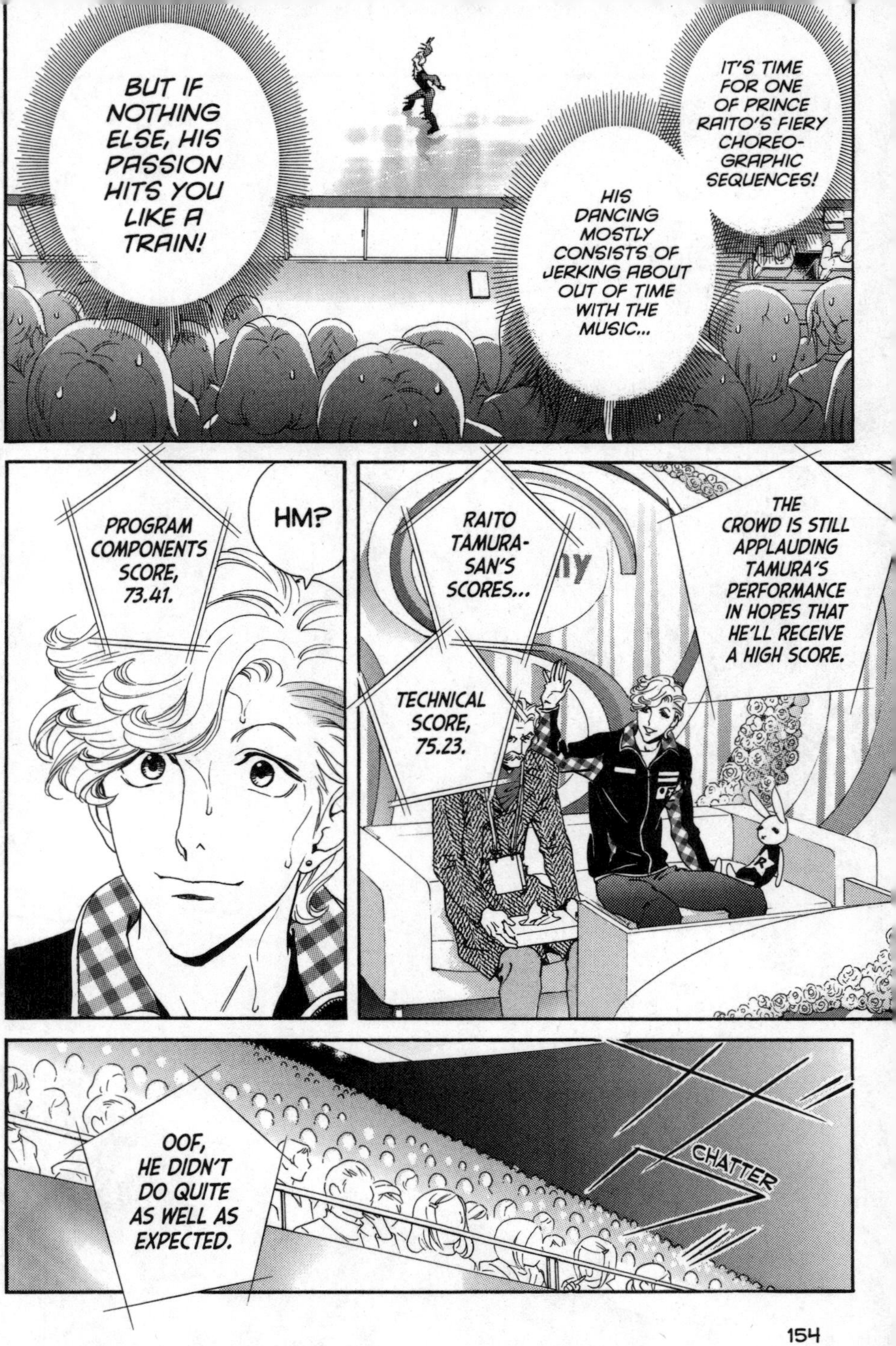
IT'S TIME FOR ONE OF PRINCE RAITO'S FIERY CHOREO-GRAPHIC SEQUENCES!
HIS DANCING MOSTLY CONSISTS OF JERKING ABOUT OUT OF TIME WITH THE MUSIC...
BUT IF NOTHING ELSE, HIS PASSION HITS YOU LIKE A TRAIN!
THE CROWD IS STILL APPLAUDING TAMURA'S PERFORMANCE IN HOPES THAT HE'LL RECEIVE A HIGH SCORE.
RAITO TAMURA-SAN'S SCORES...
TECHNICAL SCORE, 75.23.
HM?
PROGRAM COMPONENTS SCORE, 73.41.
CHATTER
OOF, HE DIDN'T DO QUITE AS WELL AS EXPECTED.

*4T: QUAD TOE LOOP **2A: DOUBLE AXEL

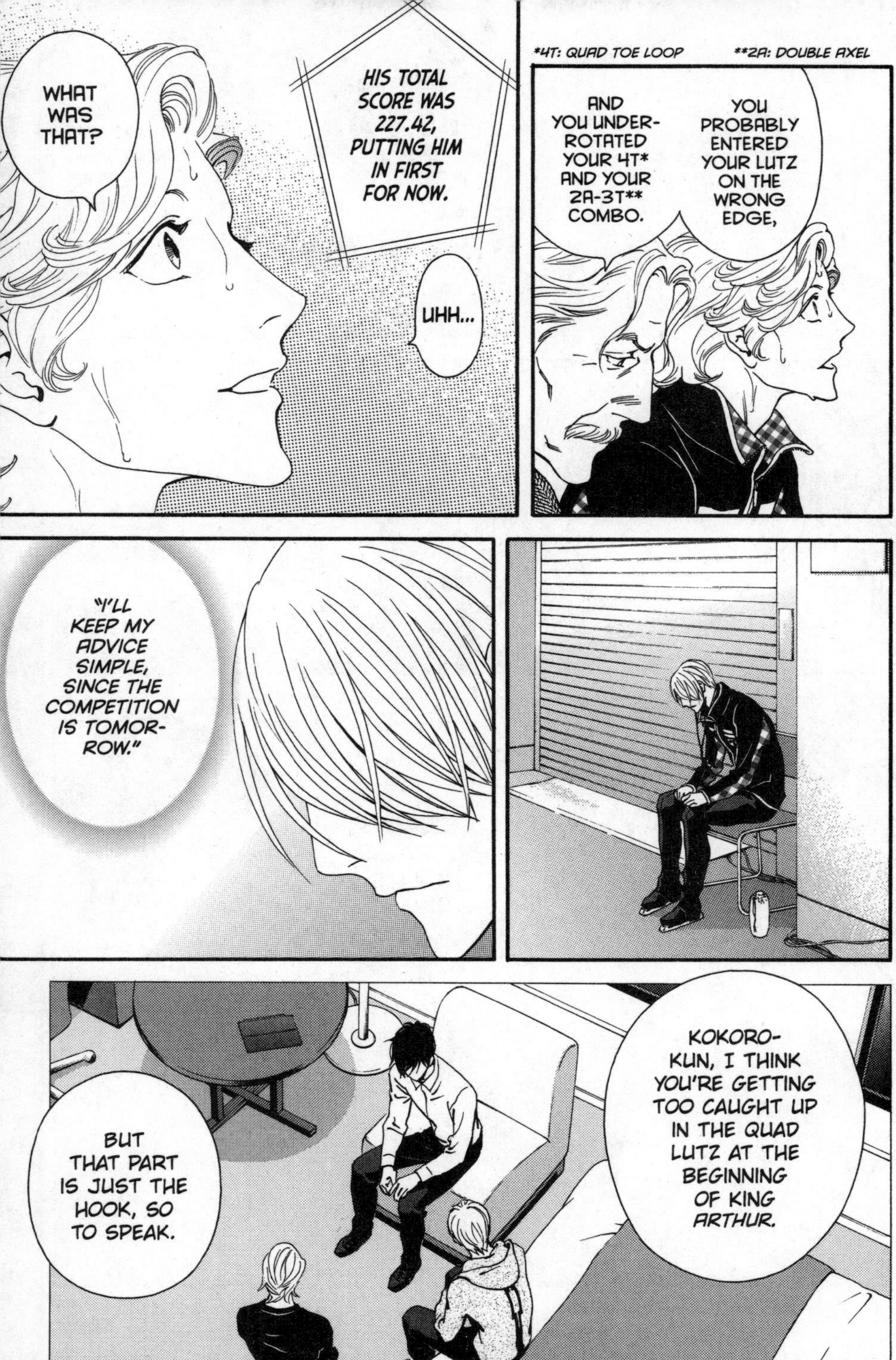
YOU PROBABLY ENTERED YOUR LUTZ ON THE WRONG EDGE,
AND YOU UNDER-ROTATED YOUR 4T* AND YOUR 2A-3T** COMBO.
HIS TOTAL SCORE WAS 227.42, PUTTING HIM IN FIRST FOR NOW.
UHH...
WHAT WAS THAT?
"I'LL KEEP MY ADVICE SIMPLE, SINCE THE COMPETITION IS TOMOR-ROW."
KOKORO-KUN, I THINK YOU'RE GETTING TOO CAUGHT UP IN THE QUAD LUTZ AT THE BEGINNING OF KING ARTHUR.
BUT THAT PART IS JUST THE HOOK, SO TO SPEAK.

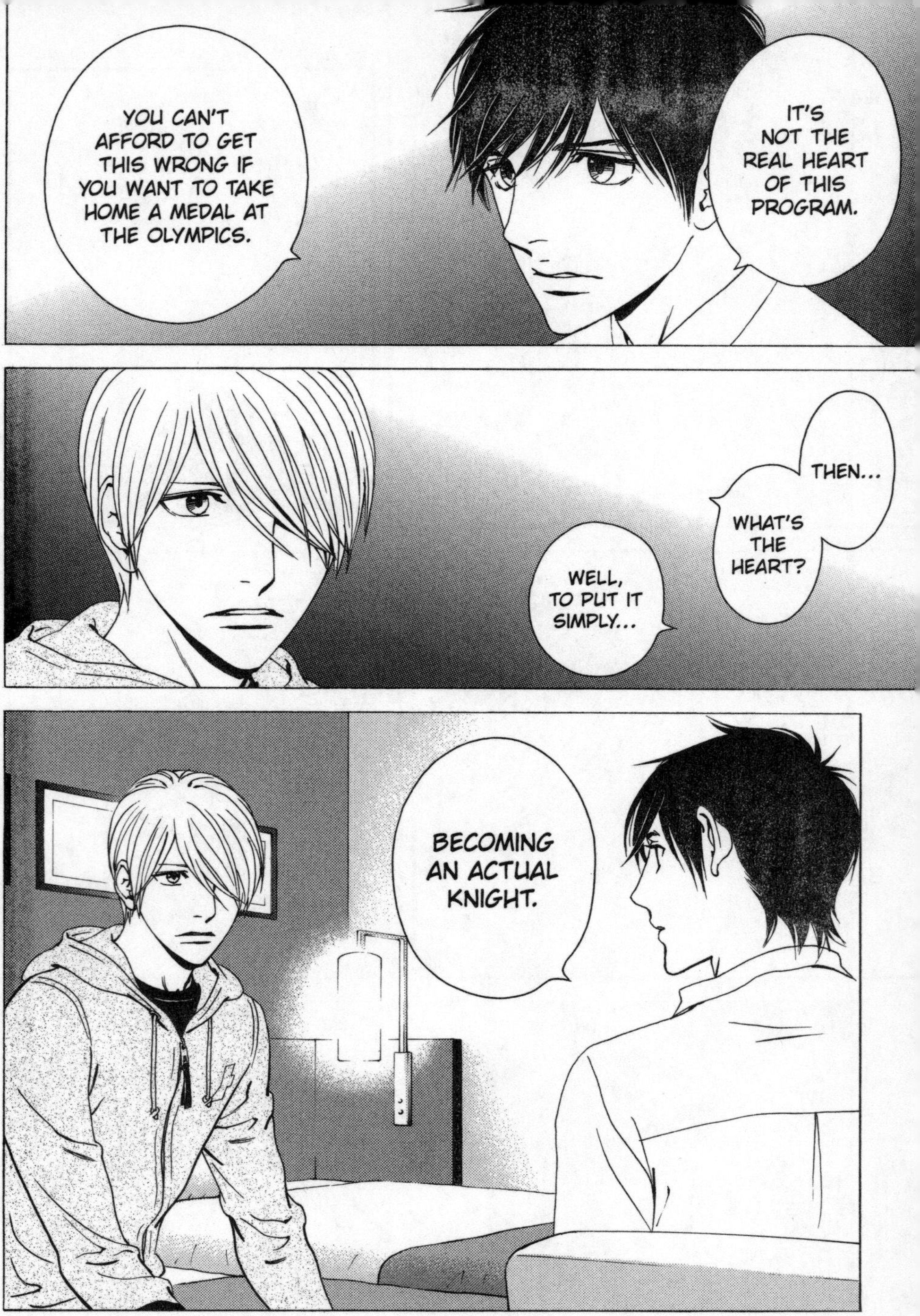
IT'S NOT THE REAL HEART OF THIS PROGRAM.
YOU CAN'T AFFORD TO GET THIS WRONG IF YOU WANT TO TAKE HOME A MEDAL AT THE OLYMPICS.
THEN...
WHAT'S THE HEART?
WELL, TO PUT IT SIMPLY...
BECOMING AN ACTUAL KNIGHT.

To be continued...

TRANSLATION NOTES

POWER WALKING, PAGE 9
More specifically, Moriyama says she was doing "Duke walking," a fitness fad from the 2000s. It was originated by Duke Saraie and popularized by his books and appearances on television. Basically, Duke walking consists of raising your hands above your head, crossing your arms, putting your palms together, and walking while leaning your body left and right and crossing your legs with each step.

SHOCKED PIKACHU, PAGE 56
Originally, Chitose says she made a face like Nanana, an open-mouthed banana who acts as a mascot for TV Tokyo. His official website is <https://www.tv-tokyo.co.jp/nanana/>. For this translation, I've changed the reference to something more likely to be familiar to English-speaking readers.

TOKUSATSU, PAGE 64
The word "tokusatsu" means "special effects," and as such, could refer to any film that makes heavy use of them, but in practice, it is usually used in reference to a certain genre of live-action movies that use such effects. Common elements include giant monsters or masked superheroes. Tokusatsu series that have gained popularity in the English-speaking world (at least in adapted form) include *Godzilla* and *Power Rangers*.

LINE, PAGE 79
Line is an internet-based messaging service primarily for use on mobile devices. It's distinguished by its wide array of expressive stickers featuring original characters as well as many from popular media franchises. While it may not be as familiar to English-speaking readers, it's used widely in Japan, as it was originally developed to facilitate communication despite overloaded cellular infrastructure following the 2011 Tohoku earthquake disaster.

MORIYAMA AND THE SYRUP, PAGE 85
The sound effect I've translated as "hngh" here, was originally a reference to figure skater Evgeni Plushenko's famous "Sex Bomb" program, which was possible thanks to Japanese's versatile onomatopoeia.

AKIHABARA, PAGE 120
Akihabara is a neighborhood in Tokyo that got its start as an electronics shopping district in the post-war Japanese economy. Since then, it has become famous worldwide as a hub for otaku culture, with many shops catering to fans of manga, video games, and the like.

Omurice, page 120
Omurice is a dish that consists of fried rice wrapped in a layer of scrambled eggs. In other words, a rice omelet!

Happi, page 121
A happi is a wide-sleeved, open-fronted shirt often worn at Japanese festivals, especially in the summer. They typically have a crest of some kind on the back, so it's likely Kokoro's dad is going to have his crew show up wearing Kijinami happi.

Oden, page 164
This is a Japanese soup with a fish-based broth that often includes hard-boiled eggs, daikon radishes, and konjac, among other ingredients.

Fried manju, page 165
Manju is a bun typically filled with red bean paste.

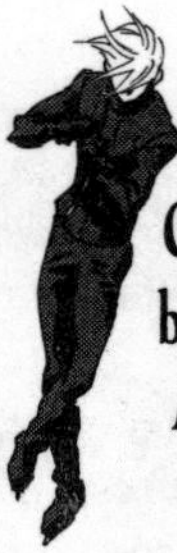

Glossary by Coach Akiyuki Kido

(based on January 2015 rules)

Ice Dancing (page 61)
Similar to singles and pairs, ice dancing is a category of figure skating competition. Skaters participate in teams of one man and one woman. It is a beautiful, unique style of skating that was inspired by ballroom dancing. Rhythm, musicality, and footwork are given priority in ice dancing, and there are those who argue that it requires the most skill of any kind of figure skating competition.

World Championships (page 61)
The World Figure Skating Championships, also known as Worlds, is the biggest event of the skating season. The winner earns the title of world champion for that season.

World standing (page 62)
A skater's world standing is derived from the total number of points and placements they get in each competition they enter.

Japan Open (page 62)
The Japan Open is an international competition held at the start of the skating season. Japan, North America, and Europe all compete. Each region is represented by two women, two men, one pair, and one ice dancing couple. The only category is the free skate. This is also where Japan's skaters usually debut their new programs. An exhibition gala with an extravagant ice show is held after the competition, so it is like a festival that christens the beginning of the new season.

ISU Grand Prix (page 62)
The ISU Grand Prix is a series of six competitions held between October and December: Skate America, Skate Canada, the Cup of China, the Trophée Eric Bompard (France), the Rostelecom Cup (Russia), and the NHK Trophy (Japan). The order they're held in varies by year.

4Lz (page 62)
This is an abbreviation of quadruple Lutz., named after the Austrian skater Alois Lutz, the first person to perform this jump. The Lutz is considered the second hardest jump after the Axel. To perform this jump, a skater uses their right toe pick (the front of the skate's blade where it has teeth) to launch themself into the air from their left skate's back outside edge. Because of the difficulty of skating on this edge, many skaters make an edge error. Note that the roles of each foot are reversed for skaters who spin clockwise.

4T (page 66)
This is an abbreviation of quadruple toe loop., which is considered to be the easiest jump. The skater uses their left toe to launch themself into the air from their right skate's back outside edge. To date, no one has managed to execute this jump with more than four revolutions, and only a select few skaters can do even that.

Short program (page 70)
The short program is a segment in which the skaters have up to two minutes and fifty seconds to perform eight predetermined elements, such as jumps, spins, or steps.

Three jumps (page 70)
The six jumps in figure skating are the toe loop, Salchow, loop, flip, Lutz, and Axel. In the short program, the following jumps are required: 1) a triple-triple or triple-double jump combination, 2) a triple jump following a step, and 3) a double or triple Axel. In the free skate, the skater may perform up to eight jumps, one of which must be an Axel. No more than three jump combinations are allowed, and only one of those can consist of three jumps.

Technical score (page 70)
The technical score is determined by the technical elements included in the program and their quality. Jumps, spins, steps, and other elements each have a base value, which is modified by a grade of execution (GOE) to get the technical score. The GOE is the average of the modifiers assigned by the judges, excluding the highest and lowest. These modifiers have one of seven values between negative and positive three.

Program components score (PCS or presentation score) (page 70)
For this score, skaters are evaluated on the basis of five program components: skating skills, transitions, performance, composition, and interpretation. A skater's final score is the total of their program components score (PCS) and their technical score.

Free skate (page 71)
In the free skating competition, skaters get to choose what elements and moves to use. Still, to ensure a well-rounded program, there are rules about what jumps, spins, and steps are required, as well as restrictions on the number of them allowed. In women's singles, this segment lasts four minutes, and in men's singles, it lasts four minutes and thirty seconds.

Penalty (page 73)
There is a rule that restricts the number of jumps of a given type that a skater is allowed to attempt. Colloquially, it's known as the Zayak rule. The name is in reference to Elaine Zayak, who became world champion with a program focused on repeatedly doing triple toe loops.

Under-rotate (page 73)
Under-rotation is the failure to include the necessary number of revolutions in a jump. A jump that's under-rotated by half a revolution or more is downgraded and has the base value of a jump with one fewer revolutions.

Olympic entries (page 73)
A country can have at most three entries in figure skating competitions at the Olympics. Each country's number of entries is determined by the placements of their skaters at the World Championships the previous year. Each placement has a point value. Places 1 through 15 are worth a number of points equal to the placement, places 16 through 24 are each worth 16 points, and places from 25 and on are worth 18 points. A country's number of entries for the next year is based on these points and their number of entries for the current year in the following manner:
- Three entries: Three entries if the combined placement score of their two top-performing skaters is 13 or less, or two entries if it's 28 or less.
- Two entries: Three entries if the combined placement score is 13 or less, or two entries if it's 28 or less.
- One entry: Three entries if their placement score is 2 or less, or two entries if it's 10 or less.

The multiple entries are distributed automatically, and the remaining countries get the leftover entries in order of placement. A country that fails to get any entries for the Olympics by this means can get one entry by placing well in a designated Olympic qualifying event (for example, the German Nebelhorn Trophy for the Sochi Olympics).

Popping jumps (page 74)
Popping a jump is when a skater accidentally does fewer rotations than they intended.

Minor competition (page 74)
An international competition recognized by the International Skating Union (ISU), but put on by a given country's local governing body for ice skating.

Unofficial record (page 91)
Only scores from competitions put on by the ISU are recognized as official records.

GOE (page 91)
Grade of execution. This is a score modifier of between negative and positive three assigned to a skater's execution of each element in their program.

Flying sit spin (page 93)
To perform a flying sit spin, a skater leaps into a one-legged squat in which they spin with their free leg extended out.

Triple Axel (3A) (page 93)
There are six different jumps in figure skating. An Axel is the only one that begins with the skater facing directly forward (on the forward outside edge). It's the most difficult jump, and a triple Axel requires three and a half midair rotations. Midori Ito was the first woman in Japan to successfully execute this jump.

Jump combination (page 102)
A jump combination is when a skater performs a jump and then immediately performs another from the foot they land on. Since jumps are landed on the right skate's back outside edge (or the left skate's if you're spinning clockwise), all jumps after the first in a combination are limited to either the toe loop or the loop jump. If the skater weaves footwork between their jumps, it's called a jump sequence instead.

Final (page 104)
The six highest-ranking skaters in the ISU Grand Prix go on to compete for first in the Final.

Footwork (page 105)
A skater's footwork is the way they weave together steps with turns and other elements. Moves such as the Mohawk, the chasse, the crossroll, and the Choctaw are steps, whereas the three turn, loop turn, rocker, counter, bracket, and twizzle are turns. A combination of steps and turns is called a step sequence.

Open practice (page 106)
Open practice is typically held on the day before, or the day of, a competition. It's the skaters' last chance to polish their routines, and they're free to participate or not at their discretion. The technical panel—which consists of a technical specialist, an assistant technical specialist, and a technical controller—is required to watch and familiarize themselves with the skaters' programs.

Six-minute warm-ups (page 111)
At the beginning of a competition, each group gets six minutes on the ice to practice.

Salchow (page 152)
This jump is executed from the left foot's back inside edge by lifting the right foot forward and to the left. The way both feet face outward just before takeoff is a unique feature of the Salchow jump. It is typically considered an easy jump because its entrance from the back inside edge makes rotating less difficult. Still, although they are rare, there are some skaters who consider it to be their most difficult jump, often owing to personal difficulty skating on their back inside edge. It was named after the Swedish skater Ulrich Salchow.

Loop (page 152)

For this jump, the skater both takes off from and lands on only their right foot. With their left leg crossed in front of their right, they jump from the right skate's back outside edge.

Flip (page 153)

To perform this jump, the skater rides the back inside edge of their left skate and uses their right toe to launch themselves into the air. It is sometimes called the toe Salchow. Due to the relative difficulty of maintaining a vertical axis, this jump's base value is almost as high as that of the Lutz. Note that the roles of each foot are reversed for skaters who spin clockwise.

Choreographic sequence (page 154)

For this step sequence, the skater is allowed a great deal of freedom in choosing their components and is scored on the sequence as a whole.

Akiyuki Kido was born on August 28th, 1975. He represented Japan in ice dancing at the 2006 winter Olympics in Turin, Italy. He took fifteenth place, the highest Japan had ever placed in ice dancing at the time. Today, he works as a coach at the Shin-Yokohama Skate Center.

Knight of the Ice Skater Profile 7

7	Ilia Sokurov	

Height:

181 cm

Blood type:

AB

Birthday:

December 16th

Place of origin:

Moscow

Strongest element:

Jumps

Strongest jump:

Loop

Most difficult jump performed to date:

Quadruple Salchow

Strength:

His jumps are both high and long, with a lot of hang time

Weakness:

He gets hurt fairly often when he's not on the ice

Hobby:

Anime

Talent:

Systema (Russian martial arts, but done in his own way)

Family composition:

Two parents and three older sisters

Favorite food:

The *oden* from a certain Tokyo vending machine

Least favorite food:

Salmon roe (it's kind of creepy)

Notes:

He's very serious about wanting to marry a
Japanese girl

Divided Opinion

6

A very angry brother

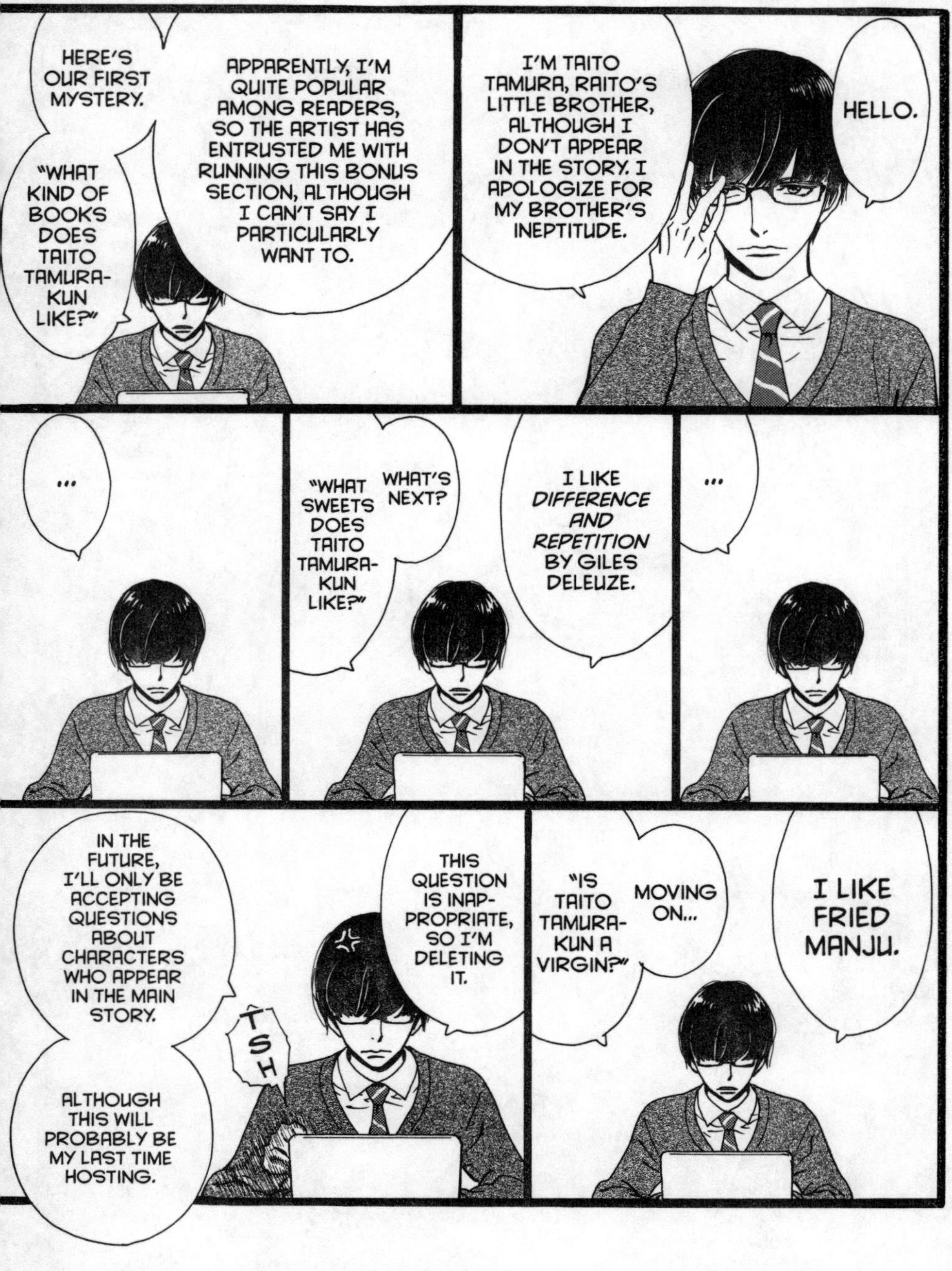

HELLO.
I'M TAITO TAMURA, RAITO'S LITTLE BROTHER, ALTHOUGH I DON'T APPEAR IN THE STORY. I APOLOGIZE FOR MY BROTHER'S INEPTITUDE.
APPARENTLY, I'M QUITE POPULAR AMONG READERS, SO THE ARTIST HAS ENTRUSTED ME WITH RUNNING THIS BONUS SECTION, ALTHOUGH I CAN'T SAY I PARTICULARLY WANT TO.
HERE'S OUR FIRST MYSTERY.
"WHAT KIND OF BOOKS DOES TAITO TAMURA-KUN LIKE?"
...
I LIKE *DIFFERENCE AND REPETITION* BY GILES DELEUZE.
WHAT'S NEXT?
"WHAT SWEETS DOES TAITO TAMURA-KUN LIKE?"
...
I LIKE FRIED MANJU.
MOVING ON...
"IS TAITO TAMURA-KUN A VIRGIN?"
THIS QUESTION IS INAP-PROPRIATE, SO I'M DELETING IT.
TSH
IN THE FUTURE, I'LL ONLY BE ACCEPTING QUESTIONS ABOUT CHARACTERS WHO APPEAR IN THE MAIN STORY.
ALTHOUGH THIS WILL PROBABLY BE MY LAST TIME HOSTING.

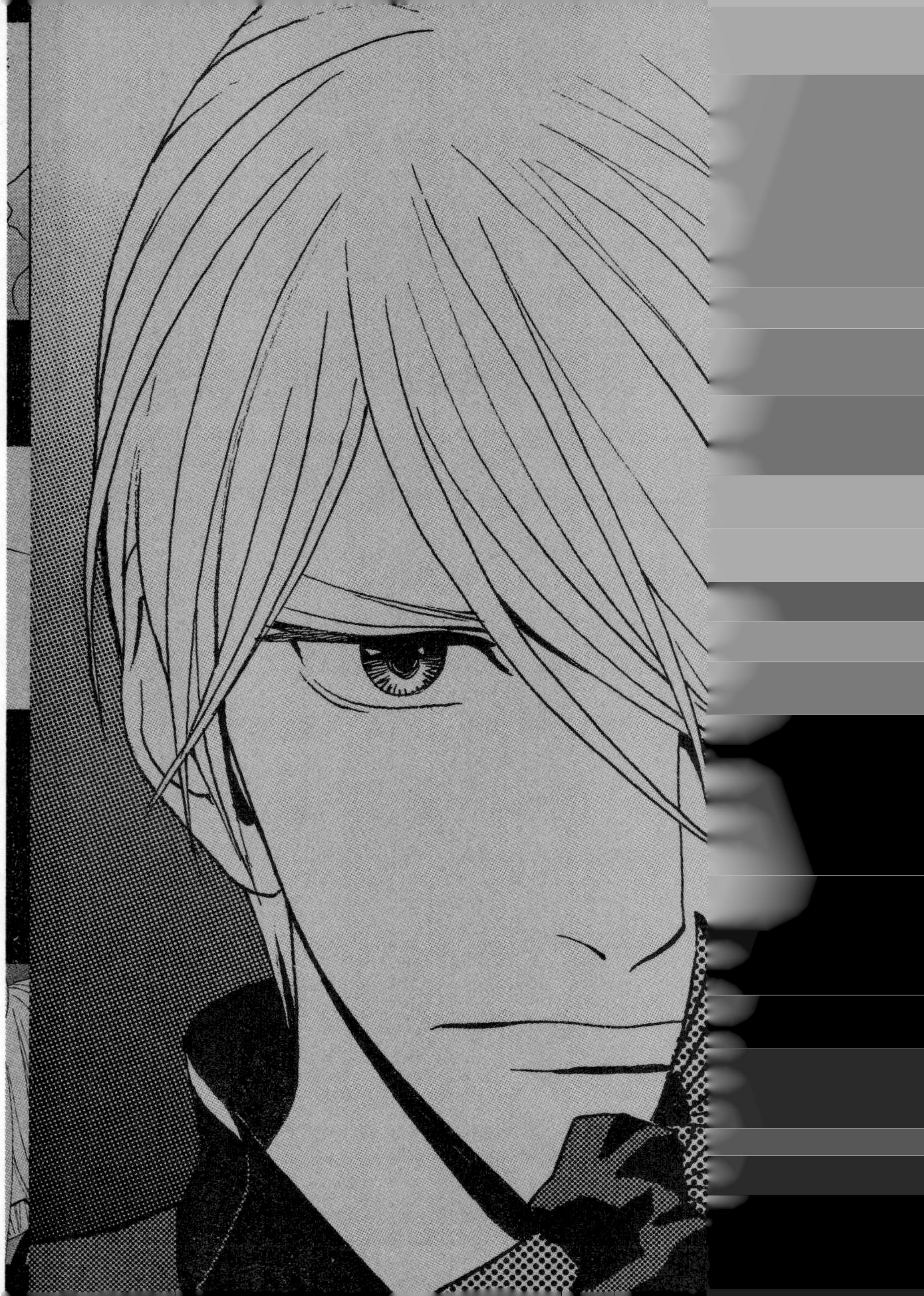

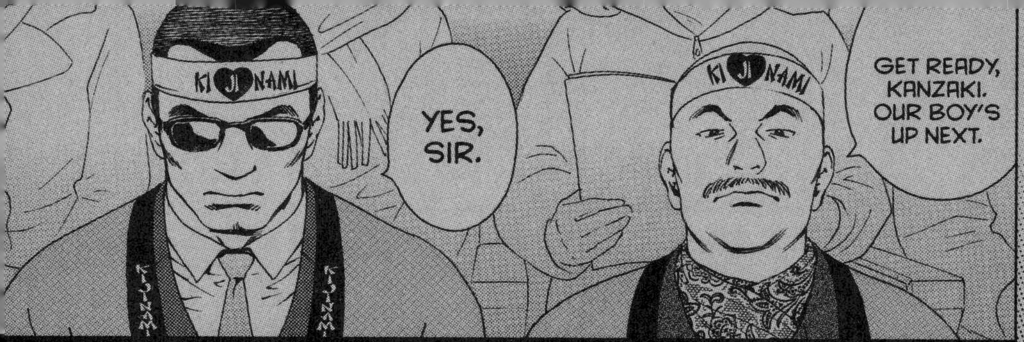
GET READY, KANZAKI. OUR BOY'S UP NEXT.
YES, SIR.

Thanks to the expressiveness of his performance, Kokoro advances to the Grand Prix Final, where he gets ready to take the ice for his free skating program. But with all eyes on him, will he be able to turn into the "actual knight" his choreographer wants him to? Then, a new challenge arises for him and Chitose...?!

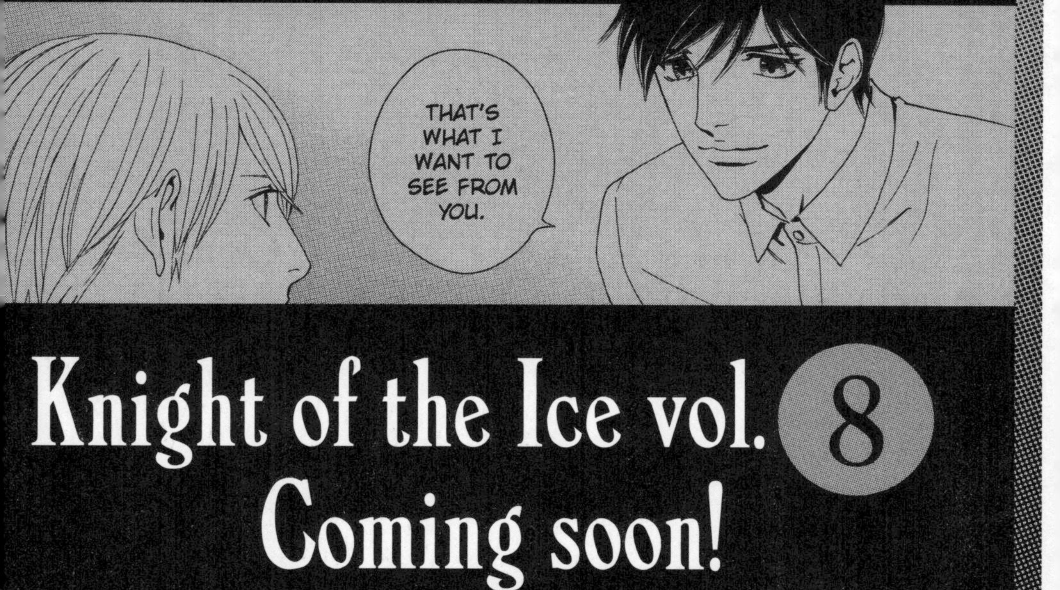
THAT'S WHAT I WANT TO SEE FROM YOU.

Knight of the Ice vol. 8 Coming soon!

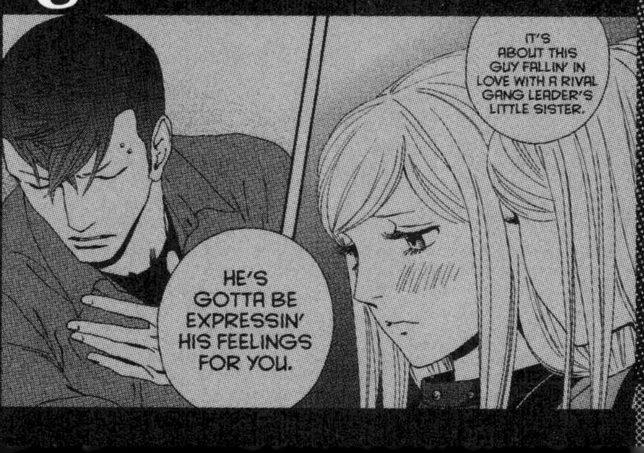
IT'S ABOUT THIS GUY FALLIN' IN LOVE WITH A RIVAL GANG LEADER'S LITTLE SISTER.
HE'S GOTTA BE EXPRESSIN' HIS FEELINGS FOR YOU.

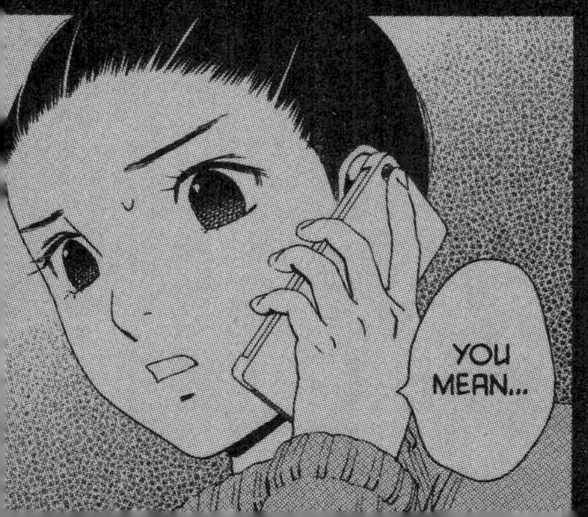
YOU MEAN...

A SMART, NEW ROMANTIC COMEDY FOR FANS OF *SHORTCAKE CAKE* AND *TERRACE HOUSE!*

A romance manga starring high school girl Meeko, who learns to live on her own in a boarding house whose living room is home to the odd (but handsome) Matsunaga-san. She begins to adjust to her new life away from her parents, but Meeko soon learns that no matter how far away from home she is, she's still a young girl at heart — especially when she finds herself falling for Matsunaga-san.

PERFECT WORLD

Rie Aruga

> A TOUCHING NEW SERIES ABOUT LOVE AND COPING WITH DISABILITY

An office party reunites Tsugumi with her high school crush Itsuki. He's realized his dream of becoming an architect, but along the way, he experienced a spinal injury that put him in a wheelchair. Now Tsugumi's rekindled feelings will butt up against prejudices she never considered — and Itsuki will have to decide if he's ready to let someone into his heart...

"Depicts with great delicacy and courage the difficulties some with disabilities experience getting involved in romantic relationships... Rie Aruga refuses to romanticize, pushing her heroine to face the reality of disability. She invites her readers to the same tasks of empathy, knowledge and recognition."
—Slate.fr

"An important entry [in manga romance]... The emotional core of both plot and characters indicates thoughtfulness... [Aruga's] research is readily apparent in the text and artwork, making this feel like a real story."
—Anime News Network

THE WORLD OF CLAMP!

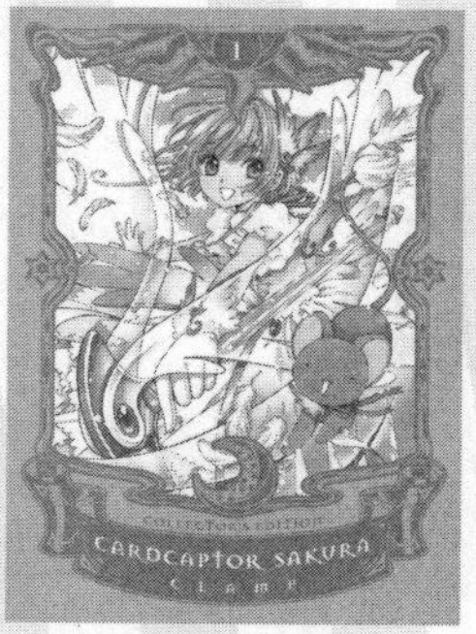
CARDCAPTOR SAKURA
Cardcaptor Sakura Collector's Edition

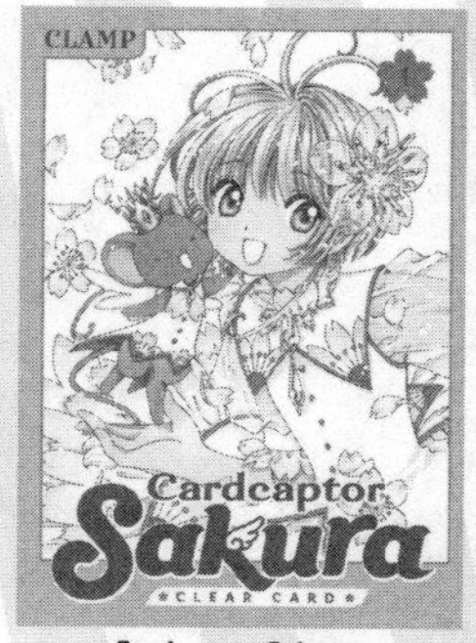
CLAMP
Cardcaptor
Sakura
CLEAR CARD
Cardcaptor Sakura: Clear Card

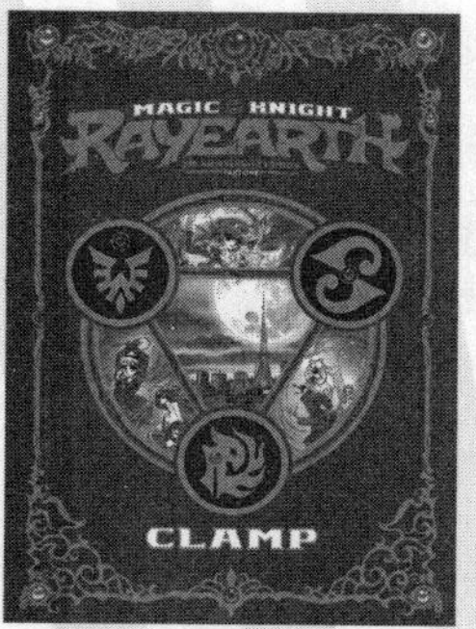
MAGIC KNIGHT
RAYEARTH
CLAMP
Magic Knight Rayearth 25th Anniversary Box Set

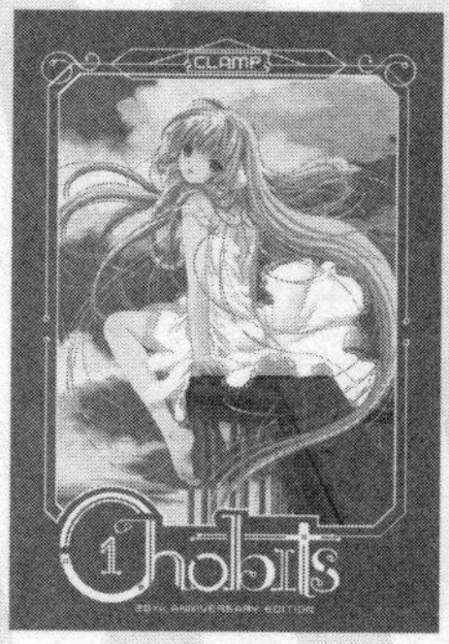
CLAMP
Chobits
Chobits

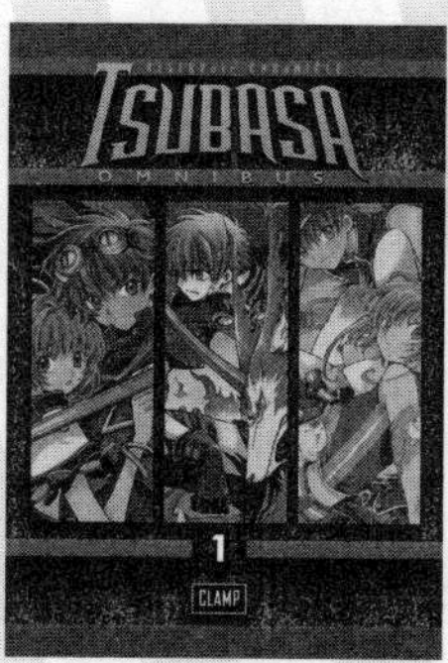
TSUBASA
OMNIBUS
1
CLAMP
TSUBASA Omnibus

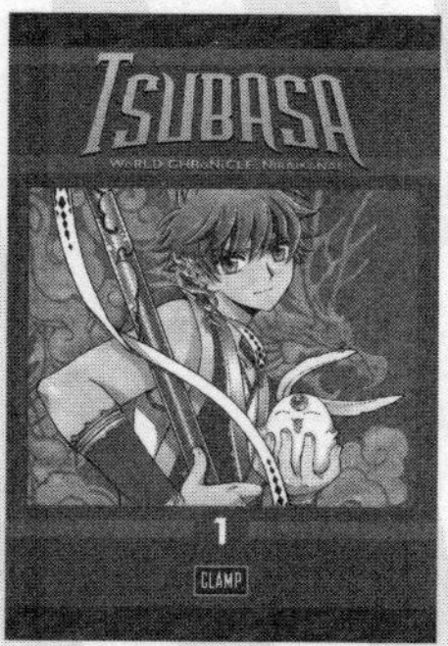
TSUBASA
1
CLAMP
TSUBASA WoRLD CHRoNiCLE

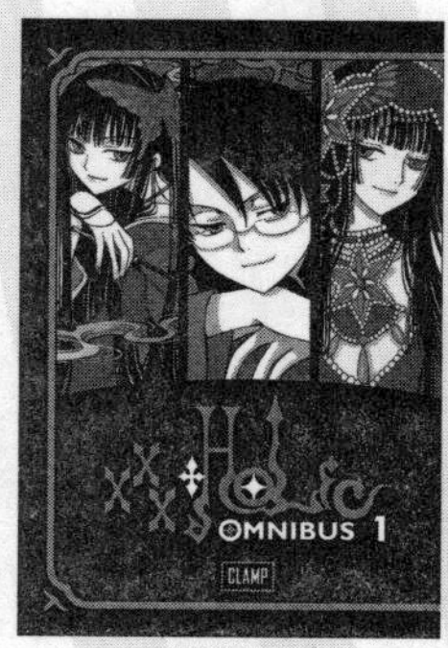
xxxHOLiC
OMNIBUS 1
CLAMP
xxxHOLiC Omnibus

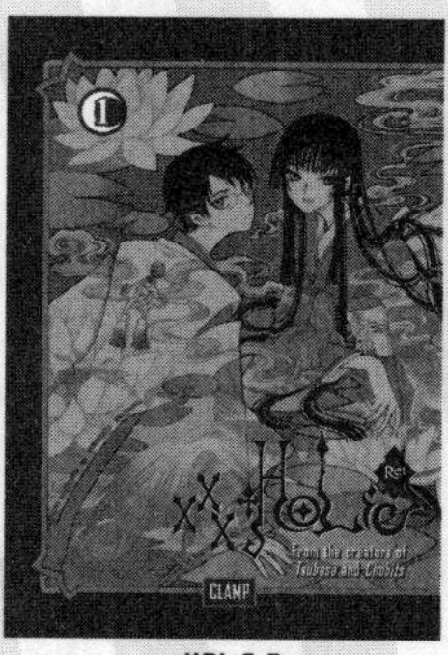
1
xxxHOLiC
Rei
CLAMP
xxxHOLiC Rei

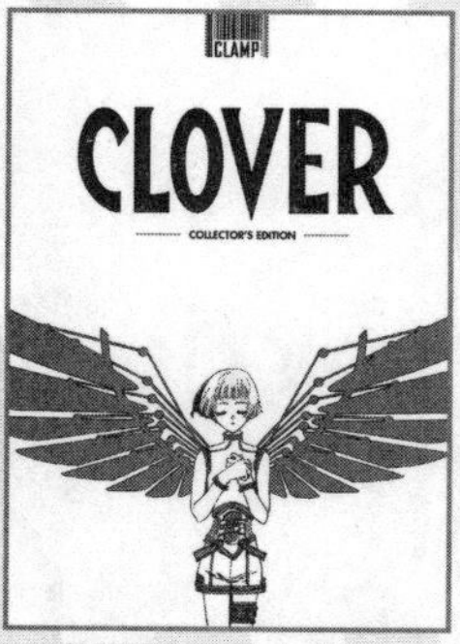
CLAMP
CLOVER
COLLECTOR'S EDITION
CLOVER Collector's Edition

KC KODANSHA COMICS

Kodansha Comics welcomes you to explore the expansive world of CLAMP, the all-female artist collective that has produced some of the most acclaimed manga of the century. Our growing catalog includes icons like *Cardcaptor Sakura* and *Magic Knight Rayearth*, each crafted with CLAMP's one-of-a-kind style and characters!

The prestigious Dahlia Academy educates the elite of society from two countries; To the East is the Nation of Touwa; across the sea the other way, the Principality of West. The nations, though, are fierce rivals, and their students are constantly feuding—which means Romio Inuzuka, head of Touwa's first-year students, has a problem. He's fallen for his counterpart from West, Juliet Persia, and when he can't take it any more, he confesses his feelings.

Now Romio has two problems: A girlfriend, and a secret...

Boarding School *Juliet*

By Yousuke Kaneda

"A fine romantic comedy... The chemistry between the two main characters is excellent and the humor is great, backed up by a fun enough supporting cast and a different twist on the genre." –AiPT

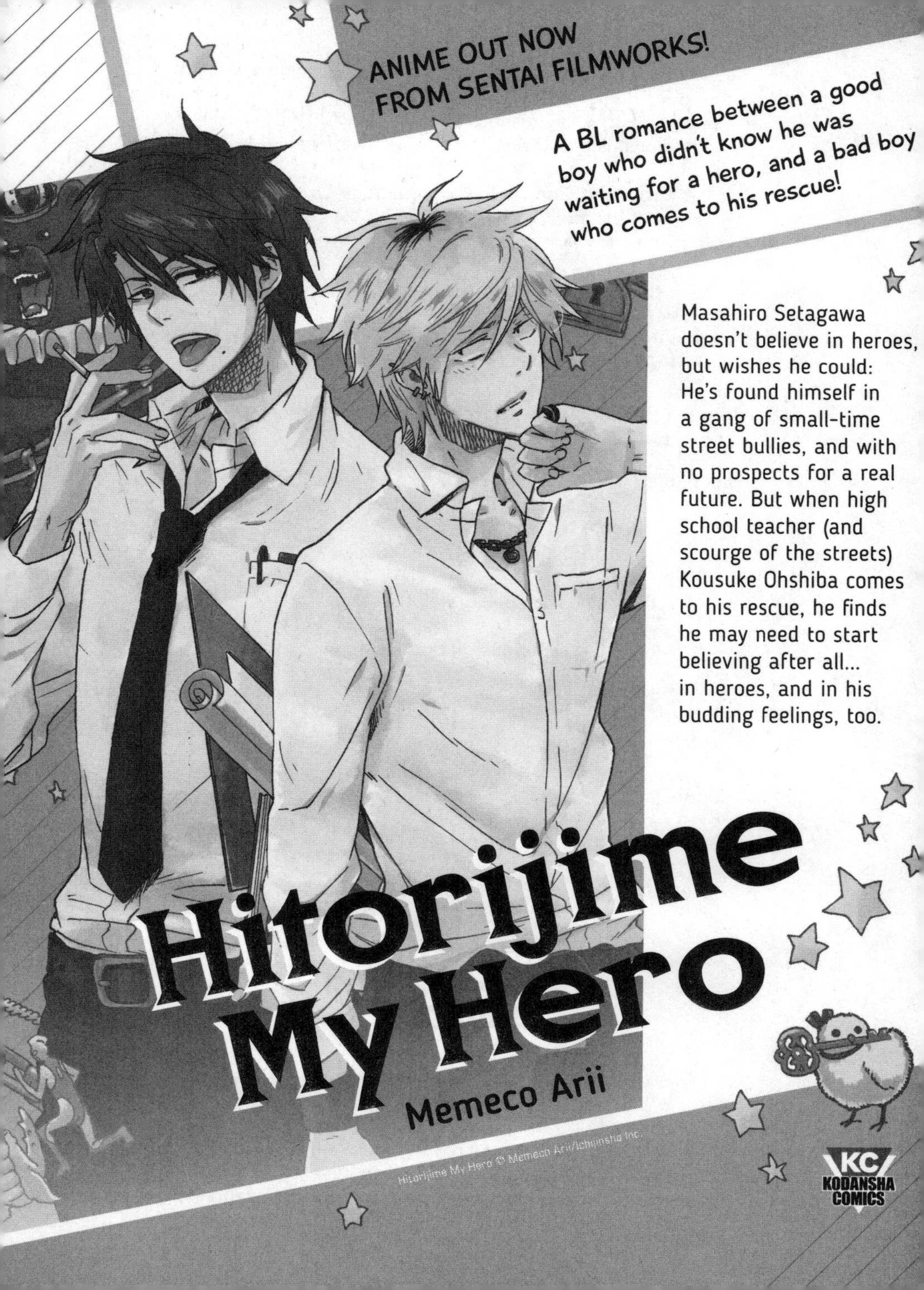
ANIME OUT NOW
FROM SENTAI FILMWORKS!
A BL romance between a good boy who didn't know he was waiting for a hero, and a bad boy who comes to his rescue!
Masahiro Setagawa doesn't believe in heroes, but wishes he could: He's found himself in a gang of small-time street bullies, and with no prospects for a real future. But when high school teacher (and scourge of the streets) Kousuke Ohshiba comes to his rescue, he finds he may need to start believing after all... in heroes, and in his budding feelings, too.
Hitorijime My Hero
Memeco Arii
Hitorijime My Hero © Memeco Arii/Ichijinsha Inc.
KC
KODANSHA COMICS

A Kodansha Comics Trade Paperback Original
Knight of the Ice 7 copyright © 2015 Yayoi Ogawa
English translation copyright © 2021 Yayoi Ogawa

All rights reserved.

Published in the United States by Kodansha Comics, an imprint of Kodansha USA Publishing, LLC, New York.

Publication rights for this English edition arranged through Kodansha Ltd., Tokyo.

First published in Japan in 2015 by Kodansha Ltd., Tokyo as *Ginban Kishi*, volume 7.

ISBN 978-1-64651-084-9

Printed in the United States of America.

www.kodanshacomics.com

1st Printing
Translation: Rose Padgett
Lettering: Jennifer Skarupa
Editing: Tiff Joshua TJ Ferentini
Kodansha Comics edition cover design by Phil Balsman

Publisher: Kiichiro Sugawara

Director of publishing services: Ben Applegate
Associate director of operations: Stephen Pakula
Publishing services managing editors: Alanna Ruse, Madison Salters
Assistant production managers: Emi Lotto, Angela Zurlo